The Old English Penitentials and Anglo-Saxon Law

Some of the earliest examples of medieval canon law are penitentials – texts enumerating the sins a confessor might encounter among laypeople or other clergy and suggesting means of reconciliation. Often they gave advice on matters of secular law as well, offering judgments on the proper way to contract a marriage or on the treatment of slaves. This book argues that their importance to more general legal-historical questions, long suspected by historians but rarely explored, is most evident in an important (and often misunderstood) subgroup of the penitentials: those composed in Old English. Though based on Latin sources – principally those attributed to Theodore, Archbishop of Canterbury (d. 690) and Halitgar of Cambrai (d. 831) – these texts recast them into new ordinances meant to better suit the needs of English laypeople. The Old English penitentials thus witness to how one early medieval polity established a tradition of written vernacular law.

Stefan Jurasinski is Associate Professor of English at The College at Brockport, State University of New York. His work has appeared in *Law and History Review*, the *Journal of Legal History*, the *Review of English Studies*, and other periodicals. He is the coeditor of *The Old English Canons of Theodore* (with R. D. Fulk, 2012), which won the Publication Prize of the International Society of Anglo-Saxonists for the best edition of the 2012–13 biennium. He was an American Council of Learned Societies Fellow for the 2014–15 academic year.

Studies in Legal History

EDITORS

Felice Batlan, *Women and Justice for the Poor: A History of Legal Aid, 1863–1945*
Stefan Jurasinski, *The Old English Penitentials and Anglo-Saxon Law*
Sophia Z. Lee, *The Workplace Constitution from the New Deal to the New Right*
Michael A. Livingston, *The Fascists and the Jews of Italy: Mussolini's Race Laws, 1938–1943*
Mitra Sharafi, *Law and Identity in Colonial South Asia: Parsi Legal Culture, 1772–1947*

The Old English Penitentials and Anglo-Saxon Law

STEFAN JURASINSKI
The College at Brockport, State University of New York

CAMBRIDGE
UNIVERSITY PRESS

CAMBRIDGE
UNIVERSITY PRESS

Shaftesbury Road, Cambridge CB2 8EA, United Kingdom

One Liberty Plaza, 20th Floor, New York, NY 10006, USA

477 Williamstown Road, Port Melbourne, VIC 3207, Australia

314–321, 3rd Floor, Plot 3, Splendor Forum, Jasola District Centre, New Delhi – 110025, India

103 Penang Road, #05–06/07, Visioncrest Commercial, Singapore 238467

Cambridge University Press is part of Cambridge University Press & Assessment, a department of the University of Cambridge.

We share the University's mission to contribute to society through the pursuit of education, learning and research at the highest international levels of excellence.

www.cambridge.org
Information on this title: www.cambridge.org/9781107083417

First published 2015

A catalogue record for this publication is available from the British Library

Library of Congress Cataloging-in-Publication data
Jurasinski, Stefan, author.
The old English penitentials and Anglo-Saxon law / Stefan Jurasinski.
pages cm. – (Studies in legal history)
ISBN 978-1-107-08341-7 (hardback)
1. Law, Anglo-Saxon. 2. Law – England – History. I. Title.
KD554.J87 2015
340.5′50942–dc23 2014047362

ISBN 978-1-107-08341-7 Hardback

To the memory of my father, Eugene Jurasinski (1929–2009)

Contents

Acknowledgments

This book originates in work undertaken nearly a decade ago with R. D. Fulk on an edition of the *Old English Canons of Theodore*. Our initial research impressed on me the need for a book-length study of the whole corpus of Old English penitentials, an underappreciated set of texts whose significance to the legal history of pre-Conquest England had yet to see much discussion outside of Allen J. Frantzen's pioneering studies. At the outset, then, I should acknowledge a very great debt to Professor Fulk for his generosity in offering to collaborate on an edition that would so reshape my interests in the years that followed.

Given its long period of development, it has been inevitable that portions of this book would appear elsewhere. A few paragraphs of Chapter 1 recast some of the points made in "The Old English Penitentials and the Law of Slavery," in *English Law before Magna Carta: Felix Liebermann and "Die Gesetze der Angelsachsen,"* ed. Stefan Jurasinski, Lisi Oliver, and Andrew Rabin (Leiden, The Netherlands: Brill, 2010), pp. 97–118. A section of Chapter 2 condenses the arguments of two prior articles: "Sanctuary, House-Peace, and the Traditionalism of Alfred's Laws," *The Journal of Legal History* 31 (2010): 129–47, and "Violence, Penance, and Secular Law in Alfred's Mosaic Prologue," *Haskins Society Journal* 22 (2011): 25–42. Some paragraphs of Chapter 6 rework portions of "Madness and Responsibility in Anglo-Saxon England," in *Peace and Protection in the Middle Ages*, ed. David Rollason and T. B. Lambert (Toronto and Durham, UK: Durham University Centre for Medieval Studies/Pontifical Institute for Mediaeval Studies, 2009), pp. 99–120. Chapter 5 is a revised version of "'Sick Maintenance' in Earlier English

Law," in *Capital and Corporal Punishment in Anglo-Saxon England*, ed. Jay Paul Gates and Nicole Marafioti (Rochester, NY: Boydell and Brewer, 2014), pp. 74–91. Translations from foreign languages are my own unless otherwise indicated; the original language is given only for quotations from primary texts. Where translations are not in dispute and cannot reasonably be improved upon, I quote those given by the editors of standard editions, my having done so indicated by "ed. and transl." in the citation. I regret very much that Rob Meens's *Penance in Medieval Europe: 600–1200* appeared just as work on this book was ending, which will explain its absence from the bibliography.

A sabbatical granted for the fall semester of 2011 made completion of the book possible, and I thank J. Roger Kurtz, our department chair at the time, for his support of my application. Colleagues at other institutions helped in various ways. R. D. Fulk's comments on an early version of Chapter 2 refined its argument considerably. Lisi Oliver and Andrew Rabin read the book in manuscript and gave excellent suggestions. Reports by the two referees for Cambridge University Press proved valuable. One of them – Paul Hyams – shed his anonymity to share with me his more detailed remarks on the manuscript, which offered many improvements in wording and helped me to situate better the argument of the manuscript within the broader concerns of historical scholarship. The referee who remained anonymous was a sharp-eyed hunter of errors and infelicitous phrases. It is impossible to state adequately my gratitude to the series editor, Michael Lobban, who read multiple drafts of the manuscript and offered detailed suggestions at each stage. The book assumed much of its present form under his patient guidance and owes him a great share of any virtues it may possess. The work of Christine A. T. Dunn, who copyedited the manuscript and suggested many improvements in phrasing, and Kanimozhi Ramamurthy, who oversaw the production of the book with great care, is also gratefully acknowledged. For permission to reproduce images, thanks are due to the Parker Library (with particular gratitude to Gill Cannell), the British Museum, and the British Library.

Over the years of writing, I have benefited from conversations and written exchanges with Lisi Oliver, Andrew Rabin, Daniela Fruscione, Bruce O'Brien, Bryan Carella, Nicole Marafioti, Jay Gates, Abigail Firey, Michael Elliot, and Helen Foxhall-Forbes, among others. I do not know how to account for the fact that not much of it was written before the birth of my son in 2009, and that work on the book is coming to a close as my daughter approaches age three. The fun of watching them grow and learn has, I suppose, been inherently motivating. They were spared listening to me talk about the book, though my wife, Aurora, was not so lucky. She offered essential guidance on how to frame its argument that sometimes harmonized uncannily with that of the series editor.

Introduction

Legislation, Custom, and the Sources of Early English Law

This book considers early English law from an unaccustomed point of view. Its focus is on texts not traditionally ascribed much worth as evidence of legal history. It was occasioned in part by historians' long-held doubts about the trustworthiness of royal legislation as a witness to legal practice. The reception of this more familiar set of texts affords some lessons about how hard it is to say anything with assurance about law in the Anglo-Saxon period, even with its wealth of textual evidence. Some words about royal legislation thus may not be out of place before our attention shifts in subsequent chapters to a decidedly different kind of prescriptive text that emerged in early England.

Long the standard place to begin for those interested in the workings of English law before the Norman Conquest, laws issued by Anglo-Saxon kings were some of the first of the post-Roman world to be written in the vernacular.[1] Unlike most other vernacular texts that likewise appeared early in pre-Conquest England, royal laws show an almost continuous development over four centuries and are attested in a broad range of manuscripts. These signs of their ostensible importance to their contemporaries, along with a seeming lack of other kinds of evidence, gave the Anglo-Saxon laws a prominent place in some of the

[1] While other Germanic languages, such as Old Saxon and Old High German, would be employed for literary and pastoral purposes, Continental vernaculars show no comparable range of uses until the later Middle Ages (a time during which, paradoxically, few official documents would be composed in English). The situation does not hold for Ireland, however, whose vernacular writings on law and penance attained great sophistication well before England's: see Allen J. Frantzen, *The Literature of Penance in Anglo-Saxon England* (New Brunswick, NJ: Rutgers University Press, 1983), 113.

earlier learned writings on the origins of English common law. Indeed, their centrality to the history of English law was never taken for granted as much as it was between the reign of Elizabeth I and the last decades of the eighteenth century.[2]

Yet the reception of the Anglo-Saxon laws in later years did not live up to expectations set by its first commentators. Though historians of the nineteenth and twentieth centuries were poised to benefit from brilliant editions of royal legislation by both German and British scholars, little was made of them. From Pollock and Maitland's *History of English Law before the Time of Edward I* (1898) and Theodore F. T. Plucknett's *Concise History of the Common Law* (1956) to S. F. C. Milsom's *Historical Foundations of the Common Law* (1969) and R. C. van Caenegem's *Birth of English Common Law* (1988), one finds only the most cursory discussions of Anglo-Saxon royal lawmaking or, as is more often the case, none at all.[3] That Anglo-Saxon law was relegated to the first chapter of the most celebrated of these texts – Pollock and Maitland's *History* – and left to Pollock to complete on his own (to Maitland's lasting disappointment) suggests that talking about it at all when addressing the development of English legal institutions was, at times, something of an obligatory nuisance.[4]

How it became commonplace for leading specialists in English legal history to ignore the first four hundred years of legislation in English

[2] On the Elizabethan reception of Anglo-Saxon legislation, the standard text is now Rebecca Brackmann, *The Elizabethan Invention of Anglo-Saxon England: Laurence Nowell, William Lambarde, and the Study of Old English* (Woodbridge, UK: D. S. Brewer, 2012). See also William Blackstone, *Commentaries on the Laws of England. A Facsimile of the First Edition of 1765–1769*, 4 vols. (Chicago: University of Chicago Press, 1979), I: 66. Here Blackstone locates the origins of English common law in the royal laws of Anglo-Saxon kings, principally Alfred's.

[3] Plucknett's *Concise History* (London: Little, Brown & Co., 1929; repr. 1956) spends a mere five pages on the period before the Conquest. It is safe to say that these results may be duplicated in studies not mentioned here, as is evident from Wormald's observations of 1999: "It is a remarkable, indeed an appalling fact that hardly more has been written on early English law since 1916 [the year in which the final volume of Felix Liebermann's *Gesetze der Angelsachsen* appeared] than in the century before" (Wormald, *The Making of English Law: King Alfred to the Twelfth Century* [Oxford: Blackwell, 1999], 24). One notable exception to the tendency described is *Essays in Anglo-Saxon Law,* eds. Henry Adams, Henry Cabot Lodge, Ernest Young, and J. Laurence Laughlin (Boston: Little, Brown, & Co., 1876), a remarkable collection whose influence from German philology caused it to be ignored in the years that followed. The *Oxford History of the Laws of England* (2003–10), which has no volume devoted exclusively to Anglo-Saxon law, has nonetheless taken major steps toward remedying the neglect of these materials.

[4] See Patrick Wormald, "Frederic William Maitland and the Earliest English Law," *Law and History Review* 16 (1998), 1–25 at 4.

is not easy to understand. That the Norman Conquest was so sweeping in its outcomes as to constitute, according to some historians, the effective beginning of English legal history does not wholly explain the omission of these materials, which are known to have held great interest at least for Maitland.[5] And though the study of Old English has never formed a part of most historians' training, some of the authors mentioned previously were perfectly capable readers of Old English.[6] For a sense of what determined the fortunes of Anglo-Saxon law in English legal historiography, we should perhaps look outside of received ideas and institutional obstacles, and consider instead the likelihood that pre-Conquest legislation could never compare favorably as a subject of scholarly inquiry with the wealth of English legal writing that postdates the rediscovery of Justinian's *Digest* in the twelfth century.[7] It was the sheer oddness of Anglo-Saxon legislation – about which more will be said in later sections of the present chapter – that ensured it would be the province of philologists rather than historians. And this was a misfortune in itself, one not ameliorated until the last decades of the twentieth century by the virtually solitary labors of Patrick Wormald. Because the Anglo-Saxon laws for the most part lack the literary qualities that made the late-medieval legislation of Frisia, Iceland, and Norway of interest beyond the ambit of legal-historical scholarship, even philological works devoted to their contents would hardly outnumber those written by historians.[8] Jakob Grimm seems not to have had Anglo-Saxon laws much

5 See Frederic William Maitland, "The Laws of the Anglo-Saxons," *The Quarterly Review* 200 (1904), 139–57. On the effects of the Conquest and subsequent French influence, see Paul Hyams, "The Common Law and the French Connection," *Proceedings of the Battle Conference on Anglo-Norman Studies* 4 (1982), 77–92.

6 In the United States, Anglo-Saxonists in departments of English and linguistics vastly outnumber their counterparts within departments of history, a count of the latter usually not exceeding the single digits. Some reasons for this situation, having mainly to do with irresponsible use of Anglo-Saxon materials for ideological ends by historians of the nineteenth century, are explored in Robin Fleming, "Henry Adams and the Anglo-Saxons," in *The Preservation and Transmission of Anglo-Saxon Culture*, ed. Paul Szarmach and Joel T. Rosenthal (Kalamazoo, MI: Medieval Institute, 1997), 13–36.

7 On the reception of Roman law during the eleventh and twelfth centuries in Western Europe, see Frederick Pollock and Frederic William Maitland, *History of English Law to the Time of Edward I*, 2 vols., 2nd ed. (Cambridge: Cambridge University Press, 1899; repr. 1968), I: 21–4; F. Wieacker, "*Ratio scripta.* Das römische Recht und die abendländische Rechtswissenschaft," in *Vom römischen Recht* (Leipzig: Köhler & Amelang, 1944), 195–284; Q. Breen, "The Twelfth-Century Revival of the Roman Law," *Oregon Law Review* 24 (1944–5), 244–87; T. F. T. Plucknett, "The Relations between Roman Law and English Common Law Down to the Sixteenth Century," *University of Toronto Law Journal* 3 (1939–40), 24–50.

8 Representative of earlier scholars' interest in alliterative formulae and other "poetic" elements of legislation in Germanic vernaculars is Dorothy Bethurum, "Stylistic Features of the Old English Laws," *Modern Language Review* 27 (1932), 263–79.

on his mind as he wrote "Von der Poesie im Recht" (1816), a study that would determine the direction of some later scholarship in its focus on ferreting out traces of oral culture he felt were present in much written legislation.[9] In his likewise influential *Deutsche Rechtsalterthümer* (1828), he would find the *Sachsenspiegel* and other late sources more certain guides to early Germanic habits of mind than the laws of Æthelberht or Alfred.[10] Departures from Grimm's assumptions were few in subsequent decades, and the habits engendered by his work are perhaps most evident in the handful of references to Anglo-Saxon law in Heinrich Brunner's otherwise sweeping *Deutsche Rechtsgeschichte* (1906).[11]

The influence of both Grimm and Brunner upon Felix Liebermann, the preeminent editor of Anglo-Saxon royal legislation, would shape the reception of these texts into the present. Their approach is evident throughout his *Gesetze der Angelsachsen* (1903–16), an edition (standard to this day) that deals deftly with philological matters but retreats for the most part from any claims about the overall significance of this corpus.[12] The view that Anglo-Saxon law offers more to the philologist than the historian would remain virtually intact in the years that followed. Thus scholars have spent much of the twentieth century scratching their heads over the meanings of *hapax legomena* and other obscurities much as Liebermann did in the commentary of his great edition, treating the Anglo-Saxon laws as an immense fund of lexical oddities and exotic customs.[13]

That the Anglo-Saxon laws have spent the entirety of their modern reception outside the focus of the two scholarly fields most disposed to make sense of them is indeed a deplorable thing. But it is not certain that earlier historians are wholly to be blamed for abandoning them. To

[9] Jakob Grimm, "Von der Poesie im Recht," *Zeitschrift für geschichtliche Rechtswissenschaft* 2 (1816), 25–99.

[10] References to Anglo-Saxon laws are outnumbered in this study by citations of Icelandic laws and compilations in other later Germanic vernaculars. Some attention is paid to *Beowulf,* held at this time (as it is occasionally now) to offer a view of early Germanic custom. See Jakob Grimm, *Deutsche Rechtsalterthümer* (Göttingen: Dieterichsche Buchhandlung, 1828), 42, 731.

[11] On Brunner's disappointment with Anglo-Saxon materials, see Wormald, *Making*, 15.

[12] For an amusing critique of Liebermann's method, see James Campbell, "Observations on English Government from the Tenth to the Twelfth Century," *Transactions of the Royal Historical Society* 25 (1975), 39–54 at 44.

[13] And this, among other things, they undoubtedly are. Exemplary studies along these lines include Carole Hough, "The Widow's *Mund* in Æthelberht 75 and 76," *JEGP* 98 (1999), 1–16; Lisi Oliver, "*Cyninges fedesl:* The King's Feeding in Æthelberht ch. 12," *Anglo-Saxon England* 27 (1998), 31–40.

the extent that royal legislation does possess the literary elements that so fascinated earlier scholars, even these features have presented problems of their own for the few historians bold enough to mine these texts for knowledge of early institutions. It is precisely because so many royal codes seem reflective of the personalities and ambitions of the kings under whose names they circulated that most modern scholars doubt they were understood as normative in the manner of Frankish legislation. Being unmentioned within records of disputes, even the grandest of law books, such as those issued by Alfred and Cnut, seemed to Wormald little more than ritual enactments of royal authority without real effect beyond the confines of the court, each perhaps echoing some of the chest beating that had surrounded the issuance of Æthelberht's laws "according to the examples of the Romans" (*iuxta exempla Romanorum*) centuries prior.[14] If the preparation of written law was indeed one of the stock gestures of Germanic kingship, intended more to authenticate royal power than to guide disputants through the minutiae of litigation, then Old English legislation demands a treatment very different from what is found in some scholarly writing, where a clause is trotted out for a quick sense of what was to be expected during the reign of Ine, Alfred, or Cnut without much regard for neighboring clauses or the overall aims of the code in which it occurs.

Nor can it be denied that genuine deficiencies in this corpus have made it unattractive to historians as a source of evidence. One who hopes to find in the legislation of Alfred or Cnut the sorts of details amply attested in the laws of Visigothic Spain, Lombard Italy, or Carolingian Francia will be disappointed. Most Old English royal legislation also shares an irritating tendency to avoid statements of abstract principle. Toward the end of the Anglo-Saxon period, and particularly during the reign of Æthelred II (d. 1016), much of what we are convention-bound to call "legislation"

[14] The claim is made often in Wormald's work. See especially his "*Lex Scripta* and *Verbum Regis:* Legislation and Germanic Kingship from Euric to Cnut," in *Early Medieval Kingship*, ed. P. H. Sawyer and I. N. Wood (Leeds, UK: Leeds University Press, 1977), 105–38; repr. in Wormald, *Legal Culture in the Early Medieval West: Law as Text, Image and Experience* (London: Hambledon, 1999), 1–43; also *Making*, 148, where Wormald observes of the Fonthill Letter, "[W]ritten law was apparently irrelevant, though Alfred's imposing *domboc* (incorporating Ine's laws) must have been issued only a few years before the episode." But see the qualifications urged in Levi Roach, "Law Codes and Legal Norms in later Anglo-Saxon England," *Historical Research* 86 (2013), 465–86. The sole account of Æthelberht's conversion and subsequent promulgation of written laws, whence comes the famous description of these laws' basis in Roman examples, is in *Bede's Ecclesiastical History of the English People*, ed. Bertram Colgrave and R. A. B. Mynors (Oxford: Clarendon, 1969), 150–1 (2.5).

amounts to little more than responses to domestic crises precipitated by Scandinavian raiding – pleas for national penance and behavior worthy of Christians so as to win back God's favor.[15]

With such encumbrances facing the historian of early English law, it is unsurprising that some scholars have sought in recent decades to expand the range of sources with which legal behaviors may be reconstructed beyond books of royal legislation.[16] Attention has focused principally on records of litigation embedded in charters, chronicles, and other prose texts.[17] While these texts pose problems of their own, being more often prepared by the winners of the disputes they memorialize, they at least allow us to descend from the ideals attested in royal legislation to the realities of law as it was understood by those who made use of it for their own ends.[18] They also show that the conduct of law in this period owed less to royal initiative than would be the case in later years.[19]

[15] On this see Chapters 3, 106–9, and 6, 176–77.

[16] John Hudson points out why historians ought to cast a wider net: "The categorization of certain affairs as legal does not make law at this time completely distinct from the rest of social life, nor give it as much autonomy as exists for modern or even later medieval law. Clearly the legal business of courts might have been hard to distinguish from their other activities, and not all arguments put forward in law cases were distinctively 'legal' in nature." See Hudson, *The Formation of the English Common Law* (London: Longman, 1996), 6.

[17] See, e.g., Patrick Wormald, "Charters, Law and the Settlement of Disputes in Anglo-Saxon England," in *The Settlement of Disputes in Early Medieval Europe*, eds. Wendy Davies and Paul Fouracre (Cambridge: Cambridge University Press, 1986), 149–68; repr. in idem, *Legal Culture*, 289–311. Andrew Rabin has also noted "the shortcomings of any approach [to pre-Conquest legal history] that assumes the extant corpus of early English law to be a fixed canon with clear boundaries and settled criteria for inclusion or exclusion"; see his "Ritual Magic or Legal Performance? Reconsidering an Old English Charm against Theft," in *English Law before Magna Carta*, 177–98 at 178. Rabin's studies in particular have gleaned much from nonlegislative sources about the practice of law within the Anglo-Saxon kingdoms, an approach exemplified in such studies as "The Wolf's Testimony to the English: Law and Witness in the *Sermo Lupi ad Anglos*," *JEGP* 105 (2006), 388–414; "Old English *forespeca* and the Role of the Advocate in Old English Law," *Mediaeval Studies* 69 (2007), 223–54; "Female Advocacy and Royal Protection in Tenth Century England: The Legal Career of Queen Ælfthryth," *Speculum* 84 (2009), 261–88.

[18] "[T]he vast majority of known suits had clergy on at least one side. Hardly less obviously, all these documents were composed by the winning party (nearly always a church), and make no pretence of impartiality." Wormald, *Making*, 146.

[19] Along with the fact that royal laws go unmentioned in these texts, instances of royal intervention suggest a very different pattern from what obtained during the Angevin period, when ministers of Henry II meddled without invitation in disputes over property, on which see Hudson, *Formation of the English Common Law*, 52–7. Significantly, Alfred becomes involved in Helmstan's case as narrated in the Fonthill Letter only when petitioned by Ordlaf. See Nicholas Brooks, "The Fonthill Letter, Ealdorman Ordlaf and Anglo-Saxon Law in Practice," in *Early Medieval Studies in Memory of Patrick Wormald*,

This book argues that Old English compilations on penance – a set of sources made use of occasionally by Liebermann to illuminate questions of Anglo-Saxon law, but cursorily and sometimes unreliably – may contribute more to such efforts than is typically assumed. Why legal historians have not done much with them is suggested by the unprepossessing nature of the texts. Though Old English penitential canons have been available to scholars in modern editions for nearly two centuries, we still cannot always be sure how they differed from other normative texts or how and when they were used. Matters are not helped by the fact that the most recent of these editions – with "recent" here meaning the early 1930s – do little to clarify their backgrounds and much to hinder their further use by historians. Yet the long omission of these materials from scholarly discussions of earlier English law has been costly. Given their focus on everyday life and their characteristic willingness to compromise when the ideals of bishops meet the practical realities of local custom, vernacular penitentials composed in pre-Conquest England offer a sense of how legal conventions were realized in practice that is for the most part unavailable either in royal legislation or in the narrative accounts of litigation sometimes found in diplomatic records. As we will see, they clarify much that royal legislation leaves obscure. To my knowledge, this book is the first to focus exclusively on the Old English penitentials, though its work is somewhat anticipated by chapters of Thomas Pollock Oakley's *English Penitential Discipline and Anglo-Saxon Law in Their Joint Influence* (1923). Many of Oakley's claims, as will be shown particularly in Chapter 1, stand very much in need of reassessment after nearly a century of uncritical repetition.

SEARCHING FOR "ANGLO-SAXON LAW"

Before explaining why royal legislation should be read in light of the texts considered here, as has been done hardly at all in most published scholarship, it will be necessary to make clear what I mean by the term *Anglo-Saxon law*, which will surface throughout the present study.[20] Those familiar with early English legal history may know why incautious use of the term is sometimes cringe inducing. For a sense of the problems

eds. Stephen Baxter, Catherine Karkov, Janet L. Nelson, and David Pelteret (Aldershot, UK: Ashgate, 2009), 301–18.

[20] The marginal status of these texts is perhaps evident in the handful of pages in Wormald's *Making* given to discussion of penitentials, even when these co-occur with, or serve as sources for, provisions of more explicitly secular legislation.

it poses, there is perhaps no better witness than the following quotation from Pollock and Maitland's *History*, one of the major legal-historical works of the past two centuries:[21]

> It suffices to know that, in its general features, Anglo-Saxon law is not only archaic, but offers an especially pure type of Germanic archaism.... The staple matter of judicial proceedings was of a rude and simple kind. In so far as we can trust the written laws, the only topics of general importance were manslaying, wounding, and cattle-stealing.... As to procedure, the forms were sometimes complicated, always stiff and unbending. Mistakes in form were probably fatal at every stage. Trial of questions of fact, in anything like the modern sense, was unknown.

Many of these observations reflect scholarly habits that became widespread toward the end of the nineteenth century. At this time, literary and legal historians alike were given to searching Old English texts for what they suggested about the prehistoric "Germanic" past without equal attention being given to what they may have meant when they appeared.[22] One of the results was a kind of confidence about what the past may have looked like common to those under no obligation to address specifics. In the case of Pollock and Maitland's *History,* the tendency yields a series of rather sweeping generalizations implicitly meant to apply to a period stretching from about the year 600 (when the first written book of laws appeared in English) to 1020 (the year in which Cnut's laws were promulgated).

Today, most of us would doubt any generalizations about a span of time that might encompass the reign of James I and the invention of the Internet. Yet scholars have long done just this for the legal environment of Anglo-Saxon England. Only in the last few decades have scholars seen anything in the laws of pre-Conquest England but hopeless conservatism and formalism. That law as we find it in the extant memorials might instead have arisen from conflicts between competing groups is something not often considered in scholarship of the past or even of the present. Given its implied indifference to local circumstances, social hierarchies, or the fact of ethnic difference (a subject of increasing importance with

[21] This amalgam of quotations (part of a larger group assembled in Wormald, "Charters, Law and the Settlement of Disputes in Anglo-Saxon England," 149–50, and criticized on different grounds) is drawn from Pollock and Maitland, *History of English Law*, I: 38, 44. Pollock and Maitland's *History* is still routinely cited in scholarly publications on earlier English laws, and it is not unusual to see some of its claims repeated without suspicion, particularly by those specializing in later periods who may not know better.

[22] The movement is now often dismissed, though its extreme manifestations are perhaps too often treated as the norm. On its influence upon English legal history, see Wormald, *Making*, 11–20.

the settlement and ultimate conquest of England by the Danes in the latter half of this period), the term *Anglo-Saxon law* has helped enable this impression of stagnancy and uniformity, a convenient shorthand whose inadequacies might be more apparent were it not so long in use.[23]

Yet the term is not easily abandoned, and not simply because there are no convenient alternatives. Certainly the notion of traditional folk law on which Pollock's claims rest may not be rejected outright. The question, perhaps, is whether Anglo-Saxon legislation was ever disposed to deliver this to us – something perhaps hinted at in Pollock's reluctance to "trust the written laws." Though Anglo-Saxon England (to use another problem term) produced legal prose in astonishing abundance – an achievement made more remarkable by the fact that virtually all of it is in Old English – this corpus of legislation appeared at a time in which writing was available to a relatively tiny subset of the population: namely, clerical elites and the kings and lay magnates they were willing to instruct.[24] We should naturally expect it to disclose the interests of this rather narrow group at the expense of others.

WRITTEN AND TRADITIONAL LAW

Such an impression is confirmed by examination of the prologues often affixed to these texts by the kings and counselors who authorized their promulgation. In the claims to unique authority voiced in these prologues, traces of earlier conflicts over who gets to make law – and the related question of the medium in which it should be situated – seem still to reverberate.[25] As we will see, the sources in question give no reason to believe that such conflicts ceased as the centuries wore on. We may take as an example of such uncertainties the varied words with which the

[23] See, e.g., Jerome Hall's *General Principles of Criminal Law* (Indianapolis: Bobbs Merrill, 1960), 78. In many respects, this study handles the Anglo-Saxon period admirably, its defect being simply those of the dominant works of its day.

[24] Matthew Townend urges that "we must be careful to think in terms of an England that was truly Anglo-Scandinavian." See his *Language and History in Viking Age England: Linguistic Relations between Speakers of Old Norse and Old English*, Studies in the Early Middle Ages 6 (Turnhout, Belgium: Brepols, 2002), 210. On the difficulties of ascribing collective identity to the speakers of disparate Germanic dialects inhabiting the separate kingdoms we are now in the habit of calling "Anglo-Saxon England," see Sarah Foot, "The Making of *Angelcynn:* English Identity before the Norman Conquest," *Transactions of the Royal Historical Society* 6th ser. 6 (1996), 25–49.

[25] I take as a foundational assumption for what follows here Paul Hyams's claim (made in reference to different aspects of royal legislation) that "The progressive strengthening of royal aspirations is easily visible in the extant law codes." Hyams, *Rancor and Reconciliation in Medieval England* (Ithaca, NY: Cornell University Press, 2003), 72.

English designated "law." It is sometimes pointed out that Modern English "law" descends from no word in the native Anglo-Saxon lexicon.[26] Its Old English ancestor, *lagu*, is probably a loan from the Prehistoric Old Norse plural noun **lagu* (attested in written Old Icelandic as *lög*), which arrived in England no earlier than the first waves of Scandinavian invasion and settlement toward the end of the eighth century.[27] Its adoption in the English legal lexicon seems to have been slow. Only during the disastrous reign of King Æthelred II, who watched the crown fall to the Norse conqueror Swein Forkbeard and would be succeeded by Swein's son Cnut, would *lagu* make a secure place for itself alongside other terms traditionally used by Anglo-Saxon legislators to describe official decrees.[28] Though commonly seen as evidence for the English absorption of Norse ways from the increasingly dominant Danish population, it seems fair to wonder whether the etymological connection of this noun with verbs meaning "to lay down" (Old Norse *leggja*, Old English *lecgan*) perhaps lent it some appeal to legislating kings given the role implicitly granted by the term to individual agency rather than immemorial custom.[29] Indeed, it may have resolved a terminological problem that had strewn with obstacles the first steps along the path toward royal dominance of lawmaking.

The way in which some of the older words are used discloses uncertainties over how, and by whom, law should be made that are not as apparent in later texts. The two most important of the nouns in question

[26] The Norse descent of the term is assumed in Sara M. Pons-Sanz, *Norse-Derived Vocabulary in Late Old English Texts: Wulfstan's Works, a Case Study* (Amsterdam: John Benjamins/University Press of Southern Denmark, 2007; repr. 2012), at 124 and *passim;* but her doubts in a subsequent publication (*The Lexical Effects of Anglo-Scandinavian Linguistic Contact on Old English* [Turnhout, Belgium: Brepols, 2013], 80, 84) should be borne in mind.

[27] This and subsequent etymological observations owe much to the *Oxford English Dictionary*, ed. James A. H. Murray (Oxford: Clarendon, 1902), s.v. "law." For a broader overview of language contact between the English and Danish populations, see Townend, *Language and History in Viking Age England*. The matters considered here receive a brief but illuminating discussion in William Ian Miller, "Of Outlaws, Christians, Horsemeat, and Writing: Uniform Laws and Saga Iceland," *Michigan Law Review* 89 (1991), 2081–95 at 2081–2.

[28] On the Scandinavian vocabulary of some Æthelredian laws, see Charlotte Neff, "Scandinavian Elements in the Wantage Code of Æthelred II," *Journal of Legal History* 10 (1989), 285–316 at 288–9 and *passim.*

[29] That the Norse form had the meaning "statute" upon adoption by the English was suggested in Charles Sweet, "The History of the Word 'Law' [II]," *Law Magazine and Review*, n.s. 3 (1874), 644–58 at 645.

were *ǣ(w)* and *dōm*, and they appear to have meant very different things. Old English *ǣ* is commonly glossed in scholarly writing as "traditional law" and opposed conceptually to *dōm*, a trace of whose meaning ("judgment") survives in Modern English "doomsday" and in the verb "deem" (a descendant of the *i*-mutated verb *dēman*, "to judge").[30] In the Anglo-Saxon period, *dōm* seems to have specifically connoted "decree (made by an individual)": thus Alfred and his successors call his compilation of laws a *domboc* ("book of judgments").[31] Its associations with royal lawmaking in particular may be evident from the panel of the Franks Casket depicting the sack of Jerusalem by Titus in AD 70. Here the word *dōm* appears in Runic writing in the lower-left margin, adjacent to an image of a ruler sitting in judgment.

According to Richard Abels, most recent commentary holds that the Franks Casket "could have been made at any of the great monasteries of early-eighth-century Northumbria," leaving its usage, however uncertain, of some value for understanding the earliest English legislation we possess.[32] Here, perhaps, we see how closely it was associated with royal initiative before coming to refer more generally to legislation.[33] Bearing all of this in mind, we may now consider how these terms are employed in the prologue to an early Kentish collection of ordinances of the late seventh century. In spite of the writer's best efforts to treat these words

[30] Use of the terms thus offers no exact parallel to French, where *lois* refers to "written laws" and *droit* to "law generally": see Hudson, *Formation of the English Common Law*, 3. The chasm between the Old English terms is wider than in French given the association of *dōm* specifically with royal decrees.

[31] The long vowel in *dōm* would make it a candidate at some point during the sixteenth or seventeenth century for the "Great Vowel Shift," a phonological change involving the raising of all long vowels that would in this instance yield Modern English "doom": the Old English form would have rhymed with Modern English "home." According to Patrick Wormald, *æ* "has strong connotations of accepted law" and is perhaps a synonym of *þeaw*, "custom," a word used in similar fashion by the Kentish king Wihtræd in his laws: see Wormald, *Making*, 95. The point differs little from that made in *Die Gesetze der Angelsachsen*, 3 vols., ed. Felix Liebermann (Halle, Germany: Niemeyer, 1903–16), III: 18, where Liebermann glosses *ǽ* as "Frühere Gesetze, jedoch wohl ungeschriebene," "Earlier laws, but probably unwritten." Lisi Oliver arrives at similar conclusions on the basis of Indo-European etymology: see Oliver, *The Beginnings of English Law* (Toronto: University of Toronto Press, 2001), 134.

[32] Richard Abels, "What Has Weland to Do with Christ? The Franks Casket and the Acculturation of Christianity in Early Anglo-Saxon England," *Speculum* 84 (2009), 549–81 at 564. The relevant panel is described briefly at 557.

[33] Use of the term to designate law would cease by the second half of the tenth century, when it was overtaken by *lagu*. See Pons-Sanz, *Norse-Derived Vocabulary in Late Old English Texts*, 86.

FIGURE 1. Detail from the Franks Casket, back panel.
(Photograph: © Trustees of the British Museum.)

as near synonyms, it will be evident that they react toward one another like two negatively charged magnets:[34]

Hloþhære 7 Eadric,	*Hlothhere and Eadric,*
Cantwara cyningas,	*kings of the men of Kent,*
ecton þa ǽ	*extended the laws*
þa ðe heora aldoras	*that their ancestors*
ær geworhton	*earlier made*
ðyssum domum	*with these judgments*
þe her efter sægeþ.	*which are stated hereafter.*

The preface to Hloþhere and Eadric's laws, often overlooked but dense with significance, suggests that if there was a distinction between traditional folk law (*ǣ*) and royal law (*dōm*) in the early English legal vocabulary, legislators appreciated at an early date the necessity of obscuring it. I have presented the text in lines of verse in order to highlight the poetic qualities noted by Liebermann, whose observation that this preface is an example of deliberately alliterative prose suggests that we should pay close attention to this feature of the text.[35] The alliterations in this case seem crafted

[34] The text is drawn from what is now the standard edition, Oliver's *Beginnings of English Law*, 126. Oliver's translation has influenced my own. Her overview of the historical circumstances surrounding the appearance of these laws (117–21) is the best to date; here she notes that the laws need not be dated to their brief period of joint rule (673–84), which ended with a conspiracy by Eadric that proved fatal to his brother.

[35] *Gesetze*, ed. Liebermann, III: 18. In presenting the preface in this way, I understand that it does not show anything like full conformity to the rules of alliterative verse. But there can be no doubt that the preface is at least designedly reminiscent of verse as it would

to overcome the sort of resistance that we might expect to have greeted the promulgation of written law in its first decades of use among the people of Kent.[36] The words with which *ǽ* alliterates, *aldoras* and *ær*, bear associations with tradition and antiquity. Simultaneously, however, the preface presents these ancestral *ǽ* as things made (*geworhton*, "wrought") through the efforts of particular people (while remaining vague about who these people were: prior Kentish kings or Kentish forefathers in general?). The prologue concludes with an assertion of the appropriateness of the new forms – written "dooms" that effectively limit the range of persons capable of producing and authorizing law – as conduits of these ancient customs. We may suspect that whoever wrote this knew something of the unease that accompanied the issuance of written law and saw in the associations of alliterative verse, itself a practice of pre-Christian antiquity, just the sort of appeal to tradition that might quiet those rankled by the shift from traditional to written and royally authorized law.

The defensiveness of the preface shows that the advent of written vernacular law in England does not simply start a camera rolling on ancient practices proceeding much as they had generations prior. Rather, the preface suggests that written law was seen as a contentious innovation needing to be couched in a rhetoric of traditionalism in order to seem harmless. It also points to the difficulties of knowing where, exactly, "Anglo-Saxon law" is to be found. Simply because a Kentish chieftain styled himself a king and began issuing written ordinances in the manner of Frankish monarchs did not make these ordinances law. Underlying the triumphalism of the preface is an awareness that others might challenge the right of these kings to alter long-observed practices, or ask by what privilege (or by what means in a polity devoid of anything like a coercive state apparatus) any elite figure might claim to issue ordinances his fellows were bound to observe. Its task, achieved primarily by rhetorical means, is to give the appearance that only the outward form of the law has changed. That the author of the preface sought such an impression is, perhaps, evident in his diction. The verb *ecton*, the preterite plural of *eacan*, may certainly be glossed "add to, extend," as is common

have been known among the people of seventh-century Kent. An analogue is perhaps furnished by the style of some Old English charms, brief and orally derived texts that combine the features of prose and verse. On the nature of these texts, see Karen Louise Jolly, *Popular Religion in Late Saxon England* (Chapel Hill: University of North Carolina Press, 1996).

[36] The laws of Hloþhere and Eadric seem to have been preceded only by those issued by Æthelberht in the first years of the seventh century.

practice. But its connotations were in all likelihood not those of the Modern English words with which it is rendered. The verb, along with its "inchoative" variant *eacnan*, had associations with pregnancy. An *eacniende wif* was a pregnant woman and an *eacnung* a fetus.[37] We can see how carefully the scribe has chosen his words. Hloþhere and Eadric have "extended" the ancestral law of the Kentish people in such a way that their codification bears the same relation to what came before it as children to their parents. While the laws of these kings may have differed in appearance from those of their ancestors, they nonetheless perpetuated their most essential properties.

The efficacy of the strategy just described is perhaps attested by its subsequent use. The prologue to the laws of Wihtræd, datable to the year 695, echoes that of Hlothere and Eadric, though without alliterative embellishment: "Þær ða eadigan fundon mid ealra gemedum ðas domas 7 Cantwara rihtum þeawum æcton, swa hit hyr efter segeþ," "There the great men devised, with the consent of all, these decrees, and added to the just customs of the Kentish people, as it hereafter says and declares ...."[38] Already in this text we can discern the shrinking domain of traditional law. Whereas Hlothere and Eadric claimed to have done no more than add to the great body of *ǽ* produced by their ancestors, Wihtræd feels obligated to perpetuate only what he deems the *just* customs (*rihtum þeawum*) of prior unwritten law.

Assurances that royal codes inaugurated no real changes to long-observed norms are not confined to the early period of Anglo-Saxon lawmaking. Those in the preface to Alfred's *domboc*, issued not long before the king's death near the close of the ninth century, differ from similar gestures in subsequent legislation by being the last to make use of the triad (*ǽ*, *dōm*, and *eacan*) found in prior Kentish laws.[39] By this

[37] *Gesetze*, ed. Liebermann, I: 32–3 (*El.* 18).

[38] Text and translation are from Oliver, *The Beginnings of English Law*, 152–3. My emphasis.

[39] The terms do not arrive until the conclusion of Alfred's preface, and their manner of appearance is quite removed from the Kentish examples discussed: "Þis sindan ða domas þe se ælmihtega God self sprecende wæs to Moyse 7 him bebead to healdenne; 7 siððan se áncenneda Dryhtnes sunu, ure God, þæt is hælend Crist, on middangeard cwom, he cwæð, ðæt he ne come no ðas bebodu to brecanne ne to forbeodanne, ac mid eallum godum to ecanne; 7 mildheortnesse 7 eaðmodnesse he lærde," "These are the judgments that almighty God was speaking himself to Moses and bade him keep; and afterward the only-begotten son of the Lord, our God, that is the Savior Christ, entered the world, he said, that he did not come to break or to suppress those commandments, but to increase them with all good [laws?]; and he taught mercy and humility." *Gesetze*, ed. Liebermann, I: 42. The quoted passage renders Matthew 5:17, in which Christ asserts that he has come not to destroy (*soluere*) but to fulfill (*adimplere*) the Torah.

time, Alfred could look back on a three-hundred-year tradition of English legislation, augmented by the laws of his West-Saxon "kinsman" Ine, whose seventh-century code may in turn show influence from Wihtræd.[40] Alfred's *domboc* would be the most grandiose contribution to this tradition yet, rivaled in scope only some 130 years later by the massive compilation of secular and ecclesiastical ordinances penned by Wulfstan, Bishop of London and Archbishop of York (d. 1023), for the Danish conqueror Cnut. Between the close of the seventh century and end of the ninth, written law seems to have become an aspect of tradition, which is perhaps why Alfred claimed the influence not of a vague set of *aldoras* but of specific lawgiving monarchs. Yet the need to neutralize the claims of unwritten law is still perceptible.[41] The *domboc* begins with an elaborate and free paraphrase of legal clauses from Exodus, a portion of the text meant perhaps to situate the origins of law entirely in things written and thereby cleanse lawmaking of the older associations borne by *ǣ*.[42] As Wormald notes, this word loses its ancient significance for the first time in Alfred's prologue, becoming by this point in its semantic trajectory just another term for written law.[43]

Alfred is as careful as his predecessors to play the game of seeming not to have tampered with venerable custom. In describing his purposes in preparing the *domboc*, Alfred says that he "dared not presume" (*ne dorste geðristlæcan*) to "put in writing at all much" (*awuht fela on gewrit settan*) of his own laws, having merely "gathered together" from the laws of his "forebears" (later identified as Æthelberht, Ine and Offa) those that "pleased him most" (*togædere gegaderode 7 awritan het, monege þara þe ure foregengan heoldon, ða ðe me licodon*).[44] Most commentators on

40 The influence of Wihtræd's laws on Ine is considered in *The Laws of the Earliest English Kings*, ed. and trans. F. L. Attenborough (New York: Russell and Russell, 1963), 3.

41 Such motives seem in keeping with the emphasis on literacy among judges attributed to Alfred in the final chapter of *Asser's Life of King Alfred*, ed. William Henry Stevenson (Oxford: Oxford University Press, 1959), 93–4.

42 The nature of the "Mosaic Prologue" will be considered in greater detail toward the beginning of Chapter 2.

43 "In the general legal sense, the word seems to be used only in the seventh century and in antithesis or parallel to *dom*.... But A[lfred] Int[troduction] 49:1, where it means Christ's Law ... usher[s] in its late Saxon usage for almost any aspect of the Divine Law ...." Wormald, *Making*, 95n330. The passage in question refers to the apostles sent to Antioch and Syria "Cristes æ to læranne," "To teach Christ's law" (*Gesetze*, ed. Liebermann, I: 42). Only in Alfred's paraphrase of Acts 15 does the success of their efforts depend solely on their use of writing.

44 See *Gesetze*, ed. Liebermann, I: 46. This and subsequent quotations from Alfred's *domboc* are from Liebermann's text of the earliest manuscript witness, CCCC 173 ("The Parker Manuscript"). The translation owes something to Wormald's in *Making*, 277.

Alfred's laws have found this statement misleading.[45] The laws of Æthelberht do not survive recognizably in Alfred's; Ine's appear only as an appendix.[46] As for Offa's, to go beyond speculation is impossible, because these do not survive and may never have existed.[47] There is, however, a great deal about Alfred's laws that must have been entirely new. As we will see in Chapter 2, his *domboc* is suffused like those of no king before him with the influence of ecclesiastical discipline: it is the first English code to attempt a large-scale adoption of canon law. It seems fair to wonder whether Alfred's defensiveness is in proportion to his ambition.

Both the Kentish and West-Saxon prefaces to royal legislation suggest that kings in the period before the Conquest enjoyed quite limited authorization to issue laws in their own name. At the very least, for a king to acknowledge having done so was unseemly, something that remained the case even for a conqueror such as Cnut.[48] Ordinances authorized by a king and his *witena gemot*, a body of counselors typically made up of bishops and lay magnates, competed with older habits and practices whose influence could never be wholly eradicated.[49] What were they, and where are they to be found? Here again, the evidence of legislation is likely deceptive. As an example, we may take the feud, whose traditional vocabulary of wergild and *bōt* (the latter being payment for lesser injuries) is, perhaps, the most familiar feature of law in Anglo-Saxon England.[50]

[45] As Wormald (*Making*, 279) has noted most recently, Alfred's claim to have appropriated these earlier laws, not daring to add any of his own, should be read skeptically; the ordinances of the *domboc* appear almost entirely of Alfred's own devising.

[46] See the overview given in *Gesetze*, ed. Liebermann, III: 33.

[47] Wormald argues (*Making*, 106–8) that Alfred may have had in mind "the report by the papal legates, George of Ostia and Theophylact of Todi, of the *capitulare* they laid before Ælfwold's Northumbrian council, then before Offa and the southern English." Even if this argument is accepted, the resemblances between this document and Alfred's laws do not seem particularly close, and the question of the presence of Offa's ordinances in the *domboc* rightly remains a matter of debate.

[48] Upon his accession Cnut agreed to uphold "the laws of Edgar": see *The Anglo-Saxon Chronicle, Vol. 6: MS D*, ed. G. P. Cubbin (Cambridge: D. S. Brewer, 1996), 63.

[49] The point was made more forcefully by Wormald toward the beginning of his career but seems no less salient now: "[T]he production and recording of written law tended to be inspired by ideological ambitions: the feeling that it was appropriate for the leaders of a civilised and Christian people to do as the Romans and Israelites had done.... There is thus no question that early medieval legal texts are mere clerical fantasies, without relevance to the law as it was issued and enforced in Anglo-Saxon England." See Wormald, "Æthelred the Lawmaker," *Ethelred the Unready: Papers from the Millenary Conference*, BAR British Series 59, ed. David Hill (Oxford: British Archaeological Reports, 1978), 47–80 at 49.

[50] Old English *bōt* survived into the Early Modern period with only a trace of its legal sense, having the somewhat vaguer meaning "remedy" when used by the speaker

From the outset, Anglo-Saxon kings sought through their written laws to limit the violence associated with the feud, perhaps because of the influence of the Church, perhaps because of the difficulties inherent in governing territories perpetually rattled by small-scale warfare.[51] They did so as verse texts continued to extol the virtues of vengeance done well, much as they had, in all likelihood, long before verse was ever put to writing.[52] Throughout the Anglo-Saxon period and beyond, the feud rested on its own set of laws, practices, and beliefs, and these are, as Hyams and others have shown, more solidly attested in imaginative literature than in legislation.[53] Pre-Conquest royal legislation is, at best, a record of attempts to curb their excesses, offering few insights about the norms that underlay them.

Once we leave the feud, it becomes harder to tell what traditional laws observed among the Anglo-Saxons may have looked like. For a sense of these norms, most scholars have relied on royal legislation in spite of its quietly antagonistic relationship with customary law. Some have hoped to find the most vigorous traces of traditional observances in the laws issued by King Æthelberht of Kent in 597. Æthelberht's is one of the few works of legislation to bear no authentic prefatory material at all.[54] In spite of its preservation only in the twelfth-century *Textus Roffensis* alongside all other Kentish royal laws issued during the seventh century, we can be sure that this collection of ordinances is the earliest surviving English

of Shakespeare's 29th sonnet, who "trouble[s] deaf heav'n with [his] bootless cries": *Shakespeare's Sonnets*, ed. Stephen Booth (New Haven, CT: Yale University Press, 1977), 28–9. On the feud as an institution, see William Ian Miller, "Choosing the Avenger: Some Aspects of the Bloodfeud in Medieval Iceland and England," *Law and History Review* 1 (1983), 159–204.

51 One ordinance characteristic of this tendency occurs in the laws of Edmund (r. 939–46), where it is urged that only those guilty of homicide, as opposed to their kin as well, be targets of retaliatory vengeance; a provision in keeping with those found in various laws issued on the Continent. For the text, see *Gesetze*, ed. Liebermann, I: 186–7. The extent to which royal laws such as Alfred's placed restraints upon violence remains somewhat disputed: see Chapter 2, 57–62.

52 As is evident in the story of the grisly vengeance perpetrated on his captor Niðhad by Weland, which was commemorated in Norse and English verse alike and appears even on a panel of Franks Casket – rather incongruously alongside a depiction of the Adoration of the Magi. On Anglo-Saxon responses to the Weland legend, none of which seems to have been negative, see Abels, "What Has Weland to Do with Christ?," 566–7.

53 See Hyams, *Rancor and Reconciliation*, 59–66.

54 The simple rubric with which it begins – *Þis syndon þa domas þe Æðelbirht cyning asette on Agustinus dæge*, "These are the judgments that Æthelbeorht established in the time of Augustine [of Canterbury]" – is almost certainly a later addition. On this see Oliver, *The Beginnings of English Law*, 83.

text of any sort not composed in the Runic alphabet.[55] And as might be expected for a text this old, the laws of Æthelberht contain a number of usages unattested elsewhere in the Old English corpus and offer evidence of economic and social arrangements so different from what obtained in later periods that they must be traditional.[56] They are also the most tight-lipped of early English laws, being composed in the simple "if-then" style favored at the time by Frankish legislation. Even this feature, however, potentially marks them as something new. The nature of their dependence on Frankish models has never been clear, but the possibility that some are outright importations from Francia seems difficult to deny outright when we consider an example such as the following:[57]

LAWS OF ÆTHELBERHT: (61) Gif hrif wund weorðeþ, XII scill gebete. (61.1) Gif he þurhðirel weorðeþ, XX scill gebete.	LEGES ALAMANNORUM: (55) Si autem interiora membra vulneratus fuerit, quod "hrevovunt" dicunt, cum 12 solidis conponat. (56) Si transpunctus fuerit, cum 24 solidis conponat.
If the belly becomes wounded, let [the offender] compensate with twelve shillings. If he [the victim] should be pierced through, let [the offender] compensate with twenty shillings.	*If, however, he should be wounded in his internal organs, which [the Alamanni] call "hrevovunt," let the offender compensate with twelve solidi. Should he be pierced through, let him compensate with 24 solidi.*

Wormald observed that Æthelberht's laws stick closely to the overall organization of the *Leges Alamannorum*, one of the plethora of tribal laws issued on the Continent over the course of the seventh and eighth

[55] The earliest Runic inscriptions in English may date from the fifth century: see Karl Schneider, "Six Old English Runic Inscriptions Reconsidered," in *Nordica et Anglica: Studies in Honor of Stefán Einarsson*, ed. Allan H. Orrick (The Hague: Mouton, 1968), 37–52; Fred Robinson, "Old English," in *Early Germanic Literature and Culture*, ed. Brian Murdoch and Malcolm Read (Rochester, NY: Camden House, 2004), 205–34 at 206. The standard edition of Æthelberht's laws is to be found in Oliver, *The Beginnings of English Law*, 60–116. An even earlier date than that favored by Oliver and other specialists is suggested in H. G. Richardson and G. O. Sayles, *Law and Legislation from Æthelberht to Magna Carta* (Edinburgh: University of Edinburgh Press, 1966), 1–12, 157–69.

[56] This is manifestly the case with its descriptions of marriage and the status of the *esne*, discussed in more detail in Chapters 2 and 3 of the present study.

[57] *Leges Alamannorum*, MGH Leges Sectio I, Tom. 5/1, ed. Karl Lehmann; rev. ed. Karl August Eckhardt (Hanover: Hahnsche Buchhandlung, 1966), 126. The parallel was earlier noted by Liebermann: see *Gesetze*, ed. Liebermann, III: 12.

centuries, and he held it to have been influenced by some Frankish source common to both.[58] This feature of Æthelberht's laws, when considered alongside close parallels such as the one given in the preceding text, suggests doubts about their ability, however remarkable their survival from the earliest period of English prose composition, to offer a wholly unobstructed view of pre-Christian traditions. These earliest of English laws may in some respects have been Frankish, at least in inspiration.[59]

At the other end of the Anglo-Saxon period, we find legislation even more dominated by learned texts and clerical ideals. One of the few substantial changes discernible in later legislation is the increased use of mutilation rather than execution, a development that, according to Katherine O'Brien O'Keeffe, shows some of the ways in which Anglo-Saxon ruling elites "sought to extend the reach of law inward into the soul."[60] Concern for the offender's spiritual condition seems to have motivated such measures. Particularly during the later Anglo-Saxon period, bishops were inclined to oppose execution as it denied to wrongdoers the possibility of contrition, though there were as well principled objections to the involvement of any cleric in the shedding of blood.[61] The new concern for the inward condition of the violent is routinely held to coincide with the involvement of Wulfstan in writing royal legislation, a prelate whose work shows deep awareness of both Latin and Old English canons on penance. We will see in Chapter 2 some reasons why this periodization should be questioned; for now, it may be said that pastoral handbooks composed in Old English exhibit an interest in the inward nature of culpability that must antedate the career of Wulfstan and like-minded prelates.

That historians have so long been inclined to "trust the written laws" for a sense of the norms observed by the greater share of the population

[58] See Wormald, *Making*, 97.

[59] The point has been made repeatedly over the years, one prominent argument in its favor being J. M. Wallace-Hadrill, *Early Germanic Kingship in England and on the Continent* (Oxford: Clarendon, 1971), 36–9. On the relationship of early Kent and the Frankish kingdoms, which appears in many respects to have involved at times slavish mimicry of the latter by the former, see Alban Gautier, "Manger et boire à la mode étrangère: adoption, adaptation et rejet des pratiques festives continentales dans la Grande-Bretagne du VIIe siecle," *Médiévales* 51 (2006), 37–52.

[60] See Katherine O'Brien O'Keeffe, "Body and Law in Late Anglo-Saxon England," *Anglo-Saxon England* 27 (1998), 209–32 at 230.

[61] On this see James W. Earl, "Violence and Non-Violence in Anglo-Saxon England: Ælfric's 'Passion of St. Edmund,'" *Philological Quarterly* 78 (1999), 125–49 at 133. See also Nicole Marafioti's excellent "Punishing Bodies and Saving Souls: Capital and Corporal Punishment in Late Anglo-Saxon England," *Haskins Society Journal* 20 (2008), 39–57.

is, in part, owing to habits stretching back to the initial reception of these texts. Though the Norman Conquest would put an end to the use of English in laws and other official documents, Anglo-Saxon royal legislation, by then representing nearly half a millennium of unbroken tradition, would remain a source of fascination to England's new French-speaking elite, becoming an object of sustained study as late as the reign of Henry I (r. 1100–35).[62] The myth of royal legislation as an unmediated source of Anglo-Saxon law in some respects owes its birth to these scholars, if only because translating these texts into Latin effectively made them the principal means by which antiquarians of the later Middle Ages would learn about legal conditions in pre-Conquest England. Until the reign of Elizabeth I, the laws of Alfred and his successors would be known through *Quadripartitus*, a translation into Latin of these and other legislative texts completed during the twelfth century by an author whose first language was probably not English.[63] This text would shape more than any other the scholarly reception of the Old English royal laws upon their rediscovery by Matthew Parker and his circle.[64]

An underlying assumption of the following chapters, shared by recent as well as older studies, is that discerning the nature of "Anglo-Saxon law" involves something more than consulting the relevant passages of royal legislation. We have seen that texts of this sort are sometimes so given to evasions and rhetorical sleight of hand, so bound up in the personal reputations of the kings who authorized them, that they cannot be

[62] On the study of pre-Conquest law during the first half of the twelfth century, see Wormald, *Making*, 224–9 and *passim*. For Wormald, "The reign of Henry I was the most important period in the history of Old English law from 1066 itself to the reign of Elizabeth. What was then done to preserve and transmit its memorials in large measure determined what was known of it for the next four and a half centuries" (228). On the nature of this tradition, see Bruce R. O'Brien, "The *Instituta Cnuti* and the Translation of English Law," *Anglo-Norman Studies* 25 (2003), 177–97.

[63] On *Quadripartitus*, the major translation into Latin of Old English ordinances, see Felix Liebermann, *Quadripartitus. Ein englisches Rechtsbuch von 1114* (Halle, Germany: Max Niemeyer, 1892); Richard Sharpe, "The Prefaces of *Quadripartitus*," in *Law and Government in Medieval England and Normandy: Essays in Honour of Sir James Holt*, ed. George Garnett and John Hudson (Cambridge: Cambridge University Press, 1994), 148–72; idem, "The Dating of *Quadripartitus* Again," in *English Law before Magna Carta*, 81–96; Bruce R. O'Brien, *Reversing Babel: Translation among the English during an Age of Conquests, c. 800 to c. 1200* (Newark: University of Delaware Press, 2011), 125–7. The late-medieval reception of *Quadripartitus* is considered in Jeremy Catto, "Andrew Horn: Law and History in Fourteenth-Century England," in *The Writing of History in the Middle Ages: Essays Presented to Richard William Southern*, ed. R. H. C. Davis (Oxford: Clarendon, 1981), 367–91.

[64] See Chapter 1, 37.

used for such purposes without the utmost caution. Subsequent chapters will make evident some of the ways in which trusting the pronouncements of kings and bishops has left us with an inadequate and sometimes naïve understanding of earlier English institutions. Chapter 1 examines the reception of the Old English penitentials from the twelfth to the twenty-first centuries, a period in which these texts move from being seen as prescriptive sources of great importance for knowledge of Anglo-Saxon law to mere faulty translations of their more prestigious Latin exemplars. Chapter 2 explores the ways in which our often-imperfect knowledge of Anglo-Saxon institutions has been used, sometimes mistakenly, to assign them their places in the chronology of early English prose. Chapter 3 discusses the law of slavery, a subject that seems to have prompted the authors of Old English penitentials to depart from the language of their sources more than any other, perhaps because English and Frankish attitudes toward slaves were difficult to reconcile for much of the Anglo-Saxon period. Chapter 4 shows that the Old English penitentials, by both granting more room to customary observances and exceeding their sources in rigor, adumbrate a set of views on marriage that complicates standard histories of this institution. Chapter 5 traces the development of "sick-maintenance," an institution arguably of Indo-European descent, through layers of transmission in Latin and English canons. Here it is shown that variations from source material, rather than indicating the translator's failure to understand the Latin, show us instead his dependence upon ideas attested elsewhere within the early Germanic world, revealing in the process a distinctly English variant of this institution. In Chapter 6, the concern of the Old English penitentials with a matter long assumed to have been irrelevant to pre-Conquest legal history – mental culpability – is considered at length. This chapter draws on verse and narrative literature to demonstrate the ways in which the Old English penitentials, in rejecting notions of spiritual pollution underlying their sources, disclose an understanding of mental liability rather more intricate than those conventionally attributed to Anglo-Saxon England.

1

The Old English Penitentials and Their Reception

For much of the earlier Middle Ages, priests and bishops throughout Western Europe readied themselves to administer the sacrament of penance with some of the most ambitious encyclopedias of vice ever composed in any language, the *libri poenitentiales*.[1] Outside of Ireland, where pastoral writings in the vernacular appeared early, these texts were composed in an accessible Latin. Their compilers indulged in few innovations, collecting judgments from earlier authorities and organizing them by topic to aid the work of confessors. In their pages, clerics could find a range of sins unflinchingly catalogued and linked with recommended periods of fasting (or, occasionally, other means of satisfaction) as well as more general observations on pastoral questions. The "tariffs" assigned in these texts to various infractions are among our principal witnesses to ecclesiastical law in the period before consistory courts or the systematic compilations of Burchard of Worms (ca. 965–1025), Ivo of Chartres (ca. 1040–1115), and Gratian (d. 1160).[2]

[1] The standard overview of this corpus remains Cyrille Vogel, *Les "libri paenitentiales,"* Typologie des sources du moyen âge occidental 27 (Louvain: Institut d'études médiévales, 1978; repr. with supplement by Allen Frantzen, 1985); see also idem, *En remission de péchés. Recherches sur les systèmes pénitentiels dans l'Eglise latine*, ed. Alexandre Faivre (Aldershot, UK: Variorum, 1994).

[2] For an overview of the state of ecclesiastical law in the earlier Middle Ages, the essential reference is R. H. Helmholz, *The Oxford History of the Laws of England, Vol. 1: The Canon Law and Ecclesiastical Jurisdiction from 597 to the 1640s* (Oxford: Oxford University Press, 2004), ch. 1 ("The Anglo-Saxon Church"). See also Roy Flechner, "An Insular Tradition of Ecclesiastical Law: Fifth to Eighth Century," in *Anglo-Saxon/Irish Relations before the Vikings*, ed. James Graham-Campbell and Michael Ryan (Oxford: Oxford University Press, 2009), 23–46 at 23–4. On the state of canon law before Gratian, see Jean Werckmeister, "The Reception of the Church Fathers in Canon Law," in *The Reception of*

At some point no later than the first quarter of the eleventh century, unknown clerics began to compose versions of the main *libri poenitentiales* in Old English. As is the case with a number of other prose genres, these anonymous forays into matters of ecclesiastical law are among the earliest attempts to use any Western European vernacular for such purposes. They confront us with a number of still-unresolved questions, the most important being whether these translated texts enjoyed greater authority than their Latin sources in their numerous cases of disagreement. All subsequent chapters of the present study will consider the relationship of these Old English collections of penitential canons, which have received little scholarly attention in comparison to their Latin counterparts, to the wider stream of normative literature that appeared in English between the seventh and eleventh centuries. Before embarking upon a more detailed discussion of the texts and their backgrounds – the main concerns of the present chapter – it will be useful to consider first a characteristic example of how many of these Old English penitential canons interact with their sources.

Our text deals with what is now called "co-sleeping" with infants, a practice whose dangers were well appreciated in this period if the frequency with which it is mentioned gives any indication. Common in penitential manuals composed at this time are provisions such as the following:[3]

Si laici infantem suum obpresserint, annum I in pane et aqua peniteant, II a vino et carne et abstineant se a luxuria tempus penitentiae.

"If a layperson should suffocate his child, let him perform a penance of one year of bread and water, two from wine and meat, and let him abstain from the pleasures of women for the duration of the penitential fast."

Si quis uir aut mulier infantem suum opresserint, III annos peniteat, I ex his in pane et aqua.

"If a man or woman should suffocate their child, let them do penance for three years, one of these on bread and water."

Given the evidence of another collection of canons offering a more expansive treatment of this offense, it seems unlikely, in spite of the remedies prescribed, that such unfortunate couples were to be held fully responsible

the Church Fathers in the West, Vol. 1: From the Carolingians to the Maurists, ed. Irena Backus (Leiden, The Netherlands: Brill, 1997; repr. 2001), 51–82.

3 The first (with plural verbs rendered more idiomatically as singular) is cap. VI, 20 of the *Excarpsus Cummeani:* see *Bußordnungen der abendländischen Kirche*, ed. F. W. H. Wasserschleben (Halle and der Saale: Graeger, 1851), 479; the second is cap. 14 of the *Poenitentiale Oxoniense I*, edited most recently in *Paenitentialia minora Franciae et Italiae saeculi VIII–IX*, ed. Raymond Kottje, L. Körntgen, and U. Spengler-Reffgen (Turnholt: Brepols, 1994), 90.

by confessors.[4] But ambivalence is apparent as well. The rather steep penance is the same as that imposed for the abduction of widows and virgins or for deliberate abortion.[5] And while the verb chosen to describe what was done to the child – *opprimere* – had the conventional meaning "crush, press," it was also a standard term for sexual assault.[6] Both circumstances give added significance to the requirement that the penitent abstain from wine and *luxuria*, a medieval euphemism for illicit carnal relations, during the three years' fast.[7] The death of the child may have been unintended, but it took place in that most unhallowed setting – the bed of a not necessarily married couple – and was perhaps brought on by their drunken torpor. Neither circumstance would have gained the couple much sympathy from a priest.

The associations just described seem to have played upon the mind of the anonymous author of an Old English treatment of this problem:[8]

> Gif se læweda man his agen ċild ofþrycce and acwelle, fæste an [gear on] hlafe and [on] wætere, and þa twa forga flæsc and ealu, and forhæbbe hine fram ælcum wife, þa hwile þe he þa dædbote do.
>
> "If a layman crushes and kills his own child, let him fast for a year on bread and water, and then for two years forego flesh and ale, and let him keep himself from every woman for the time in which he does penance."

The translator's response to the Latin suggests much about his purposes. That he sought to adjust its requirements to English conditions is evident in his substitution of "ale" for "wine." A requirement that the penitent avoid the company of "each" or "every" woman during the period of expiation seems to imply that even a father residing with his children was not likely to restrict himself to their mother. The clause may thus allude to the practice of concubinage, which some have argued had deep roots among the Anglo-Saxons.[9]

[4] The accidental nature of the offense is established in caps. 25–30 of *Poenitentiale Oxoniense II* (*Paenitentialia minora Franciae et Italiae saeculi VIII–IX*, ed. Kottje et al., 195–6), where drunkenness or negligence are considered as aggravating factors.

[5] See caps. 30 and 32 of the *Poenitentiale Oxoniense I*, in *Paenitentialia minora Franciae et Italiae saeculi VIII–IX*, ed. Kottje et al., 91.

[6] As late as the second half of the fourteenth century, the rape of a virgin by the "lusty bacheler" of the Wife of Bath's Tale is described as "oppressioun": *The Riverside Chaucer*, 3rd ed., ed. Larry D. Benson (Boston: Houghton Mifflin, 1987), 117 (ll. 883–9).

[7] For a contemporaneous definition of *luxuria* see *Paenitentiale Pseudo-Theodori*, ed. Carine Van Rhijn (Turnhout: Brepols, 2009), 10–11 (c. viiii).

[8] *The Old English Canons of Theodore*, ed. R. D. Fulk and Stefan Jurasinski, EETS ss. 25 (London: Oxford University Press, 2012), 6 (A 32).

[9] For a discussion of concubinage, see Chapter 4, 139–148.

Of equal interest, given their implications for the relative status of these Old English compilations, are signs of dissatisfaction with the Latin original. It is no doubt because of the ambiguity of *opprimere* that the Old English author substitutes a phrase meaning "crushes *and kills*." The clause thus represents an attempt to improve upon its source rather than simply to translate it, and it is possible that such a motive underlies as well his expansion on the source's reference to *luxuria*.

That the Latin was so meddled with in the course of translation perhaps attests to the importance given the Old English canon by its author. Because this was not a matter dealt with by secular law, concerned as it was primarily with wrongs inflicted by members of one kin-group upon another, remedies imposed by priests would be in this case the only official forms of redress.[10] As no treatment of this offense occurs in the principal source of his collection, its inclusion probably required the compiler to consult other texts for a suitable exemplar. We may not be mistaken in thinking that the goal of this and similar efforts undertaken throughout his text was a book of canons superior in his view to those found in Latin.[11]

In the course of responding to these kinds of exigencies, the translator also found himself, perhaps without knowing it, crafting a valuable witness to the ways in which a private misfortune acquired public consequences. His adjustments of his text to the conditions of his time show the hazards of assuming the Latin evidence to be fully representative of English conditions. They also attest to the apparent freedom with which these anonymous translators involved themselves in the production of written law even as English kings and their counselors sought to make this activity their exclusive domain. Concerned as they are with matters less lofty than feuds between rival kin-groups or disputes over the descent of land – the main preoccupations of legislation and charters – these collections of Old English canons, particularly when the attention of their

[10] The absence of official punishments of those who slay their kin is noted in *Gesetze*, ed. Liebermann, III: 44 (*Alf. El.* 14 n.2). The nature of the Germanic legislative tradition, of which the Anglo-Saxon royal codes formed a part, has been summarized as follows: "The Germanic personal injury tariffs … require that the primary payment for personal injury be rendered to the victim and the family. Legally, injury was no longer a governmental, but a personal affront, and compensation was accordingly assigned directly to the kin-group, although an additional fine payable to the common coffer could be assessed as a penalty for disturbance of the peace to offset the costs of the trial." See Lisi Oliver, *The Body Legal in Barbarian Law* (Toronto: University of Toronto Press, 2011), 10.

[11] The translator's method of adaptation differs little from what is evident in some Latin penitentials that made use of earlier materials: see *Paenitentiale Pseudo-Theodori*, ed. Van Rhijn, xxx–xxxii.

translators drifts away from Latin sources, are sometimes quite eloquent about the things we would most like to know about what it meant to live and die among the laity of Anglo-Saxon England. They can reveal much – about marriage and household affairs, the treatment of bound laborers, and even the subjective aspects of wrongdoing – provided we are aware of some of the problems that have attended their use in the past.

THE LITERATURE OF PENANCE AND SECULAR LAW

Collections of penitential canons composed in Old English survive in a number of manuscripts dating from the period before the Norman Conquest.[12] They are not always easy to classify, in part because of the heterogeneity of their Latin sources. Though the *libri poenitentiales* that circulated from the sixth to the twelfth century were ostensibly devoted to the reconciliation of penitents, the terms with which modern commentators inevitably describe these texts – "handbooks of penance," "manuals for confessors," and the like – are sometimes inadequate guides to their contents.[13] The earliest of the collections to be so labeled in modern editions, such as the *Excerpta de libris Romanorum et Francorum*, are scarcely distinguishable from contemporaneous works of secular law, imposing fines rather than penances for various acts of violence.[14] This pattern holds for much of the

12 The manuscripts containing Old English penitential materials, with their conventional *sigla* and the dates and provenances assigned them in N. R. Ker, *Catalogue of Manuscripts containing Anglo-Saxon* (Oxford: Clarendon, 1957) and Helmut Gneuss, *Handlist of Anglo-Saxon Manuscripts* (Tempe: ACMRS, 2001), are as follows: **Bx** (Ker 10, Gneuss 808): Brussels, Bibliothèque Royale, MS 8558–63 (s. xi^{1}), southeastern; **C** (Ker 53, Gneuss 73): Cambridge, Corpus Christi College MS 265 (s. xi^{med}), Worcester; **D** (Ker 49B, Gneuss 66): Cambridge, Corpus Christi College MS 201 (s. xi^{med}), Winchester; **N** (Ker 186, Gneuss 363): London, British Library, Cotton Tiberius A.iii (s. xi^{med}), Canterbury; **O** (Ker 45B, Gneuss 59): Cambridge, Corpus Christi College, MS 190 (s. xi^{med}, xi^{2}), Exeter; **X** (Ker 338, Gneuss 644): Oxford, Bodleian Library, MS Junius 121 (s. xi$^{3/4}$), Worcester; **Y** (Ker 343, Gneuss 656): Oxford, Bodleian Library, MS Laud Misc. 482 (s. xi^{med}), Worcester.

13 The point is forcefully made in Abigail Firey, *A Contrite Heart: Prosecution and Redemption in the Carolingian Empire* (Leiden, The Netherlands: Brill, 2009), 65–6: "Scholars seeking the origins of the practices of Christian confession and penance promoted the idea that the 'penitentials' were 'little handbooks' to be used by priests in the pastoral care of their flocks, despite the manuscript evidence that few of these texts circulated as 'little handbooks' and the textual evidence that they seem more closely associated with either monastic communities or bishops." It should be borne in mind that, while this statement may hold for Continental witnesses to this tradition, Old English penitentials exhibit sure signs of use for pastoral purposes (as will be shown in the present chapter).

14 This text, edited as the "Canones Wallici" in what remains the standard edition, is datable to the sixth or seventh century. For canons from this collection exemplary of this

later literature and attests to the uncertain boundaries between ecclesiastical and secular jurisdiction in this period. The two-book penitential drawn in some fashion from the instructions of Theodore of Tarsus, Archbishop of Canterbury (d. 690), whose influence on the Old English branch of this tradition exceeded that of other texts, frequently takes up questions more relevant to ecclesiastical governance than pastoral care, such as the proper consecration of churches or the behavior of priests and bishops.[15] In several cases, Theodorean canons establish rules for the conduct of marriage or the management of an estate, and do so without imposing any sort of penitential tariff.[16] Other clauses intervene directly in the practices of feuding with no explicit disapprobation.[17]

It is perhaps because their concerns routinely stretched beyond the imposition of penances that Theodorean canons and other penitentials would appear alongside secular legislative texts in later manuscripts prepared both in England and on the Continent.[18] Their focus on matters

tendency, see *The Irish Penitentials*, ed. and trans. Ludwig Bieler (Dublin: Dublin Institute for Advanced Studies, 1963; repr. 1975), 138–9 and 154–5. On the date of this text, see Léon Fleuriot, "Un fragment en Latin de très anciennes lois bretonnes armoricanes du VIe siècle," *Annales de Bretagne* 78 (1971), 601–60; David Dumville, "On the Dating of the Early Breton Lawcodes," *Études Celtiques* 21 (1984), 207–21.

15 Though it is customary to attribute the two-book penitential (hereafter *PT*, with provisions cited by book, chapter, and clause) and related compilations that circulated under his name to Theodore – a practice that will be continued in the present study given the lack of convenient alternatives – the appearance in writing of judgments attributed to the prelate no earlier than the middle of the eighth century makes their direct descent from his instruction rather unlikely. On the transmission of Theodorean judgments, see John T. McNeill and Helena Margaret Gamer, *Medieval Handbooks of Penance* (New York: Octagon, 1938; repr. 1965), 179–82; Michael Lapidge, "The School of Theodore and Hadrian," *Anglo-Saxon England* 15 (1986), 45–72 at 48; the most thorough discussion to date is to be found in Roy Flechner, "The Making of the Canons of Theodore," *Peritia* 17–18 (2003), 121–43. All Theodorean compilations are quoted throughout the present study from *Die Canones Theodori Cantuariensis und ihre Überlieferungsformen*, ed. Paul Willem Finsterwalder (Weimar: H. Böhlau, 1929). Application of the term *penitential* to the Theodorean compilations is somewhat infelicitous given their frequent concern with matters having nothing to do with the reconciliation of penitents; with its exclusive focus on matters of ecclesiastical discipline, the second book of Theodore's two-book penitential is virtually no "penitential" at all.

16 These ordinances and their English versions will be considered at length in subsequent chapters. Marriage, it should be noted, was no sacrament when these canons were prepared and was even viewed with disdain by some leading ecclesiastics, being considered a wholly secular institution that at best might be molded into a form more amenable to ascetic ideals.

17 This is most famously the case in *PT* I, iv, 1, which lightens the penitential obligation of a homicide who compensates the kin of his victim with wergild.

18 In two vernacular manuscripts composed in England (CCCC 265 [s. xi^{med}]; CCCC 190 ["O"]), laws share space with vernacular manuals for confessors, though it should be

of secular law places the Latin penitentials at some remove from their descendants in the High Middle Ages, the *summae confessorum*, most of which were composed in response to the IV Lateran Council (1215) and its requirement of annual auricular confession for the laity.[19] What role the earlier *libri poenitentiales* may have played in the confessional encounter as practiced in England seems far from certain.[20] In spite of their circulation under the names of Irish and Anglo-Saxon ecclesiastics, the major examples of this tradition, including the compilations drawn from Theodorean teachings, saw wider circulation in Francia than in England. For this reason, scholars increasingly view these texts as products of Carolingian culture that retain only a faint connection to the insular world, their association with heroes of the Anglo-Saxon church indicating little more than the high regard in which English learning was held.[21] Add to this their feeble claims to "official" authority – by the ninth century, the bishops of Paris and Châlon wanted nothing to do with them – and it becomes difficult to say what direct role Latin penitentials may have played in English pastoral care.[22] Such problems only mount when we

said that the legal content of these collections appears rather slight when they are compared with other manuscripts datable to roughly this time in which royal legislation is a nearly exclusive concern (such as CCCC 383). The most detailed discussion remains Wormald, *Making*, 210–24.

[19] See Pierre Payer, *Sex and the New Medieval Literature of Confession, 1150–1300* (Toronto: Pontifical Institute of Mediaeval Studies, 2009); also Alexander Murray's brilliant "Confession before 1215," *Transactions of the Royal Historical Society*, 6th s., 3 (1993), 51–81.

[20] Although practices concerning the confession and expiation of wrongs were doubtless features of the corporate lives of the earliest Christians, teachings on the sacrament of penance, and indeed its status as such, were uncertain until the twelfth century, with the latter being only intermittently acknowledged: see McNeill and Gamer, *Medieval Handbooks*, 17–18. In the Catholic tradition, evidence that the sacerdotal administration of penance was instituted by Christ is to be found in passages such as John 20:21–23 (NRSV): "Jesus said to them again, 'Peace be with you. As the Father has sent me, so I send you.' When he had said this, he breathed on them and said to them, 'Receive the Holy Spirit. If you forgive the sins of any, they are forgiven them; if you retain the sins of any, they are retained.'" (See also Matthew 16:19 and 18:18.) The scriptural background was familiar to the authors of the Latin penitentials from the earliest phase of their development: see McNeill and Gamer, *Medieval Handbooks*, 15; Frantzen, *Literature of Penance*, 9.

[21] Firey's is the most recent study to cast doubts on the insular origins of the major penitentials, emphasizing instead their relation to Frankish circumstances: see *A Contrite Heart*, 66–7.

[22] Their destruction had been urged by the councils of Châlon in 813 and Paris in 829 given their erroneous content and the uncertain descent of their provisions. For the Châlon council, see *Concilia Ævi Karolini*, ed. Albert Werminghoff, MGH Conc. 2.1 (Hanover: Hahnsche Buchhandlung, 1906), 281 (cap. 38); Paris: *Concilia Ævi Karolini*, ed. Albert Werminghoff, MGH Conc. 2.2 (Hanover: Hahnsche Buchandlung,

consider that English penitential rites prior to the Conquest show signs of differing from what was typical in Francia, making practices attested across the Channel a poor basis for the reconstruction of Anglo-Saxon norms. Whereas public penance for the gravest sins was preferred on the Continent, Latin penitentials translated into English make virtually no references to it.[23] And though an attempt either to introduce or revive public penance is evident in the writings of Wulfstan, it has been argued that this rite, should it have been practiced at all, may have been available to the English as one of a few "options in a wider penitential spectrum" whose details have yet to be adequately understood.[24]

That the Latin penitentials say so little about the nature of confession and so much about matters lying wholly outside the ambit of pastoral care has made these texts some of the few works of ecclesiastical legislation to have received regular attention from historians of English secular law. A major commentator on the penitential of Theodore, for example, was also the preeminent editor of the Anglo-Saxon laws, and much later scholarly discussion of the penitentials occurred wholly within the context of secular legal history.[25] The formal properties shared by English secular legislation and penitentials perhaps make this an inevitable development. As A. W. B. Simpson noted some decades ago, "There is an obvious similarity between the penitentials that set out to assign to each sin the exactly appropriate penance, and the early laws that attempted to set

1908), 633 (cap. 32): "Ut unusquisque episcoporum in sua parochia eosdem erroneos codicellos diligenter perquirat et inventos igni tradat, ne per eos ulterius sacerdotes imperiti homines decipiant." These are discussed in Frantzen, *Literature of Penance,* 98–9, who considers the anomalous survival of private penance in England an effect of public penance having never established itself in the British Isles as it had on the Continent.

[23] Theodore's penitential is itself uncertain of the nature of penitential rites among the English, observing that "Reconciliatio ideo in hac provincia publice statuta non est quia et publica penitentia non est," "Reconciliation is not publicly established in this province since public penance is also absent" (*PT* I, xiii, 4). Finsterwalder was of the opinion that "in hac provincia" refers to Northumbria; see *Die Canones Theodori Cantuariensis*, 158–63.

[24] See M. Bradford Bedingfield, "Public Penance in Anglo-Saxon England," *Anglo-Saxon England* 31 (2002), 223–55 at 224.

[25] See Felix Liebermann, "Zur Herstellung Canones Theodori Cantuarensis," *Zeitschrift der Savigny-Stiftung für Rechtsgeschichte* 43 [Kanonistische Abteilung 12] (1912), 387–409 (the great editor's only major foray into matters of canon law); Thomas Pollock Oakley, *English Penitential Discipline and Anglo-Saxon Law in Their Join Influence* (New York: Columbia University, 1923); and more recently, Carole Hough, "Penitential Literature and Secular Law in Anglo-Saxon England," *Anglo-Saxon Studies in Archaeology and History* 11 (2000), 133–41.

out for each wrong the precisely appropriate compensation."[26] Simpson went on to repeat the suggestion made often in prior scholarship that the style of the earliest penitentials may account in some way for the form assumed by the first laws to have been promulgated in English.[27]

In spite of such observations, most legal historians have not regarded penitentials as texts of central importance to understanding the legal situation of early England.[28] Scholars' relative indifference toward them probably owes something to the thesis popularized by Oakley nearly a century ago that law and penance were in a state of cooperation for much of the later Anglo-Saxon period, with penance at some point – most obviously during the reign of Alfred – being made to serve the ends of the secular state.[29] According to Oakley, requirements in the laws of Alfred and subsequent kings that offenders undertake penance in addition to secular means of expiation reflect the overall movement of most Western European polities from a period of relative lawlessness, in which "[p]rivate vengeance was still allowed in some cases" and "the executive machinery for enforcing the law was weak," to one in which monarchs and lay magnates realized that "the pressure exerted against malefactors by the secular government needed reinforcement and supplementing."[30] For Oakley, penitential sanctions acted above all as instruments of social control, having no other function than extending into the lives of laypersons the reach of an otherwise feeble state:[31]

> This aid was rendered by the Church, through religious sanctions and safeguards to strengthen legal procedure, provisions which backed secular enforcement, and supplementary penalties for delinquents. Ecclesiastical discipline was the natural means used for this cooperation, and the chief instrument for such discipline was penance.

[26] A. W. B. Simpson, "The Laws of Ethelbert," in *On the Laws and Customs of England: Essays in Honor of Samuel E. Thorne*, ed. Morris S. Arnold et al. (Chapel Hill: University of North Carolina Press, 1981), 3–17 at 17.

[27] Simpson here repeats a conventional view (disparaged by Vogel as "une exagération et une erreur," but held by generations of scholars) that the penances imposed by these texts bear some relation to wergilds prescribed in secular legislation: see Vogel, "Composition légale et pénitence tarifée," in idem, *En remission de péchés*, 294.

[28] Penitentials play no great role in Wormald, *Making*, which confines itself primarily to observations about the appearance of such texts in manuscripts of legislation (210–23). There is little detailed discussion of the contents of either Latin or Old English penitentials.

[29] Some of Oakley's arguments are anticipated in *Gesetze*, ed. Liebermann, II: s.v. "Pönitenz."

[30] "The Cooperation of Medieval Penance and Secular Law," *Speculum* 7 (1932), 515–24 at 515–16. Similar points are made throughout his monograph, *English Penitential Discipline*.

[31] "Cooperation," 516.

That Oakley's observations played some role in determining the priorities of legal-historical scholarship is plain. If penitential sanctions in this era served merely to "supplement" norms agreed upon by secular authorities, then the work of devising such norms must have been the exclusive domain of the kings under whose names most pre-Conquest legislation circulated, leaving bishops and their own prescriptive writings the mere agents of royal prerogatives.

Oakley's thesis has not, to my knowledge, received much in the way of critical evaluation. Yet many of his assertions cannot avoid seeming dated in light of contemporary scholarship. The uncertain relationship between the earlier penitentials and confession appears of itself to upset the foundations of Oakley's claim that these texts furnished the means by which otherwise toothless secular ordinances would be enforced.[32] As Abigail Firey has noted, bishops and other clerics of the eighth century seem not to have made use of these texts for the purposes supposed by Oakley and his contemporaries. Of particular interest to Firey are the manuscripts produced by Arno, Archbishop of Salzburg (ca. 750–821), in whose compilations penitential canons sit side-by-side with the *Lex Baiwariorum*. To Firey, "[t]he manuscript context of the penitentials is fully in keeping with the textual evidence … that indicates that many, if not most of these texts were to be read as learned law: they seem to have been material for the study of problems, posed as hypothetical cases, that could serve to test a priest's understanding of the principles to be applied in assessing the conditions and needs of penitents."[33] Arguments that Latin penitentials were of little relevance to confession have of course met resistance.[34] But the fact that some penitentials traveled in manuscripts alongside texts of unambiguously secular law probably has something to do with their authors' tendency to dwell on matters having little to do with penance. Thus the role envisaged for these sources by Oakley – mere "reinforcement" of royal legislation with penitential remedies – does not quite square with the nature of these texts as understood in scholarship of the present day.

[32] Certainly few historians today share Oakley's confidence in saying that "[penitentials] were manuals for the use of priests, and contained detailed lists of penances prescribed for various sins. They were constantly used by bishops and priests in imposing penances for various kinds of immorality, paganism, heresy, insubordination to ecclesiastical authority and for a whole detailed category of sins" (Oakley, *English Penitential Discipline*, 14).

[33] See Firey, *A Contrite Heart*, 194–5.

[34] For a skeptical response to the view that the major Latin penitentials were mere episcopal "commonplace books," see Rob Meens, "Penitentials and the Practice of Penance in the Tenth and Eleventh Centuries," *Early Medieval Europe* 14 (2006), 7–21.

Further problems are posed by Oakley's tendency – shared, perhaps, by many of his generation – to imagine the governance of Anglo-Saxon England as a more orderly and centralized process than was likely the case in this or any early medieval polity. Certainly his description of "Church" and "State" as discrete and unified entities does not agree with what is known of the tug-of-war between clerical estates that reached its apex during the Benedictine Reform.[35] Evidence from this period suggests no harmonious relationship between England's secular and regular clergy. The few writings we possess regarding the condition of the former – the most prominent being a series of directives authored by Wulfstan – primarily disparage them. Priests are admonished about keeping concubines, bearing weapons in church, and ignorantly stammering through baptismal formulas, among other offenses.[36] In making such accusations, Wulfstan appears to have been repeating one of the commonplaces of the Benedictine Reform; a movement, it should be noted, that seems to have depended entirely on royal patronage to stay afloat.[37] Thus there is little to suggest either the sort of top-down organization Oakley seems to impute to the pre-Conquest church or a collaborative

[35] The revival of English monasticism in the later tenth century, a movement inspired in part by parallel developments on the Continent, saw the revival of the Benedictine Rule as the model of coenobitic life and a remarkable flowering of literary production. Although the movement enjoyed royal support, its achievements were not made without injury to those who had prospered under the old dispensation – most obviously, the secular canons from whom Æthelwold, bishop of Winchester (d. c. 998), wrested control of the Old Minster. At least once an attempt was made to poison the bishop, and his ferocity was noted even by those who admired him: see Dom David Knowles, *The Monastic Order in England*, 2nd ed. (Cambridge: Cambridge University Press, 1963), 39n2; Michael Lapidge, "Æthelwold," in *The Blackwell Encyclopaedia of Anglo-Saxon England*, ed. Michael Lapidge et al. (Malden, MA: Blackwell, 1999), 19.

[36] On the rather poor reputation of priests in later Anglo-Saxon England, see especially John Blair, *The Church in Anglo-Saxon Society* (London: Oxford University Press, 2005), 491–4. For the text of the "Northumbrian Priests' Law," which addresses primarily the range of vices held endemic to some members of this estate, see *Gesetze*, ed. Liebermann, I: 380–5; also *Wulfstan's Canons of Edgar*, ed. Roger Fowler, EETS 266 (London: Oxford University Press, 1972). Much of this text as well is taken up with the failings of the secular clergy, which Fowler notes were among Wulfstan's chief concerns because "they had received less attention than the regular clergy in the Church reforms since Edgar's time" and because "earlier reform had scarcely touched the Northern province" (xlvii).

[37] See Shashi Jayakumar, "Reform and Retribution: The 'Anti-Monastic' Reaction in the Reign of Edward the Martyr," in *Early Medieval Studies in Memory of Patrick Wormald*, eds. Baxter et al., 2009, 337–52. This study explores "why the close connection between monastic interests and the royal prerogative began to unravel so quickly after July 975 [the time of King Edgar's death]" (339).

relationship between this church (itself little more than a congeries of competing interests) and "the State" (whatever this was).[38]

Oakely's argument is most visibly flawed in its dealings with the Old English penitentials, which were by and large ignored in his study in favor of Latin compilations.[39] Because he used without suspicion what was in his day the standard edition of the vernacular penitentials – the full hazards of which will be discussed subsequently – Oakley was in no position to appreciate just how much these texts in particular fail to accommodate his ingenious model of social control. When it is borne in mind that the Old English penitentials, in their departures from their source texts, contain some of the few normative statements to survive from the Anglo-Saxon period on matters such as the liability of the insane, the formation and dissolution of marriage, the epistemology of homoerotic behavior, the legal rights of slaves, and a range of other subjects important to our sense of the norms governing daily life in the British Isles prior to the Conquest, it is easy to see just how incomplete our knowledge of

[38] Remarks by Sarah Hamilton are perhaps apposite here: "The phrase 'the Church' itself rests on a misconception about the context in which bishops and clergy worked in the early Middle Ages, assuming a unification of purpose and an acceptance of a degree of papal authority which did not occur before the twelfth century. We cannot assume that we know how far bishops saw their rural clergy, or how they understood their role, or what their role was. Before the twelfth century the early medieval Church seems more characterized by the diversity of the different areas and different groups within it than by any sense of unity." See Hamilton, *The Practice of Penance, 900–1050* (Woodbridge, UK: Boydell, 2001), 22. The "social control" thesis popularized by Oakley, as Frantzen noted decades ago, faces similar difficulties. Given the rather inchoate notions of kingship and state power likely to have obtained in the polities within which these texts circulated, statements to this effect project onto these texts attitudes more characteristic of the twentieth century than the tenth. On this aspect of Oakley's thesis, see Frantzen, *Literature of Penance*, 10. Elsewhere (3), Frantzen describes the history of the "social control" thesis, tracing it ultimately to the work of Henry Charles Lea, who in Frantzen's opinion could not get beyond a tendency to see "penance as oppressive ... suppress[ing] what we might now call anti-social urges with the threat of severe punishment." That notions of state power peculiar to the nineteenth and early twentieth centuries gave to some scholarship published at this time a distorted view of antique institutions is argued in David A. E. Pelteret, "Should One Include Unnamed Persons in a Prosopographical Study?," in *Prosopography: Approaches and Applications: A Handbook*, Prosopographica et Genealogica 13, ed. K. S. B. Keats-Rohan (Oxford: Unit for Prosopographical Research, 2007), 183–96 at 183–5.

[39] Though still highly useful if read with some caution, Oakley's *English Penitential Discipline* devotes a mere four pages (131–5) to sustained discussion of the Old English texts, most of which amounts to a cursory overview of scholarly opinion. They are employed hardly at all in his discussion of English secular law and its interactions with penitential sanctions.

both the written and implicit law of early England, as well as its general cultural history, must be in their absence.[40]

Indeed, it is quite possible that the Old English penitentials exceed their Latin sources in importance for the historian of English law. That the vernacular penitentials offer a more direct disclosure of English circumstances is evident in their tendency to translate Latin compilations rather loosely. Canons having no known sources in any of the extant Latin handbooks, of which there are several, may shed yet more light on aspects of early English law not discussed in materials more routinely consulted. That these canons often conform to peculiarities of Anglo-Saxon law and culture attested in other prescriptive texts makes it very likely that they were authored by English clerics who felt free to make their own contributions to the tradition of ecclesiastical law. That ecclesiastical law was at the time a category broad enough to encompass matters having nothing to do with the pastoral care of penitents was an effect both of gaps in secular law and of the tendency of Latin penitentials to claim for themselves the territory of secular jurisdiction.[41]

Rather than see the literature of penance as the enforcement mechanism of royal pronouncements, we should perhaps regard royal and ecclesiastical law in this era as parallel forms of normative literature that become progressively intertwined over the course of the Anglo-Saxon period. As will be evident throughout the present study, many of the Old English penitentials give expression to norms that were not voiced by royal legislation and yet must have enjoyed the status of customary law. The fact that these texts often favor customary over ecclesiastical norms – as will be illustrated particularly in Chapter 3 – shows their authors to be doing

40 These matters have begun to receive discussion only within the past few decades. On the Old English penitentials' discussions of homoeroticism, see Frantzen, *Before the Closet: Same-Sex Love from "Beowulf" to Angels in America* (Chicago: University of Chicago Press, 1998), cap. 4; R. D. Fulk, "Male Homoeroticism in the Old English *Canons of Theodore*," in *Sex and Sexuality in Anglo-Saxon England: Essays in Memory of Daniel Gillmore Calder*, eds. Carol Braun Pasternack and Lisa M. C. Weston (Tempe, AZ: ACMRS, 2004), 1–34; on mental illness, see Alexander Murray, *Suicide in the Middle Ages, Vol. 2: The Curse on Self-Murder* (Oxford: Oxford University Press, 2000), 254–6; Stefan Jurasinski, "Madness and Responsibility in Anglo-Saxon England," in *Peace and Protection in the Middle Ages*, eds. David Rollason and Tom Lambert (Toronto: Pontifical Institute of Mediaeval Studies, 2009), 99–120. For slavery, see Chapter 3 of the present study, where a full biography of recent works is given.

41 I have made this argument elsewhere: see "The Old English Penitentials and the Law of Slavery," in *English Law before Magna Carta*, eds. Stefan Jurasinski, Lisi Oliver, and Andrew Rabin (Leiden, The Netherlands: Brill, 2010), 97–118; also "Madness and Responsibility in Anglo-Saxon England." In what follows, I draw on and expand the arguments made in these papers.

something other than imposing rules from without upon a population that did not share them, as Oakley's study in particular would have us expect.[42] We cannot even be sure that these canons reflect the consensus of bishops or other members of Anglo-Saxon England's clerical elite. In the following pages, it will be demonstrated that the Old English penitentials do more to shore up seigneurial rather than royal prerogatives and show a greater concern with traditional law than with legislation issuing from the royal court. If these texts were intended to aid "the State" in enforcing the ideals of kings and bishops, such purposes cannot have guided their composition from start to finish given the many instances in which they appear to side with folk observances over norms urged by more official sources of authority. These arguments may not be ventured, however, without some attention being first given to the editorial history of these texts, which did much to shape the assumptions that commentators bring to them.

THE RECEPTION OF THE OLD ENGLISH PENITENTIALS

The first persons to examine the Old English penitentials seem to have sought in these texts knowledge of pre-Conquest law. As is the case with royal legislation, the post-Conquest reception of the Old English penitentials begins with the *Leges Henrici Primi*, a curious text perhaps intended to aid Norman magnates in their struggle to understand the customs and legal terms of the people they had subjugated.[43] Though legislative texts loom large among the sources appropriated by the *Leges*, it

[42] That royal legislation, including that of Alfred, might have depended upon penitential canons for its provisions rather than simply employing penance to "reinforce" provisions of its own devising is an aspect of this corpus somewhat in dispute. See Hough, "Penitential Literature" (where the influence of penitentials upon secular law prior to the career of Wulfstan is viewed as unlikely); Audrey Meaney, "Old English Legal and Penitential Penalties for Heathenism," *Anglo-Saxons: Studies Presented to Cyril Roy Hart*, ed. Simon Keynes and Alfred P. Smyth (Dublin: Four Courts, 2006), 127–58 at 131–3 (where such influence is tentatively held to have occurred). Evidence not discussed by either Hough or Meaney in favor of such influence is considered in Jurasinski, "Violence, Penance, and Secular Law in Alfred's Mosaic Prologue," *Haskins Society Journal* 22 (2010), 25–42; idem, "Sanctuary, House-Peace, and the Traditionalism of Alfred's Laws," *The Journal of Legal History* 31 (2010), 129–47. The question will be taken up in Chapter 2.

[43] The text's editor holds it to have been meant by the author to serve as "a treatise which would embrace quite widely the law of his day" (see *Leges Henrici Primi*, ed. and trans. L. J. Downer [Oxford: Clarendon Press, 1972], 3). Discussion of this aspect of the *Leges* has been sparse: see Oakley, *English Penitential Discipline*, 134 (where its author

perhaps reveals the author's attitude toward his evidence that a number of its chapters reproduce not royal legislation but Latin and vernacular penitentials.[44] The appearance of such texts in this compendium may indicate something more than its author's having made indiscriminate use of the normative materials found in pre-Conquest manuscripts. For the Anglo-Saxons to have consulted older penitentials probably seemed strange to an immigrant from the Continent, where the ninth-century episcopal condemnations of these texts presumably were of more effect than in pre-Conquest England.[45] The survival of these compilations in the vernacular may have added to their fascination for the author of the *Leges* given his taste for the exotic and archaic.[46] When it is borne in mind that the clauses appearing in his collection consider principally wrongs done to and by members of various clerical estates, and that even wrongs of this magnitude are in some cases dealt with by private penance – a measure unlikely to have been favored on the Continent for such offenses – we can perhaps see why the author of the *Leges* added material from penitentials to his assemblage of English oddities alongside explications of *healsfang* and *flymenfyrm*.[47] He probably saw them

is referred to as "a canonist of the early Norman period" and its use of the *Scriftboc* appears to go unrecognized).

44 Such is the case for caps. 68.6–12; 70.16–17; 72.1–2; 73.1–6 (derived from the *Old English Penitential* and *Scriftboc*); 75.5. That the remainder of these are in Downer's view derived from the *Penitential of Pseudo-Theodore* (a fellow-traveler with the Old English penitentials in some manuscripts) suggests that the translator's acquaintance with this body of texts was quite limited. I hope to return to derivation of these clauses in a future publication. Use of canonical sources (though not of the Old English texts considered here) in the *Leges* is closely considered in Bruce Brasington, "Canon Law in the *Leges Henrici Primi*," *Zeitschrift der Savigny-Stiftung für Rechtsgeschichte. Kanonistische Abteilung* 92 (2006), 288–305.

45 Kottje notes that the copying of penitentials by Halitgar of Cambrai and Hrabanus Maurus ends "rather abruptly" in the middle of the twelfth century and attributes this development to the Gregorian reform and its aftermath. See Raymund Kottje, *Die Bussbücher Halitgars von Cambrai und des Hrabanus Maurus: Ihre Überlieferung und ihre Quellen*, Beiträge zur Geschichte und Quellenkunde des Mittelalters 8 (Berlin: De Gruyter, 1980), 254 and n. 7.

46 On this element of the *Leges*, see Hudson, *The Formation of the English Common Law*, 249–50; O'Brien, "The *Instituta Cnuti* and the Translation of English Law," 197.

47 E.g., caps. 68.7 and 68.9–11 appear to enjoin remedies of private penance on those guilty of homicide. A standard feature of later Frankish penitential discipline is the so-called Carolingian dichotomy, a regime requiring public penance for public sins and private penance for private sins. Public penance underwent a revival by Frankish bishops during the ninth century, and its consequences were permanent and severe for those obliged to undergo it. On the "dichotomy," admittedly a problematic construct given the public nature even of ostensibly "private" penitential remedies, see Hamilton, *The Practice of Penance*, 4–7, 34–8. For the public penance likely prescribed for deliberate homicide in

as revealing less about the workings of the church than about the peculiarities of folk law among the English. Some penitential clauses quoted within the *Leges* refer to instances of unintentional homicide, and it may be assumed that they were seen as shedding light on English attitudes regarding mental liability, one of this author's main preoccupations.[48]

The *Leges Henrici Primi* would be copied into the fourteenth century, and its influence, along with *Quadripartitus*, extended even into the Elizabethan era, during which the latter in particular would help Laurence Nowell and William Lambarde to make sense of Old English legislation.[49] But penitentials would not again accompany legal materials in any collection until the middle of the nineteenth century, with the publication of Benjamin Thorpe's *Ancient Laws and Institutes of England* (1840).[50] While Thorpe's edition potentially made possible the reintroduction of these texts to scholars whose interests extended beyond the field of church history, its eccentric handling of them would ensure their neglect. The problems began with Thorpe's assignment of convoluted titles to the Old English penitentials and failure to note in some instances the distinctions between them. While Thorpe acknowledged two such compilations, the *Confessionale* and *Poenitentiale Ecgberti*, associating both with the eighth-century bishop Ecgbeorht (d. 766) on the basis of an incipit occurring only in the *Confessionale*, it would become clear long afterward that this corpus was more varied than Thorpe had assumed.[51] Not until 1934 – almost a century later – would Robert Spindler's edition

the period of the *Leges*, see the penitential attributed to Bartholomew of Exeter (d. 1184), in Adrian Morey, *Bartholomew of Exeter, Bishop and Canonist* (Cambridge: Cambridge University Press, 1937), 210 (cap. xli); McNeill and Gamer, *Medieval Handbooks*, 348. Bartholomew's approach is close to that of Halitgar in its preference for conciliar judgments over those attributed to Irish and English clergy.

48 His discussion of unintentional homicide is a portion of this text often discussed in modern scholarship; see, e.g., Pollock and Maitland, *History of English Law*, I: 54–5.

49 That the *Archaionomia* contains in some instances translations by Nowell from *Quadripartitus* into "Elizabethan Old English" has been known since Kenneth Sisam's "The Authenticity of Certain Texts in Lambarde's *Archaionomia* 1568," *Modern Language Review* 18 (1923), 98–104; 20 (1925), 253–9; repr. in idem, *Studies in the History of Old English Literature* (Oxford: Clarendon, 1953), 232–58.

50 For a discussion of these prior editions, see Frantzen, "Sin and Sense: Editing and Translating Anglo-Saxon Handbooks of Penance," in *Making Sense: Constructing Meaning in Early English*, eds. Antonette diPaolo Healey and Kevin Kiernan (Toronto: Pontifical Institute of Mediaeval Studies, 2007), 40–71 at 43–4.

51 "Þas capitulas Ecgbryht, arcebisceop on Eoforwic, awende of Ledene on Englisc, þæt þa ungelæredan hit mihton þe eð understandan," "Ecgbeorht, archbishop of York, translated these chapters from Latin into English, so that the unlearned might more easily understand them." *Das altenglische Bussbuch*, ed. R. Spindler (Leipzig: Bernhard Tauchnitz, 1934), 170.

of the *Confessionale* recognize the *Canons of Theodore* as an independent set of texts, establishing thereby the existence of three penitentials in Old English.[52] Later work, however, would continue to obscure these materials as it sought to shed light on them. While Spindler's contemporary Josef Raith, also an affiliate of the program in English Philology at the University of Munich, would do a great service to scholarship by preparing an edition of the *Poenitentiale* (henceforth *Old English Penitential*), he would edit as an appendix to this text a series of canons that merit consideration in their own right. Not until Fowler's edition of this group of canons, to which he gave the title *Handbook for the Use of a Confessor* (henceforth *Handbook*), would the range of texts to be included within this corpus become sufficiently clear.[53] Thus it was only by the mid-1960s that scholars would acknowledge the circulation of at least four vernacular penitentials during the Anglo-Saxon period: the *Scriftboc*, the *Canons of Theodore*, the *Old English Penitential*, and the *Handbook*.[54]

While commentary has tended to ignore the differences between them, each of the Old English penitentials relies on its own set of Latin canons and treats its anchor texts rather differently. Yet neither the sources nor the styles of translation manifest in the Old English penitentials has received much comment beyond the primarily descriptive account in Allen Frantzen's important *Literature of Penance in Anglo-Saxon England* (1983).[55] Differences between them are most apparent with regard to the Latin materials employed. The *Scriftboc* and *Canons* rely on fairly archaic collections of Latin ordinances, principally those attributed to Archbishop Theodore. These exist in a variety of versions, and it seems

[52] The *Canons* are edited in their entirety for the first time in *The Old English Canons of Theodore*, eds. Fulk and Jurasinski. It should be conceded that the integrity of the Old English penitentials is not immediately apparent upon examination of the manuscripts: canons omitted in some manuscript witnesses are present in others, leaving the establishment of discrete texts to a large extent a matter of editorial judgment. Such instances are discussed in Frantzen, "Sin and Sense," 42n10. In spite of these difficulties, I see no reason to assume that these texts cannot be discussed, with some qualifications, as distinct from one another in meaningful ways. They have suffered in transmission only slightly more than the laws of Cnut or Alfred, e.g., the extant witnesses of which in some cases differ substantially from one another and omit significant portions of text.

[53] The standard edition remains R. Fowler, "A Late Old English Handbook for the Use of a Confessor," *Anglia* 83 (1965), 1–29.

[54] The discussion in Frantzen, *Literature of Penance* (133) acknowledges each member except the *Canons*. But the omission, which attests to the uncertain status of this text, would not occur in Frantzen's subsequent work.

[55] Discussion of the Old English penitentials is confined to 133–41 in this study.

possible that the *Scriftboc* and *Canons* sometimes employ more than one of the Theodorean compilations. Matters are also complicated by frequent use in these texts of penitential canons attributed to Cummean, a figure about whom much less is known, and whose teachings seem to have been incorporated early into the cycle of Theodorean canons.[56]

A different set of sources underlies *The Old English Penitential*. Most of its chapters are drawn from the collection authored by Halitgar of Cambrai at some point prior to 831, the year of his death. Halitgar's collection is a document of the Carolingian reform of penitential discipline, composed at the instigation of Ebbo of Rheims. Its author reaches back to fourth-century councils for suggested remedies, relegating canons attributed to Irish missionaries or heroes of the Anglo-Saxon church to the sixth book of his collection. This he called a "Roman Penitential," and his claim to have copied it *de scrinio Romanae ecclesiae* seems meant to justify further use of such disreputable materials.[57] Though the slim evidence available does not preclude its earlier circulation, Halitgar's collection seems not to have been available in England before the outset of the tenth century, when portions were copied by a scribe of St. Augustine's Abbey in Canterbury.[58] If no precise date for the *Penitential* is indicated by its contents, its use of clauses from the *Scriftboc* makes the priority of the latter text beyond doubt.

The *Handbook* is unique in its appearing to rely on vernacular source material alone: most of its canons derive from the *Penitential*, and these are in several cases recast in ways that alter the style but not the import of their exemplars. Modern scholarship has detected in this collection the

[56] For a summary of prior speculations on the identity of Cummean, see McNeill and Gamer, *Medieval Handbooks*, 98–9.

[57] Among the early sources employed by Halitgar are the councils of Elvira (ca. 300) and Ankara (314); use is also made of the council of Nicæa (325). On the background of the penitential, see especially Kottje, *Die Bussbücher Halitgars von Cambrai und des Hrabanus Maurus*. The standard edition, used throughout the present study, remains that of H. J. Schmitz, *Die Bussbücher und die Bussdisciplin der Kirche*, 2 vols. (Mainz: Franz Kirchheim Verlag, 1883–98), I: 465–489 (the "Roman Penitential"), 719–32. Others have not followed Schmitz in accepting Halitgar's claim, disparaged by Wasserschleben (*Bußordnungen*, 58), to have found the materials of book six in a Roman archive: see Schmitz, *Bussbücher*, I: 466–70; Wasserschleben, *Bußordnungen*, 72–7; Oakley, *English Penitential Discipline*, 18–19; McNeill and Gamer, *Medieval Handbooks*, 295–7; Vogel, *Les "libri paenitentiales,"* 81–2.

[58] Philip Rusche, "St. Augustine's Abbey and the Tradition of Penance in Early Tenth-Century England," *Anglia* 120 (2002), 159–83. This article finds evidence for awareness of Halitgar's and Theodore's penitentials in the 930s and 940s, somewhat earlier than is assumed in most standard histories of penance in Anglo-Saxon England. As will be discussed in Chapter 2, it is conventionally held (though with increasing qualifications in more recent literature)

fingerprints of Wulfstan.[59] With the *Handbook*, the production of vernacular manuals for confessors seems to have come to an end. Though we should be suspicious of any narrative seemingly embodied by such scant evidence, it is tempting to see in these texts, as Frantzen has suggested, an increasing disregard for Latin sources that may indicate that the vernacular canons were coming to rival them in prestige.[60]

The style of these handbooks is another area in which profound differences are apparent. Before this can be discussed, we must consider yet another way in which Thorpe's edition made consideration of this aspect of the Old English penitentials unnecessarily difficult. Although Thorpe translated the Anglo-Saxon laws into English and provided for each of his editions copious explanatory notes, his treatment of the Old English penitentials differed pronouncedly. For reasons of decency, Thorpe chose to translate these texts into Latin and to leave them without any interpretive commentary in spite of the difficulties these texts often pose.[61] The first of these choices would initiate a chain of misunderstandings ultimately leaving scholarly knowledge of the Old English penitentials in somewhat worse shape for much of the twentieth century than it had been in the nineteenth. While F. W. H. Wasserschleben granted a place to the Old English penitentials in his *Bußordnungen der abendländischen Kirche* (1851), the standard edition of much of the Latin penitential corpus into the present, he reproduced not the Old English but Thorpe's Latin translation.[62] In the years that followed, many scholars

that penitentials were not much in use in England until the Benedictine Reform was firmly established. Rusche's article is a major challenge to this thesis.

59 Such connections, having long been suspected, are considered in Catherine Cubitt, "Bishops, Priests and Penance in Late Anglo-Saxon England," *Early Medieval Europe* 14 (2006), 41–3 at 53–4; Melanie Heyworth, "The 'Late Old English Handbook for the Use of a Confessor': Authorship and Connections," *Notes and Queries* 54 (2007), 218–22.

60 See Frantzen, "Sin and Sense," 42.

61 Thorpe was naturally concerned that the contents of penitentials would give offense to Victorian readers: "For reasons which will be manifest on perusal, it was deemed advisable to give a corrected Latin version ... in preference to an English one" (*Ancient Laws and Institutes of England*, 2 vols., ed. Benjamin Thorpe [London: Eyre and Spottiswoode, 1840], I: xvin1). It should be noted that Thorpe's Latin translation relies to some extent on the edition prepared over a century before by David Wilkins, *Concilia Magnae Britaniiae et Hiberniae* (London: Gosling, Gyles, Woodward, Davis, 1737). The ultimate origins of this Latin translation remain unknown, though it is certainly not of the pre-Conquest era or even of the Middle Ages. Frantzen has suggested plausibly that it may derive from the work of Elizabethan antiquaries given that Wilkins apparently "regarded the Latin as a translation contemporary with the Old English version": see "Sin and Sense," 47.

62 *Bußordnungen*, ed. Wasserschleben, 42–4 and 300–18.

would assume Thorpe's translation to be the medieval Latin source on which the Old English texts had supposedly depended.[63] Soon the latter were in danger of being eclipsed by rival texts in Latin that had never existed. Helena M. Gamer and John T. McNeill's *Medieval Handbooks of Penance* (1938), relied upon by generations of English-speaking scholars and still of great use to any student of this corpus, would assert erroneously the existence of Latin and Old English versions of the *Scriftboc* in Cambridge, Corpus Christi College 190.[64] (Similar assumptions had been made decades prior by Arthur West Haddan and William Stubbs.[65]) With some of these penitentials now being assumed to have had a contemporaneous Latin equivalent, few scholars bothered to consider the Old English where discussion of these texts surfaced at all.

Not until well into the twentieth century would the Old English penitentials again be edited in their original language. But editions by Spindler and Raith, however much they succeeded in clearing away the obscurities of Thorpe's earlier treatment, ultimately established further obstacles to the study of these texts. The most characteristic feature of the Old English penitentials – their tendency to recast rather profoundly the language of their Latin sources – was often dismissed by these editors as evidence of the ignorance of the translators.[66] Thus commentary on the *Scriftboc* in Spindler's edition was confined to sorting out the sources read and misread by the translator. Whether these divergent renderings of the Latin might have been made with a purpose was a possibility rarely, if ever, entertained. The effects of Spindler's approach were apparent in a review of his edition by C. L. Wrenn, one of the few notices of this text to appear in English.[67] Perhaps because Spindler had asserted that

63 See, e.g., Frank Barlow, *The English Church, 1000–1066* (London: Longmans, 1963), 264n5, where the *Scriftboc* and *Penitential* are regarded as potentially forming a part of the tradition of Frankish penitentials.

64 McNeill and Gamer, *Medieval Handbooks*, 243: "The Confessional of Egbert was published by Wilkins from the eleventh century Codex Corpus Christi College, Cambridge, 190, which contains both Anglo-Saxon and Latin versions."

65 See their *Councils and Ecclesiastical Documents Relating to Great Britain and Ireland*, 3 vols. (Oxford: Clarendon, 1871; repr. 1964), III: 415.

66 Raith concluded that the divergences of the *Penitential* from its sources could be explained only by its reliance on a now-lost Latin penitential: see *Die altenglische Version des Halitgar'schen Bussbuches*, ed. Josef Raith (Hamburg, 1933; repr. Darmstadt: Wissenschaftliche Buchgesellschaft, 1964), xxix. Because of his assumption that the translator was reluctant to meddle with the language of his sources, Spindler several times emends out of existence the *Scriftboc*'s departures from its source materials, and shows little interest in how these might reflect the circumstances of the translator.

67 C. L. Wrenn, "Review of Robert Spindler, *Das altenglische Bussbuch*," *Review of English Studies* 12 (1936), 244–6.

the "sacrosanct handling of source material" (*sakrosankte Behandlung des Quellenmaterials*) characteristic of the author of the *Scriftboc* was "in sharpest contrast with the practice of the Halitgar-translator, who, as much as may be known, often departs quite indiscriminately from his exemplar," Wrenn would assert that "the O[ld] E[nglish] translation in Dr. Spindler's chosen text is remarkably literal."[68] There is, in fact, nothing consistently "literal" about the style of translation evident in the *Scriftboc*, which suggests that Wrenn had paid greater attention to Spindler's introductory notes than to the text.

How Spindler came to his own conclusions about the translation practices evident in the *Scriftboc* is somewhat harder to understand. Rather than yielding even in the most extreme cases of divergence to the more reasonable conclusion that its author might not always have sought to reproduce sense-for-sense the penitentials of Theodore and other luminaries of the early English Church, his commentary attributes clauses unfaithful to the Latin to a kaleidoscopic range of possible sources.[69] Both Spindler and Raith were also given to speculation on the possible influence of now-lost intermediary Latin collections that perhaps resembled the Old English canons more closely than their known sources. Raith concluded that the idiosyncrasies of the *Old English Penitential* could be explained only by reliance on such a lost Latin compilation:[70]

> Has the translator assembled himself from all possible penitentials the canons to be rendered, or has he simply translated a penitential that by chance is for us no longer extant? I hold the latter assumption to be correct: the translator had lying before him a Latin penitential corresponding to that of Pseudo-Egbert that he translated after a fashion.

Statements of this sort, of course, cannot be refuted in any definitive way. As happens once every few decades, vanished texts may indeed appear and require reconsideration of old views.[71] I think, however, there are few reasons for scholars to continue to worry about whether a lost Latin

[68] *Das altenglische Bussbuch*, ed. Spindler, 14; Wrenn, "Review," 244.

[69] The situation of these texts is thus not unlike that of those considered by Stephanie Hollis and Michael Wright, who note that "The relative neglect of much of the secular prose corpus is, at least in part, attributable to the view that it consists of little more than debased translations of Latin compilations." See Hollis and Wright, *Old English Prose of Secular Learning* (Woodbridge, UK: D. S. Brewer, 1992), 10.

[70] *Die altenglische Version*, ed. Raith, xxix.

[71] See, e.g., Mechthild Gretsch, "The Taunton Fragment: A New Text from Anglo-Saxon England," *Anglo-Saxon England* 33 (2004), 145–93; Aidan Conti, "The Taunton Fragment and the Homiliary of Angers: Context for New Old English," *Review of English Studies* n.s. 60 (2008), 1–33.

source accounts for the anomalous translations in these texts. We may consider the analogy of what has happened over the past several decades in studies of the Alfredian Boëthius. This text translates its source as freely as some Old English penitentials, and it was long assumed that its divergences might be traced to one or more of the Latin commentaries that attached themselves to *De consolatione philosophiae* over the course of the Carolingian Renaissance. However, an article published decades ago by Joseph S. Wittig put this theory to rest to the satisfaction of most scholars.[72] It is now customary to assume that the author or authors of the Alfredian translations were content to work in relative freedom from their sources, and that this was a translation practice acceptable in scholarly circles for much of the Anglo-Saxon period. Instructive in this regard are the remarks of Hans Sauer, who observes in Old English prose translations approaches ranging from strict adherence to the language of sources to virtual independence from them:[73]

> At the beginning of the scale are the interlinear glosses, which follow their examples word-for-word; then come the independent translations as made, for example, by King Alfred and his circle – sometimes quite faithful to the language of their sources, sometimes freely paraphrasing and commenting upon them; finally we have works whose authors so profoundly reworked and altered the underlying Latin sources that they may be more easily regarded as independent compositions: among these may be counted above all many of the writings attributed to Ælfric and Wulfstan.

One may, of course, quibble with the details of Sauer's assessment. The Alfredian version of Augustine's *Soliloquies*, for example, may easily be placed in the third category of virtually "independent compositions" along with his rendering of Boëthius. In this respect, what was possible at the end of the Old English period seems just as likely to have occurred centuries prior. But Sauer's remarks, which confirm in any case what most specialists in Old English studies know intuitively, should alert us to a fact seemingly lost on many scholars of the nineteenth and early twentieth centuries: hunting down the sources of every eccentric translation of a Latin text may in some cases hide from us the true nature of the translator's work. The implications for the texts considered in the present study are plain. While earlier scholarship, preoccupied with a

72 Joseph S. Wittig, "King Alfred's Boethius and Its Latin Sources: A Reconsideration," *Anglo-Saxon England* 11 (1983), 157–98.

73 Hans Sauer, *Theodulfi Capitula in England. Die altenglischen Übersetzungen, zusammen mit dem lateinischen Text*, Münchener Universitätschriften 8 (Munich: Wilhelm Fink, 1978), 118–19.

supposed lost Latin *Vorlage*, shrank from looking too closely at divergent translations in the Old English penitentials, the analogy of other translations from this period suggests that such worries were unnecessary. Indeed, Frantzen has noted that Spindler erroneously "disregarded the possibility that Anglo-Saxon translators, or the ecclesiastical authorities for whom they worked, might have had reason to alter penances and work as editors themselves."[74] This is an observation of significance to the study of early law, for it suggests that the Old English penitentials may be considered a series not of translations but of normative texts in their own right. This conclusion is borne out by a brief examination of passages not considered in Frantzen's study or any other of which I am aware.

We may begin with the text assumed by its most recent editor to stick closely to its sources, the *Scriftboc*. One clause illustrative of the independence even of this translation reworks *PT* I, iv, 4:

Si laicus alterum occiderit odii meditatione, si non vult arma relinquere, peniteat VII annos, sine carne et vino III annos.

"If a layman slays another with hatred in his thoughts, if he will not give up his arms, let him do penance for seven years, for three [of these] without meat or wine."

In the translator's hands, the result is as follows:[75]

Gyf man slyhð oðerne on morð on eorran mode and mid behydnysse, fæste IV gear; sum willað VII.

"If a man slays another in [an act of] *morð* and with a wrathful mind and with concealment, let him fast four years; some wish for seven."

The clause is plainly a synthesis of ecclesiastical and secular norms. To the established canonical sanction on homicide committed maliciously (*odii meditatione*) the translator has added an element of his own legal tradition: the taboo form of homicide known as *morð*, here defined as "concealment" (*behydnysse*) following upon an act of homicide.[76] Widely known to historians of English penal law, this norm is in evidence throughout the corpus of Germanic legislative texts, as in *Grágás* cap. 88 ("En þa er morð ef maðr leynir eða hylr hræ eða gengr eigi í gegn," "And that is murder if a man conceals or hides the body, or does

[74] Frantzen, "Sin and Sense," 56.

[75] *Das altenglische Bussbuch*, ed. Spindler, 186 (cap. XIX.20.a).

[76] The Old English word is the ancestor, by way of Medieval Latin *murdrum*, of Modern English "murder." See Bruce R. O'Brien, "From *Morðor* to *Murdrum:* The Preconquest Origin and Norman Revival of the Murder Fine," *Speculum* 71 (1996), 321–57.

not confess").[77] We may assume that this principle of Germanic folk law has here attached itself to the *Scriftboc*'s discussion of *morð*.[78]

In view of the relative scarcity of evidence concerning Anglo-Saxon law, minor changes such as this one may bear great significance. Prior to the laws of Cnut, the term *morð* occurs only within compounds, a circumstance prompting one commentator to suppose that it had no legal meaning in England until the eleventh century, having arrived in Cnut's legislation perhaps through the influence of Scandinavian languages.[79] The portion of the *Scriftboc* quoted in the preceding text potentially undermines such speculations and is, in any case, of great interest for historians of Anglo-Saxon law given its capacity to narrow down the meaning of this otherwise rather uncertain term. Yet it has not been recognized as such in any legal-historical publication of which I am aware.[80] The clause suggests grounds for dissent from the view that Old English *morð* did not refer "exclusively, or even generally" to secret killings.[81] In any case, neglect of these texts omits potentially crucial evidence by which Anglo-Saxon legal conventions might be reconstructed.

Another clear adjustment of ecclesiastical law to secular norms is found in the *Old English Canons of Theodore*. Here we see the translator doing something rather different as he draws on canons in multiple

77 *Grágás: Islændernes Lovbog i Fristatens Tid*, ed. Vilhjálmur Finsen (Copenhagen: Det nordiske Literatur-Samfund, 1852), 153.

78 In making here and elsewhere in this study the claim that some Old English penitentials relied sporadically on unwritten Germanic norms, I am mindful of the skepticism, already noted earlier, with which historians now view the notion of "Germanic law." Having no desire to restore the excesses of some nineteenth-century scholarship, I think the notion that members of closely related speech communities might share certain legal norms, some of which may be traceable to a period prior to their separation into distinct groups, is uncontroversial; where the norms in question involve a shared lexicon (as in *morð*, *nið*) it seems a matter of common sense.

79 Horst Haider Munske, *Der germanische Rechtswortschatz im Bereich der Missetaten* (Berlin: De Gruyter, 1973), 46–7.

80 See *Gesetze*, ed. Liebermann, II: s.v. "Mord," where this clause goes unmentioned; likewise E. G. Stanley, "Words for the Dictionary of Old English," in *The Dictionary of Old English: Retrospects and Prospects*, eds. M. J. Toswell and Antonette di Paolo Healey (Kalamazoo, MI: Medieval Institute, 1998), 33–56 at 48–51.

81 O'Brien, "From *Morðor* to *Murdrum*," 343. In this O'Brien follows Munske and Johannes C. H. R. Steenstrup, *Normannerne*, 4 vols. (Copenhagen: Klein, 1876–82), IV (*Danelag*): 279 (whence Munske appears to have derived his argument). I would not dispute O'Brien's more general and quite important claim that *morð* might refer to slayings other than those done secretly, repeated with seeming approval in John Hudson, *The Oxford History of the Laws of England, Vol. II: 871–1216* (Oxford: Oxford University Press, 2012), 166. That it could take on broader meanings does not require us to assume the loss of the more restrictive sense evident in this clause of the *Scriftboc*.

collections – much as he did in the clause considered at the outset of this volume – to arrive at a syncretic version of his own. The first source is cap. II, 12 of the *Penitential of Cummean:*[82]

Qui per turpiloquium uel aspectu coinquinatus est, non tamen uoluit fornicari corporaliter, .xx. uel .xl. diebus iuxta qualitatem peccantis peniteat.

"He who because of lewd conversation or looking [at a woman] is polluted, but did not wish to sin corporeally, let him do penance for twenty or forty days in accordance with the gravity of the sin."

The second is *PT* I, viii, 1:

Sacerdos si tangendo mulierem aut osculando coinquinabitur, XL. dies poeniteat.

"A priest who is polluted by touching a woman or kissing her – let him fast for 40 days."

The rendering of these clauses in the *Old English Canons of Theodore* seems to show that this translator as well felt free to depart from the language of his sources:[83]

Gyf mæssepreost for his geþohtum weorðeð besmiten, fæste twentig daga. Gyf he gehrine þa breost mid his hand, fæste þreo wucan.

"If a priest becomes polluted as a result of his thoughts, let him fast for twenty days. If he touches breasts with his hand, let him fast for three weeks."

Here, opportunities to probe the conscience of a penitent regarding "lewd speech" and "kissing" are foregone for the sake of clarity, while the translator reduces the rather uncertain offenses referred to in his sources to a single wrong attested only in secular legislation. Some analogue may be furnished by caps. 11 and 18 of Alfred's code, both of which prescribe restitutions for the behavior inveighed against in the *Canons*, though the context here envisaged is that of sexual assault:[84]

[11] Gif mon on cirliscre fæmnan breost gefó, mid V scill. hire gebete. [11.1] Gif he hie oferweorpe and mid ne gehæme, mid X scill. gebete.

"If a man seizes the breast of a 'churl' woman, let him compensate her with five shillings. If he overpowers her but does not violate her, let him compensate her with 10 shillings."

Among Alfred's influences may have been cap. 26. 4 of the *Lex Salica*, which establishes that to touch uninvited the hand, arm, or breast of a free woman was a serious offense.[85] The occurrence of this prohibition in

[82] *The Irish Penitentials*, ed. and trans Bieler, 114. This clause is discussed in more depth in Chapter 6, 185–86.

[83] *Canons*, eds. Fulk and Jurasinski, 7 (A 42–3).

[84] *Gesetze*, ed. Liebermann, I: 56.

[85] See *Lex Salica. 100 Titel-Text*, ed. Karl August Eckhardt (Weimar: Böhlau, 1953), 143.

both the *Lex Salica* and Alfred's code makes this prohibition in all likelihood an element of folk law that therefore may not owe its appearance in the *Canons* to external textual influences.

Though both are given to free translation, the *Scriftboc* and *Canons* do not depart from the laconic style of their sources. Such is decidedly not the case with the *Old English Penitential*, whose author is on many occasions unable to refrain from elaborating on his anchor texts with inventive and often somewhat florid digressions. A characteristic example is his rendering of cap. 99 of the Council of Carthage:[86]

Oblationes dissidentium fratrum neque in sacrario neque in gazofilatio recipiantur.

"The offerings of disputing brothers are not to be received either at the altar or in the treasury."

For the author of the *Penitential*, this simple rule, reliant on Matthew 5:23–24, will not suffice:[87]

Soðlice nis nanum cristenum men alyfed, þæt he on godes cyrcean gode lac offrigie þa hwile þe he nið oððe andan oððe ænige unðwærnesse on his heortan hæbbe wið his ðone nehstan; forðam his lac ne beoð gode andfenge, ærþam þe he hine sylfne geðwærie 7 gegladige wið his nehstan.

"Truly it is not permitted to any Christian that he should make a good offering in God's church while he has in his heart any anger or jealousy or any ill will toward his neighbor; therefore his offerings will not be well received, until he should reconcile himself and come to agreement with his neighbor."

The source merely establishes a precept of ecclesiastical governance, urging priests not to accept the offerings of those in dispute with one another. The *Penitential* turns this rule back on the communicant: he must scrutinize himself not only for anger or the peculiarly Germanic kind of hatred known as *nið*, but for any trace of ill will toward his neighbor (*ænige unðwærnesse*) before approaching the altar lest his sacrifice be profaned. The translator will not have his reader in any doubt over what is meant by "discord" and so fleshes out all that is implicit in the Latin. It will be seen subsequently that free translations elsewhere in the *Penitential* either clarify what the translator considered moments of vagueness in earlier penitentials or force them into agreement with his own stringent standards. The tendency to "spiritualize" the contents of Halitgar as is done

[86] *Bussbücher*, ed. Schmitz, I: 728 (IV.xxxi).

[87] *Die altenglische Version*, ed. Raith, 33 (cap. 27). The situation is not unlike that of Chaucer's Wife of Bath: "In al the parisshe wif ne was ther noon / That to the offrynge bifore hire sholde goon; / And if ther dide, certeyn so wrooth was she / That she was out of alle charitee." *The Riverside Chaucer*, ed. Benson, 30 (ll. 449–52).

here is also evident elsewhere in the *Penitential*. Repeatedly its author mentions the temptations of the devil where there is no such reference in his source, attributes motivations to actions about which Halitgar had been silent, and manifests a particular concern for the moral implications of the slightest movements of the soul.[88] Of all the Old English penitentials, it exhibits the greatest sensitivity to the "inner life."

The clauses considered in the present chapter and those to be discussed subsequently show that ecclesiastical canons composed in English were more susceptible to secular legal influences than their Latin sources (many of which wandered into territory having little to do with pastoral care). Why this should be the case is a question that allows for no single answer. Because the Old English penitentials respond to a range of pastoral questions, we should probably assume that the routes by which secular custom came to find a home in these texts were as varied as the problems they address. Among the range of possible solutions, some of which will be considered throughout the present volume, one is perhaps suggested by the manuscript settings of these texts. Three of the four Old English penitentials are preceded by instructions for a confessor – our strongest indication that, while the frequency of auricular confession and the nature of penitential rites observed at this time remain matters of uncertainty, Old English penitentials were copied at least initially without any "antiquarian" aims, being meant simply to aid priests in the cure of souls.[89] Their preservation in MS Y (Laud Misc. 482) gives further evidence of the uses to which they were once put. This portable, unadorned manuscript has long been recognized as just the sort of book that would have assisted a priest in his daily work. Its inclusion of Latin offices for the sick and the dying along with penitential texts – "a unique combination in the surviving Anglo-Saxon material," according to Victoria Thompson – perhaps gives some sense of the circumstances under which confession was heard at this time.[90] Likewise significant is

[88] See *Die altenglische Version*, ed. Raith, 25 (II.17), 26 (II.19), 39 (III.6), 41 (III.11): all are additions by the translator of "þurh deofles costnunga" ("through the temptations of the devil") where nothing of the sort is present in the source text.

[89] See Rob Meens, "The Frequency and Nature of Early Medieval Penance," in *Handling Sin: Confession in the Middle Ages*, York Studies in Medieval Theology II, eds. Peter Biller and A. J. Minnis (York: York Medieval Press, 1998), 35–62 at 54: "Our sources do not permit us to recreate the procedure of penance as it functioned in practice, let alone to establish its frequency with any precision, since such texts are normally of a normative type." One of the few certainties is that confession both of grave and minor sins was urged during Ash Wednesday; see Hamilton, *The Practice of Penance*, 38–9.

[90] Victoria Thompson, "The Pastoral Contract in Late Anglo-Saxon England: Priest and Parishioner in Oxford, Bodleian Library MS Laud Miscellaneous 482," in *Pastoral Care*

the careful rendering in some of these manuscripts of colored or shaded initials indicating the boundaries between canons. This manner of presenting the text, likely intended for ease of reference, is found even in Cambridge, Corpus Christi College 190, a witness to Wulfstan's "commonplace book." These texts seem to have been copied with the understanding that they would see regular use by presbyters and bishops alike.

That Old English penitentials were copied even in the late Anglo-Saxon period specifically to aid in pastoral care may tell us something about how they came to acquire traces of popular law. As Firey has shown, priests in Francia may have enjoyed some liberty to adapt remedies to the circumstances of the penitent: if penitentials often seem to have offered unsatisfying solutions to the problems they consider, it is perhaps because they were meant as aids to memory, or to establish the boundaries of the acceptable.[91] Such notions of sacerdotal authority were no doubt familiar to the authors of the Old English penitentials, and it is quite likely that these texts and their divergences from sources reflect the accumulated wisdom of priests who understood the limitations of Frankish handbooks for English circumstances. The latitude granted to priests to adapt remedies to the conditions of penitents is evident, for example, in the *ordo confessionis* appearing toward the beginning of the *Handbook:*[92]

> And geþengc ðu þæt þu ne scealt næfre gelice deman þam rican and þam heanan, þam freon and þam þeowan, þam ealdan and þam geongan, þam halan and þam unhalan, þam eadmodan and þam ofermodan, þam strangan and þam unmagan, þam gehadodum and þam læwedum. Ælce dæde sceal gesceadwis dema wislice toscadan, hu heo gedon si and hwar oððe hwænne.
>
> "And know that you shall never judge alike the rich and the poor, the free and the servile, the old and the young, the healthy and the sick, the modest and the proud, the powerful and the weak, those in orders and those of the laity. Of each deed the discerning confessor shall wisely distinguish how it was done and where or when."

A number of the Old English canons so far discussed may be understood as attempts to adjust the remedy to the "where" of the offense: thus

in Late Anglo-Saxon England, Anglo-Saxon Studies 6, ed. Francesca Tinti (Woodbridge, UK: Boydell, 2005), 106–20 at 106.

91 See Firey, *A Contrite Heart*, 203–4. As Firey notes, the canons of Châlon were in part an attempt to replace the tradition of sacerdotal latitude with more rigorously text-based procedures for penance. Given that Anglo-Saxon England was, as far as may be known, untouched by such debates, it may be assumed that the situation for confessors within the pre-Conquest English church remained close to what obtained in Francia before the reaction against penitentials.

92 See Fowler, "Handbook," 19.

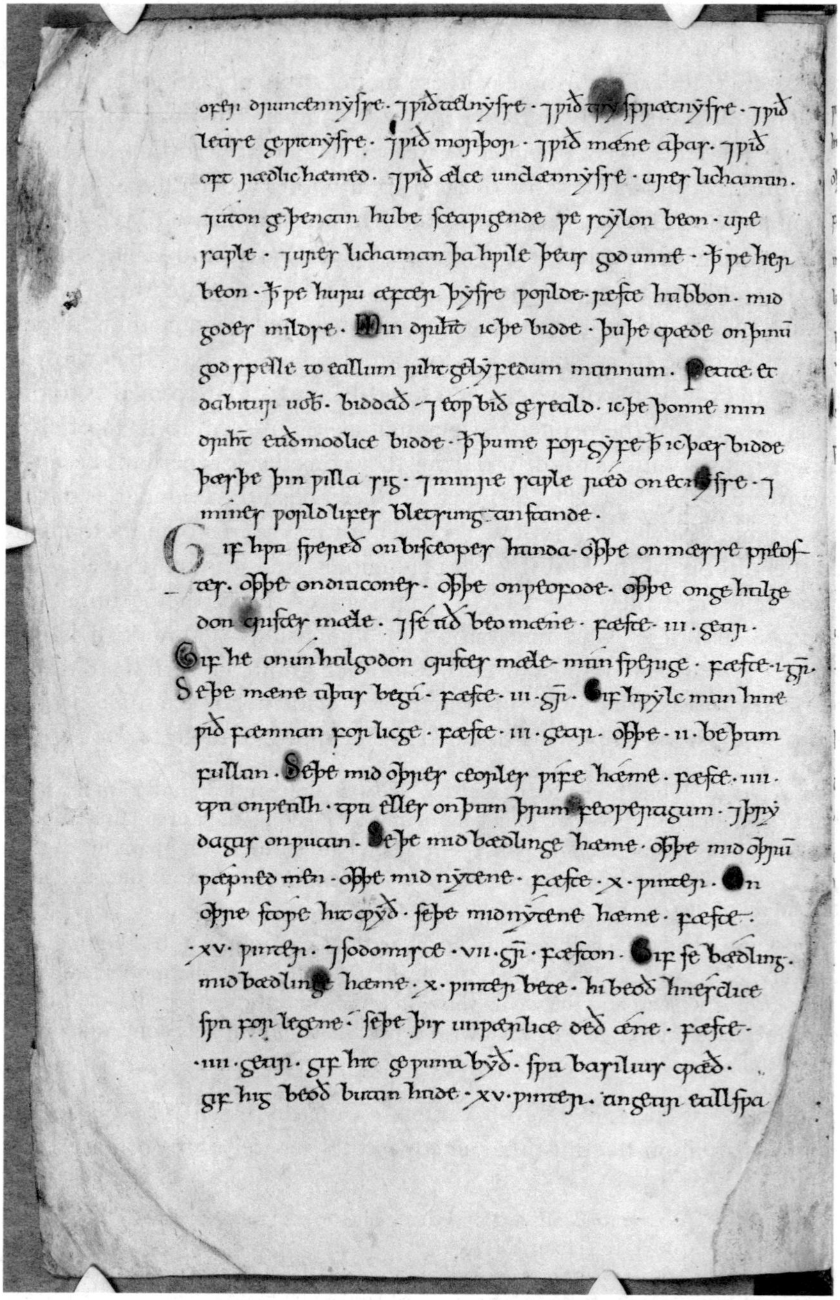

FIGURE 2. This page (CCCC 190, p. 416) shows the transition from a brief formula for confessors (ed. Fulk and Jurasinski, *The Old English Canons of Theodore*, 77–78) to the B-text of the *Canons of Theodore*, where the shaded initials become more numerous. (Photograph: Courtesy of the Master and Fellows of Corpus Christi College, Cambridge.)

"wine" becomes "ale" and an instance of homicide turns into *morð*. But it is of no less significance for the present study that the confessor in the passage just quoted is designated as a *dema* ("judge"). The explicitly judicative role assumed for confessors suggests for this clerical estate a greater share of authority than envisaged by Oakley, one that entitled them to intervene directly in matters of secular law and devise in some cases wholly new ordinances. Whether the role of penance in secular legislation of the later Anglo-Saxon period reflects royal deference to clerics as much as a search for "reinforcement" is a question that has been too little considered in work so far published.

Indeed, we may assume that penitentials came to be written in Old English for the same reason this language served as the medium for other texts traditionally composed in Latin. To clarify Latin canons for English audiences can have been only a secondary concern in the only polity of early Western Europe to give its own written vernacular a status comparable to Latin. Moreover, one may doubt whether the *Scriftboc* was consulted primarily as an aid for understanding its Latin sources (translated, at all events, in no order that would have allowed for easy comparison with the originals) given that the Old English text received substantial glossing in MS X (Bodleian Library, Junius 121), some of it apparently done without consultation of the *Scriftboc*'s Latin source.[93] That the glossator did not rely exclusively on collation of the Old English canons with Latin exemplars further suggests that the *Scriftboc* was regarded as possessing, at least toward the end of its reception, an authority of its own, which may be among the reasons why several of its clauses would be appropriated by the author of the *Leges Henrici Primi*. This circumstance, along with its preservation in five manuscripts – few Old English prose or verse texts survive in more than one – suggests that the *Scriftboc* and other Old English penitentials were regarded by the end of the Anglo-Saxon period as guides sufficient in themselves on matters of pastoral care. The result, as I hope to show in the following chapters, is a wealth of observations on the legal attitudes of their day that so far has not been adequately explored.

[93] This generalization does not hold for all of the glosses, but some clearly do not replicate Latin sources and, perhaps more interestingly, appear to have as their object clarification of the Old English for readers in the late Anglo-Saxon period. This seems particularly to be the case with cap. XIII.16.g (where the glossator clarifies the apparently then-exotic term *þycgean*).

2

Legal Change, Vernacular Penitentials, and the Chronology of Old English Prose

Though it stands to reason that all of the Old English penitentials are unlikely to have been written at the same time given their varied styles and concerns, the problem of their chronology has attracted little sustained attention in the nearly two centuries that these texts have been available in modern editions. Of the handful of published remarks on this subject, most occur in works whose primary focus lies elsewhere.[1] Suggested dates have varied widely, with uncertainty evident even in the work of the preeminent authority on the Anglo-Saxon penitentials. Though he once considered the *Scriftboc* "probably not earlier than the reign of Alfred," Allen Frantzen has in subsequent years narrowed down the possibilities, asserting in a series of publications that all of the Old English penitentials may be dated to "the tenth and eleventh centuries."[2] According to Frantzen, this *terminus a quo* holds even for the *Old English Canons of Theodore* and *Scriftboc*, in spite of their reliance upon pre-Halitgarian materials of the sort one would not expect to travel from Francia in the aftermath of the Carolingian reform.[3] The specific tenth-century context most often envisaged for these texts is not the period shortly after Alfred's

[1] As will be seen in the pages that follow, discussions of dating have rarely amounted to more than isolated observations and conjectures in the standard editions.

[2] Allen J. Frantzen, "The Tradition of Penitentials in Anglo-Saxon England," *Anglo-Saxon England* 11 (1983), 23–56 at 42; Frantzen, "Penitentials," in *The Blackwell Encyclopaedia of Anglo-Saxon England*, 362; also Mary Clayton, "Suicide in the Works of Ælfric," *Review of English Studies* n.s. 60 (2009), 339–370 at p. 347 n. 36.

[3] His most recent treatment of the Old English penitentials endorses the first half of the tenth century as the earliest possible *terminus a quo* for the *Old English Canons of Theodore*, a text he considers "roughly contemporary with the *Scriftboc*"; see "Sin and Sense," 41.

reign but the revival of vernacular writing that followed the episcopates of Æthelwold and Dunstan toward the close of the century.[4]

Frantzen's is, of course, not the only voice to have been raised on the subject. In his *Libri paenitentiales* (1978), Cyrille Vogel had asserted (regrettably without much explanation) that the *Scriftboc* might be dated as early as the eighth century, "avant la réforme carolingienne (plutôt que vers 950/1000)."[5] (Frantzen's supplement to this volume, appearing in 1985, avoids assigning a specific date, maintaining merely that the *Scriftboc* is the earliest of the Old English penitentials and that the *Canons of Theodore* are based in some way on an early recension of the *Scriftboc*.[6]) One detects in the work of some later scholars as well a suspicion that these texts must be older. Audrey Meaney has characterized the *Scriftboc* as "of uncertain, perhaps tenth-century, date."[7] And in a 2006 article, Cubitt suggested that this handbook "may date to as early as the reign of Alfred," though without further discussion.[8]

The date urged by Frantzen has the advantage of being the safest, agreeing as it does with the least-disputed aspects of the Old English penitential corpus taken as a whole. We have seen that all manuscript witnesses date to the eleventh century and that copying of these texts seems unlikely in at least one instance to have been motivated by "antiquarian" aims.[9] Moreover, the *Handbook* appears to have been embellished with Wulfstanian phrases, a feature that has long suggested its ties to the prelate.[10] Later composition also seems inevitable for the *Penitential*, itself the principal source for the provisions of the *Handbook*, given its reliance on a text not known to have circulated in Anglo-Saxon England until the tenth century in spite of its appearance on the continent one hundred

[4] The commentary of Frantzen's online edition favors for both a date no earlier than the second half of the tenth century while leaving open the possibility of composition in the first half.

[5] Vogel, *Les "libri paenitentiales,"* 73. Here Vogel refers to the reaction against the penitentials by some Frankish bishops in the middle of the ninth century, an event before which composition of vernacular penitentials has conventionally been held impossible: see R. D. Fulk and Christopher M. Cain, *A History of Old English Literature* (Oxford: Blackwell, 2003), 125–6. On the reaction, see Frantzen, *Literature of Penance,* 94–5.

[6] Vogel, *Les "libri paenitentiales,"* 39–40.

[7] Audrey Meaney, "The *Ides* of the Cotton Gnomic Poem," in *New Readings on Women in Old English Literature*, eds. Helen Damico and Alexandra Hennessey Olsen (Bloomington: Indiana University Press, 1990), 158–75 at 161.

[8] Cubitt, "Bishops, Priests and Penance," 53.

[9] As is most plainly the case in MS Laud Misc. 482, described in Thompson, "The Pastoral Contract in Late Anglo-Saxon England."

[10] See Chapter 1, 39–40.

years prior. That the fourth book of the *Penitential* recasts canons drawn from the *Scriftboc* likewise indicates the priority of the latter, though the manuscript transmission of this portion of the *Penitential* may suggest a more complicated picture.[11]

As we will see in Chapter 3, however, when scholars have sought evidence beyond the dates of the manuscripts for proof that these texts appeared late in the development of Old English prose, the results have been less than satisfying. Because doubts have surrounded principally the *Scriftboc* and the *Canons of Theodore*, the present chapter will be occupied primarily with situating these two penitentials within the tradition of early English pastoral texts. The scant evidence available to resolve such problems precludes too much certainty. But I hope to show in the following pages that the range of probable dates of composition can be widened considerably beyond what most scholars have been willing to entertain since the early 1980s. Much of what follows will reassess in particular the arguments of Spindler. Though his edition of the *Scriftboc* had assigned both the *Scriftboc* and *Canons* to the era of the Benedictine Reform, he offered significant evidence – to be explored in more detail subsequently – that would seem, if interpreted differently, to argue against such a date.[12]

SUPPOSED OBSTACLES TO COMPOSITION PRIOR TO THE BENEDICTINE REFORM

It should be noted at the outset that, as far as the *Canons* and *Scriftboc* are concerned, the hypothesis of tenth-century composition has received only the most ambivalent support from its two principal exponents: Spindler and, in the present era, Frantzen. What made post-Æthelwoldian composition seem inevitable to Frantzen in spite of the relative archaism of the sources on which the *Canons* and *Scriftboc* rely was his assumption – shared by a fair number of specialists in Old English – that little vernacular writing of any consequence can have occurred in the mid- or late ninth century amid Viking assaults on monastic scriptoria and the general decay of Latin learning that King Alfred laments in the preface

[11] See Frantzen, *Literature of Penance*, 137–8. Here Frantzen also considers the failure of the *Canons* and *Scriftboc* to make much use of late practices allowed by the *Handbook* – such as commutations – which to him seems sure evidence for the *Scriftboc* having been composed prior to the *Penitential*.

[12] Spindler, *Das altenglische Bussbuch*, 111. As will be seen, Spindler seems not to have appreciated the full implications of this evidence, though later scholars would.

to his translation of Gregory's *Cura pastoralis*.[13] "[I]t is highly unlikely," Frantzen notes, "that the machinery of private penance would have fared well during the ninth century invasions."[14] But in spite of the disarray into which monastic life and thus Latin learning must have fallen, Frantzen does leave open the possibility that the textual "machinery of penance" was furnished nonetheless by Archbishop Fulk of Rheims, who sent to King Alfred a number of clerics schooled in Frankish penitential traditions:[15]

> Significantly Alfred's law codes were the first compiled since the eighth century and it seems likely that his enthusiasm for new legislative texts extended to ecclesiastical as well as secular law.... He could have learned about Frankish penitential traditions from one of Francia's most important authorities, Fulk, archbishop of Rheims, with whom Alfred corresponded on at least one occasion. During the long pontificate of Hincmar (d. 992) Rheims had become perhaps the most important continental centre for the production of canonical texts.

Frantzen's supposition that Frankish penitentials may have been available in Wessex through Archbishop Fulk's emissaries may enjoy more advantages than is routinely assumed. In a list of manuscripts giving "an indication of the sort of books which were imported into England in the years following King Alfred's revival of ecclesiastical life in the 890s," Michael Lapidge has included Oxford, Bodleian Library, Bodley 572 (s. ix^{in}), a manuscript first copied in Francia which contains the penitential of Cummean and other canons.[16] When it arrived in England is unknown. But given that other Frankish manuscripts seem likely to have appeared in England at the close of the ninth century, it is at least probable that Alfred's Frankish counselors came toting texts on pastoral care, most of which are now lost.[17]

Some sense of what these texts may have looked like comes from Alfred's *domboc*. Because the evidence is somewhat disputed, discussing it adequately will involve a brief departure from the Old English

[13] Frantzen, *Literature of Penance*, 122.

[14] Ibid., 126. Carole Hough has reiterated such claims, asserting that Frankish penitentials cannot have been available prior to the reform efforts of Æthelwold and Dunstan. See Hough, "Penitential Literature and Secular Law."

[15] Frantzen, "The Tradition of Penitentials," 50; also Frantzen, *Literature of Penance*, 127.

[16] Michael Lapidge, *The Anglo-Saxon Library* (London: Oxford University Press, 2006), 171.

[17] London, BL, Cotton Galba A. xviii, another manuscript copied perhaps in Rheims early in the ninth century containing the Psalterium Gallicanum, is held to have come to England during the second half of the ninth century or the beginning of the tenth (ibid., 169).

penitentials. But close consideration of Alfred's laws is warranted, for as we will see (and as some have suspected), the Alfredian era probably has more to tell us about these texts than one might think.[18] We may begin with the recasting of Exodus 22:18 ("Maleficos non patieris vivere," "Wizards thou shalt not suffer to live") in the assemblage of translated biblical ordinances with which this text begins.[19] Alfred's expanded version ("Ða fæmnan þe gewuniað onfon gealdorcræftigan 7 scinlæcan 7 wiccan, ne læt þu ða libban," "Do not allow to live those women who are accustomed to receive enchanters and magicians and witches") has struck Audrey Meaney as derived in some way from cap. I, xv, 4 of the penitential of Theodore:[20]

> Si mulier incantationes vel divinationes diabolicas fecerit I annum vel III · XL mas vel XL iuxta qualitatem culpae peniteat. De hoc in canone dicitur: qui auguria auspicia sive somnia vel divinationes quaslibet secundum mores gentilium observant <u>aut in domos suas huiusmodi homines introducunt</u> in exquaerendis aliquam artem maleficiorum penitentes isti si de clero sunt abiciantur. Si vero saeculares quinquennio peniteat.
>
> "If a woman performs diabolical incantations or divinations, she shall do penance for one year or the three forty-day periods, or forty days, according to the nature of the offense. Of this matter it is said in the canon: He who celebrates auguries, omens from birds, or dreams, or any divinations according to the custom of the heathen, <u>or introduces such people into his houses</u>, in seeking out any trick of the magicians – when these people become penitents, if they belong to the clergy they shall be cast out; but if they are secular persons they shall do penance for five years."

While Meaney does qualify this attribution, noting her own uncertainty whether "Alfred could have been acquainted with this *Penitential,* since it does not seem to have been known in England at this time," it is significant that Theodore's penitential condemns those who invite sorcerers

[18] Cubitt suggests ("Bishops, Priests and Penance," 47), after a survey of texts that begins with the Alfredian period, that "by the end of the ninth century, a developed terminology for penitential practice had already evolved," one that was "used consistently across a number of sources from different periods and provenances, from Alfred's court circle and possibly ninth-century Mercia ... through into the tenth and eleventh centuries."

[19] Unless indicated otherwise, this and all subsequent quotations from the Vulgate are drawn from *Biblia Sacra iuxta Vulgatam Versionem*, ed. R. Gryson et al. (Stuttgart, Germany: Deutsche Bibelgesellschaft, 1994); translations are from the Douay version, as edited in *The Holy Bible*, ed. R. Challoner et al. (New York: Catholic Book Publishing Co., 1950). On the likelihood of influence from penitentials on Alfred's Prologue, see Meaney, "The Ides of the Cotton Gnomic Poem," 161; idem, "Old English Legal and Penitential Penalties for Heathenism," 131–3; Jurasinski, "Violence, Penance, and Secular Law." Some of this section repeats arguments made in the last of these publications, though not in full detail.

[20] For the text of Alfred's laws, see *Gesetze*, ed. Liebermann, I: 38–9; the translation of *PT* is that of McNeill and Gamer, *Medieval Handbooks*, 198.

into their homes on the authority of another collection of ordinances (*in canone*) that might have been available to Alfred and his circle if Theodorean collections were not.[21] As McNeill and Gamer observe, the source to which Theodore seems to refer is almost certainly some form of canon 24 of the Council of Ankara (314).[22]

Other portions of Alfred's laws suggest more decisively the influence of penitential canons. One case in point is his treatment of Exodus 21:12–14, which in the original reads as follows:

> Qui percusserit hominem volens occidere morte moriatur. Qui autem non est insidiatus, sed Deus illum tradidit in manu eius, constituam tibi locum quo fugere debeat. Si quis industria occiderit proximum suum et per insidias, ab altari meo evelles eum ut moriatur.
>
> "He that striketh a man with a will to kill him, shall be put to death. But he that did not lie in wait for him, but God delivered him into his hands: I will appoint thee a place to which he must flee. If a man kill his neighbor on set purpose and by lying in wait for him, thou shalt take him away from my altar, that he may die."

Alfred makes a few significant additions:[23]

> Se mon se ðe his gewealdes monnan ofslea, swelte se deaðe. Se ðe hine þonne nedes ofsloge oððe unwillum oððe ungewealdes, swelce hine God swa sende on his honda, & he hine ne ymbsyrede, sie he feores wyrðe & folcryhtre bote, gif he friðstowe gesece. Gif hwa ðonne of giernesse & gewealdes ofslea his þone nehstan þurh searwa, aluc ðu hine from minum weofode, to þam þæt he deaðe swelte.
>
> "He who kills a man deliberately, let him die the death. But he who kills him out of necessity [or 'under compulsion'] or unwillingly or unintentionally, as God put it in his hands, and he did not lie in wait for him, let him be worthy of life and of [the opportunity for] amends by folk-right [or 'customary law'], if he should seek asylum. But if someone with desire and intent should kill his neighbor, remove him from my sanctuary so that he may die the death."

The expansion of *Qui autem non est insidiatus* as *Se ðe hine þonne nedes ofsloge oððe unwillum oððe ungewealdes* has been described as "appear[ing] to be for explanation rather than emphasis or elegance."[24] Exactly what is explained, I would add, becomes apparent once we see that the three categories of unintentional homicide Alfred inserts here

[21] Meaney, "Old English Legal and Penitential Penalties," 133.

[22] McNeill and Gamer, *Medieval Handbooks,* 198n102.

[23] *Gesetze*, ed. Liebermann, I: 30–1. My rendering of *sie he feores wyrðe & folcryhtre bote* differs from Michael Treschow's ('The Prologue to Alfred's Law Code: Instruction in the Spirit of Mercy', *Florilegium* 13 [1994], 79–110 at 92), who gives "let him be responsible for the life and its legal compensation": cf. *Gesetze*, ed. Liebermann, I: 31: "so sei er des Lebens und volksrechtlicher Busse würdig, wenn er eine Schutzstätte findet."

[24] Treschow, "Prologue," 92.

(*nedes,* "under compulsion," *unwillum,* "involuntarily," *ungewealdes,* "through negligence/carelessness") seem to reflect the taxonomies of lethal violence found in many of the Frankish penitentials that circulated on the Continent (and, perhaps, in England) in the years prior to Alfred's reign.[25] In these sources as well, the requirement of compensation for homicide as a specifically penitential remedy is routine, something that Alfred duly adds to his version of the biblical ordinance, thereby harmonizing the text with secular and ecclesiastical law.[26]

Departures from the biblical text elsewhere in Alfred's laws fall into a similar pattern. A master who beats his slave so severely that he or she dies within two days is free of penalties in the Vulgate (*non subiacebit poenąe*); in Alfred, this same master is not "entirely as guilty" (*ealles swa scyldig*) as he would be had the slave died in his own hands. It is the interior condition of the master that is at issue in this text, as is not the case in Exodus. Perhaps for this reason, Alfred expands the period in which the death of the slave is of legal relevance from one to two days (*uno die supervixerit vel duobus*) to two or three (*ðeah he libbe twa niht oððe ðreo*). That the time in which a master is liable for the violent death of his slave is, in Alfred's version, the same as that prescribed in the Council of Elvira, seems in itself evidence that this clause was influenced by the sort of canon collections long assumed to have been unavailable in ninth-century Wessex.[27]

25 See, e.g., *PT* I, iv, 3–7: "Si laicus alterum occiderit odii meditatione, si non vult arma relinquere, poeniteat VII annos, sine carne et vino III annos.... Qui per jussionem domini sui hominem occiderit, XL diebus abstineat se ab ecclesia, et qui occiderit hominem in publico bello, XL dies poeniteat. Si per iram, III annos, si casu, I annum, si per poculum vel artem aliquam, VII annos aut plus, si per rixam, X annos poeniteat," "If a layman slays another with malice aforethought, if he will not lay aside his arms, he shall do penance for seven years; without flesh and wine, three years.... One who slays a man by command of his lord shall keep away from the church for forty days; and one who slays a man in public war shall do penance for forty days. If through anger, he shall do penance for three years; if by accident, for one year; if by a potion or any trick, seven years or more; if as a result of a quarrel, ten years." *Bußordnungen*, ed. Wasserschleben, 188; trans. McNeill and Gamer, *Medieval Handbooks*, 187.

26 "Si quis pro ultione propinqui hominem occiderit, peniteat sicut homicida VII vel X annos. Si tamen reddere vult propinquis pecuniam aestimationis, levior erit poenitentia i.e. dimidio spatio," "If one slays a man in revenge for a relative, he shall do penance as a murderer for seven or ten years. However, if he will render to the relatives the legal price, the penance shall be lighter, that is, [it shall be shortened] by half the time." *Bußordnungen,* ed. Wasserschleben, 187 (*PT* I, iv, 1); trans. McNeill and Gamer, *Medieval Handbooks,* 187.

27 This clause of the Council of Elvira would subsequently receive adaptive translation in the *Old English Penitential;* the provision of the council and its treatment are discussed in more detail in Chapter 3, 96–97.

The adaptations of Exodus just described are significant to our understanding of the *domboc* as a whole. We have seen that the standard view of the relation between penance and secular law, given fullest articulation by Oakley and repeated with little variation in the years since, holds that Alfred and subsequent legislators urged penance for wrongdoers as a way of bolstering the weak enforcement mechanisms of the nascent Anglo-Saxon "state." These portions of the Prologue, however, make evident a shift of a more profound character. The recasting of Exodus 21:12–14 (on intended and unintended homicide) has long been understood to reveal something of the law of sanctuary observed in Alfred's day. And here it seems significant that Alfred does not regard, as had Ine before him, one's having reached a sacred building as alone sufficient to spare one's life.[28] In this and many other clauses of the Prologue having to do with violence, it is one's intent that is exculpatory, as is routinely the case in the literature of penance. I have argued elsewhere that this particular feature of Alfred's legislative "reforms" – his emphasis on the interior condition of the offender – affords an explanation for the otherwise perplexing provisions of cap. 42 of the code proper:[29]

Eac swelce, gif mon becume on his gefán, 7 he hine ǽr hamfastne ne wite, gif he wille his wæpen sellan, hine mon gehealde XXX nihta 7 hine his freondum gecyðe; gif he ne wille his wæpenu sellan, þonne mot he feohtan on hine. Gif he wille on hond gan 7 his wæpenu sellan, 7 hwa ofer þæt on him feohte, gielde swa wer swa wunde swa he gewyrce, 7 wite 7 hæbbe his mæg forworht.

"Likewise, if a man run across his opponent, and did not previously know him to be at home, if he will give up his weapons, he is to be kept for 30 days and his friends informed; if he will not give up his weapons, then he may fight against him. If he is willing to surrender, and to give up his weapons, and after that anyone fights against him, he [who does] is to pay wergeld or compensation for

28 "[5] Gif hwa sie deaðes scyldig 7 he cirican geierne, hæbbe his feorh 7 bete, swa him riht wisige. [5.1] Gif hwa his hyde forwyrce 7 cirican geierne, sie him sio swingelle forgifen," "If someone is condemned to death and he runs to a church, let him have his life and let him make such compensation as is deemed fitting. If someone is to be scourged and runs to a church, let the beating not be administered." *Gesetze*, ed. Liebermann, I: 90–1.

29 Nearly identical conditions are imposed (cap. 42.1) on the conduct of those who surround an adversary knowing him to be at home; I have chosen to quote the subsequent clause because it comes closer to expressing the underlying idea of these provisions. The translation given here is that in *English Historical Documents, Vol. 1, c. 500–1042*, ed. and trans. Dorothy Whitelock (London: Eyre and Spottiswoode, 1955), 380. No commentator has made adequate sense of *hæbbe his mæg forworht*, which literally means something like "he has undone his kinsman." Whitelock's assumption that the attacker has forfeited his right to vengeance is far from certain; the meaning seems rather to be that by harming a man who has abandoned his weapons he has now exposed his kin to justifiable vengeance.

wounds according to what he has done, and a fine, and is to have forfeited [the right to avenge] his kinsman [Attenborough: '[A]nd his kinsman shall forfeit his claim to protection as a result of the action']."

This clause has been referred to as an articulation of the traditional law of "house-peace," a principle in ancient Germanic law endowing the homestead with a sacral character similar to that enjoyed by pagan temples and, subsequently, ecclesiastical buildings.[30] Oddly, this claim has been accompanied by the assertion (made at greatest length by Liebermann, and without any evidence of which I'm aware) that the person so captured by his foes could expect death at their hands if unable to ransom his life in the thirty days afforded him to do so – a claim that seems based on the example of sanctuary laws postdating those in question by centuries.[31] Should this have been the case, it seems hard to suppose that the protection afforded by the homestead can have been very great at all. I have argued that we have instead an attempt by Alfred to rearticulate the customs of the feud in a way that emphasizes its inherent means of reconciliation.[32] That disputants even in cases of homicide might pacify the kin of the decedent by placing themselves in their power (the typical meaning of the legal metaphor *on hand gān*) is a feature of the feud well attested elsewhere in medieval Europe.[33] Paul Hyams finds such ritual displays of "ostentatious vulnerability" amply witnessed in Norman and later English sources as means of establishing friendship between disputants.[34] On the continent, the custom was referred to as *deditio*.[35] And it may have figured among the practices of ninth-century England's expanding Norse population, though evidence is isolated to later literary sources. In *Vatnsdœla saga*, for example, a homicide secures mercy

30 See Frederick Pollock, "The King's Peace," *Law Quarterly Review* 1 (1885), 37–50 at 39–40.

31 *Gesetze*, ed. Liebermann, III: 290 (s.v. "Asyl"); also III: 504 (s.v. "Heimsuchung").

32 See "Sanctuary, House-Peace, and the Traditionalism of Alfred's Laws."

33 The phrase alludes to the Germanic notion of protection referred to as *mund*, a word meaning "hand" that came in legal contexts simply to mean "protection." The term and its implications are considered in David Day, "Hands Across the Hall: The Legalities of Beowulf's Fight with Grendel," *Journal of English and Germanic Philology* 98 (1999), 313–24 at 315–16. The metaphor features in Roman law as well: see the explanation of *manumissio* in *Justinian's Institutes*, ed. Paul Krueger, trans. Peter Birks and Grant McLeod (Ithaca, NY: Cornell University Press, 1987), 38–9 (1.5).

34 Hyams, *Rancor and Reconciliation*, 203.

35 "From the ninth century onwards we know that disputes in both East and West Francia might be settled by means of a ritualized submission or *deditio*, as it is often termed. The core acts involved in this were the deposition of weapons, prostration and begging pardon from the offended party (most often the king)." Levi Roach, "Penance, Submission and *deditio:* Religious Influences on Dispute Settlement in later Anglo-Saxon England (871–1066)," *Anglo-Saxon England* 41 (2012), 343–71 at 351.

by reminding the kin of his victim, to whom he has abandoned himself, of their obligations under traditional law: "It is the custom of leaders to spare the lives of those who voluntarily place themselves at their mercy.... It is not like a great man, to slay a man who goes under the power of another ...." (*er þat ok höfþingja siðr, at veita þeim líf, er sjálfkrafa ganga upp a þeira náð ... er þat ok eigi stórmannligt, at stríða þeim, er á vald manns gengr*).[36] Similar notions are attested in penitential texts to which Alfred and his circle may well have had access. And these are, in the view of most commentators, merely giving expression to traditional law, perhaps that of the Celtic populations among whom private penance first took shape.[37]

A more fundamental problem haunts Liebermann's standard interpretation. To argue that an armed band who attacked a man in his home was entitled under this ordinance to slay him if dissatisfied with the payment forcibly extracted from him is to suggest that Alfred here permits a practice little removed from what codes of the tenth and eleventh century term interchangeably *hamsocn* and *husbryce*.[38] The former is defined by the twelfth-century *Leges Henrici Primi* as an offense occurring "if anyone goes with premeditation to a house where he knows his enemy to be and attacks him there, whether he does this by day or by night" (... *si quis premeditate ad domum eat ubi suum hostem esse scit et ibi eum inuadat, si die uel nocte hoc faciat*).[39] Edmund, Æthelred II, and Cnut condemn *husbryce* and *hamsocn* with unqualified severity. Æthelred specifies that those who die while engaged in such assaults should be denied Christian burial, while Cnut's code (II 62.1) stipulates that the kin of a man slain while invading another's home should expect no compensation.[40] The conclusion one might draw from this is not that the prohibition on *hamsocn* was unknown in Alfred's day. An awareness of it is perhaps indicated by the distinction made in this section of Alfred's laws between one who attacks his foe knowing him to be at home and one who mounts

36 *Vatnsdœla saga*, Íslenzk fornrit 8, ed. Einar Ólafur Sveinsson (Reykjavík: Íslenzka Fornritafélag, 1939), 15–16.

37 The obligation in question was known in their own language as *goire*, the duty of the eldest son to support his parents in their old age. The earliest penitentials, doubtless under the influence of folk law, permit this obligation, after a ritualized demonstration of his own submission, to be assumed by a homicide for his victim's family: see *The Irish Penitentials*, ed. Bieler, 243n10; also discussed in Jurasinski, "Sanctuary, House-Peace, and the Traditionalism of Alfred's Laws," 143–4.

38 That there is no real semantic distinction between the terms is argued for in Rebecca V. Colman, "*Hamsocn*: Its Meaning and Significance in Early English Law," *The American Journal of Legal History* 25 (1981), 95–110.

39 *Leges Henrici Primi*, ed. and trans. Downer, 252–3 (cap. 80.11a).

40 See IV Æthelred cap. 4.

such an assault ignorant of this fact (with the same remedy prescribed in both cases). Rather, Alfred seems to have understood that armed disputes were likely to encroach upon private dwellings but sought nonetheless to remind disputants of their obligations under traditional law to those who gave up their arms and submitted. These obligations happened to be wholly amenable to the notions of culpability drawn from ecclesiastical law for which Alfred clearly established a place in the Prologue of his *domboc*, most plainly in the recasting of sanctuary provisions in Exodus.[41] To give up one's weapons and place oneself in the power of one's foes, a remedy urged often by penitentials of this period, was to demonstrate contrition and a desire for peaceful reconciliation: wishes that even in the rough-and-tumble world of conversion-era Scandinavia seem to have been treated with respect.

THE DECAY OF LEARNING

Though the influences on Alfred's laws argued for in the preceding section perhaps require more Latin learning than is typically assumed for this period, a loose consensus has held for some time that remarks in

[41] Arguments made in "Sanctuary, House-Peace, and the Traditionalism of Alfred's Laws" are challenged in an essay by Tom Lambert ("The Evolution of Sanctuary in Medieval England," in *Legalism: Anthropology and History*, eds. Paul Dresch and Hannah Skoda [Oxford: Oxford University Press, 2012], 115–44]). Lambert asserts that a requirement of safety for the person so attacked after the passage of thirty days "cannot be inferred directly from the text" and "relies entirely on analogies, many of which are rather distant" (129n40). His assertion that the clause contains "a clearly implied threat that if the kinsmen fail to produce an appropriate compensation settlement in that time, the captive will no longer be safe from harm" is intriguing, though I doubt that anything can be understood as "clearly implied" by the muddled prose of Old English royal legislation. While I would concede that Alfred's laws were conditioned by a culture that looked favorably on vengeance, it is another thing entirely to say that this clause shows Alfred *endorsing* lethal violence in such cases (as Lambert appears to argue) or that every case in which a man guilty of homicide placed himself in the power of the decedent's kin was understood *inevitably* to result in the offender's death (as Liebermann contended). My aim was to show that this situation had outcomes Liebermann and subsequent commentators did not consider. Because Alfred chooses here – I think significantly – not to specify the outcome, it seems reasonable to assume that a violent resolution was not the only one he urged on disputants. At all events, there is no arguing against the fact that servitude in the household of the aggrieved was an expected outcome *within the feud itself* where an offender did not have the means to pay adequate compensation: see Martin J. Ryan, "Archbishop Ecgberht and his *Dialogus*," in *Leaders of the Anglo-Saxon Church: From Bede to Stigand*, ed. Alexander R. Rumble (Woodbridge, UK: Boydell, 2012), 41–60 at 55. To suggest that Alfred advocates execution in such instances would, it seems, make these ordinances wholly against the grain of tradition and at odds with the overall sense of Alfred's laws on violence.

the preface to Alfred's translation of the *Cura Pastoralis* should be taken with a grain of salt. Knowledge of Latin may well have suffered during the reign of Alfred, as has been dramatically demonstrated by Lapidge.[42] But recent as well as older scholarship has suggested that historians may have read too credulously Alfred's assessment of his age, leaving it to play an exaggerated role in modern appraisals of ninth-century learning.[43] Alfred acknowledges in his *Preface* that Latin scholarship in the kingdom of Mercia had not been wholly obliterated, something that would seem self-evident from his correspondence with Bishop Werferth and the recruitment of Mercian scholars to his circle.[44] His negative appraisal of Latin learning south of the Humber should, in any case, be considered alongside Abbot Ælfric of Eynsham's lament, almost a century later, concerning the grave ignorance of the priest with whom he began his study of Latin.[45] That Ælfric was as absorbed as Alfred in rebuilding knowledge of Latin among his contemporaries should perhaps make us question whether the era of the Benedictine reform would necessarily have been more favorable to the production of English penitentials than any other period.

Even if the worst-case scenario envisaged by Alfred's *Preface* is assumed, the obstacles to composition in the ninth century remain far from insuperable. To translate the bulk of the penitential canons to which the *Scriftboc* and *Canons* turn their attention would have required no great Latinity, nor is accurate translation, as was shown in Chapter 1,

42 Michael Lapidge, "Latin Learning in Ninth-Century England," in *Anglo-Latin Literature, 600–899* (London: Hambledon, 1996), 409–54. It should be noted, however, that even this study assembles evidence for significant scholarly activity prior to Alfred's restorative efforts. See also Nicholas Brooks, *The Early History of Canterbury: Christ Church from 597 to 1066* (Leicester, UK: Leicester University Press, 1984), 164–74.

43 See Christine Thijs, "Levels of Learning in Anglo-Saxon Worcester: The Evidence Reassessed," *Leeds Studies in English* 36 (2005), 105–31; J. Morrish, "King Alfred's Letter as a Source on Learning in England in the Ninth Century," in *Studies in Earlier Old English Prose*, ed. P. E. Szarmach (Albany: SUNY Press, 1986), 87–107.

44 Alfred says that few south of the Humber could understand the liturgy or translate a letter from Latin and notes his expectation that there were "not many beyond the Humber" who might do so either. See *King Alfred's West-Saxon Version of Gregory's Pastoral Care,* EETS o.s. nos. 45 and 50, ed. and trans. Henry Sweet (London: Oxford University Press, 1871), 3.

45 In the preface to his translation of Genesis, Ælfric describes a priest, once his *magister* in his youth, who was able only *be dæle Lyden understandan* ("to understand Latin in parts") and did not grasp the difference between the Old and New Law: see *The Old English Heptateuch and Ælfric's Libellus de Veteri Testamento et Novo, Vol. 1: Introduction and Text,* EETS 330, ed. Richard Marsden (Oxford: Oxford University Press, 2008), 3. See also James Hurt, *Ælfric*, Twayne's English Author Series 131 (New York: Twayne, 1972), 28.

their chief concern. Indeed, in their many departures from their sources, the Old English penitentials have something more in common with the Alfredian versions of the *Consolatione philosophiae* or Augustine's *Soliloquia* than with the quintessential document of the Benedictine revival, Æthelwold's rendering of the Benedictine Rule, which has been characterized by Lapidge as "a model of clarity and accuracy."[46]

Given the difficulties in assuming the second half of the ninth century to have been a black hole of learned activity with the exception of the Alfredian translations, I would suggest that the Benedictine Reform need not retain its hold on the imaginations of scholars who aim to understand the place of the *Canons* and *Scriftboc* in the chronology of Old English prose. Though nothing forbids dating these texts to the tenth century, nothing about our knowledge of the period as a whole requires it either. And the dissatisfaction with the Reform as a means of periodization evident in John Blair's 2005 monumental study, who notes that attitudes and developments conventionally adduced as characteristic of this movement are perceptible in the lifetime of King Alfred, should caution us against identifying any set of ideas too closely with a particular era.[47] Evidence of significant Latin learning was not necessarily likelier to appear after the middle of the tenth century than during the second half of the ninth, and the *Scriftboc* and *Canons* would not, in any case, merit such a label because the language of their sources was often of little concern to the translators.

LEGAL CHANGE AS A DATING CRITERION

That the hypothetical tenth-century origin of the vernacular penitentials rests on feeble foundations becomes only more apparent when we reexamine what Spindler considered the centerpiece of his argument. Spindler begins his discussion by noting that the *Scriftboc*'s most pronounced debts are to what he took to be ninth-century Frankish compilations such as the *Capitula Dacheriana* and *Canones Gregorii*.[48] (We know now that these

[46] See Lapidge, "Æthelwold," in *The Blackwell Encyclopaedia*, 19.

[47] In a synthesis of current scholarship on the Reform, Blair characterizes Eadgar as "the first king prepared to identify wholeheartedly with the Reform" and suggests the existence of "a religious culture in Eadgar's reign which, when we probe beneath the surface, starts to look less exclusive and more like that of Æthelstan's and Edmund's." The "nostalgia" for the "glorious English monastic past" that drove the work of the Reform is traced by Blair to the late ninth century: "Nostalgia in fact begins with Alfred" (347). See Blair, *The Church in Anglo-Saxon Society*, 347–52.

[48] Spindler, *Das altenglische Bussbuch*, 111.

may be considerably older.)[49] When speculations about the Benedictine Reform are left aside, Spindler acknowledges that these texts leave us with a *terminus a quo* of the ninth century. For Spindler, this is complicated by the dates of the manuscripts: "On the other hand our manuscripts belong to the eleventh century. The resulting date of composition for our text is the tenth century."[50] In support of what might otherwise seem a hastily rendered conclusion reliant on disparate bits of evidence, Spindler adduces parallel clauses from the *Scriftboc* and the *Canons* concerned with the marriage contract, each of which translates the same portion of the *Penitential of Theodore*. Given that the dates of the *Capitula Dacheriana* and *Canones Gregorii* have been pushed back significantly in the years since Spindler's edition, the clauses on marriage turn out to be all that holds Spindler's argument for a tenth-century date together.

His claims about these clauses have as far as I can tell evaded all critical scrutiny in the decades that followed. I would suggest that they offer less to Spindler's argument than he supposed. Both are concerned with the fate of a bride-price should the contracted marriage fail to occur, and each derives from a canon that probably looked something like the following:[51]

Illa autem disponsata si non vult habitare cum eo viro cui est disponsata reddatur ei pecunia quam pro ipsa dedit et tertia pars addatur; si autem ille noluerit perdat pecuniam quam pro illa dedit.

"But if she who is betrothed refuses to live with the man to whom she is betrothed, the money which he gave for her shall be paid back to him, and a third part shall

[49] Much light has been shed on the dates of these texts since Spindler's work in the early twentieth century. Thomas Charles-Edwards ("The Penitential of Theodore and the *Iudicia Theodori*," in *Archbishop Theodore: Commemorative Studies on His Life and Influence*, ed. Michael Lapidge [Cambridge: Cambridge University Press, 1995], 141–74), notes that the Theodorean rules "quoted in the A-Recension of the *Collectio Canonum Hibernensis*, compiled before 725" must have been drawn from "Finsterwalder's D, entitled *Iudicia Theodori*, but generally known as the *Capitula Dacheriana* after D'Achéry, its first editor" (142). This would push the date of the *Capitula* well beyond the ninth- or tenth-century appearance indicated by Spindler. Charles-Edwards attributes the *Canones Gregorii* as well to the phase of "direct interaction between Theodore and his pupils" while acknowledging that the *Canones* are "less well dated" (157). However, Alan Thacker has suggested that the association of these canons with Gregory the Great may owe something to Theodore's own teaching: see Thacker, "Memorializing Gregory the Great: The Origin and Transmission of a Papal Cult in the Seventh and Early Eighth Centuries," *Early Medieval Europe* 7 (1998), 59–84 at 75–6; also Flechner, "The Making of the Canons of Theodore," 124n12.

[50] Spindler, *Das altenglische Bussbuch*, 111.

[51] *PT* II, xii, 34 (also *CD* 118); trans. McNeill and Gamer, *Medieval Handbooks*, 211.

be added; if, however, it is he who refuses, he shall lose the money that he gave for her."

The *Scriftboc*'s rendering of this clause appears in Spindler's edition as follows:[52]

Gif heo nele mid þam were eardian þam ðe heo ær geweddod wæs, agyfe hi*m* eft þæt feoh þæt he for heo sealde, *and* eac ðone ðriddan dæl þæs yrfes. And gif he þ*æt* nelle, ðolige his feos; *and* seo fæmne ga on mynster oððe elcor in hire clænnesse hie halde.

"If she does not wish to dwell with the man to whom she was previously betrothed, let him be given back the money that he gave for her, and also the third portion of the inheritance. And if he [the bridegroom] does not accept this, let him lose his money; and let the woman enter a monastery or otherwise maintain herself in chastity."

Further departures from the Theodorean source are evident in the *Canons*' version:[53]

Gif beweddod mæden nele to þam þe heo beweddod bið, and wæs hire willa, forgylde þonne þæt feoh þæt heo ær underfeng, and þærto[eacan] gedo [swa mycel swa] þæs feos þryddan dæl sy, and þa magas forgyldon heora wedd; [and] gif he þonne nylle hy niman, hæbbe forseald þæt feoh þæt he sealde.

"If a betrothed maiden does not desire him to whom she is betrothed, and the betrothal was [made] with her consent, let [?her] return then the money that she previously received, and add to it as much as a third of that money, and let her kinsmen pay back their *wedd;* and if, however, he does not want her, he has lost the money that he gave."

52 III.xiv.17.d (Spindler, ed., *Das altenglische Bussbuch*, 183). The translator has added a strange condition (taken from the immediately preceding clause in *PT*) that the woman is to adopt a religious vocation, or at least remain celibate, should her prospective husband change his mind after paying the bride-price. This condition may owe something to the uncertainty of patristic and early medieval authors concerning the distinction between betrothal and marriage. On this tendency in early canon law, see Philip Lyndon Reynolds, *Marriage in the Western Church* (Leiden, The Netherlands: Brill, 1994; repr. 2001), 316–22; James Brundage, *Law, Sex, and Christian Society in Medieval Europe* (Chicago: University of Chicago Press, 1987), 132: "Sexual relations with a betrothed woman might be treated as adultery ...." (*PT* II, xii, 33 had merely stipulated that young women should have freedom in marriage, which the author reasonably saw as entailing their freedom to join a monastery if they wished.) The *Scriftboc*'s understanding of the nature of the payment also differs from what is given in the source: *PT* merely assumes an exchange of *pecunia*, whereas the language of the *Scriftboc* suggests two types of payment: the bride and her kin are to receive *feoh* ("money," or perhaps some form of chattel) and immovable, heritable property (often, but not always, the meaning of *yrfe*).

53 Fulk and Jurasinski, *The Old English Canons of Theodore*, 6–7 (A 36); square brackets indicate the readings of other manuscripts. It is noteworthy that the division of payments understood by the translator of the *Scriftboc* is absent. The nature of the wealth given up by the *magas* is therefore less clear.

Discrepancies between the three clauses may be clarified by the following table:

Poenitentiale Theodori	Scriftboc	Canons of Theodore
Bride-price returned to bridegroom should betrothal fail, with a "third part" added punitively to this amount.	Adds condition that bride in a case of failed betrothal must subsequently reside in a monastery or remain celibate; *tertia pars* becomes "third part of the [bride's] inheritance," that is, her dowry.	In addition to the return of the bride-price as stipulated in Theodore – here described as having been received directly by the bride – the bride's kin return the *wedd* (unmentioned in any possible source) to the bridegroom.

According to Spindler, the various routes by which compensation made its way to the bridegroom, and the different forms it assumed, correlate with the steps by which marriage law took shape in England:[54]

Who is the subject making restitution? In Theodore it is the arranger of the betrothal, the guardian of the bride (that is to say the kin, primarily the father), to whom according to the older folk-law of the Anglo-Saxons the bride-price was paid. Then, however, the guardian gave the bride-price to the bride only in usufruct; and in later Anglo-Saxon law the bride-price is paid no longer to the guardian, but directly to the bride herself: from a usufructary she becomes a recipient of the bride-price. Should the wedding then fail to occur, the bride is properly the one to make restitution: to *agyfe* … we may apply the subject *heo*. Thus late Anglo-Saxon legal conditions are evident in these loose translations.

Spindler's remarks rest on the consensus of his day on how the use of bridewealth had evolved among the Anglo-Saxons from the "early" to "late" period (with neither being defined within clear chronological limits). We will see the problems with this shortly. More immediately concerning is the selection of evidence. The version of the *Scriftboc*'s clause that occurs in CCCC 190, a recension roughly coeval with the other witnesses and the basis of Thorpe's edition, complicates his reconstruction. Here the subject in the main clause is the indefinite pronoun *man* "one, someone" (*agife man him eft þæt feoh þæt he for hig sealde*). The construction is probably a periphrastic rendering of Theodore's Latin

[54] Spindler, *Das altenglische Bussbuch*, 47.

passive (*reddatur ei pecunia*), leaving us with one version of this provision in which the person returning the payment is never specified.[55] It is by no means clear which witness is "better," as Thorpe's may be a somewhat earlier witness to the development of the *Scriftboc* than Spindler's base-text (MS X).[56]

Uncertainties about which party is obliged to make restitution are evident even in the textual witness preferred by Spindler. In Old English, and particularly in legislative prose, the verbs of subordinate and main clauses are given to unsignaled shifts of referent. Take cap. 31 of the laws of Ine:

> Gif mon wif gebyccge, 7 sio gyft forð ne cume, agife þæt feoh 7 forgielde 7 gebete þam byrgean, swa his borgbryce sie.

Attenborough translates the text as:[57]

> "If anyone buys a wife and the marriage does not take place, he [the bride's guardian] shall return the bridal price and pay [the bridegroom] as much again, and he shall compensate the trustee of the marriage according to the amount he is entitled to for infraction of his surety."

Because the man who purchased the wife cannot be returning the money to himself, the subject of *agyfe* in the main clause is clearly not the subject of *gebyccge* in the subordinate clause. The meaning here is presumably the same as in the periphrastic passive mentioned previously: "Let the bride-price be given back." It is just possible, then, that in the witness employed by Spindler, the subject of *nele* (*heo*) need not be the subject of *agyfe* in the following clause, particularly given the tendency of earlier Anglo-Saxon law, both in the case of Ine and Theodore, to be vague about who returns the payment. In any case, it is unlikely that she (as opposed to those in guardianship over her) would have had the authority over alienation of any property to be inherited (the likely meaning here of *yrfe*).

For its part, the Old English *Canons of Theodore* does at first appear more supportive of Spindler's thesis than the *Scriftboc*: thus Spindler

[55] So said Bruce Mitchell (though not with reference to this particular clause): "However we care to put it, it is clear that *man* + active verb form frequently represents a Latin passive in translated texts and is frequently preferred to *wesan, weorðan* + second (past) p[articiple] in original and translated texts." See Mitchell, "Old English *Man* 'One': Two Notes," in idem, *On Old English* (Oxford: Blackwell, 1988), 264–8 at 268.

[56] Frantzen's edition, here following Spindler, translates the crucial clause as "she is to give back to him the property that he gave for her" in spite of this variant.

[57] F. L. Attenborough, ed. and trans., *The Laws of the Earliest English Kings* (New York: Russell and Russell, 1963), 47.

seemingly takes the *Scriftboc* to imply what the *Canons* state explicitly with its assertion that it is the woman who received (and accordingly must return) the bride-price ("*forgylde* (scil. *heo*) *þonne þæt feoh þæt heo ǽr underfeng*").[58] But all of this is complicated by the subsequent requirement (added by the author of the *Canons* and present in none of his possible sources) that the kin also compensate the prospective husband (... *and þa magas forgyldon heora wedd*).[59] Our sense of the significance of this addition depends on the meaning of the ambiguous term *wedd* (which Thorpe perhaps wisely left untranslated [*et solvant propinqui suum "wedd"*]).[60] Though it is not as clear as one would like (apparently having the meaning "pledge" in cap. C 9 of the *Canons of Theodore*), attestations of the meaning "(monetary) pledge" for Old English *wedd* are sufficiently common to allay any doubts about the meaning of the word here.[61] The eleventh-century glossary occupying B. L. Harley 3376 (itself probably based on earlier glossaries) gives as Old English synonyms of *dos* the words *wed*, *gifu*, and *fædren feon* (the latter being an error for *feoh*).[62] We may assume that this clause simply enjoins the *magas* to repay the money with which the bridegroom sealed the agreement, most likely the *fostorlean* (as it is called in *Wifmannes Beweddung*). This is the amount due to those who raised the bride, which the bridegroom is to pledge (*weddige*) to her kin.[63] Thus the reference in the *Canons* to her earlier receipt of a payment may not indicate what Spindler suggests: she receives both a direct, possibly minor payment – a payment at least in movables, as is made more likely given its designation by *feoh* rather than

58 As quoted in Spindler, ed., *Das altenglische Bussbuch*, 47.

59 Frantzen's online edition gives "[she is to] repay the relatives the dowry." While this rendering resolves some of the difficulties suggested by Spindler, it is a great departure from the source, as *heo* cannot be the subject of the third-person plural verb.

60 Thorpe, *Ancient Laws*, 352.

61 "Gif beweddod mæden wiðsace þam þe heo beweddod bið, ga þanne on mynster oððe hira maga wedd gelæste," "If a betrothed maiden should refuse the man to whom she is betrothed, let her go then into a religious house or fulfill the pledge of her kin [by marrying the man anyway]." The source is *PT* II, xii, 34, which, as has already been noted, established a quite different set of conditions for the betrothed woman: "Puellam disponsatam non licet parentibus dare alteri viro nisi illa omnino resistat. Tamen ad monasterium licet ire, si voluerit," "Parents may not give a betrothed girl to another man unless she flatly refuses [to marry the original suitor]; but she may go to a monastery if she wishes" (trans. McNeill and Gamer, *Medieval Handbooks*, 211).

62 *The Harley Latin-Old English Glossary*, ed. Robert T. Oliphant (Paris: Mouton de Gruyter, 1966), 144. Cf. *faderfio* in the laws of Lombard Italy, on which see J. B. Bury, *The Invasion of Europe by the Barbarians* (New York: W. W. Norton, 1927; repr. 1967), 281–2.

63 *Gesetze*, ed. Liebermann, I: 442 (cap. 2).

yrfe – and another, perhaps more substantial payment over which her kin maintain control. The latter is characteristic of the supposedly "early" phase of Anglo-Saxon law, yet its presence is self-evident in a text taken by Spindler to exemplify later attitudes toward marriage.[64]

The relation of the *Canons'* language to marriage law may, I believe, be pieced together more reliably, though the uncertainty of the evidence permits nothing like the orderly series of developments assumed in prior commentary.[65] It has already been seen that the author of the *Canons* was given to filling in what he felt to be gaps in the language of his anchor-texts.[66] This is substantially the case in this clause as well: the author's concern to "correct" Theodore is evident in his addition of *and wæs hire willa,* here giving expression to the disdain of the Church for marriages made without the consent of both parties.[67] I would suggest that in this instance the author, seeing the ambiguous passive construction in Theodore, attempts to flesh out its ambiguities by situating it within the betrothal practices of his own day.

Our own determination of what these practices were is complicated by the fact that the more detailed descriptions of the marriage contract are quite late, something that makes Spindler's confidence in reconstructing its course of development seem unwarranted. In contrast to the situation envisaged by Spindler, these almost uniformly acknowledge that betrothals were sealed with payments directly to the bride *and* to her kin.[68] We can assume that the *Canons* refer as well to this dual-payment custom. But the

[64] Reynolds, *Marriage*, 387–9, notes among the Franks both minor gifts of shoes or jewelry made directly to the bride along with more substantial gifts of immoveable property.

[65] The remarks of Diane Owen Hughes are instructive: "Germanic marriage, like marriage almost everywhere, wove a web of gifts and settlements of which we can still observe only the most substantial and enduring strands." See "From Brideprice to Dowry in Mediterranean Europe," *Journal of Family History* 3 (1978), 262–6 at 266.

[66] See Chapter 1, 24–25.

[67] On this development in ecclesiastical law see Michael M. Sheehan, "Choice of Marriage Partner in the Middle Ages: Development and Mode of Application of a Theory of Marriage," in *Marriage, Family, and Law in Medieval Europe: Collected Studies*, ed. James K. Farge (Toronto: University of Toronto Press, 1996), 87–118. The emphasis on consent – of the families of those to be married, and, most importantly, of the prospective bride and groom – characteristic of ecclesiastical law even at this early date is an inheritance from Roman juristic thought: see Philip Lyndon Reynolds, "Dotal Charters in the Frankish Tradition," in *To Have and to Hold: Marrying and Its Documentation in Western Christendom, 400–1600*, eds. Philip Lyndon Reynolds and John Witte Jr. (Cambridge: Cambridge University Press, 2007), 114–64 at 124n35.

[68] *Gesetze*, ed. Liebermann, I: 442. The so-called Kentish Marriage Agreement records a pound of gold given to the bride to induce her to accept the offer of marriage and a substantial estate. See *Anglo-Saxon Charters*, ed. and trans. Agnes Jane Robertson (Cambridge: Cambridge University Press, 1956), 150–1 (cap. LXXVII).

affinities of these texts ultimately afford no reliable means of periodization. Liebermann's summary of marriage law, itself the basis of Spindler's commentary, finds evidence for the "early" practice of "marriage by purchase" in the laws of Æthelberht and Ine – texts so archaic that they necessarily stand outside the period of consideration where the penitentials are concerned. The chief evidence for a shift in betrothal practices (whose date is never specified) comes, however, from what are probably *very* late texts, chiefly *Wifmannes Beweddung*, which may have been written during Wulfstan's lifetime.[69] Whether the change is to some extent coeval with these texts is, as Liebermann acknowledges, far from clear; he argues that the *Beweddung* is not imposing new requirements, but rather giving expression in some of its provisions to norms already recognized for some time.[70] Liebermann concedes that there is more than a little of the supposedly old practice in this text, with the kin overseeing the marriage arrangement and withholding the full amount of the *yrfe* to a widow who marries again – something that suggests that the bride does not possess the *yrfe* outright.[71] With the impetus for change being impossible to isolate, the *Canons* could give evidence of the supposedly "late" practice and still be an "early" text with respect to major events used to delimit the chronology of Old English prose, such as the Alfredian translation program and the Benedictine Reform. Alternatively, the mixture of "old" and "new" practices perceived by Liebermann in the *Beweddung* may merely suggest that the chronology of developments envisioned by historians of Spindler's day is faulty.[72] Relevant in this regard are the doubts of one major scholar over whether the existence of *Muntehe* and other marital institutions reconstructed in the nineteenth century should continue to be assumed at all. Ruth Mazo Karras notes that "efforts to treat the *dos* given to the woman as a late mutation of a primitive bride-price that went to the male guardian in return for *Munt* over the woman come up against the statement of Tacitus that the *dos* is paid to the woman (not her relatives)."[73] Evidence for the transfer of *mundium* as a feature of marriage in Anglo-Saxon England strikes Karras as spotty at best. While most

69 *Gesetze*, ed. Liebermann, III: 241–2.

70 Ibid.

71 Ibid.

72 Liebermann's model of the evolution of marriage law is taken for granted in Andreas Fischer, *Engagement, Wedding and Marriage in Old English* (Heidelberg: Carl Winter, 1986), 18–20. While *Kaufehe* is assumed to be the norm in earlier Anglo-Saxon England, "[b]y the eleventh century … marriage had developed from a contract between two men (guardian and suitor) to one in which the woman also had her say …" (19).

73 Ruth Mazo Karras, "The History of Marriage and the Myth of *Friedelehe*," *Early Medieval Europe* 14 (2006), 119–51 at 128.

normative sources of this era emphasize the centrality of the *dos* to the legitimation of marriages, they are not as clear that this payment constitutes a purchase of the same power held over the woman by her kin or guardians.[74]

Most damaging to Liebermann's and hence Spindler's thesis is evidence unremarked by either that payment of the bride-price directly to the bride was indeed conceivable in the "early" period of Anglo-Saxon marriage law as well, if by "early" we mean the era prior to the Benedictine Reform. This occurs in the partial translation of Exodus that precedes the laws of Alfred. Here Alfred employs the same loose style of translation seen in the preceding text, freely changing the provisions of Mosaic law to agree with the norms of his own day.[75] And so in describing what is to be done when a slave girl is given in marriage, Alfred translates the Vulgate's "providebit puellae nuptias et vestimenta et pretium pudicitiae non negabit," "He shall provide her a marriage, and raiment, neither shall he refuse the price of her chastity" as "do hiere gyfta, locige þæt hio hæbbe hrægl 7 þæt weorð sie hiere mægðhades, þæt is se weotuma agife he hire þone," "[A]nd let him see that she have raiment, and that which is the worth of her maid-hood, that is, the dowry; let him give her that" [Thorpe], a more overt designation of the bride as the recipient of the dowry than was present in his source.[76] The woman in question has no family to speak of and is thus the only possible recipient of the *weotuma*.[77] Liebermann's suggestion in his commentary that this is not a "real" betrothal seems little more than a way to preserve the fragile integrity of his theory concerning the development of betrothal practices in early England. In any case, it has been seen once again that the barriers to composition prior to the Benedictine Reform rest on no solid foundation.

DIALECT

If circumstantial evidence does not favor composition in the later tenth century as strongly as often supposed, linguistic evidence, as has been noted even by those who advocate tenth-century dates for the *Scriftboc*

74 Karras, "The History of Marriage," 128–9.

75 See Jurasinski, "Violence, Penance, and Secular Law." For a full discussion of this portion of the *domboc*, see Jurasinski, "Slavery, Learning and the Law of Marriage in Alfred's Mosaic Prologue," in *Secular Learning in Anglo-Saxon England*, eds. László Sándor Chardonnens and Bryan Carella, *Amsterdamer Beiträge zur älteren Germanistik* 69 (2012): 45–64.

76 Here, it should be noted, Thorpe is using "dowry" to refer to the payment made by a bridegroom to a woman (or her kin) in earlier Germanic law.

77 *Gesetze*, ed. Liebermann, I: 31–2. She had previously been sold into slavery.

and *Canons*, makes identification of these texts with the Benedictine Reform exceedingly difficult. Of the two, the *Scriftboc* has received by far the greater share of scholarly attention. While the language of the manuscripts was in the main Late West Saxon, Spindler suggested that this can have been "in no way also the language of the archetype" (*keineswegs auch die Sprache des Archetyps*) and went on to assert the presence in much of the text of the Mercian scribal dialect, which is generally agreed not to have been in more than extremely limited use beyond the year 900.[78]

It should be noted that Spindler appears to sidestep the implications of this Mercian substrate for the dating of the text, acknowledging only its usefulness as a means of localization. What matters, according to Spindler, is the absence of Early West Saxon forms, traces of which would surely have been present in the text had it been composed prior to the tenth century.[79] This claim is hard to reconcile with what we know about Old English scribal dialects. The distinction between "Early West Saxon" and Mercian forms is much less clear than Spindler indicates given the role of Mercian clerics in the Alfredian revival of Old English prose; for this reason, some scholars have treated both dialects as more or less coextensive.[80] His conclusion that the text must have been composed during the Reform in an "East-Mercian Benedictine monastery" tied somehow to Worcester seems, in any case, a nonstarter given the disuse into which this dialect had fallen by the early tenth century.[81] It has already been seen that Spindler's assumed date was in part owing to his view that the

[78] Spindler, *das altenglische Bussbuch*, 112; on the Mercian dialect and the chronology of Old English writing, see A. Campbell, *Old English Grammar* (Oxford: Clarendon, 1959; repr. 1962), §§11–14; Thomas E. Toon, "The Social and Political Contexts of Language Change in Anglo-Saxon England," in *English in Its Social Contexts*, eds. Tim William Machan and Charles T. Scott (Oxford: Oxford University Press, 1992), 28–46.

[79] Spindler, *das altenglische Bussbuch*, 112: "On the other hand, the main portion of our penitential, if it had come into existence earlier, would most likely have entered the Early West Saxon scribal domain perhaps in the ninth century or even already in the time of Egbert, and would have preserved individual traces of it, which is, for example the case with *Beowulf*.... Thus our determination of the date given above may find further support from this consideration."

[80] Campbell, *Old English Grammar*, § 19, notes the impossibility of establishing "geographical limits to Mercian," and indeed most studies have cautioned against understanding Old English dialects in geographical terms (though this is indeed possible for later English texts). T. F. Hoad ("West Saxon Dialect," in *The Blackwell Encyclopaedia of Anglo-Saxon England,* 472), notes the opinion of many that the distinction between Early and Late West Saxon "results at least in part from the intrusion of features from other dialects, chiefly Mercian."

[81] Spindler, *das altenglische Bussbuch*, 114.

Canones Gregorii and *Capitula Dacheriana* were relatively late sources – a view shown in recent years to be illegitimate. Had this not been the received opinion of Spindler's lifetime, the presence of Anglianisms in the *Scriftboc* might have led him to a different set of conclusions.

The significance of the *Scriftboc*'s dialect features remains unclear in present-day commentary. While Frantzen would find Spindler's assertions about the origins of the *Scriftboc* dubious in his study of 1983, scholarship in general has shown reluctance to view an admixture of Anglian forms in texts whose dialect is predominantly Late West Saxon as evidence of composition prior to the tenth century.[82] Yet some have contended, without referring to this text in particular, that the presence of such forms probably deserves more serious consideration than it is given in Frantzen's work. Further arguments for the *Scriftboc*'s Anglian origins were made by Franz Wenisch in 1979, and Frantzen has noted with seeming approval Wenisch's conclusions while appearing to concede that the presence of Anglianisms in this text may pose a genuine obstacle to supposing its tenth-century origins.[83] Some remarks are therefore in order on the relevance of these forms to dating, for it is evident that they have not yet received a coherent assessment.[84]

My purpose in this section is not to offer arguments for or against proposed linguistic tests for dating Old English texts – a matter ably dealt with by other specialists, and requiring a lengthy discussion of matters extraneous to the subject of this book – but rather to suggest the possibility of some future consensus on what the linguistic peculiarities of the texts considered in this chapter might suggest about when they were composed. Though the use of dialect criteria to localize and date texts has become one of the more contentious practices in contemporary Old English studies, certain areas of agreement among disputants may illuminate the texts under consideration in this study. While some

[82] "[A]lthough some Mercian forms are present, no research has yet established that they were retained from a copy of the 'Scriftboc' written earlier than the tenth century." Frantzen, *Literature of Penance*, 134.

[83] Frantzen ("Sin and Sense," 62n59) cites without apparent disagreement the argument of Franz Wenisch, *Spezifisch anglisches Wortgut in den nordhumbrischen Interlinearglossierung des Lukasevangeliums* (Heidelberg: C. Winter, 1979), 63 and 327, who notes that the vast majority of Anglian words in the vernacular penitential corpus are to be found in the *Scriftboc*. Frantzen mentions a few of these in his note and seems to regard them as genuine. But remarks in the most recent version of his online edition appear to retreat entirely from this position, adopting instead the orthodox view of a tenth-century *terminus a quo*.

[84] Frantzen notes in *Literature of Penance* (134n36) his attention to consider the dialect of the *Scriftboc*, but no such study has appeared.

handbooks suggest that Old English prose produced before the activities of Alfred and his circle was fundamentally trivial, there can be no doubt that composition of nonverse, nonglossarial texts in Old English antedates the reign of Alfred by nearly three centuries and that the result was something more than "a small amount of legal writing," as one survey describes pre-Alfredian prose.[85] Though the evidence is confined exclusively to the twelfth-century *Textus Roffensis*, there must have been a lively tradition of legislative prose composition for the duration of the seventh century, as the Kentish texts that survive uniquely in this manuscript show a century-long development from rudimentary to highly coordinated syntax, something that may indicate a transition from oral to bookish modes of lawmaking.[86] Moreover, a small number of Mercian texts (such as the *Old English Martyrology*) may be assumed uncontroversially to belong as well to this pre-Alfredian (or, in some cases, Alfredian) corpus.[87] Efforts to draw works whose dialects are more mixed into this Mercian tradition have been inhibited over the last several decades by the assumption that Anglianisms outside of texts securely datable to the pre-Alfredian era may merely constitute variations within the scribal dialect of Wessex, a view popularized by Karl Bülbring in the early twentieth century and made more attractive of late by the reluctance of many scholars to date Old English texts more than a few years prior to their surviving manuscripts.[88] This is a recent and heavily contested development among Anglo-Saxonists, one that their colleagues in departments of classics would no doubt find puzzling given the fair number of

85 This is the remark of Michael Alexander, who likewise says that "Old English prose literature was called into being by King Alfred ..." (1) and asserts that aside from Kentish legal texts all that was written before the reign of Alfred "does not deserve to be called prose" (167). See Alexander, *A History of Old English Prose* (Peterborough, ON: Broadview, 2002), a recasting of his earlier *Old English Literature* (London: 1983; repr. Schocken, 1987), where these remarks appear verbatim.

86 See Oliver, *The Beginnings of English Law*, 34–41; also Patrick Wormald, "*Inter cetera bona ... genti suae*: Law-making and Peace-Keeping in the Earliest English Kingdoms," *La Giustizia nell'Alto Medioevo* (Spoleto: Centro Italiano di Studi sull'altio Medioevo, 1994), II: 967–93.

87 Among the most resistant studies to the dating implications of Anglianisms in prose texts is Janet Bately, "Old English Prose before and during the Reign of King Alfred," *Anglo-Saxon England* 17 (1988), 93–138. But even this article grants that "[t]he corpus of vernacular prose literature that can be safely attributed to the period before 900 ... consists of two or three Mercian texts (the *Dialogues* and possibly the Martyrology and Bede) and seven West Saxon ones .... Almost all of these texts seem to have been composed during the last thirty years of the ninth century" (118).

88 On this see R. D. Fulk, "Anglian Dialect Features in Old English Anonymous Homiletic Literature: A Survey, with Preliminary Findings," in Susan M. Fitzmaurice and

Roman texts (such as Varro's *de lingua Latina* or the poems of Catullus) that survive only in Carolingian or later witnesses.[89]

Much of the reluctance of present-day scholars to acknowledge the usefulness of dialect criteria for dating probably comes from the poor reception of Vleeskruyer's edition of the life of St. Chad, whose claims are often overstated.[90] It is regrettable that this study has come to be seen as the standard argument in defense of a broad, possibly pre-Alfredian tradition of Mercian prose. Certainly the existence of an Anglian scribal dialect in use no later than the first quarter of the tenth century had elsewhere been demonstrated in studies whose worth has yet to be similarly assailed. In a 1951 article, for example, Jackson J. Campbell showed that scribes who copied the several versions of the Old English Bede made a deliberate effort to substitute West Saxon for Anglian forms in later stages of the text's transmission.[91] An essay by Carolin Schreiber has demonstrated a similar pattern of substitutions in the surviving manuscripts of the Old English *Pastoral Care*.[92] That a certain number of words (such as the conjunction *nymðe* "unless" or the noun *mennen* "female slave") can be securely assigned either to the Anglian dialect or to an early phase of West Saxon prose has yet to be challenged even by studies whose attitude toward dialectology as a tool for dating is less than sanguine.[93] Nor has the existence of an Early West Saxon vocabulary – the archaism of which is manifest in substitutions by Late West Saxon scribes – suffered serious challenges, even if the particulars of this dialect remain in dispute. All of

Donka Minkova, eds., *Studies in the History of the English Language IV: Empirical and Analytical Advances in the Study of English Language Change*, Topics in English Linguistics 61 (Berlin: De Gruyter, 2008), 81–100; Fulk, "Localizing and Dating Anonymous Prose: The Evidence of Old English Legislation," in *English Law Before Magna Carta*, 59–80.

89 All extant copies of Varro's *Lingua Latina* are derived from the eleventh-century *Codex Laurentianus*. See Varro, *On The Latin Language*, 2 vols., ed. and trans. Roland G. Kent (Cambridge, MA: Harvard University Press, 1938), xii. Catullus affords an even more remarkable example, all witnesses having been prepared no earlier than the late fourteenth century: see *The Poems of Catullus*, ed. and trans. Guy Lee (Oxford: Oxford University Press, 1990), ix–x.

90 *The Life of St. Chad: An Old English Homily*, ed. R. Vleeskruyer (Amsterdam: No rth-Holland, 1953).

91 Jackson J. Campbell, "The Dialect Vocabulary of the Old English Bede," *Journal of English and Germanic Philology* 50 (1951), 349–72.

92 Carolin Schreiber, "Dialects in Contact in Ninth-Century England," in *Bookmarks from the Past: Studies in Early English Language and Literature in Honour of Helmut Gneuss*, eds. Lucia Kornexl and Ursula Lenker (Frankfurt: Peter Lang, 2003), 1–32.

93 On these and other potential archaisms of the *Scriftboc* see Spindler, *Das altenglische Bussbuch*, 117–18. Perhaps the most outwardly compelling of these items is *mennen*, a rare word in later West Saxon prose that seems to have been misunderstood by the

this is germane to the present discussion, because even those who would date the *Canons* and *Scriftboc* to the tenth century agree that years of copying by West-Saxon scribes failed to remove a small but significant substrate of words typically considered archaic in other prose texts; these are not to be found in the *Penitential* or the *Handbook*.[94] While such evidence may of itself not suffice to date or localize these texts, its occurrence alongside other nonlinguistic features appearing to indicate composition prior to the era of the Reform reasonably seems to increase the probability of such a date. These will be considered in what remains of this chapter.

DATING THE CANONS *AND* SCRIFTBOC

Much of the discussion so far has attempted to show the weaknesses of some prevailing assumptions regarding the place of the Old English penitentials in the development of Anglo-Saxon prose. In what follows, I hope to discuss this matter more constructively and suggest new criteria for establishing the chronology of these texts. Fortunately, a set of texts posing analogous problems has received much more attention than the Old English penitentials. Readers familiar with debates over the dating of the Vercelli and Blickling homilies may have already noticed that the

copyist of MS Y (Oxford, Bodleian Library, MS Laud Misc. 482), who renders the term with the nonsensical *gemaennan* at V.6.h. It is interesting that later scribes seem to have regarded this as an old-fashioned term: the scribe of the *Textus Roffensis,* e.g., renders *mennen* as *þeowwifman* (*Gesetze*, ed. Liebermann, I: 31–2).

94 On *mennen* (*Canons* A 110; *Scriftboc* V.6.h, 177) see Wenisch, *Spezifisch Anglisches Wortgut*, 303. On *morðor* (*Canons* A 83, 118 [MS Y substitutes *morð* in both cases]; *Scriftboc* I.a.h., 171; XII.15.f, 181), see Robert J. Menner, "The Anglian Vocabulary of the Blickling Homilies," in *Philologica: The Malone Anniversary Studies*, ed. Thomas Austin Kirby and H. B. Woolf (Baltimore: Johns Hopkins University Press, 1949), 56–64 at 58. On *nymðe* (*Scriftboc* XIV.17.c, 182; XVII.19.1, 184) see Campbell, "Dialect Vocabulary"; Robert J. Menner, "The Anglian Vocabulary of the Blickling Homilies," 58. A full description of the somewhat more disputed Anglian phonological, morphological, and lexical features of the *Canons* occurs in Fulk and Jurasinski, *The Old English Canons of Theodore.* I am uninterested here in rehearsing the arguments in favor of the reality of the Anglian dialect as something more than a "register" occasionally adopted by writers of later Old English prose, nor do I think it would be worthwhile to argue against the claim (made in Bately, "Old English Prose," 105–7) that the discovery of isolated Anglian forms in Old English texts known to be later somehow renders all dialect tests useless. Great learning has been summoned in defense of both positions, and one senses (particularly where *Beowulf* is concerned) that more argument is unlikely to change minds. I will say that, for the purposes of the present study, the presence of words, Anglian or not, which are regularly the objects of substitutions in later witnesses, is a likely indicator – by no means the only one we should consider – of a text's date.

scholarly reception of these texts mirrors much of what has been said about the Old English *Canons* and *Scriftboc*. Here as well the Reform looms large as a means of periodization, and often without yielding satisfactory results. Though the two manuscripts in which these homilies appear – Vercelli, Biblioteca capitolare CXVII and Princeton, Princeton University Library, Scheide Library 71, respectively – are both datable to a period no earlier than the second half of the tenth century, the homilies have long been understood to show signs of earlier composition. Determining just how early they are requires that we examine them in light of what can be known about the evolution of doctrine in the Anglo-Saxon church. As Abbot Ælfric inveighed against apocryphal and heterodox statements in homilies, those containing such elements have traditionally been held to predate the Reform or at the very least to be aberrant. The presence of Anglianisms in such texts, when combined with evidence of eccentric or heterodox beliefs (particularly those associated with Irish ecclesiastical culture), has been seen by Donald Scragg as well as a succession of earlier commentators as strong evidence for composition prior to the Reform.[95]

This view has been critiqued in an insightful paper by Nancy M. Thompson. Her most trenchant criticism is that this method does not supply us with a very clear sense of what the theology of the pre-Reform church would have looked like, instead assigning whatever appears heterodox or redolent of paganism (such as charms and prognostics) to the pre-Reform era even as these nonstandard varieties of belief are likely to have persisted into the tenth century and beyond.[96] Thompson is right to note the hazards inherent in assuming the Reform and its leading exponents to have succeeded in combating superstitious practices as much as

[95] See Nancy M. Thompson, "Anglo-Saxon Orthodoxy," in *Old English Literature in Its Manuscript Context*, ed. Joyce Tally Lionarons (Morgantown: West Virginia University Press, 2004), 37–66. It should be said that D. G. Scragg's view, as Thompson notes, has varied over time. While initially endorsing the view that "the Vercelli Book and the Blickling Homilies ... are our two principal witnesses to the state of homiletic writing in English before the work of Ælfric appeared" (315) – a statement held by Thompson to locate these texts "in the unreformed past" (42) – his subsequent edition of the Vercelli homilies sees in the vocabulary of this text the influence of Æthelwoldian reformers. See Scragg, "The Homilies of the Blickling Manuscript," *Learning and Literature in Anglo-Saxon England*, ed. Michael Lapidge and Helmut Gneuss (Cambridge: Cambridge University Press, 1985), 299–316; *The Vercelli Homilies and Related Texts,* EETS o.s. 300 (Oxford: Oxford University Press, 1992), xxxix.

[96] Thompson also rightly suggests that the orthodoxy of Ælfric and Wulfstan has been overstated; the term, she suggests, is something of an anachronism given that the work of both preceded "a push to systematize doctrine and punish deviance" that "would not occur until well into the twelfth century" (46).

they would have us believe.[97] It can be safely assumed on such grounds that the apparent eccentricities of the Vercelli and Blickling homilies do not require us to assume the archaism of these texts.[98]

We do, however, possess some sense of tendencies other than those singled out by Thompson that might have set the pre-Reform church apart from that of Ælfric's era. It is well-known, for example, that Ælfric chides secular clergy who consulted the Old Testament for guidance on a variety of pastoral matters. In his letter to Æthelweard on the hazards of reading and translating the Old Testament, Ælfric complains of indifference to the distinction between the Old and New Law.[99] It may be that his homily for January 1 expresses concern that too-literal reading of scripture might lead to a revival of circumcision among his contemporaries.[100]

These curious developments may be read as products of the ignorance into which some clergy must have fallen during the ninth and tenth centuries, perhaps as a consequence of the relentless Scandinavian raiding that had depleted the wealth of monastic estates. Alternatively, they may show traces of the contempt for members of the secular clergy evident in many writings associated with the Benedictine Reform.[101] But surely it is relevant to our understanding of such remarks that practices derived from the Old Testament circulated among the English during the era of conversion as well. It is thus possible that these blundering apprehensions of biblical law owe something to ideas disseminated in the earliest decades of missionary activity among the English.

97 This is a point made repeatedly by Roy Liuzza in his *Anglo-Saxon Prognostics: An Edition and Translation of Texts from London, British Library, MS Cotton Tiberius A .iii.* (Cambridge: D. S. Brewer, 2010). Here it is argued that "not all clerics shared the views of more narrowly orthodox writers like Ælfric, who vigorously and repeatedly condemned the use of auguries and divination" (viii).

98 Indeed, the most recent edition of the Blickling homilies is extraordinarily cautious about the dating of these texts, holding them to "emanate from the threshold" of the Reform (xxiii). *Blickling Homilies*, ed. and trans. Richard J. Kelly (New York: Continuum, 2003).

99 See n. 45; also Melinda J. Menzer, "The Preface as Admonition: Ælfric's Preface to Genesis," in *The Old English Hexateuch: Aspects and Approaches*, eds. Rebecca Barnhouse and Benjamin C. Withers (Kalamazoo, MI: Medieval Institute, 2000), 15–40 at 17.

100 Presumably, Ælfric would not have pointed out that circumcision is no longer permitted to Christians unless he feared that his contemporaries might think otherwise. The remark should perhaps be read in the context of his other statements against observance of the Old Law. See *The Homilies of Ælfric*, ed. and trans. Benjamin Thorpe (London: Ælfric Society, 1844–6), I, 94–5.

101 On the negative appraisal of the secular clergy by Reform-era sources, see Julia Barrow, "The Clergy in English Dioceses c. 900–c. 1066," in *Pastoral Care in Late Anglo-Saxon England*, ed. Francesca Tinti (Rochester, NY: Boydell, 2005), 17–26 at 17.

Indeed, the very confusion bemoaned in Ælfric's writings was at one time encouraged by those who introduced the English to Christian precepts. Flora Spiegel has discussed the curious recommendation of Pope Gregory the Great to Abbot Mellitus that the recently converted English be urged to build huts made from branches – a practice in imitation of the Jewish festival of Sukkot – to accompany their annual sacrifice of cattle.[102] His aim in urging this practice, Spiegel suggests, was "first [to] bring the English up to the intellectual level of the Jews, with knowledge of the Law, the Old Testament, and the concept of a single deity and Creator" before subsequently introducing them to the subtleties of Christian doctrine.[103] That the Anglo-Saxons remained throughout their history in the habit of imagining themselves as the people of biblical Israel in their literature is well-known.[104] But material evidence that these structures were actually fashioned by the English shows, according to Spiegel, that the much-discussed "typological correspondence between the Anglo-Saxons and the Jews was not simply an exegetical conceit constructed from patristic sources"; rather, it was an idea that governed the earliest efforts to convert the English and that can perhaps be expected to have left some traces on their habits of mind.[105]

Such habits may already have been somewhat entrenched given the likely circulation in England of Levitical precepts prior to the missionary activities organized by Gregory. Such is the argument of Rob Meens, who notes that "[i]n Ireland, Cornwall and Wales" in the years before Augustine's mission, "attitudes seem to have been much more in line with Old Testament rules of ritual purity, while in Rome, such rules were interpreted spiritually."[106] Meens speculates that, if Gregory the Great in his

[102] Flora Spiegel, "The *tabernacula* of Gregory the Great and the Conversion of Anglo-Saxon England," *Anglo-Saxon England* 36 (2007), 1–13.

[103] Ibid., 5.

[104] This is a matter of some interest in current Old English studies, most discussion being launched by Nicholas Howe, *Migration and Mythmaking in Anglo-Saxon England* (South Bend, IN: Notre Dame University Press, 2001).

[105] Spiegel, "The *tabernacula* of Gregory the Great," 1.

[106] Rob Meens, "'A Relic of Superstition': Bodily Impurity and the Church from Gregory the Great to the Twelfth-Century Decretists," in *Purity and Holiness: The Heritage of Leviticus*, eds. M. J. H. M. Poorthuis and J. Schwartz (Leiden, The Netherlands: Brill, 2000), 284. See also Meens, "Ritual Purity and the Influence of Gregory the Great in the Early Middle Ages," in *Unity and Diversity in the Church*, Studies in Church History 32, ed. R. N. Swanson (Cambridge, MA: Blackwell, 1996), 31–43, and the similar arguments in Matthew Innes, "'Immune from Heresy': Defining the Boundaries of Carolingian Christianity," in *Frankland: The Franks and the World of the Early Middle Ages. Essays in Honour of Dame Jinty Nelson*, eds. Paul Fouracre and David Ganz (Manchester, UK: University of Manchester Press, 2008), 101–25 at 110.

Libellus Responsionum admonishes Augustine's converts not to understand literally biblical assertions that menstruating and recently delivered women were ritually unclean, it is probably because his mission found itself confronting attitudes toward purity drawn from the Pentateuch. Ultimately such views were seen by Gregory as obstacles to the full conversion of the people of Kent. While Gregory likewise conceded that these states were polluting,

> for Gregory it was inward convictions that counted, not outward behavior. Women should make up their own mind: when they decided not to approach the body and blood of the Lord when menstruating, they were to be praised, but when they got carried away by the love of the sacred mystery they were not to be prevented from going to church or from receiving communion.[107]

Given that habitual reliance on the laws of the Old Testament seems to have persisted into Ælfric's day and become one of the principal targets of this reform-minded abbot, the presence of such attitudes in a normative text, particularly when occurring in conjunction with other features associated with earlier phases of Anglo-Saxon prose, may very well suggest something about when it was composed. And it is interesting in this regard that evidence of the strict biblicism described by Meens is not evenly distributed among the Old English penitentials. We find it most in the *Canons*. Its main source, the *Penitential of Theodore*, is understood by commentators as critical of the rigid purity code of the early English church, reassuring its readers, for example, that unclean foods consumed unintentionally are not defiling.[108] Theodore's penitential does not, of course, represent a full break with the past. On matters of ritual purity, Theodore does seem to make concessions to views disdained by the *Libellus*. The most dramatic of these is Theodore's refusal of communion to menstruating women.[109]

For the compiler of the *Canons*, it would seem that even these concessions would not suffice. He turns this prohibition into one directed against women who are *on gebyrdtidum*, a phrase that probably means "in the time of childbirth."[110] Thus he flatly contradicts Theodore's allowances for such women to receive the Eucharist (II, xii, IV) while making no mention

107 Meens, "A Relic of Superstition," 284–5.

108 *PT* I, vii, 7.

109 Ibid., xiv, 17.

110 I find unconvincing the Toronto *DOE*'s gloss of this phrase as "the time when nature ordains menstruation." The entry seems to rest on the assumption that the *Canons* aimed to render Theodore accurately, a view that this study argues throughout to be unreliable.

in this clause of menstruation, which had been the translated canon's actual concern.[111] (That the subsequent clause [A 114] seems to refer to menstruation while its source is manifestly concerned with the period of purification after childbirth is further evidence of the translator's disregard for his sources in formulating purity regulations of his own.) It seems quite likely that A 113 was revised to accommodate the language of Leviticus, for here (12:1–8; 15:19–32) pregnancy and menstruation are equated as polluting states that prevent women from entering the temple. The *Canons* are certainly more conservative on this question than their source, and perhaps they look back to the kinds of attitudes critiqued in Gregory's *Libellus*.

As will be shown in Chapter 3, other departures from the language of sources are suggestive of an earlier text. Such is the case, for example, with its treatment of the abstention from labor on Sunday, which was revived during the archiepiscopate of Wulfstan along rather different lines than are evident in the *Canons*.[112] Clues to the date at which the *Canons* appeared may also be afforded by what its translator chooses not to change. The sale of children into slavery by their parents, for example, is a practice unlikely to have been tolerated by the later Anglo-Saxon period given denunciations of the practice by Wulfstan; the later *Old English Penitential* also shows disapproval of the practice.[113]

At all events, the archaism of the *Canons* is demonstrated most dramatically by its preservation (with slight changes) of Theodore's complaints about the Irish Church. Theodore (II, ix, 1) asserts that those ordained by the Irish are to be reconfirmed by English bishops because the Irish "in pascha et in tonsura adunati aecclesię catholicę non sunt" ("are not in unity with catholic practice with respect to the observance of Easter and the tonsure"). The *Canons* (A 33) change this into a statement that the Irish "ne þa eastro[n] swa ne healdað [swa we healdað]" ("do

[111] A 113: "Wif on gebyrd[um monða] tidum ne gange heo on cyrcan, ne to husle ne gangan naðer ne nunnan ne læwede; gif hy þonne geþristlæcan, þreo wican fæsten," "A woman who is near to giving birth is not to enter a church, nor is she to receive communion whether she is religious or of the laity; if she dares to do so, let her fast for three weeks." The source is *PT* I, xiv, 17: "Mulieres autem menstruo tempore non intrent in ecclesiam neque communicent nec sanctimoniales nec laicae si presumant tribus ebdomadibus ieiunent," "Women during their times of menstruation are not to enter the church nor receive the Eucharist, neither religious nor lay; if they presume to do so let them fast for three weeks." The *Canons* contradict *PT* II, xii, 4: "Mulieri quoque licet per omnia ante communicare quando debet peperere," "Women also are entirely permitted to receive communion before they should give birth."

[112] See the laws of Edward and Guthrum (*Gesetze*, ed. Liebermann, I: 132 [cap. 8]) and Cnut (*Gesetze*, ed. Liebermann, I: 344, caps. 46–7).

[113] See Chapter 3, 111–12.

not keep Easter as we do"). The Paschal controversy was certainly not timely during the eleventh century – the era of our extant manuscripts – but it was as late as the close of the ninth century.[114] That the compiler of the *Canons* felt it appropriate to recast this statement into language with greater immediacy than Theodore's shows that he was not mechanically substituting word-for-word equivalents of the Latin: to him, the Paschal controversy was among the concerns of the present day. This would be, to say the least, highly improbable in a text of the Benedictine Reform. In this and other instances, the *Canons* seem quite out of place in the tenth-century context supposed by most who have commented upon it, and its archaism may explain why, when compared to others, its influence on later ecclesiastical lawmaking seems to have been so minor.

Given the foregoing, we may assert some tentative conclusions. It has been seen that even advocates of a later date concede that the *Canons* and *Scriftboc* contain a substantial amount of Anglian forms unlikely to have surfaced in these texts should they have been composed more than a couple of decades after the death of Alfred. Both also treat various matters in ways characteristic of the era before the Reform. Their one shared manifestation of supposed change regarding the law of marriage is much harder to set in a chronology of legal developments than typically assumed given the appearance of supposedly "late" practices in early texts (such as Alfred's Mosaic Prologue) and "early" practices in late texts (such as *Wifmannes Beweddung*). Most surveys of Old English prose concerned with dating have nothing to say about the *Scriftboc* and *Canons*. But ground for their inclusion among the small group of Alfredian or even pre-Alfredian prose texts seems at least as solid as other texts whose membership in this category is less disputed. Reasons for assigning them a date much later than the last decades of the ninth century reside principally in the dates of the manuscripts. Given the appearance of very early texts in very late manuscripts within and outside of the Old English tradition, arguments from the dates of manuscripts have little to recommend them.

There is little doubt that the Benedictine Reform movement with which these texts are routinely associated, in addition to being linguistically irreconcilable with them, sheds little light on their contents. With the

114 Wesley Stevens notes that the Bedan method for calculating the date of Easter would not be accepted everywhere in the British Isles until the ninth century. See Stevens, "Easter Controversy," in *The Blackwell Encyclopaedia*, ed. Lapidge et al., 1999, 157; also William North, "History, Tradition, and Authority in Bede's Interpretation of the Council of Whitby, 664," *Anglo-Saxon* 1 (2007), 1–53 at 2–3.

exception of Archbishop Wulfstan and his contemporary Ælfric – both of whom surface fairly late in the history of this movement – ecclesiastics of the Reform seem to have had no more interest in penance among the laity than their forebears. It is difficult to see why this movement, absorbed as it seems to have been in restoring monastic life, should have provided the impetus for composing the earliest of these texts.

Given the lack of linguistic or historical evidence that the *Canons* and *Scriftboc* could have surfaced so late in the history of Anglo-Saxon prose, we may look elsewhere for the reasons why some ecclesiastics undertook the writing and copying of vernacular penitentials. Here we are not without some circumstantial evidence. It has already been shown that a new concern with penance was among Alfred's principal legislative innovations. If the stipulations of his code are to be taken seriously – and Alfred's *domboc*, significantly, is the only royal legislation to which later codes allude – penance plays a role in the administration of justice during Alfred's kingship more significantly than ever before.[115] For those priests and bishops engaged in carrying out the agenda urged by the king and his circle (some of whom were drawn from the diocese of Rheims, a center for the writing of penitentials in the ninth century), textual support presumably would have been necessary. And given concerns about the degraded state of Latin learning, the most natural language in which to situate these textual aids would have been English.

That these texts have their origins in efforts, perhaps Alfredian, to strengthen the enfeebled mechanisms of pastoral care seems a more plausible way to account for their origins than to assume their dependence upon the ideologies of the Reform – a connection whose rationale, in any case, has never been made explicit by scholarship. Such a date conforms both with the dialect evidence (dialect mixture being itself a typical feature of the Alfredian translations) and with the idiosyncratic pastoral concerns of the *Scriftboc* and *Canons*.

Frantzen has astutely observed that the writing of penitentials in Old English "had the slightly odd effect of furnishing English bishops with new material which was, in fact, quite old, or at least old-fashioned"; "the 'Scrift boc,'" he notes, "is an excellent example: obviously new to the English in the tenth century, it was based on texts similar to those which the Paris Council of 829 had scorned."[116] The evidence presented

[115] Each of the Alfredian clauses (caps. 1.2, 1.8, 5.4, and 14) whose concern with penance is beyond dispute is discussed in Hough, "Penitential Literature."

[116] Frantzen, *Literature of Penance*, 147–8.

builds on this and similar suggestions by proposing that the *Scriftboc* (and *Canons*) seem archaic because they probably are. Absent the assumption that Latin penitentials were unavailable in the years before the reform – a claim, as has been shown, from which one may now cautiously dissent on a number of grounds – we need no longer go to great lengths to explain why such "old-fashioned" texts as the earliest Old English penitentials were appearing so late, and in a dialect hardly used by tenth-century scribes.

3

The Law of the Estate

Bishops, Masters, and Slaves

Anglo-Saxon England differed little from other premodern societies in making extensive use of captive labor. Though the beginnings of the practice as it was known to the English are to be found in periods prior to the introduction of writing and thus beyond the reach of scholarly inquiry, its demise – or, at the very least, the point at which bishops and secular elites might no longer tolerate it – comes abruptly in the decades following the Norman Conquest.[1] The condemnation of English slavery by the bishops assembled at Westminster under Archbishop Anselm of Canterbury (1033–1109) has long been held to mark the official end of the institution, by then at least seven centuries old. The language with which they did so is in itself remarkable for offering up an unusual parallel to modern rhetoric on the subject. The bishops demand "[n]e quis illud nefarium negotium, quo hactenus homines in Anglia solebant uelut bruta animalia uenundari, deinceps ullatenus facere praesumat," "that no one should in the future take part in the evil trade by which hitherto in England men have customarily been sold like brute beasts" – a rebuke so clear in its moral reasoning that it would be repeated by English and American abolitionists.[2]

[1] According to David Pelteret, slavery was probably not "a significant social feature" among the Germanic peoples of the continent until they entered into close contact with the Roman Empire. For the Germanic settlers who grew numerous in Britain by the fifth century, however, the traffic in slaves was already a familiar and important facet of economic life. See Pelteret, "Slavery in Anglo-Saxon England," in *The Anglo-Saxons: Synthesis and Achievement*, eds. J. Douglas Woods and David A. E. Pelteret (Waterloo: Wilfrid Laurier University Press, 1985), 117–33 at 118.

[2] For the text of the Council of Westminster (1102), see William of Malmesbury, *Gesta Pontificum Anglorum*, ed. and trans. Michael Winterbottom (Oxford: Oxford University Press, 2007), 192–3 (i.64.5); also *Eadmeri historia novorum in Anglia, et opuscula duo,*

This and similar denunciations of English slavery in the period after the Conquest invite a number of questions about the dominant views of servitude before the Norman hegemony. Did the bishops' attitudes show any continuity with those of their pre-Conquest predecessors? Or was theirs an outsider's perspective, as would seem to be implied by the designation of this practice as one peculiar to the English?[3] What did the Anglo-Saxons think of their slaves? Any answers must, of course, vary in accordance with the nature of the sources consulted. But in surveying what has so far been said on the subject, one cannot but be surprised by its relative paucity and by its indebtedness to things said long ago. According to David Pelteret, the longest treatment of this subject prior to his own monumental volume of 1995 was John Mitchell Kemble's *Saxons in England* (1849) – only a chapter of which was devoted to servitude.[4] Kemble's study was the first since 1818, and no substantial work of scholarship devoted to the practice of slavery would follow Kemble's for nearly thirty years.[5]

It is true that the picture does not seem quite so bleak when German scholarship is taken into consideration. An entry concerned with

de vita Sancti Anselmi et quibusdam miraculis eius, ed. Martin Rule (London: Eyre & Spottiswoode, 1884), 143. After quoting this passage in its entirety, Samuel Wilberforce, in his *History of the Protestant Episcopal Church in America* (New York: Stanford and Swords, 1849), asserts: "This must be the Church's rule on the banks of the Mississippi, as it was on those of the Thames" (300).

3 Reasons to doubt any similarly tender feelings for the plight of slaves among the English abound – even where we would least expect them. Christopher Dyer has described the thinking of St. Wulfstan of Worcester, another conventional champion of the interests of slaves, as much more complicated than is typically understood, being often characterized by "an assumption of aristocratic superiority, combined with some concern for the welfare of the poor" as well as horror at the "monstrous" strength of the laboring classes (147–8): see Dyer, "Bishop Wulfstan and His Estates," in *Wulfstan and His World*, eds. Julia S. Barrow and N. P. Brooks (Aldershot, UK: Ashgate, 2005), 137–49.

4 John Mitchell Kemble, *The Saxons in England*, 2 vols. (London: Longman, Brown, Green and Longmans, 1849; rev. ed. Walter de Gray Birch, 1876), I: 185–227 (cap. VIII). Of the significance of Kemble's volume to the study of slavery in Anglo-Saxon England, Pelteret notes that "His survey included a treatment of slaves which is still the longest and most wide-ranging treatment of this Anglo-Saxon class yet written." See Pelteret, *Slavery in Early Mediaeval England* (Woodbridge, UK: Boydell, 1995), 5.

5 Samuel Heywood, *A Dissertation upon the Distinctions in Society, and Ranks of the People, under the Anglo-Saxon Governments* (London: W. Clarke and Sons, 1818), 355–424 (cap. VI); Frederic Seebohm, *The English Village Community* (London: Longman, Green & Co., 1876; 2nd ed. 1883). Heywood's elegant survey may still be read with profit, and Seebohm's conclusions about the origins of some English agricultural practices retain considerable authority among present-day historians, as is noted in Susan Oosthuizen, "The Anglo-Saxon Kingdom of Mercia and the Origins and Distribution of Common Fields," *Agricultural History Review* 55 (2007), 153–80 at 158–9.

slavery in the legal encyclopedia occupying the second volume of Felix Liebermann's *Gesetze der Angelsachsen* is probably longer than Kemble's chapter and certainly more sweeping in the range of materials described.[6] Nonetheless, Pelteret is right about the importance that Kemble's work would have for later scholars. Being the least read portion of a notoriously daunting edition, Liebermann's *Sachglossar* would do little to stimulate interest in slavery during the twentieth century. The handful of scholars who did make use of Liebermann's discussion of slavery employed it mainly as a concordance to the major legal sources while showing little curiosity about the arguments buried in its dense pages of heavily abbreviated German.[7]

Liebermann's entry was itself undermined by its inattention to the Old English penitentials as well as its dependence upon some of the same "Germanist" ideas that had prevailed during Kemble's career.[8] Thus the Old English penitentials, which say a great deal about slavery, have received attention from historians of this institution for only two decades, and sporadically at that.[9] The present chapter argues that these texts require some doubts about the relative moral enlightenment historians have long assumed for the leading figures of the pre-Conquest English church. First, however, it will be necessary to discuss the assumptions that came to govern the study of Anglo-Saxon slavery in the nineteenth century, some of which remain with us today.

As David Wyatt has recently observed, Kemble's understanding of Anglo-Saxon slavery cannot be understood apart from the circumstances of his age.[10] He was one of a generation of scholars for whom a disinterested approach to the historical study of servitude seemed impossible. As was evident in studies such as Henry Sumner Maine's *Ancient Law*

[6] Noteworthy as well is Ignaz Jastrow, *Zur strafrechtlichen Stellung der Sklaven bei Deutschen und Angelsachsen* (Breslau [Wrocław]: W. Köbner, 1878).

[7] Exceptions come, unsurprisingly, from the German-speaking world: see, e.g., Karl Jost, *Wulfstanstudien*, Schweizer anglistische Arbeiten 23 (Bern: A. Francke, 1950), 42.

[8] Liebermann's reliance upon the ideas of Jakob Grimm and his contemporaries is discussed in Wormald, *Making*, 23.

[9] The Old English penitentials are considered in Pelteret, *Slavery*, 101–5; more recently they have received discussion in David Wyatt, *Slaves and Warriors in Medieval Britain and Ireland, 800–1200*, The Northern World 45 (Leiden, The Netherlands: Brill, 2009). Though superb in many respects, the discussion here is not systematic and greater attention is paid to Latin sources: see 54, 132, 151.

[10] See Wyatt, *Slaves and Warriors*, 3, 11. Pelteret's criticisms focus on Kemble's "Germanist" approach (acquired from his mentor, Jakob Grimm, with whom he had studied at Göttingen) and his consequent reliance on continental sources to flesh out the details of the institution: see *Slavery*, 6–7.

(1861), historical inquiry into slavery was at the time felt to be inextricable from the pressing question of its morality. The notion of slavery as "a primitive family institution" sometimes encountered in the United States was to Maine "pregnant with an admission of the moral defensibility of Negro-servitude."[11] American slavery and its abolition would also seize the attention of the young Frederic Seebohm, who would go on decades later to author a series of penetrating studies of early English agrarian life.[12]

Though England had rejected the trade in slaves in 1807, and the practice of slavery in 1833, events in America could only complicate the efforts of a historian tasked as Kemble was with describing in primarily laudatory terms a society in which slavery was ubiquitous.[13] To this challenge Kemble seems to have responded more than once with mere boosterism. In his *Saxons in England*, we find the Anglo-Saxon church simultaneously credited with efforts to make the lot of slaves less miserable and exculpated for the apparent failure of these measures: "The Christian clergy indeed did all they could to mitigate its hardships, but when has even Christianity itself been triumphant over the selfishness and the passions of the mass of men?"[14] Though Kemble here acknowledges the harsh treatment of some slaves in early England with a forthrightness not to be found in the work of later scholars, Kemble situates the dominance of such conditions outside of what most would recognize as the "official" beginning of the Anglo-Saxon period: the conversion of King Æthelberht and the establishment of an archiepiscopal see at Canterbury. Conceding that in its earliest state English slavery granted to the master absolute power over the life of his slave, Kemble admonishes us that "[t]hese remarks apply, no doubt, in their full force, only to our pagan forefathers; but even Christianity itself did not at once succeed in rooting out habits which its divine precepts of justice and mercy emphatically condemn."[15] Thus surfaced the notion of Anglo-Saxon slavery

[11] Henry Sumner Maine, *Ancient Law: Its Connection with the Early History of Society and Its Relation to Modern Ideas* (Boston: Beacon, 1861; repr. 1963), 158.

[12] Seebohm's early interests in the matter of slavery are evident in *The Crisis of Emancipation in America* (London: Alfred W. Bennett, 1865), a work intended for fellow members of the Religious Society of Friends in England. Pelteret observes (*Slavery*, 6–7) that Seebohm's later contributions to the study of Anglo-Saxon slavery were "poles apart from Kemble's"; his *English Village Community* (1876) would emphasize the continuity of English practices with those of the Romans in contrast to Kemble's arguments for the basis of English servitude in Germanic institutions.

[13] Heywood had directly compared New World slavery with that of the Anglo-Saxons in his *Dissertation*, 363–4.

[14] Kemble, *Saxons in England*, I: 208.

[15] Kemble, *Saxons in England*, I: 186.

as somehow exceptional when compared with that of the New World and, in any case, under constant if ineffectual assault from an ecclesiastical establishment that succeeded at least in making conditions less brutal than they might otherwise have been. Such sentiments would be expressed with less restraint a little more than a decade later in John Thrupp's study of 1862, *The Anglo-Saxon Home: A History of the Domestic Institutions and Customs of England from the Fifth to the Eleventh Century.* According to Thrupp, "The Christian clergy no sooner obtained power in England, than they exerted it to the utmost, to put an end to the foreign slave trade.... From the earliest period the Christian clergy used their influence, not only to diminish the severity of slavery, but to limit its extent."[16] Thrupp's assertions show how eagerly other British historians embraced Kemble's arguments as they watched a former colony self-destruct over the question of slavery less than a century after it had secured its autonomy.

As slavery faded from view, so, it would seem, did much of the interest in its early history. Nor would conditions be ripe for a reappraisal of Kemble's ideas during most of the twentieth century. Where slavery is mentioned at all by scholars of this period, most of whom witnessed firsthand the calamities of World War II, their tone, as has been noted by Wyatt, is typically recuperative, with most studies allowing for slavery only an insignificant role in Anglo-Saxon economic life.[17] These judgments must have been soothing in the aftermath of the war. But they are in essence Victorian coinages, outlasting their age primarily because few scholars were interested in replacing them.

The studies of Pelteret and, more recently, Wyatt perhaps signal an end to this period of neglect.[18] Yet their reappraisals of Kemble's thesis have not wholly clarified the extent to which the moral questions surrounding slavery troubled the Anglo-Saxon church.[19] Sympathy for maltreated slaves is certainly evident in the various texts that furnish the basis of present-day

[16] John Thrupp, *The Anglo-Saxon Home: A History of the Domestic Institutions and Customs of England, from the Fifth to the Eleventh Century* (London: Longman, Green, Longman and Roberts, 1862), 129–35.

[17] David Wyatt, "The Significance of Slavery: Alternative Approaches to Anglo-Saxon Slavery," *Anglo-Norman Studies* 23 (2001), 328–47. This tendency is, perhaps, most evident in the work of Frank Merry Stenton. As is noted by Wyatt and others, of the more than seven hundred pages of his great *Anglo-Saxon England*, only four discuss slavery, and none at much length.

[18] Another skeptical response to this view is Ross Samson, "The End of Early Medieval Slavery," in *The Work of Work: Servitude, Slavery and Labor in Medieval England*, eds. Allen J. Frantzen and Douglas Moffat (Glasgow: Cruithne Press, 1994), 95–123.

[19] On the role of the broader Church in shaping the early law of slavery, see Paul Allard, "Slavery," *The Catholic Encyclopedia*, Vol. 14 (New York: Robert Appleton, 1912), 36–9.

speculation. We find it expressed in materials as diverse as the homilies and laws of Wulfstan and the miracles of St. Swithun. While little is known about what the latter had to say on the subject of slavery – or anything else, for that matter – we may at least credit his apparition with intervening repeatedly on behalf of slaves.[20] Yet outright objections to the institution, as both Pelteret and Wyatt acknowledge, are absent from the legal and homiletic writings of early English ecclesiastics.[21]

The relative silence of ecclesiastical sources on moral questions surrounding slavery is illuminated by the fact, considered at some length by Pelteret, that slaves labored on monastic holdings as well as secular estates.[22] To be sure, traces of disdain for the practice of keeping slaves on monastic and ecclesiastical estates are not wholly absent. Writing to Pope Zacharias in 751 concerning the establishment of the monastery at Fulda, Boniface observed with some pride the presence there of "uiros stricte abstinentie, absque carne et uino, absque sicera et seruis, proprio manuum suarum labore contentos," "men of strict continence, [who have abjured] meat and wine, cider and slaves, content with the labor of their own hands."[23] Yet however much they were preached, the virtues of manual labor, so manifest to an idealist such as Boniface, meant little to generations of monks accustomed to having others do the work. The penitential of Theodore (II, viii, 3) observes without apparent disapproval that, while Greek monks did not keep slaves, Roman monks did. The abject dependence upon captive labor that resulted from such arrangements is expressed with touching innocence in a sermon of Abbo of Saint-Germain-des-Prés that is likely to have served as a source for Wulfstan's *Sermo ad Anglos*:[24]

Nostri homines uillani et serui et ancille et toti qui nostras uillas tenebant et nostras terras arabant unde nos et uictum et uestimenta habere deberemus, et

[20] See Pelteret, *Slavery*, 58. It should be noted that while Lantfred does lament the cruelty of the punishments administered to a slave girl, his language implies that such measures might have been appropriate had the girl not been punished "because of a small transgression" (*pro paruo … commiso*); see *The Cult of St. Swithun*, ed. and trans. Michael Lapidge (Oxford: Clarendon, 2003), 288–9. It will be shown that this is very much in keeping with the attitude of normative sources discussed in this chapter.

[21] Pelteret, *Slavery*, 252–3; Wyatt, *Slaves and Warriors*, 29.

[22] See Pelteret, *Slavery*, 121, 158, and 256 (where it is noted that "Peterborough Abbey still reported them on its estates as late as the 1120s").

[23] See *Die Briefe des heiligen Bonifatius und Lullus*, MGH Epistolae selectae 1, ed. Michael Tangl (Berlin: Weidmannsche Verlagsbuchhandlung, 1916), no. 86, 193; also the discussion in Franz Staab, "Bonifatius, die *regula sancti patris Benedicti* und die Gründung des Klosters Fulda," *Archiv für mittelrheinische Kirchengeschichte* 57 (2005): 55–69.

[24] Edited in James E. Cross and Alan Brown, "Literary Impetus for Wulfstan's *Sermo Lupi*," *Leeds Studies in English* 20 (1989), 271–91 at 281. The translation is my own, but influence from Cross and Brown's has been unavoidable.

unde nos caballos et arma comparabamus, iam sunt mortui aut captiuati. Quale opus habemus nos sine illis hominibus? Nos non scimus neque terras arare neque seminare neque uineas putare aut fodere. Quid faciemus nos modo?

"Our men – villains and slaves and slave-women and all those who used to maintain our estates and ploughed our lands from which we had both food and clothing, and from which we purchased horses and arms – now are dead or captive. What work we have without those men! We don't know how to plough the earth or sow seeds or prune or cultivate vines. What should we do now?"

It is hard to imagine English monks as vexed by scruples about the morality of forced labor should they have enjoyed anything like the life of ease described here by Abbo. Yet present-day commentators, even while acknowledging grave doubts about the claims of Kemble and others who attributed opposition to slavery to the English Church, have for the most part been content to suggest that its most influential bishops at the very least urged compassion for those in bondage.[25] Thus has the Church retained its role in more recent scholarship as ultimately an agent of slaves' liberation, if by means less direct than those alleged by Kemble. According to Pelteret, by imposing on slaves the same moral and festal obligations as the free, the Church (largely through the agency of Wulfstan) was able to establish among the English the notion of slaves and free persons as equals before God, an idea that would lead in time to sentiments such as those expressed at the Westminster council.[26] Elsewhere in Pelteret's study the Church is credited with acting in early English society as the sole protector of slaves from physical harm given its "more humane perception of the slave."[27] Though Wyatt has recently emphasized the failure of Wulfstan's efforts at reforming English life, he nonetheless attributes to the prelate "concerns regarding the morally corrupting effects of slave ownership" while allowing that he "clearly

[25] See Pelteret, *Slavery*, 90–1: "[T]he equality of all before God and the Grace shown by Him to His 'slaves' led Wulfstan to be concerned about the welfare of those at the bottom of the social hierarchy in general, and slaves in particular.... Wulfstan interpreted this equality of all to mean that in the secular realm everyone should receive equal protection under the law.... In Wulfstan's view, the slave was not, however, a chattel but a fellow human being on the lowest rung of the social ladder." As a description of Wulfstan's ideals as expressed in tracts such as *Episcopus* – the sense, it should be noted, in which Pelteret's remarks are intended – these remarks are undoubtedly correct. However, it is worth mentioning here that Wulfstan in the passage referred to by Pelteret is urging lords to protect *nydðeowan* or "penal slaves," a class of persons who, according to Wyatt, "are often referred to separately from the mass of other slaves. They appear to have received preferable treatment as they were more likely to be manumitted upon the death of their master." See Wyatt, "The Significance of Slavery," 329n8.

[26] Pelteret, *Slavery*, 252.

[27] Ibid., 91, 103–5.

recognized the humanity" of slaves.[28] Both authors thus permit the English Church to keep the place assigned it by Kemble as guardian, however ineffectual and double-minded, of the rights of slaves.

The foregoing remarks do not deny the substantial departures from Kemble's views in recent historiography. Both Pelteret and Wyatt concede that Kemble's assessment of the English Church relied on a faulty understanding of the complex relationship of Christian tradition to the slaveholding world in which it was born.[29] The Victorian sentimentality in Kemble's imagined picture of a medieval Church viewing slavery as one of the abuses of its age has not gone unnoticed. Yet the weight of tradition favored those who had no qualms about slavery, and to an extent not always readily acknowledged. Nowhere among ancient or medieval conciliar decrees would English bishops of the eleventh century or earlier have found precedent for the explicit condemnation of slavery Kemble imputes to them. In scripture, they would likewise have found little ground to oppose slavery, as has often been noted.[30] Inasmuch as the New Testament addresses the issue at all, we find not only explicit toleration of slavery, but also disdain expressed by the Apostle for the "slavish" and "demeaning" nature of the manual labor with which he was obliged to support himself.[31] Such an attitude, as one biographer notes, was shared by most educated and well-off

[28] Wyatt, *Slaves and Warriors*, 286–7.

[29] It should be said that Pelteret appears to see the relationship of the Church to slavery in a somewhat gloomier light toward the end of his study (particularly at 255–6) than he does elsewhere, particularly in his discussion of Wulfstan or the supposedly humanizing effect of the penitentials. His concluding remarks acknowledge "contradictory attitudes" among the English clergy that make sense only if it is borne in mind that the Church was both "an organisation which followed a set of *administrative* principles" and "a collection of individual Christians who followed a set of *moral* principles" (255). The "moral principles" turn out to revolve around the inherent goodness of manumitting slaves.

[30] Jennifer Glancy argues that "we cannot presume Matthew supposes the punishments that slave owners commonly visit on their slaves to be excessive" and observes throughout her study the likeness of the Gospels and the Pauline Epistles to other literatures of late antiquity in their shared indifference to moral questions surrounding the keeping of slaves: see Glancy, *Slavery in Early Christianity* (Oxford: Oxford University Press, 2002), 120. Some caveats are in order, however. While it has become a commonplace that the writings of the New Testament offered no negative judgments of slavery, remarks on the subject in 1 Peter 2:18–21 do not admit of being read in the sense described. To be urged to submit to injustice after the example of Christ does not alter the fact that one has been made nonetheless the victim of a wrong. The famous injunction for slaves to obey their masters in Ephesians 6:5–7 similarly urges patient suffering. Close consideration should be given to the social vision of Galatians 3:28 as well.

[31] His occupation is so characterized in I Corinthians 9:19 and 2 Corinthians 11:7, respectively. For a discussion, see Jerome Murphy-O'Connor, *Paul: A Critical Life* (Oxford: Oxford University Press, 1996), 85. In 1 Corinthians 4:12, 2 Corinthians 6:5; 11:23, 27, Paul mentions his occupation "among the unfair hardships of his life."

persons in the late-antique world.[32] All of this invites questions about the true nature of the inheritance of the English church from antiquity on matters of slavery. While members of the regular clergy in England conventionally styled themselves "servants" (*ðeowas*) of Christ, as Paul had done, disdain both for those compelled to work and for manual labor must have accompanied this gesture. The views of Boniface may not be taken as representative. We should, perhaps, not be surprised if leading Anglo-Saxon ecclesiastics were able to entertain contradictory and perhaps irreconcilable views of those whose lot was to be made to perform others' labor, particularly given remarks such as those of Abbo of Saint-Germain-des-Prés.

Such ambivalence may be evident where it has not so far been widely recognized in the work of Ælfric, abbot of Eynsham. It is true that his celebrated *Colloquy* offers us a poignant view of a young servant's life of hard labor – one of the few instances in all of Old English literature in which a slave speaks.[33] But Ælfric's *Grammar* illustrates, as Elizabeth Stevens Girsch has shown, Latin accidence with the range of violent responses that a slave might expect of his masters.[34] It is hard not to think that this curious, perhaps playful moment in the *Grammar*, in which *meum seruum flagello* ("I beat my slave") and *meos seruos diligo* ("I love my slaves") serve as examples of pronoun declensions, shows something of the conflicted emotions that surrounded the maintenance of this institution.[35] Even in his at times more sympathetic *Colloquy* we find the notion of abandoning one's occupation likened to sin: in a harmonious society, members of each stratum are obliged only to accept their condition and exercise their duties without complaint:[36]

> Siue sis sacerdos, siue monachus, seu laicus, seu miles, exerce temet ipsum in hoc, et esto quod es, quia magnum dampnum et uerecundia est homini nolle esse quod est et quod esse debet.

According to Murphy, "No one bred to a craft would speak of it in this way. Paul's stance is that of those whose inherited status preserved them from physical work."

32 Murphy-O'Connor, *Paul: A Critical Life*, 88–9.

33 For a discussion and analysis of this portion of the *Colloquy*, see Pelteret, *Slavery*, 64–5; for the passage, see *Ælfric's Colloquy*, ed. G. N. Garmonsway, 2nd ed. (London: Methuen, 1947), 20–1 (ll. 22–35).

34 "Metaphorical usage, Sexual Exploitation, and Divergence in the Old English Terminology for Male and Female Slaves," in *The Work of Work*, ed. Moffat and Frantzen, 30–54 at 36. These examples are not present in Ælfric's source: see *Excerptiones de Prisciano: The Source for Ælfric's Latin-Old English Grammar*, ed. David W. Porter (Woodbridge, UK: D. S. Brewer, 2002).

35 The examples may owe something to Ælfric's Latin learning, or to attitudes inherited from the Roman world. According to William Fitzgerald, "Being beaten is one of the most important things that literary slaves do" in Roman literature: see *Slavery and the Roman Literary Imagination* (Cambridge: Cambridge University Press, 2000), 32

36 *Ælfric's Colloquy*, ed. Garmonsway, 41–2 (ll. 240–3).

"Whether you are a priest, or a monk, or a layperson, or a soldier, exert yourself in this activity, and be what you are, for it is a great loss and a shame for a man not to wish to be what he is and what he must be."

Though the abbot does not refer specifically to servitude in this passage, its language suggests that Ælfric is unlikely to have seen injustice in the condition of the slave whose depiction in the *Colloquy* is nonetheless affecting.[37] One thus finds in the work of this contemporary of Wulfstan a mix of what may be genuine sympathy with an understanding that the subordinate classes should expect, as much as the oblates of a monastery, to do their work under threat of violence.

THE CHARACTER OF ENGLISH SLAVERY

Further complicating our efforts to understand supposed ecclesiastical denunciations of slavery are uncertainties about the kinds of pressures that native tradition must have exerted upon any attempts by bishops to elevate the status of slaves. Scholars have long suspected that, among the English, slavery may have assumed a character somewhat different from what prevailed across the Channel. It has long been pointed out that traditional slavery probably lasted longer among the Anglo-Saxons than it would elsewhere in Western Europe, where it was being replaced by the aggregate of relationships for which *feudalism* is the inevitable if not the best term. The divergent forms of labor obtaining among the English and their Norman conquerors may even, according to Stenton, have become a site of conflict between the two peoples – something that may explain the tone of the Westminster assembly:[38]

Slavery of the thorough-going English type seems to have been a rare condition in contemporary Normandy, and there are indications that in some parts of England many slaves were emancipated by their Norman masters, and provided with houses and plots of land on which to live as dependant cottagers.

Little evidence has been summoned in support of Stenton's thesis, which probably owes something to Kemble's assumption that slavery was particularly harsh among the pre-Conversion English. The evidence of royal legislation paints a decidedly mixed picture. The laws of Æthelberht

[37] The slave says of his work, "[N]on est tam aspira hiems ut audeam latere domi pro timore domini mei ... O! O! magnus labor. Etiam, magnus labor est, quia non sum liber," "There is not a winter bitter enough that I might dare stay home due to my fear of my master ... Oh! Oh! It's hard work. Indeed, it is hard work, because I am not free." See ibid., 20–1 (ll. 24–35).

[38] F. M. Stenton, *Anglo-Saxon England*, 472.

suggest that a slave referred to as an *esne* enjoyed the right to marry.[39] Yet the laws of Hlothhere and Eadric, set to writing only decades afterward, show the *esne* receiving treatment identical to that of a slave in cases of homicide: here, the offending slave is to be handed over to the kin of the deceased, acting as a kind of payment. If an *esne* was somehow different from a slave – the typical term for which was *ðeow* – the distinction seems not to have been everywhere recognized. As for the notoriously brutal penalties urged in the laws of Æthelstan (r. 925–39) against slaves who engaged in theft, even these provisions are balanced with others seemingly "acknowledg[ing] that the slave could be a principal in a legally recognized act and was answerable at law for it" and urging merciful treatment for the servile in other contexts.[40]

Thanks to the studies of Pelteret and Wyatt, we now know that the Old English penitentials afford further insights into the legal status of slaves. Both scholars are in relative agreement that they evince an Anglo-Saxon church concerned to protect slaves from wanton violence.[41] While this is broadly true, I would suggest that the Old English penitentials also confirm in ways that have yet to be appreciated Stenton's view that slavery in England was somehow more 'thoroughgoing' than across the Channel. In a 2010 essay, I assembled various statements from Old English penitentials that show the translators of these texts recasting their sources in ways unfavorable to slaves.[42] For example, the requirement of Halitgar's penitential that a woman who beats a slave girl to death receive penance in accordance with whether her actions were deliberate is radically changed once rendered into the vernacular. The Latin reads as follows:[43]

Si qua femina furore zeli accensa flagellis verberaverit ancillam suam, ita ut infra diem tertium animam cruciatu effundat, et quod incertum sit voluntate, an casu occiderit; si voluntate, post septem annos, si casu per quinquennii tempore acta legitime poenitentia a communione placuit abstineri; quod si infra tempora constituta fuerit infirmata, accipiat communionem.

"If a woman in the heat of jealousy (or rage) whips her maidservant so that within three days the latter gives up her soul under the torture, so that it is uncertain whether her mistress killed her intentionally or accidentally: if intentionally,

[39] This and subsequent observations on the language of slavery owe much to Pelteret's summary account, an appendix to his *Slavery*, 271–3.

[40] Ibid., 85.

[41] Both Pelteret (103–5) and Wyatt consider the Old English penitentials proof of ecclesiastical hostitility to the excesses of slavery.

[42] Jurasinski, "The Old English Penitentials and the Law of Slavery."

[43] The source text is cap. 5 of the Council of Elvira as it appears in Halitgar's penitential: see *Bussbücher*, ed. Schmitz, I: 723 (IV.v).

she should refrain from communion after seven years, and after five if accidentally, having performed the appropriate penance. If during either of these periods of penance she becomes ill, let her receive communion."

In the Old English version, the penance is to be assessed in accordance with the guilt or innocence of the slave, not the mistress who has slain her:[44]

Gif hwylc wif for hwylcum lyðrum andan hire wifman swingeð, & heo þurh þa swingele wurð dead, & heo unscyldig bið, fæste seo hlæfdige VII ger, gif heo þonne gewitnesse hæbbe, þæt heo scyldig sy, fæste heo III ger.

"If a woman because of some loathsome jealousy beats her bondwoman, and she [the slave] dies because of the beating, and she is innocent, let the woman fast for seven years; if she should have knowledge that [the slave] was guilty, let her fast for three years."

The pattern is repeated in a clause on masters who beat their slaves to death without first seeking formal judgment against them.[45] The translator imagines that the slave has been so treated because of his engagement in theft – a condition not present in his source – and allows for the killing to be somewhat excusable if witnesses affirm that the slave is culpable (*forworht*):[46]

Be þam men þe his þeowan ofslyhð for þyfþe butan his hundredes gewitnesse. Gif hwylc man his æht ofslehð, & he nane gewitnesse næbbe þæt he forworht sy, butan he hine for his hatheortnesse & for gymeleaste ofslyhð, fæste II ger.

"Concerning the man who kills his slave for theft without knowledge of the hundred. If a man kills his 'possession,' and he has no witness that he [the slave] was guilty, but rather he killed him out of anger and because of carelessness, let [the master] fast for two years."

This rendering amounts to an ecclesiastical affirmation of owners' power of life and death over their slaves. That seigneurial authority was not to be meddled with by outsiders is perhaps emphasized by the translation of *servum proprium* ("one's own slave") as *æht* ("possession").[47] It is

44 Departures from the source text in this passage are described by Raith but never connected with similar treatments in other vernacular penitentials: see *Die altenglische Version*, ed. Raith, 17 (cap. 3).

45 The source is Halitgar's version of a canon of the Council of Agatha (506): "*De his qui servos suos extra judicem necant.* (Ex concilio Agatense, cap. XXXV): Si quis servum proprium sine conscientia judicis occiderit, excommunicationem vel pœnitentiam biennii reatum sanguinis emundabit," "Of those who kill their slaves without legal process … If someone kills his own slave without the knowledge of a judge, he will atone for the guilt of blood either with excommunication or a two-year penance." *Bussbücher*, ed. Schmitz, I: 723 (IV.iv).

46 *Die altenglische Version*, ed. Raith, 17n4.

47 Pelteret (*Slavery*, 261) holds the term to be "a general word for property," observing that "It was used especially of land, but also of moveables such a[s] cattle." It would seem

possible that this clause was composed in response to a treatment of this situation in the *Scriftboc* that exhibits even less concern for the welfare of the slave, imposing a mere one-year penance on a master who kills his own bondman.[48]

The *Old English Penitential* is not alone in making the guilt or innocence of the slave the main criterion of the master's culpability for violence. As I argued, a willingness to excuse the ordinarily inexcusable when a slave is "guilty" is an addition so frequently made within the penitential corpus that we should wonder whether it constitutes an aspect of what some might call a "discourse" of servitude prevailing among the early English. A case in point is the treatment of Theodore's condemnation of masters who take money from their slaves. One version of the *Canons* adds that this offense is to be punishable only in the absence of known offenses by the slave (*butan forworhtum*).[49] This statement and those mentioned earlier recall Wulfstan's assertions, both in his legislation and in his *Sermo ad Anglos*, that the sale of slaves abroad is a crime particularly grievous when those so treated are *unforworhte*.[50] The evidence

on the basis of such evidence that connotations of disparagement may be present in this instance.

[48] See *Das altenglische Bussbuch*, ed. Spindler, cap. XIX.20.c (186): "Swa hwylc swa his man ofslea, fæste I gear." Spindler suggests that this clause, which likewise translates the chapter of the Council of Agatha mentioned previously, must originate in some external source (58). Given the tendencies outlined here, however, I think it may be assumed that this clause reflects attitudes toward slaves attested elsewhere in the corpus of Old English penitentials.

[49] "Nis nanum men alyfed, þæt he genime on his þeowe ænig feoh butan his willan and buton forwyrhtum, gif he hit mid rihte gestryneð," "It is permitted to no man that he seize from his slave any money without the latter's consent and without wrongdoing [?on the part of the slave], if he obtains it rightfully." The source is *PT* II, xiii, 3: "Non licet homini a servo suo tollere pecuniam quam ipse labore suo adquesierit," "It is not allowed for a man to take from his slave money which the latter has acquired through his own effort"; for the Old English versions, see *Ancient Laws and Institutes*, ed. Thorpe, 238–9 (where the phrase *buton forwyrhtum* is relegated to the textual apparatus); for reasons never made clear, it occurs in the body of the text in *Quellen und Forschungen zur Geschichte der teutschen Literatur und Sprache*, ed. F. Mone (Aachen & Leipzig, 1830), 518 (c. 109), as it does in Fulk and Jurasinski, *The Old English Canons of Theodore*, 5 and n. (A24).

[50] Wulfstan, *Sermo ad Anglos:* "[E]arme men syndan sare beswicene 7 hreowlice besyrwde 7 ut of þysan eard wide gesealde swyþe unforworhte fremdum to gewealde," "Wretched [impoverished?] men are sorely deceived and horribly tricked and sold out of this land, [though] quite innocent, into the power of strangers." See *The Homilies of Wulfstan*, ed. Dorothy Bethurum (Oxford: Clarendon, 1957), 262. See also Æthelred V, 2; VI, 9: "[U]res hlafordes gerædnes 7 his witena is, þæt man Cristene men 7 unforworhte of earde ne sylle, ne huru on hæðene þeode, ac beorge georne þæt man þa sawla ne forfare þe Crist mid his agenum life gebohte," "[I]t is the decree of our lord and his councilors, that Christian men who are innocent of crime shall not be sold out of the land, least of all to

of the Old English penitentials proves Liebermann right in his suspicion that Wulfstan means in this portion of the *Sermo* to excuse the selling of condemned slaves to the heathen.[51] That Wulfstan found acceptable the *Penitential*'s reworkings of Halitgarean materials is perhaps manifest in his preservation of the clause concerning the mistress and her slave girl with only slight alterations in the *Handbook for the Use of a Confessor*, a text likely to have been prepared by the prelate.[52] Even in this egregious allowance for maltreatment of slaves, which radically recasts an ancient canon, Wulfstan seems to have found nothing objectionable. His acceptance of these attempts to vitiate the modest rights of slaves, I suggested, require us to qualify assertions that the Old English penitentials "sought to afford slaves some protection against abuse at the hands of their owners" and that the English Church, at Wulfstan's urging, attempted when possible to improve slaves' conditions.[53]

My purpose at present is to consider the significance to our understanding of slavery of clauses touched on only briefly in the aforementioned essay that probably deserve greater scrutiny. Before discussing the first of these – a clause on the observance of Sunday in the *Old English Canons of Theodore* – some discussion of its background may be necessary, as the significance of this text depends very much on the way in which it responds to legislative tradition, the nature of which has yet to be made entirely clear in published scholarship. It will be shown that the tendencies described previously are manifest in this clause as well, yielding a text that sheds light both on attitudes toward slavery and the

the heathen, but care shall diligently be taken that the souls which Christ bought with his own life be not destroyed)." See *The Laws of the Kings of England from Edmund to Henry I*, ed. and trans. Agnes Jane Robertson (Cambridge: Cambridge University Press, 1925), 78–79; *Relatio* (an eleventh-century Latin paraphrase of Æthelred's laws): "Nemo etenim pro pecunię commutatione alicuius quempiam Christianum insontem ex patria eiciat, sed nec paganorum dominio subdat: nefas igitur est, ut quos Christus sanguinis sui effusione redemit, Iudeorum uel gentilium uinculis sint inretiti," "Let no one for someone's exchange of money drive some innocent Christian from his homeland, nor indeed subject him to the dominion of pagans; for it is abhorrent, that those whom Christ bought with his spilled blood should be bound in the snares of Jews and gentiles." *Gesetze*, ed. Liebermann, I: 251.

51 *Gesetze*, ed. Liebermann, II: 693 (12g). Liebermann has been often criticized for making this suggestion: see "The Old English Penitentials and the Law of Slavery," 110–11.

52 Fowler, "A Late Old English Handbook for the Use of a Confessor," 21 (ll. 154–6). It should be said in Wulfstan's defense that the *Penitential*'s additions to the clause concerning the fatal beating of a male slave are not preserved, though the result nonetheless is not one particularly favorable to slaves.

53 Pelteret, *Slavery*, 104. I have critiqued the often-made assertion of Wulfstan's opposition to the sale of slaves to pagans in "The Old English Penitentials and the Law of Slavery," 110–12.

changing nature of laws concerning the behavior of free persons and slaves during liturgical holidays. When examined in conjunction with legislative evidence, it will be seen that the clause from the *Canons* further demonstrates the relative severity of English attitudes toward slaves along with a corresponding leniency toward the free. It does so in ways that may be correlated with earlier periods of English legislation. Indeed, regulations on the observance of Sunday potentially disclose much about the relative status of slaves and free persons because these tended prior to the tenth century to be concerned with enforcing an abstention from "servile labor," a preoccupation of much Germanic legislation during the pre-Carolingian era.

PRIOR LAWS ON SUNDAY OBSERVANCE

We may begin by noting that reference to the Sunday repose from labor in the Theodorean cycle on which the *Canons* rely is in itself an anomaly. The principal influences upon the Theodorean canon collections – the earlier collections of Uinniau, Columbanus, and Cummean – say little about Sunday even though the interest of other Irish ecclesiastics in this subject appears to have been quite keen.[54] Outside of Ireland, elite clergy during much of the early Middle Ages held reservations about making Sunday into a kind of Sabbath.[55] Theodore's judgments were issued amid some uncertainty over the obligations of Christians and, as we will see, attempt to negotiate between competing ideas.

The story of how Sunday became a "Sabbath" in medieval Western Europe requires treatment in greater detail than is possible here; what follows is a mere sketch of what is agreed upon. Sunday became the principal day for corporate worship in late antique Christianity – the "Lord's day" of Revelation 1:10 – because tradition held it to be the day of Christ's resurrection. But Constantine's establishment in 321 of Sunday (in his language, the *dies solis*) as a *feria* – a state holiday requiring rest from from work – would have a greater influence upon subsequent legislation.[56] That this *feria* was understood to honor the Sun as a deity was no obstacle to its persistence under difference auspices. Among some early Christian writers, Sunday had

[54] See Dorothy Haines, *Sunday Observance and the Sunday Letter in Anglo-Saxon England* (Woodbridge, UK: D. S. Brewer, 2010), 17–19; Wilhelm Thomas, *Der Sonntag im frühen Mittelalter* (Göttingen, Germany: Vandenhoeck & Ruprecht, 1929), 51–2.

[55] L. L. McReavy, "The Sunday Repose from Labor," *Ephemerides theologicae Lovaniensis* 12 (1935), 291–323 (with Irish materials discussed at 322).

[56] Haines, *Sunday Observance*, 4–5.

already come to acquire associations with the Sabbath, and these would yield in time a set of restrictions on the behavior of Christians that would prove impossible to eradicate in spite of resistance from episcopal assemblies such as the Council of Orléans (538), which complained that such regulations were more Jewish than Christian:[57]

Quia persuasum est populis die Domineco agi cum caballis aut bubus et veiculis itinera non debere neque ullam rem ad victum praeparari vel ad netorem domus vel hominis pertenentem ullatenus exerciri, quae res ad Iudaicam magis quam ad Christeanam observantiam pertenere probatur, id statuimus, ut die Dominico, quod ante fieri licuit, liceat.

"Because the people are persuaded that on the Lord's day they may not go out on horses or in ox-drawn carts nor prepare anything for food nor apply themselves in any fashion to anything having to do with the cleaning of their home or their own person, which is shown to pertain more to Jewish than to Christian observance, we determined, that on the Lord's day, what was permissible to do before is [again] permissible."

That this provision, even after condemning these practices, goes on to permit them in as much they facilitate lay attendance of the Mass is exemplary of clerics' deep ambivalence. As was seen in Chapter 2, Gregory the Great had sometimes been disposed to permit and even encourage the observance of Jewish ceremonies (such as Sukkot) and legal ordinances among the recently converted as a means of initiating them into Christian sensibilities. But even he expressed suspicion of attempts to institute a Sunday "Sabbath" along with some willingness to tolerate its least extreme manifestations.[58]

In later centuries, most elite churchmen would learn to stomach observance of the "Lord's day" as a Sabbath and perceive its practical advantages while urging in their sermons that the legal portions of the Torah be understood spiritually and allegorically.[59] The earlier secular laws of Western Europe suggest that such remonstrations were received with indifference.[60] In time, the common practice was to interpret the Third Commandment with an emphasis on the version occurring in Deuteronomy (where the Sabbath rest is made a memorial of slavery in Egypt) over that in Exodus

57 Ibid., 8–9; the council is edited in *Concilia aevi Merovingici,* MGH Concilia 1, ed. F. Maasen (Hanover: Hahnsche Buchhandlung, 1893), 82 (cap. 31).

58 McReavy, "The Sunday Repose from Labor," 317.

59 On the ambivalence of Paulinus of Aquileia, see Thomas, *Der Sonntag,* 70–1. The tension seems to have been felt acutely by Ælfric: see *Ælfric's Catholic Homilies,* EETS ss. 5, ed. Malcolm Godden (London: Oxford University Press, 1979), 114–15.

60 In noting the biblicism of early Frankish pronouncements, Thomas notes that it is unclear whether the "lex" on which they claim to be grounded is Mosaic or prior territorial law and doubts whether the compilers knew themselves: see Thomas, *Der Sonntag*, 66.

(where it is tied to God's rest from creation). Its observance, however, was to be guided not by the strict prohibition of all work found alike in Exodus and Deuteronomy, but instead by the rules for appointed festivals expounded in Leviticus 23:7, which had required on these occasions a somewhat qualified abstention from "servile work" (*opus servile*), contrasting them (at 23:3) with the complete cessation of labor that was to accompany the Sabbath.[61] Just what constituted these proscribed *opera servilia* differed from text to text. One shared characteristic of laws promulgated within the territories of the Frankish Empire is a literal-minded tendency to understand this phrase as referring to the work of slaves.[62] This development is particularly evident in the language of the eighth-century *Lex Baiwariorum*. Though this text is often quoted in studies of the medieval Sunday, it is basic to an understanding of the tradition and thus reproduced here *in extenso*:[63]

Si quis die dominico operam servilem fecerit liber homo, id est, bovem iunxerit et cum carro ambulaverit, dextrum bovem perdat; si autem secaverit foenum aut collegerit aut messem secaverit aut collegerit vel aliquod opus servile fecerit die dominico, corripiatur semel vel bis, et si non emendaverit, rumpatur dorsus eius L percussionibus. Et si iterum praesumpserit operari die dominico, auferatur de rebus eius tertia pars, et si nec cessaverit, tunc perdat libertatem suam et sit servus qui noluit in die sancto esse liber. Servus autem pro tali crimine vapuletur. Et si non emendaverit, manum dextram perdat, quia talis causa vetanda est quae Deum ad iracundiam provocat [...]

"If a free person does servile work on Sunday, that is, if he should yoke oxen and go about in a cart, let him lose the right-hand ox; if, however, he cuts or collects hay or cuts or collects a harvest or does on a Sunday any sort of servile work, let him be warned once or twice, and if he does not correct himself [perhaps 'make compensation'], let him be beaten upon his back with fifty blows. And if he again

61 McReavy, "The Sunday Repose from Labor," 308. The prohibitions in Leviticus are phrased differently from the explanation of the Sabbath in Deuteronomy 5:14, where the emphasis is on abstention from *all* work as a memorial of the servile conditions of captivity in Egypt. Thomas finds the first nonallegorical usage of *opus servile* in the work of Martin of Braga; see *Der Sonntag*, 29.

62 Haines, *Sunday Observance*, 6–8. Nancy M. Thompson observes that the language of Frankish legislation urging that Sundays and other holy days be "sabbatized ... suggests that the directive was aimed specifically at the labouring classes": see "The Carolingian *de festiuitatibus* and the Blickling Book," in *The Old English Homily: Precedent, Practice, and Appropriation*, Studies in the Early Middle Ages 17, ed. Aaron J. Kleist (Turnhout, Belgium: Brepols, 2007), 97–120 at 106.

63 *Leges Baiwariorum*, MGH Leges Sectio I, Tom. 5/2 ed. Ernst von Schwind (Hanover: Hahnsche Buchhandlung, 1926), 349–51 (cap. VII, 4). The translation is somewhat indebted to Theodore John Rivers, *Laws of the Alamans and Bavarians* (Philadelphia: University of Pennsylvania Press, 1977), 137, though this rendering is not without problems (see following text). See also the similar provision in *Leges Alamannorum*, ed. Lehmann and Eckhardt, 98 (cap. XXXVIII).

should dare to work on Sunday, let the third part of his property be taken away. And if he still does not cease, then let him lose his freedom and become a slave who did not wish to be free on a holy day. However, let a slave be beaten for such a crime. And if he does not mend his ways, let him lose his right hand, as such acts are prohibited that incite God to anger. . . ."

Along with its attention to spelling out what constitute *opera servilia*, a new emphasis is evident. The main concern of the Bavarian clause is the free man (*liber homo*) who performs *operam servilem*.[64] A repeat offender, having not been corrected of this behavior even by scourging (*rumpatur dorsus eius*), sees his punishments culminate in his being reduced to servitude: "tunc perdat libertatem suam et sit servus qui noluit in die sancto esse liber." The logic of this law seems reminiscent of secular measures meant to police the mingling of slaves and free persons, as in the Frankish requirements that those who take slaves in marriage be reduced to slavery.[65] We may suspect that the purpose of the Sunday ordinance, as in these cases, was likewise as much to maintain the boundaries between slaves and free persons as to forestall God's wrath.

McReavy has argued that Theodore's treatment of this institution resists the forms of sabbatarianism manifest in Frankish legislation.[66] Certainly it avoids specific reference to the *opera servilia*, perhaps because of their inherent ambiguity. Instead, it is engagement in a variety of occupations having little or nothing to do with the work of agricultural slaves that places one in violation of the Sunday repose.[67] The Theodorean canon is as follows:[68]

Qui operantur die dominico greci prima vice arguunt secunda tollunt aliquid ab eis tertia vice partem tertiam de rebus eorum aut vapulant vel VII diebus peniteant.

64 This aspect of the clause is disguised somewhat by Rivers's rendering, where its opening sentence is translated "If anyone does servile work on Sunday, for a freeman...." It is plain that *quis* belongs with *liber homo*: the clause is not concerned simply with listing punishments for the various social classes, but with the particular problem of the *liber homo* who does slavish work.

65 See *Lex Salica*, MGH Leges Sectio I, Tom. 4/2, ed. Karl August Eckhardt (Hanover: Hahnsche Bucchandlung, 1969), 54 (cap. XIV.10): "Si quis ingenuus ancilla aliena priserit in coniugio, mallobergo bonimo, ipsi cum ea in seruicio implicetur"; discussed in Kemble, *Saxons in England*, I: 194.

66 McReavy, "The Sunday Repose from Labor," 322.

67 At *PT* II, viii, 1, Theodore asserts that Greeks and Romans were permitted on Sundays to engage in sailing and riding, and could ride in a carriage only to church; they were not permitted to make bread or to bathe.

68 *PT* I, xi, 1. Cap. 14 of *Cap. Dacheriana*, a possible source for several of the *Old English Canons of Theodore*, has *tollunt ... et vapulant* and thus seems to require harsher measures.

"Regarding those who work on Sunday: the Greeks will argue with them on the first occasion, on the second take something from them, on the third [take] a third of their possessions or beat them or [require] that they do penance for seven days."

According to McReavy, Theodore's attribution of these views to Greeks rather than to the scriptures (another departure from much Frankish legislation) implied that they were not to be understood as wholly binding on the English.[69] In other portions of his penitential, Theodore was satisfied merely to offer suggestions to priests while granting them the final say in matters of pastoral care, so the motives McReavy imputes to Theodore seem consistent with the general character of Theodore's legislative style.[70] One may conclude on the basis of this admittedly slim evidence that Theodore's enthusiasm for observance of the Sabbath was not much greater than that of the pope who had sent his predecessor to Kent less than a century prior.

The laws of the Kentish king Wihtræd and the West-Saxon king Ine, contemporaries of Theodore who consider Sunday regulations at some length, indicate that Theodore's judgments were offered amid conditions not unlike those implied by the Bavarian ordinance quoted earlier. Though neither the Latin phrase nor a vernacular equivalent is used in Ine, the focus remains implicitly on the prohibited *opera servilia*. Yet these laws give the impression that a number of the ostensibly free classes were servile for the purposes of Sunday.[71] Particularly hard to pin down is the social situation assumed by the early Kentish ordinance. We have seen that the *esne* of the early Kentish laws seems to have occupied a place between outright slavery and freedom given his right to marry.[72] His precarious position

[69] McReavy, "The Sunday Repose from Labor," 322–3.

[70] *PT* II, x, 1–5, e.g., is plainly made up of suggestions for the conduct of priests concerning the insane.

[71] Ine 3–3.2: "Gif ðeowmon wyrce on Sunnandæg be his hlafordes hæse, sie he frioh, 7 se hlaford geselle XXX scill. to wite. Gif þonne se ðeowa butan his gewitnesse wyrce, þolie his hyde [oððe hydgyldes]. Gif ðonne se frigea ðy dæge wyrce butan his hlafordes hæse, ðolie his freotes [oððe LX scll'; 7 preost twyscildig]." "If a slave works on Sunday by his lord's command, he shall become free, and the lord shall pay a fine of 30 shillings. If, however, the slave works without the cognizance of his master, he shall undergo the lash or pay the fine in lieu thereof. If, however, a freeman works on that day, except by his lord's command, he shall be reduced to slavery, or [pay a fine of] 60 shillings. A priest shall pay a double fine." See *Gesetze*, ed. Liebermann, I: 13 and 90, respectively; trans. Attenborough, *Laws of the Earliest English Kings*, 37.

[72] Wihtræd 9–11: "Gif esne ofer dryhtnes hæse þeowweorc wyrce an sunnan æfen efter hire setlgange oþ monan æfenes setlgang, LXXX scætta se dryhtne gebete. Gif esne deþ his rade þæs dæges, VI se wið dryhten gebete oþþe sine hyd. Gif friman þonne an ðane

may illuminate the status of the *frigea* referred to in Ine whose Sunday labor is culpable only if done *butan his hlafores hæse*, "without his lord's permission." That the same phrase is used to indicate the condition under which Wihtræd's *esne* may incur penalties for Sunday labor suggests that the freedom of Ine's *frigea* may have been nominal at best.

Strangely little is said in either of these ordinances about how the more elite members of free society are to comport themselves in spite of this being a focus of continental legislation. It is noteworthy that these early Kentish and West-Saxon laws give the free person caught laboring a way to avoid enslavement through his payment of a fine – an option not explicitly available in the *Lex Baiwariorum* though characteristic of other texts.[73] The indifference of these laws to the behavior of nonlaboring classes in any case shows them not to have been influenced by Theodore.[74]

Extant royal legislation goes nearly silent on the Sunday rest after the laws of Ine and Wihtræd before the subject reemerges during the mid-tenth century as a major concern.[75] Now attention shifts to the activities even of the highest orders of free society, with punishments for this class ranging from severe fines to enslavement (though never, perhaps

forbodenan timan, sio he healsfange scyldig; 7 se man se þæt arasie, he age healf þæt wite 7 þæt weorc." "If a servant, contrary to his lord's command, does servile work between sunset on Saturday evening and sunset on Sunday evening, he shall pay 80 sceattas to his lord. If a servant makes a journey of his own [on horseback] on that day, he shall pay 6 shillings compensation to his lord or undergo the lash. If a freeman works during the forbidden time, he shall forfeit his *healsfang,* and the man who informs against him shall have half the fine, and [the profits arising from] the labour." *Gesetze,* ed. Liebermann, I: 13; trans. Attenborough, *Laws of the Earliest English Kings,* 27. On the status of the *esne,* which underwent a series of changes throughout the Anglo-Saxon period, see Pelteret, *Slavery*, 271–4.

73 The option is available to free persons in the *Lex Frisionum* and *Pactus Legis Salicae,* on which see Haines, *Sunday Observance*, 6–7.

74 The disparity between Theodorean treatments and those occurring in these early secular laws is noted in Lisi Oliver, "Royal and Ecclesiastical Law in Seventh-Century Kent," in *Early Medieval Studies in Memory of Patrick Wormald*, 97–112 at 108–10.

75 Or just a century if Ine's laws are understood to have applied to the population of ninth-century Wessex, which seems doubtful; see Pelteret, *Slavery*, 82. The authenticity of Ine's laws is argued for in Wormald, *Making*, 103 and 278–80. It is intriguing that Ælfric of Eynsham seems to reject his contemporaries' obsession with shunning servile labor by interpreting this prohibition in a wholly spiritual sense: "Oðer restendæg is us toweard. þæt is ece líf. on ðam bið an dæg buton ælcere nihte. on þam we ús gerestað ecelice. gif we nu ðeowtlicera weorca. þæt sind synna geswicað," "We may anticipate another rest-day, that is eternal life, in which there will be one day without any night, wherein we will rest eternally, if we now cease from servile works – that is to say, our sins." *Ælfric's Catholic Homilies*, ed. Godden, 118–19. The equation of "servile works" with "sins" is probably taken from Augustine's commentary on the Gospel of John, discussed in Haines, *Sunday Observance*, 4.

significantly, beatings). These new regulations on Sunday observance are understood to bear the influence, not of Theodore, but of Carolingian capitularies offering a more searching view of the Sunday repose than was evident in the earlier *Leges barbarorum*. The approach is perceptible as early as the *Admonitio generalis* (789). Here the Sunday repose requires abstention from a wide range of activities, being understood as a time in which all classes would attend Mass and receive instruction in the faith.[76] No longer was it an occasion merely for the avoidance of the *opera servilia*, as it had been for the *Lex Baiwariorum* as well as the seventh-century laws of Wessex and Kent. Now the repose was to bring slave and aristocrat alike under visible subjection to God's law, in the process, perhaps, making the differences between them less significant.[77]

King Æthelstan appears to have been the first to attempt widening the scope of prohibited Sunday activities after the fashion of Carolingian capitularies. Cap. 24.1 of II Æthelstan, an ordinance assigned conventionally to the years 926–30, banned Sunday markets with a penalty of loss of goods and a fine of thirty shillings.[78] (The resulting amercement was not too far from what Ine and Wihtræd had demanded for a free laborer who works on Sunday.) The innovation seems to have been premature, for within a few years, we find the directive repealed in IV Æthelstan 2; it is just possible that the drafter of these ordinances, Archbishop Wulfhelm, was unable to enforce them and compelled to retreat.[79] Thus the situation of Sunday law in the first half of the tenth century may have been little different from what obtained in the late seventh and early eighth centuries in England.

Not until the eleventh century would the reshaping of English Sunday law initiated by Æthelstan have lasting effects. In one of his earliest enactments, the so-called Laws of Edward and Guthrum (1002), Wulfstan reasserts the ban first articulated in II Æthelstan against Sunday markets and preserves its punishments.[80] When he revisits this subject during the reign of Æthelred, we find a range even of leisure occupations forbidden, the motive for which was a sense that the affluent should be compelled

[76] Carolingian influence on later practice is noted in Haines, *Sunday Letter*, 23, and its character described on 15–16. For the Sunday regulations of the *Admonitio generalis*, see *Capitularia regum francorum I*, MGH Legum Sectio II, Capitularia I, ed. Alfred Boretius (Hanover: Hahnsche Bucchandlung, 1883), 61 (cap. 81).

[77] That the intent was to forestall divine wrath is evident from V Æthelred 26.

[78] Haines, *Sunday Letter*, 21.

[79] Sarah Foot takes the view that this reform of Sunday observance "proved unworkable." See *Æthelstan: The First King of England* (New Haven, CT: Yale University Press, 2011), 145. Wormald notes (*Making*, 291n130) that the situation of these Æthelstanian clauses may be more complicated than typically assumed. I hope to revisit questions surrounding these laws in a future publication.

[80] *Gesetze*, ed. Liebermann, I: 132–3 (caps. 7–9.1).

to join with those who labored for them in observance of fasts if England was to be spared divine wrath.[81]

We have seen that Sunday legislation in England begins with something close to the earlier Frankish practice, as outlined in the *Lex Baiwariorum*, with Sunday conceived of primarily as an occasion for abstention from servile labor and thus of the greatest consequence for slaves and dependent free laborers. Not until the lifetime of Wulfstan does English secular law adopt a position closer to Theodore's, with the Sunday repose now encompassing the activities of free persons as much (perhaps more) than those in servitude.[82] Only one or two features of English legislation on the Sunday repose seem to have remained constant through centuries of change. While the *Lex Baiwariorum* and the penitential of Theodore assert that beatings are to be available as punishments for free persons who refuse to observe the Sabbath, nowhere are beatings for the free offender even suggested as a penalty in either Wihtræd's or Ine's laws. That the situation persisted in Wulfstan's legislation even as the prelate sought to align English observance with Carolingian models suggests it was an element of English custom.[83] In addition, neither the enactments of Wihtræd and Ine nor those of Æthelstan and Wulfstan permit a free person merely to be scolded on the first offense. Instead, free persons seem to have been expected immediately to undergo the full penalty. All of these variations may be schematized as follows:

Sunday Legislation in England and Francia

	Immediate Punishments for the Free?	Punishments Confined to Servile Work Only?	Beatings Administered to Free as Well as Slaves?
Lex Baiwariorum	N	Y	Y
Poenitentiale Theodori	N	N	Y
Kentish and early West Saxon laws	Y	Y	N
Later (Wulfstanian) English laws	Y	N	N

[81] See VI Æthelred 22.1, which bans on Sunday markets, meetings, hunting, and other "worldlicra weorca," translated by Robertson (97) as "secular employments." Hunting in particular would have been understood as an aristocratic amusement.

[82] Haines notes that Ine's and Wihtræd's laws "are most closely related to the Germanic law codes of the Continent"; Haines, *Sunday Letter*, 20.

[83] "Edward and Guthrum" caps. 7–9.1 threaten free persons with fines or enslavement should they fail to pay them and slaves with beatings that may be avoided by payment.

We may now turn at last to the clause of the *Canons* mentioned earlier, whose response to Theodore's penitential reflects, I would argue, a particular phase of the tradition outlined in the foregoing discussion:

Ða ðe wyrceað sunnandæge, æt þam forman cyrre Grecas hy ofercidað; æt þam oðrum cyrre, nimað hwæthwæge þæs þe hy wyrcean; æt þam þriddan cyrra þæne þriddan dæl þæs þe hi mid gescyldigað; and gif hit syn þeowe men, and hi hit heora willan don, syn hy beswungene; and gif hit syn freo men, fæsten hy seofonniht flæsce and ealað.

"Of those who work on Sunday, the Greeks chide them on the first occasion; on the second, they take from them whatever they are working on; on the third, they take away a third of the things with which they have incurred guilt: and if they are slaves, and they do it of their own volition, they are beaten; and if they are free men, they are to fast for seven days on bread and ale."

In spite of its alteration of its source, this clause has attracted little comment. Haines confines herself to an observation that the canon "adapts the punishment for a third offense to what looks like something closer to the secular legal codes: slaves are to be flogged and freemen to do seven days of penance."[84] I am not sure, however, that all changes in this clause show influences wholly external to the tradition of vernacular penitentials. Indeed, the behavior of other members of this tradition regarding Sunday observance and questions of slavery makes a strict division between secular and ecclesiastical law difficult to discern. Instead, a range of norms seems to have come into effect. The suspicion inherent in many vernacular penitentials that continental canons offered too much leniency toward slaves is corrected here by adding the requirement that a slave be beaten. The characteristically English resistance to the notion of treating free persons in the manner of slaves where the Sunday repose was concerned, which was more a matter of custom than formal law, is dealt with by eliminating the requirement that a thrice-offending free person be beaten. Indeed, the translator's desire to insulate free persons from punishment is perhaps evident in one change likely to be overlooked. Whereas both Theodore and the Bavarian ordinance had prescribed for thrice-offending freemen the loss of a third of their possessions ("partem tertiam de rebus eorum" [Theodore], "auferatur de rebus eius tertia pars" [*Lex Baiwariorum*]), the *Canons* reduce this to loss of "a third of the things with which they have incurred guilt," a qualification close to the statement in Wihtræd cap. 11 seeming to require that an informant

Not once does any English legislation suggest that free persons who violate the Sunday repose should be beaten.

[84] Haines, *Sunday Observance*, 31.

be given the profits from the offender's work.[85] When we consider this clause of the *Canons* solely in terms of its additions to the Theodorean text, we see that its translator reacted to Theodore's provisions by writing into them something of the atmosphere of earlier English secular law in particular, where the conduct of the laboring classes is the chief concern (as it is not in Theodore) and where free offenders are to be spared the humiliation of bodily punishments or losing too great a share of their belongings for infractions. The translator's retention of the mild seven-day penance for the offending freeman likewise seems harmonious with the pre-Æthelredian state of English "Sabbath" law.[86] For such leniency to have been countenanced during Wulfstan's career seems improbable.

Given the possibility established in Chapter 2 that the *Canons* were composed in advance of the Benedictine Reform, this clause may give some sense of why Æthelstan's attempt to ban activities other than the traditional *opera servilia* fell on deaf ears. As long as the Sunday repose was a matter principally affecting slaves and dependent laborers – as the *Canons* hasten to add in their version of Theodore's clause – the business of aristocratic life could go on without hindrance. Not until the catastrophes of Æthelred's reign, apparently, would English magnates be willing to forego activities of their own in the hope of restoring divine favor for what remained of the English-speaking portion of England.[87] Thus the Sunday clause in the *Canons* is not merely an ordinance showing influence from secular law. Its language echoes the earlier stages of secular law on Sunday observance, in which keeping Sunday properly meant keeping one's slaves and dependent laborers from working and suffering the consequent losses rather than doing some of their work oneself.

SLAVERY AND THE HOUSEHOLD

It has been seen that ordinances ostensibly directed at enforcement of the Sunday repose show a concern, unremarked in prior scholarship, to

85 Both II Æthelstan (cap. 24.1) and Wulfstan's "Laws of Edward and Guthrum" (cap. 7) stipulate that a freeman engaging in trading on Sunday is to lose the goods in question ("þolige þæs ceapes"). Other forms of Sunday labor when performed by the free are remedied with fines, with failure to pay leading to penal slavery. See *Gesetze*, ed. Liebermann, I: 164, 132.

86 A seven-day penance would have been seen as remarkably trivial in the later period outlined by Haines, particularly given Wulfstan's reliance upon severe fines or enslavement.

87 On the crises of Æthelred's reign and the liturgical reforms undertaken in response, see Simon Keynes, "An Abbot, an Archbishop, and the Viking Raids of 1006–7 and 1009–12," *Anglo-Saxon England* 36 (2007), 151–220 at 171 and 184.

maintain clear boundaries between slaves and free persons. Such measures are perhaps to be expected in an environment in which the status of some laborers, as was the case with the *esne*, might be uncertain. What remains of this chapter will consider another set of remarks long held to show the compassion of Anglo-Saxon bishops for the unfree. These are found in Wulfstan's *Sermo ad Anglos*, among whose major themes the treatment of the free in a servile manner figures prominently. A case in point is his denunciation of those who have sold their kin into slavery:[88]

> Eac we witan georne hwær seo yrmð gewearð þæt fæder gesealde bearn wið weorðe 7 beorn his modor, 7 broþor sealde oþerne fremdum to gewealde; 7 eal þæt syndan micle 7 egeslice dæda, understande se þe wille.
>
> "Also we are very much aware of the occurrence of the crime in which a father sells his son for money, and a son his mother, and a brother sells another into the power of strangers; and these are all heavy and terrible deeds; let him understand who will."

That Wulfstan found this practice particularly abhorrent is suggested by its placement immediately after the rather hideous anecdote concerning a group of men who purchase a slave collectively for use as a prostitute only to sell her later "for money" (*wið weorðe*). Commentary on this portion of the *Sermo* has been sparse. Bethurum's edition offers the only published observations on its treatment of the sale of kin of which I am aware:[89]

> The Confessional of Egbert 27 says that if compelled by the greatest necessity (probably the danger of starvation) a father may sell into slavery a son seven years old or under, but not one older than that unless the son is willing. The Penitential of Pseudo-Egbert forbids the selling of kindred under the same penalty as selling Christians to the heathen.

With its conjecture that a father would be driven only by near-starvation to sell his son into slavery, Bethurum's note lends itself to the view that

88 *The Homilies of Wulfstan*, ed. Bethurum, 270–1.

89 *Homilies of Wulfstan*, ed. Bethurum, 362. In fact there are not one but two instances in which vernacular penitentials express approval for the sale of kin into slavery, the second of which occurs in the *Canons*. If we include the source of the provisions in the *Scriftboc* and *Canons*, the penitential of Theodore, three canons found in English manuscripts give their permission for members of one's family to be sold. See *Das altenglische Bussbuch*, ed. Spindler, 183 (cap. XV.18.c): "Se fæder his sunu gyf him mycel ðearf bið, he hine mot in þeowet gesyllan, oððæt he bið VII-wintre; ofer þæt, butan þæs sunu willan he hine ne mot syllan"; *Canons of Theodore* A 133: "Se fæder mot his sunu for mycelre nydþearfe on þeowet gesyllan oð þæt he bið seofonwintre, ac syððan he ne mot buton his willan." Both are derived from (and translate with little variation) *PT* II, xiii, 1: "Pater filium suum necessitate coactus potestatem habet tradere in servitium VII annos. deinde sine voluntate filii licentiam tradendi non habet," "If he is compelled by necessity, a father has

there was no real difference between how the *Scriftboc* and the *Penitential* viewed this practice.[90] (The text in question says only that such an act might be motivated by "great need.") Her remarks differ little from those made by Liebermann, who had claimed that the *Penitential* prescribes excommunication for this offense.[91] A more complex situation becomes evident upon direct examination of the text:[92]

Gif hwylc cristen man his agen bearn oððe his nehstan mæg wið ænigum wurðe sylle, næbbe he nænne gemanan mid cristenum mannum ær he hine alysed hæbbe of þam þeowdome; gif he þonne hine begitan ne mæge, dæle swa mycel feoh for hine swa he ær mid him nam 7 alyse oðerne of þeowdome 7 gefreoge þæne 7 fæste VII wican on hlafe 7 on wætere; 7 gif he þæs gestreones næbbe þæt he hine alysan mæge, fæste þonne XXVIII wicæna on hlafe 7 on wætere.

"If any Christian man sells his own child or his near kinsman for any amount of money, he is not to associate with Christian men before he has released him [his kinsman] from servitude; if, however, he may not redeem him, let him give as much money as he received for him and release another [person] from slavery and manumit him and fast for seven weeks on bread and water; and if he does not have the money with which to free him, let him then fast for twenty-eight weeks on bread and water."

We can see that, for those wishing to make amends, the offense is potentially remediable with a twenty-eight-week fast, not excommunication. Yet the text begins with an unqualified condemnation of those who sell their kin, a clear departure from the practice of earlier penitentials. The zeal of the author becomes all the more evident when we consider the relationship of this clause to the text it reworks. The source of this clause, a chapter of Halitgar's "Roman Penitential," does not address the sale of one's children; rather, it requires penance of one who *parentem suum vendiderit*.[93] Latin *parens* may refer to one's immediate progenitor or to one's relative – but never, of course, to a child. In the source, therefore, the wrong most likely consisted of extreme filial impiety; no norm is articulated here against the sale of *all* kin. In having his version refer specifically to the offense of selling one's own child or near kinsman, the author of the *Penitential* established a category of offense not known

the power to sell his son of seven years of age into slavery; after that, he has not the right to sell him without his consent" (trans. McNeill and Gamer, *Medieval Handbooks*, 211).

90 On the sale of one's kin in cases of famine, see Wyatt, *Slaves and Warriors*, 26 and n. 107.

91 For his part, Liebermann misquotes the Theodorean clause underlying cap. XV.18.c of the *Scriftboc* and cap. A 133 of the *Canons:* the version he adduces, *Pater filium potestatem habet tradere in servitium 14 annorum, deinde non,* occurs in no member of the Theodore cycle of which I am aware (*Gesetze,* ed. Liebermann, II: 708 [5a]).

92 *Die altenglische Version,* ed. Raith, 57 (cap. IV.21).

93 *Bussbücher*, ed. Schmitz, I: 487; also *Bußordnungen*, ed. Wasserschleben, 374.

to his predecessors and thus turned his back on previous vernacular canons, which had allowed for this very practice. His rejection of older views, as will be shown in Chapter 4, is in keeping with his responses to the rules set forth by earlier penitentials on the conduct of the newly married.

That the *Canons* and *Scriftboc*, in allowing for parents to sell their kin into slavery, argue for something that the Reform-era English church would find increasingly distasteful seems an inevitable conclusion. While the possibility that allowances for the sale of kin might still be made in the later period must, of course, be acknowledged, these clauses, when joined to others that seem reflective of earlier conditions, seem to indicate authorship in a period closer to that of their Theodorean source, in which such behavior was countenanced by the Church, than to the Benedictine Reform, in which these transactions were denounced. In condemning the sale of kin in his *Sermo* without qualification, Wulfstan may well have been giving voice to views that surfaced late in the history of the Anglo-Saxon church.

AN ECCLESIASTICAL REFORM OF SLAVERY?

This chapter has shown that English prescriptive sources appear to share in their treatments of slavery a concern that clear lines be established between slaves and the free, and above all that free persons never endure treatments typically allotted to slaves. This is a concern evident in Frankish legislation that seems only to have grown more intense once it found roots in English soil. Such a tendency, along with the aggressive restoration of seigneurial prerogatives over the unfree found throughout the corpus of Old English penitentials (and in opposition to the language of their sources), perhaps provides us some framework through which to view Wulfstan's condemnation of those who sell their kin into slavery. In the study referred to at the outset of this chapter, I expressed some doubts about the view, frequently maintained over the course of the twentieth century, that Wulfstan was in any sense the reformer of slavery that Whitelock and others made him out to be. I continue to doubt such claims for Wulfstan, primarily because it has yet to be shown that his remarks on slavery, however much they may go against the grain of earlier normative statements, are any different in their motivation from the essentials of the tradition against which they react. All readers of Wulfstan's *Sermo* known that it culminates in an episode concerning a slave who, fleeing to the Danes, returns to enslave his master 'through

God's anger'.[94] Elsewhere, Wulfstan narrates with horror that, should a slave escape to the Danes and return to slay his master, he would be obliged to pay no wergild; should, however, the master slay his former slave in self-defense, he would be obliged to pay for him as if he were free.[95] In the midst of World War II, Whitelock influentially characterized Wulfstan as possessed by a desire to "stop the slave trade"; but the statements just referred to are not those of a bishop opposed on principle to the practice of slavery.[96] Wulfstan's casting the Danes as instruments of divine punishment (as had Alcuin to the monks of Lindisfarne) presumes that a rightly ordered world is one in which slave and master are each secure in their place – a view not unlike that expressed in the passage from Ælfric's *Colloquy* mentioned near the outset of this chapter. Throughout the *Sermo,* the wrongs of the English do not reside in their use and sale of slaves, nor in violent abuse of them. It is their exploitation of slaves for sexual purposes, and their habit of subjecting members of their own kin to servitude, that Wulfstan particularly condemns. Both in a sense involve the sort of commingling of slave and free bodies that English legislation strove from its earliest period to prevent. While the sale of one's kin into slavery does indeed receive increasing condemnation toward the end of the Anglo-Saxon period, and while this constitutes a genuine reform, it is not one motivated by moral concerns about slavery. Rather, it is prompted by the fear that such practices might erode the distinctions between slaves and free persons.

Such concerns are evident in Wulfstan's complaint in the *Sermo* that the *unforworhte* are being sold abroad. We may suspect that in back of this and similar statements in the Wulfstanian corpus is Deuteronomy 24:7, a clause condemning the kidnapping and sale abroad of the free.[97] That this – and not the maltreatment of those condemned to penal slavery – is the true concern of this passage becomes evident when it is viewed alongside parallel passages in penitentials to which Wulfstan would likely have had access. In its reference to those sold abroad as *sare beswicene and hreowlice besyrwde,* "sorely tricked and miserably deceived," the *Sermo* seems plainly to be more aligned with these penitential canons than with

94 "And oft þræl þæne þegen þe ær wæs his hlaford cnyt swyþe fæste 7 wyrcð him to þræle þurh Godes yrre." *The Homilies of Wulfstan*, ed. Bethurum, 271.

95 Ibid.

96 Dorothy Whitelock, "Archbishop Wulfstan: Homilist and Statesman," *Transactions of the Royal Historical Society* 24 (1942), 24–45 at 42n1.

97 "If any man be found soliciting his brother of the children of Israel, and selling him shall take a price, he shall be put to death, and thou shalt take away the evil from the midst of thee" (Douay).

secular laws dealing with this subject or earlier church councils and papal decrees that condemn the sale outright. Regino of Prüm's *Ecclesiastical Discipline* and the ninth-century *Penitential of Pseudo-Theodore* – two penitentials Wulfstan employs elsewhere in his corpus that are, for some reason, nowhere considered as direct textual sources for this portion of the *Sermo* – both prescribe severe penances for those who lure the previously free into slavery, and do so in language that Wulfstan seems closely to emulate. For example, *Pseudo-Theodore*'s "suaderit, ac in alteram regionam seduxerit" sounds very much like the *Sermo*'s similarly tautological construction. Regino's "eum blandiendo seduxerit et vendiderit et extra patriam in captivitatem miserit" is perhaps even closer.[98] Though the victim invariably ends up abroad, the ruse is not for that reason condemned: the penitential remedy is to restore him to freedom, and the additional seven years of penance are prescribed "pro illo furto," "for that theft." All of this, I think, reinforces the conclusion for which I have argued throughout the present chapter. In lamenting that the *unforworhte* were so treated, Wulfstan means no more than what he says: it's a shame when free and innocent people are treated like slaves. There is no condemnation here of the sale of guilty slaves abroad.

Whether Wulfstan's statement against the trade in Cnut's code likewise indicates his disdain for the international slave trade seems equally open to question. This provision has been somewhat less discussed but nonetheless figures significantly in arguments holding Wulfstan to have disapproved of the international trade in slaves, and so it merits brief

[98] Regino c. II.41: "Interrogandum, si aliquis hominem liberum aut servum alterius, aut peregrinum et adventitium furatus fuerit, aut eum blandiendo seduxerit et vendiderit et extra patriam in captivitatem miserit, aut si aliquis Iudaeo vel pagano Christianum mancipium vendiderit ...," "It is to be asked, whether someone has stolen either a free man or someone else's slave or a traveler, or has with deceit tricked [him] and sold him and sent him into captivity beyond his homeland, or whether someone has sold a slave to Jews or to pagans..." (Regino of Prüm, *De synodalibus causis et disciplinis ecclesiasticis*, ed. F. G. A. Wasserschleben [Leipzig: Engelmann, 1840; repr. 1964], 212); *Pseudo-Theodore* c. XXVII.4. "Si quis Christianus alterum Christianum suaderit, ac in alteram regionum seduxerit, ibique eum vendiderit pro proprio servo, ille non est dignus inter Christianos requiem habere, donec redimat eum, et reducat ad proprium locum... 5. Si quis Christianus alterum Christianum vagantem repererit, eumque furatus fuerit, ac vendiderit, non debet habere inter Christianos requiem, donec redimat eum, et pro illo furto VII annos poeniteat," "If a Christian lures another, and tricks him into traveling to another country, and there sells him as if he were his own slave, he is not worthy to be buried among Christians, until he buys him back and takes him back to his own homeland.... If a Christian should meet another who is traveling and steal him, and sell him, he may not be buried among Christians until he buys him back, and does penance for this theft for seven years" (*Bußordnungen*, ed. Wasserschleben, 611).

consideration here. The clause appears near the outset of Cnut's "secular" laws, and the version quoted in the following text is from the earliest witness to these (Cotton Nero A.i):

And we beodað, þæt man Cristene men ealles to swiðe of earde ne sylle ne on hæðendome huru ne gebringe; ac beorge man georne, þæt man þa saule ne forfare, þe Crist mid his agenum life gebohte.

Robertson translated this chapter as follows: "We forbid the all too prevalent practice of selling Christian people out of the country, and especially of conveying them into heathen lands, but care shall be zealously taken that the souls which Christ bought with his own life be not destroyed."[99] Should this indeed be the correct rendering of the clause, we would have no reason to doubt the assertion that "no exceptions" are made here for the sale of the condemned (even if the earlier laws penned for Æthelred do hint at such concessions), or Liebermann's claim that this chapter is composed in such a way "so that no one, not even a penal slave or a Celt, could be sold to the heathen."[100] But consideration of the manuscript context of this clause offers little support to the dominant view of its significance. Robertson's translation of Cnut's laws, to which Whitelock resorts with some frequency in her edition of the *Sermo* (though she does not do so explicitly here) is based upon the version occurring in one of the latest and least accurate manuscripts of Cnut's code: BL Harley MS 55, which was composed during the reign of Henry I.[101] Like its near-contemporary, CCCC 383, the Harley codex occasionally replaces the verb *beodan* "announce, command" with *forbeodan* "prohibit" (though the former does not do so in this instance). As is often the case in the editorial history of Cnut's laws, the standard translation appears to issue from the latest and seemingly least trustworthy manuscripts: we have seen that the oldest witness has *beodan*.

That Robertson's standard edition favors the probably corrupt reading *forbeodan* is, perhaps, an effect of Liebermann's editorial assumptions. The occurrence of *forbeodan* in Lambarde's *Archaionomia* (which Liebermann assumed erroneously to be based upon now-lost manuscripts), and of its equivalent in the three Latin translations composed

99 Robertson, *Laws*, 177 (II Cnut 3).

100 *Gesetze*, II: 693 sec. 12g. David A. E. Pelteret, "Slave Raiding and Slave Trading in Early England," *Anglo-Saxon England* 9 (1981), 99–114 at 110n89. For the clause in Æthelred's legislation from which this one appears to be derived, see n. 44.

101 On the date and provenance of the manuscript, see most recently Wormald, *Making*, 185–90.

after the Conquest, appear to have ensured its avoidance of further and, in my view, necessary scrutiny.[102] With Liebermann's views about the provenance of readings in Lambarde's *Archainomia* having been decisively repudiated in studies by Kenneth Sisam and Patrick Wormald, we can probably dispense with any suggestion that *forbeodan* might descend from the archetype. It seems likelier that the added prefix is one of many "corrective" emendations of the twelfth-century manuscripts, few of which seem founded on anything other than a highly imperfect understanding either of late Old English or of slavery, which by the twelfth century was a vanishing institution.[103]

For Wulfstan to have made some concession to the sale of condemned slaves would seem consistent with the logic of legislative statements in this one's immediate vicinity. Chapters 4 through 6 of II Cnut ask that various criminals and apostates be driven from the land, and similar clauses adjoin the prohibition of the sale of slaves abroad in VI Æthelred. A rendering of the first half of this chapter more sensitive to its context would be something like the following: "We command that one not sell entirely too hastily (*ealles to swiðe*) Christian men out of the country, at least [Liebermann: *wenigstens*] that they not convey them into heathen lands ...."[104] Those who own slaves are admonished to avoid the practice, but there is no outright prohibition. Because Whitelock regards the similar language with which Wulfstan addresses execution in adjacent clauses as being intended merely to "limit the application of the death

[102] *Instituta Cnuti:* "[P]rohibemus, ne Christiani gentibus extra hanc terram uenundentur nec in paganismo..."; *Consiliatio Cnuti*: "Interdicimus etiam, ne Christiani foras a patria uenundentur, presertim in paganism[um] non tradantur..."; *Quadripartitus's precipimus* must be derived from a manuscript containing *we beodaþ*, and shows that this was considered a valid reading of this clause by some of its earliest commentators. See *Gesetze*, ed. Liebermann, I: 311.

[103] In holding the language of this clause to make some allowance for the sale of slaves abroad, my views differ from those expressed in A. G. Kennedy, "Cnut's Law Code of 1018," *Anglo-Saxon England* 11 (1983), 57–82, where the language of this provision is dealt with in more detail than any study of which I am aware. Here *unforworhte* in the prior Æthelredian clause is taken to be "semantically superfluous," an impossibility given arguments presented toward the beginning of this chapter concerning the use of this term in vernacular penitentials, whose evidence has yet to be discussed in conjunction with Wulfstan's employment of it. As for *ealles to swiðe,* Kennedy doubts that it may be understood as "indicating here a more tolerant attitude to the international slave trade" (68).

[104] Liebermann's translation is not far from what I suggest here: "Und wir gebieten (verbieten A; Beschluss der Witan ist D), dass man christliche Menschen nicht allzu rasch ausser Landes verkaufe, wenigstens nicht ins Heidentum bringe; sondern ernstlich hüte man sich, dass man jene Seelen (-le G) nicht verderbe, die Christus mit seinem eigenen Leben erkauft hat."

penalty," there seem no reasons not to assign it the same meaning when applied to the sale of slaves.[105] Given William of Malmesbury's claim that the international slave trade persisted in spite of episcopal denunciations because dues from the trade swelled royal revenues – and because the trade was engaged in by members of Cnut's own household – there seem abundant reasons why Wulfstan would have adopted a more conciliatory tone where this issue was concerned.[106]

CONCLUSION

When a broader range of evidence is considered, Wulfstan's views on slavery seem little removed from those attested elsewhere in the early North Sea world. As Pelteret has recently shown, both Old English and Norse literatures represent those in servitude as somehow ontologically different from those outside of it.[107] We see in texts of this era some early signs of slaves being regarded as physically as well as morally inferior to their masters.[108] The "ideological" nature of these constructs is readily apparent: they insist on the natural basis of man-made institutions even as this is belied by the practices of enslavement, which seem routinely to have drawn into servitude those were previously free. To permit free persons to be beaten when this bore associations with slavery, and to allow free persons to sell their kin, would be to acknowledge the factitiousness of an institution held by most literate persons of this era to have been established by divine ordinance. We have seen that a drive to maintain the utter abasement of bound laborers was peculiar to the English, a major reason for the divergence of their ecclesiastical laws from those observed on the Continent. Such tendencies were not without consequences for the English. After the Conquest, some of the Norman magnates who would govern them

105 Whitelock, "Wulfstan, Homilist and Statesman," 42. That *beodan* must have the sense "command" is evident from the immediately following clause: "And we beodað, þæt man eard georne clænsian aginne on æghwylcan ende 7 manfulra dæda æghwær geswice." Perhaps because no manuscript adds *for-* to this clause, Robertson translates as follows: "And we enjoin that the purification of the land in every part shall be diligently undertaken, and that evil deeds shall everywhere be put an end to" (177).

106 See Pelteret, *Slavery*, 76.

107 Pelteret, "The Image of the Slave in Some Anglo-Saxon and Norse Sources," *Slavery and Abolition* 23 (2002), 75–88.

108 In addition to Pelteret's observances on the tendency of Anglo-Saxon and Norse literary sources to depict slaves as having dark complexions – a characteristic of demons in hagiography – we should consider the observations of Christopher Dyer mentioned toward the outset of this chapter.

would see their attitude toward bound laborers as hopelessly backward and requiring the bitter medicine of reform from without.[109] The Old English penitentials offer evidence that confirms this view, and their exclusion from consideration by Liebermann and others has long made Anglo-Saxon institutions appear more charitable to slaves than they are likely to have been.

[109] William of Malmesbury held the Norman conquest of England to be God's judgment on the English for harboring a lazy, corrupt aristocracy given to the sexual abuse of slaves as well as to selling free and slave alike to foreigners for easy gain: "Illud erat a natura abhorrens, quod multi ancillas suas ex se grauidas, ubi libidini satisfacissent, aut ad publicum prostibulum aut ad externum obsequium uenditabant," "One practice in particular was perfectly inhuman: many of them got their own serving-maids with child and, when they had sated their lust on the girls, sold them to a public brothel or to service in a foreign country." Portions of William's eulogy of Anglo-Saxon England may be indebted to Wulfstan's *Sermo ad Anglos*. See *William of Malmesbury, Gesta Regum Anglorum*, 2 vols., ed. and trans. R. A. B. Mynors, R. M. Thomson, and M. Winterbottom (Oxford: Clarendon, 1998), I: 458–9 (iii.245).

4

The Law of the Household

Marriage and Sexuality

It has long been understood that the Germanic-speaking peoples likely shared notions of married life different from, and occasionally incompatible with, those favored by the monks and bishops who sought their conversion. For a sense of these norms, scholars of the nineteenth and early twentieth centuries were content to dwell upon sources that ostensibly had little in common, considering the laws written in Latin between the reigns of Clovis and Charlemagne alongside Scandinavian legislative and narrative texts composed as late as the thirteenth century. Out of these diverse materials was built a system of marriage law that supposedly governed the thinking of Franks, Lombards, and Norwegians alike.[1]

In more recent decades, resistance to the pan-Germanic approach of earlier scholars seems to have shifted the focus of historians of medieval marriage. None of the leading surveys of this subject published over the last several years contains any substantial remarks about Old Scandinavian materials, as was commonplace prior to World War II.[2] Undoubtedly, this development has left present-day research on safer ground. While the

[1] The practice has been disparaged in Karras, "The Myth of *Friedelehe*," 127–31 and *passim:* "If we exclude the automatic assumption that everything in any 'Germanic' law code must derive from a primitive, common Germanic culture, however, it is not at all clear why the Lombard laws provide evidence for Frankish social arrangements.... The project of reconstructing prehistoric, common Germanic institutions from thirteenth-century Norse sources is dubious in and of itself." An overview of this scholarly tradition is found in Wormald, *Making*, 1–28. For reasons given earlier (see Chapter 1, n. 78), I am not sure that this approach should be dismissed entirely.

[2] An influential example is afforded by cap. 11 of Rudolf Huebner, *History of Germanic Private Law*, trans. Francis S. Philbrick (Boston: Little, Brown & Co., 1918; repr. 1968). Sparing references to Old Scandinavian (primarily Icelandic) laws on marriage occur in Reynolds, *Marriage in the Western Church,* at 111 and 351.

Leges Barbarorum impose interpretative problems of their own, they at least have the advantage of being contemporary sources, whereas Norse prose narratives – a chief fund of material for earlier scholarship – may postdate the era of Icelandic settlement by three or more centuries.[3]

Recent work on these sources has thus yielded a set of assumptions more tentative than the often-fanciful conjectures of the nineteenth century. Gone from recent studies are speculations about primitive Germanic matriarchy, for example.[4] Yet the notion of a distinctly Germanic approach to marriage has not been abandoned outright. It is now something of a commonplace that marriages among the continental Germans were more easily dissolved than they would be subsequently under church law, with most sources "regard[ing] the first year of marriage as a trial period, at the end of which the union might be terminated unless a child was conceived."[5]

The definition of marriage has also seemed to contemporary scholars more fluid than it would later be under ecclesiastical influence. Concubinage, it has been argued, existed alongside more formalized unions among various Germanic-speaking peoples and was perhaps regarded as no less able to produce legitimate children.[6] The leniency of such arrangements is perhaps an effect of all marital unions among the Franks and Lombards being contingent upon consummation, as was not the case in Roman law. Brundage offers the following blunt formulation: "Marriage in Germanic law consisted simply of sexual intercourse accompanied by an intention to live together permanently and have children."[7] Whatever freedom traditional marriage law afforded to couples appears to have been framed in such a way as to have been enjoyed principally by husbands, for in cases of adultery – perceived in this era according to Brundage as "an exclusively female crime" – men faced fewer difficulties dissolving their unions than women.[8]

Anglo-Saxon materials play a remarkably minor role in both the earlier and later phases of the search for "Germanic marriage."[9] The most

[3] For reassessments of "Germanic law" as a category, see Reynolds, *Marriage in the Western Church*, 66–101; James Brundage, *Law, Sex, and Christian Society*, 124–36.

[4] See, e.g., Herbert Meyer, "Friedelehe und Mutterrecht," *Zeitschrift der Savigny-Stiftung für Rechtsgeschichte. Kanonistische Abteilung* 47 (1927), 198–286. His arguments are discussed in Karras, "Myth of *Friedelehe*," 122.

[5] Brundage, *Law, Sex and Christian Society*, 131.

[6] Ibid., 130; see also Huebner, *History of Germanic Private Law*, 588.

[7] Brundage, *Law, Sex and Christian Society*, 130.

[8] Ibid., 132.

[9] While studies such as those of Heinrich Brunner and Karl von Amira do take note of Anglo-Saxon legislation, the approach is often selective and unsystematic.

significant surveys of medieval marriage law to be published in the last three decades say hardly a word about Old English texts, while the sole study to address the subject of marriage in Anglo-Saxon England focuses almost exclusively on lexical matters.[10] The reasons why scholarly attention has been diverted elsewhere may reside in the nature of the Old English materials. Aside from their existing in a vernacular that is not a part of every historian's training, the relative silence of royal legislation on matters of marriage when compared to analogous laws issued in Francia has probably contributed to their neglect. What little these laws have to say about marriage is of doubtful significance. One would find it hard indeed to build any kind of system out of the terse judgments of Æthelberht, for example, whose remarks on the particulars of marriage are both the most abundant of those issued by pre-Conquest legislators and the most obscure.[11]

While the Old English penitentials have a great deal more to say on this subject, here the difficulty lies in their dependence on a non-English set of sources whose provisions may not tell us much about Anglo-Saxon customs. This chapter will show that the way in which these sources are treated may afford a sense of what marriage looked like in pre-Conquest England somewhat clearer than those adumbrated by the more routinely consulted texts. For historians, perhaps the main value of the Old English penitentials resides in their further demonstrating the lack of uniform

[10] See Fischer, *Engagement, Wedding and Marriage in Old English*.

[11] A long and probably fruitless debate has surrounded the clauses in the code of King Æthelberht of Kent that discuss marriage by purchase given their use of the verb *gebycgan* "buy" to describe the acquisition of a wife, a usage occurring in other legislation and in verse texts such as *Maxims II*. See F. Mezger, "Did the Institution of Marriage by Purchase Exist in Old Germanic Law?" *Speculum* 18 (1943), 369–71; Doris Mary Stenton, *The English Woman in History* (London: George Allen, 1957), 8; Anne L. Klinck, "Anglo-Saxon Women and the Law," *Journal of Medieval History* 8 (1982), 107–21; Christine Fell, *Women in Anglo-Saxon England* (Bloomington: Indiana University Press, 1984), 56–73; Mary P. Richards and B. Jane Stanfield, "Concepts of Anglo-Saxon Women in the Laws," in Helen Damico and Alexandra Hennessey Olsen, eds., *New Readings on Women in Old English Literature* (Bloomington: Indiana University Press, 1990), 89–99 at 93–5; Meaney, "The Ides of the Cotton Gnomic Poem," 158–75; Carole Hough, "The Widow's *Mund* in Æthelberht 75 and 76," 13n27; Oliver, *The Beginnings of English Law*, 78–9, 106–9. Much of the debate is traceable to an obscure piece by S. J. Crawford, Review of W. J. Sedgefield, *An Anglo-Saxon Verse-Book*, *The Modern Language Review* 19 (1924), 104–8 at 107. In order to refute the view that *gebicge* means "buy" in *Maxims II* l. 45a, Crawford invokes *Hêliand* ll. 295–8, where it is asserted that Joseph *giboht* Mary *te bridiu:* thus "[t]here can be little doubt that *þæt hi mon beagum gebicge* is equivalent to 'to get married.'" This seems to me no transparent indication that the verb did not indicate a purchase: the *Hêliand* is, after all, a long exercise in adapting the Gospels to the customs and religious ideas of the recently converted Saxons.

customs among the Germanic-speaking peoples of early medieval Europe. While the canons to be discussed occasionally seem to corroborate the views presented at the outset of this chapter about the nature of marriage in the wider Germanic world, more often they suggest a set of norms quite independent of what seems to have prevailed in Francia and not wholly the product of clerical remonstrations.

That marriage is one of several subjects to attract instances of free translation in nearly all of the Old English penitentials makes such an inquiry possible. The present chapter will consider, in the following order, what these sources have to say about the marital contract, consummation, and acceptable forms of intimacy within marriage, each of these being a subject for which Old English translators seemingly sought to stake out positions different from those of their sources. It will conclude with a brief excursus on the relevance of this evidence to the question of whether, and for how long, concubinage was accepted in early England. Considered together, the canons to be discussed do much to illuminate the understanding of marriage likely to have prevailed among the Anglo-Saxons between the ninth and eleventh centuries, perhaps more than sources consulted in prior studies.

THE MARRIAGE CONTRACT

For all of the Old English penitentials, ensuring the consent of the bride and groom to the marriage agreement was of sufficient concern to occasion substantial rewriting of source materials. Such motives are evident in the *Scriftboc*'s recasting of marriage regulations concerning slaves in caps. XIII.16.b-c and in the clause on failed betrothals (already considered at length in Chapter 2).[12] The translator's having added to the former language acknowledging the legitimacy only of unions to which both parties agreed makes plain his interest in establishing consent as a criterion of lawful marriage. Given the role of the Church in urging that all marriages be consensual and in elevating the dignity of unions between the unfree, it is difficult to see how these requirements arrive in Old English materials as anything other than the effects of ecclesiastical influence.[13]

[12] For a discussion of the former, see Jurasinski, "The Old English Penitentials and the Law of Slavery," 113–17.

[13] The development of similar provisions in canon law on the Continent is discussed in Hartmut Hoffmann, "Kirche und Sklaverei im frühen Mittelalter," *Deutsches Archiv für Erforschung des Mittelalters* 42 (1986), 1–24.

No such easy explanation, however, accounts for the treatment of another portion of Theodore's penitential (*PT* II, xii, 33) in these same texts. The clause takes up the means by which marriages that have not yet been consummated are to be dissolved:

Si vir et mulier coniunxerint se in matrimonio et postea dixerit mulier de viro non posse nubere cum ea si quis poterit probare quod verum sit accipiat alium.

"If a man and woman join in matrimony, and subsequently the woman should say of the man that he is unable to have intercourse, if someone is able to establish that this is true, let her accept another [husband]."

In the *Canons* (cap. A 132) this clause becomes "Gif wer and wif hy gesomnien, and heo þonne secge þæt he ne mæge hæman mid hire, gif heo hit þonne gecyðan mæge þæt hit soð sy, nime hire oðerne," "If a man and a woman unite in marriage, and she should afterwards say that he is unable have intercourse with her: if she may declare [show?] that it is true, let her take for herself another." The elimination of the third party (*si quis poterit probare quod verum sit* ...), charged apparently with proving the husband's impotence, would seem to suggest that the *Canons* here offer to the wife somewhat greater freedom to dissolve the union than is present in the source.[14]

To narrow down just how much freedom is implied requires a clear sense of the meaning of *gecyðan*. Frantzen translates the verb as "say that it is true," but it is possible that in this instance the *ge-* prefix indicates a formal declaration before some sort of assembly.[15] Accordingly, the text may be understood as imposing on the woman a requirement to take an oath or make some other kind of public announcement. It hardly needs to be said that supplanting a formal investigation with an oath would not

[14] Theodore may refer here to some ancestor of the medical examination known to have been prescribed by ecclesiastical courts in the later Middle Ages for couples attempting to dissolve their marriages: see Vern L. Bullough, "On Being a Male in the Middle Ages," in *Medieval Masculinities: Regarding Men in the Middle Ages*, ed. Clare A. Lees et al. (Minneapolis: University of Minnesota Press, 1994), 31–45 at 41. A quasimedical test for impotence, to be employed when this condition was used as a ground for divorce, is attested in the laws attributed to Hywel Dda: see *The Law of Hywel Dda: Law Texts from Medieval Wales*, ed. Dafydd Jenkins (Llandysul, UK: Gomer, 1986), 59. (I am indebted to Lisi Oliver for this reference.)

[15] Roger Lass notes the etymological relationship of the prefix *ge-* to Latin *con-* and observes in its earliest usage – most explicitly in Gothic – the same sense of "collectivity or associativity" evident in the distinction between Modern German *Berg* "mountain" and *Gebirge* "mountain chain." This meaning can obtain for both nouns and verbs, though Lass concedes that in nonparticipial verb forms the presence or absence of this prefix may have connoted nothing at all. See Lass, *Old English: A Historical Linguistic Companion* (Cambridge: Cambridge University Press, 1994), 204.

have offered the wife an easier resolution of her problem than is envisaged in Theodore.[16] Nonetheless, the wife's pronouncement is not specifically identified as an oath, and dispensing with the examination required in Theodore appears in any case to leave the wife in more control of the outcome than is permitted in the Latin.

The *Scriftboc*'s handling of this clause perhaps sheds more light on the *Canons*'s departure from Theodore. Here the conditions for dissolution appear less ambiguously to favor leniency, as there is no requirement even of a formal declaration, oath or otherwise: "Wer ond wif gyf heo geðyded beoð and se wer mid heo gehæman ne mæge, þæt wif hine mot forlætan and hire oðerne niman, gif þæt on þone ceorl cuð bið," "If a man and woman are united in marriage and the man may not have intercourse with her, the woman is permitted to leave him and take another, if it is known about the man."[17] Here we have lost even the requirement of a formal declaration. If the author of the *Scriftboc* could countenance a union dissolved so easily, it stands to reason that the translator of the possibly contemporaneous *Canons* is to be believed when he asserts that the wife's formal declaration of the husband's impotence should suffice. In any case, it is surely significant that two Old English translators should have altered this canon in ways that facilitate breaking up the unconsummated marriage. That they did so under the influence of folk law is made more probable by the fact that they were written at a time when impotence was not necessarily considered ground for dissolution of marriage.[18]

While the clauses just reviewed seem to confirm that ecclesiastical laws on the indissolubility of marriage had to contend with more flexible views among the laity, the autonomy they seem to offer women should be regarded cautiously. Both of the clauses described may be considered alongside cap. C 9 of the *Canons,* which seems to contradict A 36 (discussed in Chapter 2). The former had as its source the following Theodorean canon:[19]

> Puellam disponsatam non licet parentibus dare alteri viro nisi illa omnino resistat. Tamen ad monasterium licet ire, si voluerit.
>
> "It is not allowed to parents to give a betrothed girl to another husband unless she entirely refuses [the first]. Yet she is permitted to enter a monastery if she wishes."

[16] On oaths in early England, see Robert Bartlett, *Trial by Fire and Water* (Oxford: Clarendon, 1986), 30–1.

[17] XIV.17.b.

[18] Brundage, *Law, Sex and Christian Society*, 143–5.

[19] *PT* II, xii, 34.

The situation envisaged by Theodore is that a woman refuses the man to whom she is betrothed and a subsequent suitor as well; she is to be allowed to adopt a religious vocation, but not, presumably, to entertain a third proposal of worldly marriage. The C-text of the *Canons* gives instead a harsh rule concerning the inviolability of the first marriage agreement:[20]

Gif beweddod mæden wiðsace þam þe heo beweddod bið, ga þanne on mynster oððe hira maga wedd gelæste.
"If a betrothed maiden refuses the suitor to whom she is betrothed, she must either enter a monastery or fulfill the agreement made by her kin."

It has already been said that this clause may reflect the reluctance of ecclesiastics in this era to acknowledge a substantial distinction between betrothal and marriage.[21] That the indifference of this clause to consent in marriage owes something to traditional attitudes cannot, however, be ruled out.[22]

Both the *Canons* and the *Scriftboc* preserve the stricture against women accepting subsequent husbands (even after unjust abandonment) in Theodore, a rule derived ultimately from Basil's first and second canonical letters to Amphilochius.[23] They do so while retaining a husband's entitlement to dispose of a wife guilty of fornication. Brundage's point, made without reference to the Old English penitentials, that the Germanic peoples regarded adultery as an "exclusively female crime" finds further confirmation in the sole change to the Theodorean text made by the *Canons*. While the source was concerned with the husband's fornication, stating that the wife may not leave him "even if he is a fornicator" (*licet sit fornicator*), the *Canons* gives "þeah heo forlegen beo," "even though she is an adulteress." This substitution of the feminine for the masculine pronoun may be an error, but its conformity to a pattern observed elsewhere makes it a potentially significant one. The translator

[20] *Canons,* C 9. See discussion in Chapter 2, 69n61.

[21] See Chapter 2, 66n52.

[22] See Roberta Frank, "Marriage in Twelfth- and Thirteenth-Century Iceland," *Viator* 4 (1973), 473–84 at 477, where it is noted that Icelandic law did not require consent before marriage.

[23] See *Scriftboc* XVII.19.u; *Canons,* caps. A 21–22 (= *PT* II, xii, 5–6): "Gif hwylces mannes wif bið dearnunga forlegen, þonne is him alyfed þæt he forlæte hy and nime him oðer. Nis þam wife na alyfed þæt heo forlæte hire wer butan leafe, þeah heo forlegen beo, butan Basilius demde þæt heo moste gan in mynster, gif heo wolde." "If someone's wife has secretly fornicated, then is it allowed for him to leave her and take another [wife]. The wife is not allowed to leave her husband without [his] permission, though she has fornicated, but Basil deemed that she may go into a monastery, if she wishes."

may well have thought that an allowance for the wife to depart in the event of her husband's adultery must be mistaken. Though it is difficult to know what should be made of the omission of Theodore's requirement (retained in the equivalent clause of the *Scriftboc*) that only those in a first marriage be permitted to dismiss their wives (see cap. XII.15.c.), it can probably be assumed that this reflects the hostility toward iteration of marriage evident in most pastoral texts of this period.[24]

The clauses considered in this section show traditional, perhaps "Germanic" norms concerning marriage still contending with ecclesiastical ordinances. Regarding the marriage contract, the *Canons* and *Scriftboc* for the most part stick closely to ecclesiastical precepts (cap. C 9 being a noteworthy exception), even correcting their sources so that they affirm less ambiguously the insistence on consent that has long been recognized as a hallmark of ecclesiastical law in this era.[25] But the drift away from ecclesiastical rules concerning impotence and its effects on the marriage contract corroborates Brundage's view that consummation was the *sine qua non* of "Germanic marriage." Cap. 9 of the *Canons'* C text, which had insisted (in opposition to Theodore) that a woman fulfill the marriage agreement negotiated by her kin or enter a monastery, may likewise show something of the residual force of the custom of "marriage by purchase," a practice sufficiently vital in spite of centuries of denunciation to figure among Wulfstan's complaints about English morality as late as the eleventh century.[26] Ecclesiastical remonstrations that marriages involve the consent of bride and groom are maintained in these texts, but in ways that suggest their continued competition with older practices.

CONSUMMATION

The handling of consummation in the Old English penitentials affords its own set of peculiarities. Before these can be considered, a review of the background against which the translators would have read Theodore's provisions – the direct source of nearly all those occurring in

[24] See P. M. J. Rock, "Bigamy (in Canon Law)," in *The Catholic Encyclopedia*, Vol. 2, ed. Charles George Herbermann et al. (New York: Appleton, 1907–12), 561–4.

[25] On this see Sheehan, "Choice of Marriage Partner in the Middle Ages."

[26] [74] "And ne nyde man næfre naðor ne wife ne mæden to ðam þe hire sylfre mislicige, ne wið sceatte ne sylle, buton he hwæt agenes ðances gyfan wille," "And no woman or maiden shall ever be forced to marry a man whom she dislikes, nor shall she be given for money, except the suitor desires of his own freewill to give something." Text and translation of "II Cnut" are that of Robertson, *Laws*, 212–13. On this clause see Klinck, "Anglo-Saxon Women and the Law," 111; Fischer, *Engagement, Wedding and Marriage in Old English*, 19.

Old English – will be necessary. Prior to being united in marriage, early medieval couples were advised by priests "to heed the admonitions given by the Angel Raphael to the Old Testament teacher, Tobias, and thus to spend their time in prayer and penitential exercises" for perhaps a matter of days before consummating their union.[27] The biblical instructions from which this tradition purported to descend were as follows (Tobias 6:18–22):[28]

> But thou, when thou shalt take her, go into the chamber, and for three days keep thyself continent from her, and give thyself to nothing else but prayers with her. And on that night lay the liver of the fish on the fire, and the devil shall be driven away. But the second night thou shalt be admitted into the society of the holy Patriarchs. And the third night thou shalt obtain a blessing that sound children may be born of you. And when the third night is past, thou shalt take the virgin with the fear of the Lord, moved rather for love of children than for lust, that in the seed of Abraham thou mayest obtain a blessing in children.

Reynolds notes that the instructions of the Angel Raphael occur only in Jerome's version of the Book of Tobit and suggests that "[w]e may perhaps attribute some of the peculiarities of the Vulgate version to Jerome himself," whose ascetic view of marriage was extraordinary even by the standards of his time.[29] In any case, the process by which the "nights of Tobias" entered the stream of canon law seems to have involved many false starts and resulted in a variety of practices existing side-by-side. The influential *Statuta Ecclesiae Antiqua*, a compilation of sixth-century Gaul once erroneously known as the "Fourth Council of Carthage" whose provisions appear verbatim in several later collections, advises just one night of chastity after the blessing of the couple:[30]

> Sponsus et sponsa, cum benedicendi sunt a sacerdote, a parentibus suis vel a paranymphis offerantur. Qui cum benedictionem acceperint, eadem nocte, pro reverentia ipsius benedictionis, in virginitate permaneant.
>
> "The bride and bridegroom, when they are to be blessed by a priest, should be offered [in marriage] by kin or guardians. And when they have received the blessing, let them remain in their virginity that night to show reverence for this same blessing."

27 Brundage, *Law, Sex and Christian Society*, 159.
28 Text is from *The Holy Bible*, ed. R. Challoner.
29 Reynolds, *Marriage in the Western Church*, 334–5.
30 For the text, see *Les statuta ecclesiae antiqua*, ed. Charles Munier (Paris: Presses Universitaires de France, 1960), 100 (cap. 101). Identical is the version occurring in Regino, *De synodalibus causis et disciplinis ecclesiasticis*, 271 (cap. CLII). Cap. LXXIII of Chrodegang's *Regula longior canonicorum* suggests two or three nights and makes a handful of minor additions: see *The Chrodegang Rules*, ed. and trans. Jerome Bertram (Aldershot, UK: Ashgate, 2005), 220 and 274.

Whether the canonist has in mind the "nights of Tobias" is unclear, for the text merely asserts that the couple's abstinence is meant to show "reverence" for the benediction. While the story of Tobit appears to have shaped more overtly Caesarius of Arles's thinking about marriage regulation, the result was still no outright adoption of the biblical practice.[31] The narrative appears again in the late ninth-century work of Jonas of Orléans (d. 843), serving here as an *exemplum* on the importance of continence in marriage.[32]

While these sources disagree on the length of the prescribed period of continence and the ground for its application, they are, almost without exception, united in seeing at least the night of the wedding as an infelicitous time for consummation. Given such circumstances, the recommendations of Theodore's penitential may have seemed somewhat remarkable to its earliest readers:[33]

> In primo conjugio presbiter debet missam [cantare] et benedicere ambos et postea abstineant se ab aecclesia XXX diebus; quibus peractis peniteant XL diebus, et vacent orationi; et postea communicent cum oblatione.
>
> "In a first marriage the presbyter ought to perform Mass and bless them both, and afterward they shall absent themselves from church for thirty days. Having done this, they shall do penance for forty days, and absent themselves from the prayer [better: 'devote themselves to prayer']; and afterwards they shall communicate with the oblation."

There is reason to believe that this clause would not have sat well with many ninth- or tenth-century audiences. Brundage suggests that the thirty-day period in which the couple is instructed to absent themselves from the worshiping community is meant to afford them "a short period of frolic ... dedicated to sexual exploration and delectation."[34] If this is the proper way

[31] Reynolds, *Marriage in the Western Church*, 336–7.

[32] "Audiant igitur qui uxores ducere cupiunt, qualiter angelus Raphael Tobiam de uxore sibi conjugenda instruxerit": Jonas of Orléans, *De institutione laicali*, in *Patrologia Latina*, 217 vols., ed. J.-P. Migne (Paris: Garnier, 1844–64), CVI: 171 (II.2); for discussion, see Reynolds, *Marriage in the Western Church*, 372. According to Reynolds, Hincmar of Rheims (806–82) shows awareness of the custom as well (391).

[33] *PT* I, xiv, 1; trans. McNeill and Gamer, *Medieval Handbooks*, 195. By *vacent orationi* Theodore means that the couple is to undertake a period of prayer, perhaps echoing I Corinthians 7:5, in which Paul advises married couples not to deprive one another "except perhaps by consent, for a time, that you may give yourselves to prayer" (*nisi forte ex consensu ad tempus ut vacetis orationi*). McNeill and Gamer's rendering does have something to recommend it: *vacare* can mean "to be free from labor, not busied, idle, at leisure; to have leisure or time." See *A Latin Dictionary*, eds. Charlton T. Lewis and Charles Short (Oxford: Clarendon, 1879; repr. 1951), s.v. *vacō*. But Theodore was clearly mindful of Paul's instruction as is evident from the language of *PT* II, xii, 2 (see following text, n. 47).

[34] Brundage, *Law, Sex and Christian Society*, 159.

to read the clause – and I am aware of no other possibilities having been proposed – Theodore here violates both the letter and the spirit of laws referred to previously concerning the immediate aftermath of the wedding, laws that would have held from the earliest period in which the Old English penitentials may have been written.

It is possible that this is one of Theodore's apparent concessions either to customary observances or to human frailty (something for which he is praised, on the basis of other canons, by Frank Stenton).[35] But we can be sure that its allowances for the lust of young couples should not be read as endorsements of it. While indeed afforded some space to exercise (and subsequently atone for) their appetites, the couple is barred from their fellow Christians for perhaps seventy days while so engaged. Such a measure was probably intended to protect their priest from the spiritual harm that even indirect proximity to the erotic was held in this era to pose for members of the secular clergy. Such concerns are evident in a number of sources, the most relevant of which for our purposes is canon 39 of the Council of Agde (506). This clause resurfaces in the rules for canons compiled by Chrodegang in the eighth century and thus was undoubtedly, given a much later translation of the text into Old English, known to some members of the Anglo-Saxon clergy by at least the eleventh century.[36] The notion at work here may be the same underlying proscriptions of priests sharing water with pregnant women: the fact of prior sexual activity alone was regarded as investing persons with unholy influences that might defile the priest and ultimately pollute the sacrifice of the Mass.[37] It will be seen in Chapter 6 that such notions did much to shape Anglo-Saxon notions of ritual purity.

[35] Frank Merry Stenton, *Anglo-Saxon England* (Oxford: Clarendon, 1943; repr. 1962), 140; Audrey Meaney, "Women, Witchcraft and Magic in Anglo-Saxon England," in *Superstition and Popular Medicine in Anglo-Saxon England*, ed. D. G. Scragg et al. (Manchester, UK: Manchester Centre for Anglo-Saxon Studies, 1989), 9–40 at 12: "Theodore appears always to have attempted to fit his rulings to English conditions – and to English sins. Perhaps, as a foreigner, he was able to see more clearly what was irregular, and what was excusable in the circumstances."

[36] "Presbiteri, diacones, subdiacones, uel deinceps, quibus ducendi uxores licentia non est, alienarum nuptiarum consortia euitent, neque his caetibus amisceantur ubi amatoria et turpia cantantur, aut ubi obsceni motus corporum choris et saltationibus efferuntur, ne auditus et obtutus sacris misteriis denudatus turpium spectaculorum atque uerborum contagione polluantur," "Priests, deacons, subdeacons and others who are not permitted to marry, should avoid the wedding celebrations of others; they should not attend gatherings where immoral love-songs are sung, or where people dance and strike indecent postures, otherwise their ears and eyes may be drawn away from the sacred mysteries, and they may be defiled by contact with unseemly sights and words." *The Chrodegang Rules*, ed. and trans. Bertram, 218 and 273.

[37] See cap. 6.2 of the Bigotian Penitential, in *The Irish Penitentials*, ed. Bieler, 216; for discussion see Brundage, *Law, Sex and Christian Society*, 156.

Indeed, Theodore's sense of the pollutions inherent in marital sexuality may be greater than what is evident in the writings of other ecclesiastics. Our sense of Theodore's aims depends in part on what is meant by his imposition of a forty-day fast on the couple – another element of this clause that might have struck earlier readers as unorthodox given its absence elsewhere. There is reason to suspect that the fast may have been understood to serve as a spiritual remedy for the marriage alone, as such an undertaking was necessarily the outcome of licit, but nonetheless polluting, carnal desire.[38] Carol Braun Pasternack has suggested something of this sort with her remark that the forty-day penance reflects Theodore's understanding of marriage "both as a sanctified institution and as a violation of purity."[39] It is probably no accident that the clause is immediately followed by one that assigns a year-long penance for those twice married; subsequently, we find that the thrice married are assigned seven years of penance. While Theodore was indeed more tolerant of remarriage than his contemporaries, it seems that Theodore was also more anxious than others to provide the means for the married couples' purification, and the forty-day penance probably represents the first stage of these measures.

Thus, while the remedies arrived at by Theodore for the spiritual hazards of consummation may have seemed unorthodox, we can be sure that the aims underlying them were not. Ecclesiastics of this era likely saw marriage as little more than the best possible outcome of nonetheless culpable desires, influenced as they were by a patristic tradition in which "marriage was both blessed and cursed."[40] Marriage would not become a sacrament until the twelfth century, and those who compiled these chapters may well have been receptive to Jerome's admonition that married couples who enjoyed one another excessively were, in some respects, no better than fornicators or those who consorted with prostitutes.[41]

Interpretation of Theodore's clause by the Old English translators seems, however, to have been unaffected by such subtleties of moral reasoning. However negative its view of marriage may implicitly have been, Theodore's penitential still appears (at least in Brundage's opinion) to

[38] That a required period of abstinence after the wedding ceremony constituted a de facto penance upon marriage was recognized in the first half of the twelfth century by Bishop Nifont of Novgorod: see Eve Levin, *Sex and Society in the World of the Orthodox Slavs, 900–1700* (Ithaca, NY: Cornell University Press, 1989), 167.

[39] Carol Braun Pasternack, "Negotiating Gender in Anglo-Saxon England," in *Gender and Difference in the Middle Ages*, Medieval Cultures 32, eds. Sharon Farmer and Carol Braun Pasternack (Minneapolis: University of Minnesota Press, 2003), 107–44 at 127.

[40] Reynolds, *Marriage in the Western Church*, 337.

[41] James Brundage, "Let Me Count the Ways: Canonists and Theologians Contemplate Coital Positions," *Journal of Medieval History* 10 (1984), 81–93.

leave the couple with thirty days' "frolic," and none of the justifications for this allowance implicit in Theodore's text seems to have sufficed to overcome resistance to it among those who prepared the Old English penitentials. The clause does not pass through Anglo-Saxon hands without undergoing substantial alterations.

Our overview begins with the *Scriftboc*. Given the silence of the *Canons of Theodore*, it is certainly the first, and perhaps only penitential canon in Old English to address itself to the Theodorean clause on consummation. The language with which it does so is particularly challenging:

In þære ærestan geðeodnysse weres and wifes preoste gedafenað þæt he mæssan singe and ða gesamnunga bletsige; and heo æfter þon hie ahebban, þæt hie cyrican secan, mid almessan; and ðam nihtum forðgetenum hie hi gebiddan and fæsten XL nihta and æfter ðam gan to husle. (XII.14.e)

Frantzen gives the following translation of the clause:

"In the first joining of man and woman, it is proper for the priest that he should sing Mass and bless the union; and they afterwards so comport themselves so that they visit the church with almsgiving; and when the nights have gone by they pray, and fast for 40 nights and after that go to Eucharist."

What we make of this canon depends on the interpretation of a single verb. Frantzen's treatment differs from Spindler's, who held that Old English *ahebban*, "to raise up" (probably substituted for earlier *ahabban*, "refrain (from)" in a now-lost recension, as appears to have been the case in manuscripts of the Old English Bede) renders *abstineant*, which would rule out Frantzen's "comport themselves."[42] Thus Spindler glosses *ahabban* as "abstain from one another" (*sich enthalten*) and indicates (in spite of its usually being paired with the preposition *fram*) that this verb takes the object *hie*, resulting in a translation something like "and they afterwards [should] abstain from one another, so that they visit the church with almsgiving." Possible support for this reading comes from the *Old English Rule of Chrodegang* given its use of *forhebban* to describe the same situation.[43] Spindler's view that the *Scriftboc* here uses a typical idiom for a couple's abstinence thus seems reasonably sound. His reading requires us to see the *Scriftboc* as prescribing something not advised in

[42] Raymond J. S. Grant notes such a substitution in Cambridge, Corpus Christi College 41 (known under the siglum B), a late manuscript of the Old English Bede: see Grant, *The B-Text of the Old English Bede: A Linguistic Commentary* (Amsterdam: Rodopi, 1989), 157–8.

[43] *Forhebban* renders *abstineant* in cap. LXXI (= LXXIII of the *Regula Longior*) of *The Old English Version of the Enlarged Rule of Chrodegang*, ed. Brigitte Langefeld (Frankfurt: Peter Lang, 1985), 310–11.

this clause of Theodore's penitential: a period of abstinence immediately after the wedding, perhaps patterned in some fashion on the "nights of Tobias," which, as we have seen, might assume a variety of forms. Thus the phrase *ðam nihtum forðgetenum*, though ostensibly based upon the absolute construction in the Latin (*quibus peractis*), may well have been understood to refer implicitly to the "nights of Tobias" or one of the myriad of arrangements that seem to have approximated this institution in the ecclesiastical law of this era. The almsgiving enjoined upon the couple may likewise issue from the requirement of the biblical text that Tobias and his spouse spend their time in prayer and pious acts.[44] Another trace of the Vulgate is perhaps evident in the requirement that the couple pray for one another (*hie hi gebiddan*), though it echoes as well Theodore's injunction that they devote themselves to prayer (*vacent orationi*), itself a quotation from I Corinthians 7:5.[45]

Whatever his motives, the translator's clumsy attempt to reconcile Theodore with the norms of his own day only multiplied the uncertainties of his source. The *Scriftboc*'s rendering appears to suggest that the couple must endure after their period of continence another forty days of fasting. Perhaps it was understood that these two periods were to be punctuated with at least one instance of intimacy, ideally urged on by thoughts of procreation alone; the forty-day fast assumes an act to require it. But a priest of this era would have found no such concession in the literal sense of the Old English. And we should perhaps not assume that the concession was even implicitly present. We have seen that Theodore's treatment of the wedding night was not in keeping with most pastoral regulations of this period. In any case, affording the couple some space to enjoy one another cannot have figured highly among the translator's priorities.

Indeed, the attitude of the translator toward marital sexuality is perhaps revealed in his failure (or refusal) to render accurately the sole instance in which Theodore does seem to allude, if ambiguously, to the "nights of Tobias."[46] The canon in question (*PT* II, xii, 1–2) requires that

[44] Spindler struggled to make sense of the linkage of the period of abstinence with almsgiving: "Line 200 of the Old English text … can, however, only mean 'Because they may not enter the church, they must give alms'; 'mid aelmessan' seems defective, particularly because there is no source for it in the Latin source text, and XXX 'diebus' on the other hand is not retained." Spindler, *altenglische Bussbuch*, 41. It may be of some significance that almsgiving is identified by Theodulf of Orléans as an act securing forgiveness of sins: see his *Capitula ad presbyteros parochiae suae*, in *Patrologia Latina*, ed. Migne, CV: col. 204 (cap. 36).

[45] I am assuming here the unsoundness of McNeill and Gamer's translation.

[46] That it may be understood this way has been argued by P. Saintyves ("Les trois nuits de Tobie ou la continence durant la première ou les premières nuits du mariage," *Revue*

those who are married should abstain for three days before receiving the Host.[47] It is unclear whether the canon refers to the newly married, with *antequam communicent* referring to their resumption of corporate worship, or lays down a condition to be observed throughout a couple's marriage.[48] While the latter seems likelier, the clause was susceptible (as we will see) to being understood as prescribing the proper consummation of marriage, and so it is surprising that the author of the *Scriftboc,* in giving the "nights of Tobias" no more than an implicit role in his treatment of this matter, seems not to have made the use of it that he might have.[49] Instead, the *Scriftboc*'s author (cap. XIII.16.e) follows the same impulse that led him to make a hash of the Theodorean provisions described earlier, this time using the three nights of abstinence to add to the burdens of couples preparing for a Quadragesimal fast: "Ða ðe in rihtum hæmede beoð, þreom nihtum ær ðam feowertiges nihta fæstenne

Anthropologique 44 (1944), 266–6 at 287), though the evidence is unfortunately misrepresented in his attributing the following canon (not in fact found in any member of the Theodore cycle) to "Theodore's penitential": *Ceux qui se marient doivent s'abstenir pendant trois nuits de consommer leur union.* (Saintyves inexplicably does not provide the Latin.) The quoted clause is in fact translated from Jacques Petit, *Theodori sanctissimi ac doctissimi archiepiscopi cantuarensis poenitentiale* (Paris: Lutetiae Parisiorum, 1667), 166; it occurs not in *PT* but in "a collection of pseudo-Theodoran canons" (McNeill and Gamer, *Medieval Handbooks*, 180). The passage in question (QUI IN MATRIMONIO SUNT, TRES NOCTES ABSTINEANT) is, in any event, misconstrued by Saintyves, as it constitutes merely the subheading of a chapter entitled *De quæstionibus Conjugiorum* that never advises observance of the "nights of Tobias": the chapter as a whole is concerned only with abstention prior to receiving the Eucharist and before the required fasting periods, and thus not with the immediate aftermath of the wedding. Petit's volume is extremely difficult of access, and I am grateful to James Humble of the Rare Books Library at St. Charles Borromeo Seminary for making its contents available to me.

47 The Theodorean source (*PT* II, xii, 1–2) is as follows: "Qui in matrimonio sunt III noctes abstineant se a coniunctione antequam communicent. Vir abstineat se ab uxore sua XL diebus ante pascha usque in octavas paschae. Inde ait apostolus: ut vacetis orationi," "Those who are married shall abstain from intercourse for three nights before they communicate. A man shall abstain from his wife for forty days before Easter, until the week of Easter. On this account the Apostle says: 'That ye may give yourselves to prayer.'" Trans. McNeill and Gamer, *Medieval Handbooks*, 208.

48 The former is assumed in Rosalind Hill, "Marriage in Seventh-Century England," in *Saints, Scholars, and Heroes: Studies in Medieval Culture in Memory of Charles W. Jones*, 2 vols., eds. Margot H. King and Wesley Stephens (Collegeville, MN: Hill Monastic Manuscript Library, 1979), I: 67–75 at 72.

49 To read this clause as referring to the whole of one's married life makes sense given the urging of Theodulf of Orléans in his *Capitula* that laypeople approach the altar only after having abstained for a while from *opere conjugali*: see *Patrologia Latina*, ed. Migne, CV: col. 205. The Theodorean clause gives more specific guidance. See also the attempt to disambiguate Theodore in *Paenitentiale Pseudo-Theodori*, ed. Van Rhijn, 17 (XI.1), where the applicability of this clause to the duration of one's marriage is made clear.

hi ne gesamnigan heo, and swa þæt feowertig nihta ealle oð ða nigoðan niht in Eastron," "Those who are in a proper union, they will not have intercourse in the three nights before the Quadragesima, and also during the entire forty nights until the ninth night of Easter." Spindler regarded this as an invention of the translator.[50] It is just as likely, I think, that the translator understood himself to be restating what he had earlier said about the wedding night, with the forty-day fast referring to Theodore's recommendation for the newly wedded couple. The resulting provision is, however, hopelessly garbled.

The suggestion that this is effectively the second treatment of consummation in the *Scriftboc* is lent some plausibility by the fact that the author of the *Penitential* likewise views this canon as a reference to the wedding night, perhaps after the *Scriftboc*'s muddled example. The *Penitential* translates the identical version of Theodore's clause that occurs in the fourth book of Halitgar's penitential, giving the most lucid reference to the "nights of Tobias" known to have surfaced in the Old English period (cap. 21):[51]

Halige bec tæceað hwæt ælcum geleaffullum were to donne is, þonne <he> his riht-æwe ærost ham bringeð; þæt is æfter boca tæcinge þæt hy þreora daga 7 nihta fyrst heora clænnesse healdan sceolon, 7 þonne on þone þriddan dæg heora mæssan gestandan 7 hy butu husl niman, 7 syððan heora gesynscipe healdan for gode 7 for worulde swa heora þearf sy.

"The holy books teach concerning what every faithful husband is to do when he first brings home his lawful bride; that is, according to the instruction of the books, that they should first for three days keep their chastity, and then on the third day attend Mass and both receive the Host, and afterwards keep their union before God and the world as is required of them."

The only substantial remark on this passage I am aware of is by Raith, who notes that the Latin gives no indication of relevance to the conduct of the newly married, as the clause appears in Halitgar's collection (as it does in Theodore's) alongside other strictures that held for the duration of one's marriage.[52] To Raith, the two clauses from the *Scriftboc* discussed earlier constituted "a different and in parts considerably deviant version" of the Theodorean language adduced by Halitgar.[53] But the *Penitential*'s

[50] Spindler, *Das altenglische Bussbuch*, 45.

[51] *Die altenglische Version*, 28. For Halitgar's quotation of the Theodorean clauses, see *Bussbücher*, ed. Schmitz, I: 727 (IV.xxiiii).

[52] "The prohibition of marital intercourse before the taking of Holy Communion … was fundamentally misunderstood by the translator: he makes out of it a prohibition of marital intercourse during the first three nights after the wedding (the so-called Nights of Tobias)." *Die altenglische Version*, 28.

[53] Ibid.

language admits of being seen as something other than a "misunderstanding" if we assume that its author is writing with an awareness of the *Scriftboc*'s earlier provisions, as he certainly was in the latter portion of his manual. Here the *Penitential* incorporates the "nights of Tobias" in a way that avoids the troublesome ambiguities posed by the equivalent portion(s) of the *Scriftboc*. No priest would have left the *Penitential*'s version in any doubt about what to expect of the couple. Indeed, this clause of the *Penitential* perhaps reworks the *Scriftboc* as much as it does the Theodorean provision in Halitgar as it develops themes implicitly present in its vernacular antecedent, elevating the couple's celebration of the Eucharist (implicit, as the translator understood it, in Theodore's *antequam communicent*) to a ritual acknowledgment of the couple's triumph over base desires. Indeed, this portion of the *Penitential* may constitute a second attempt (after the *Scriftboc*'s) to correct Theodore's more explicit discussion of consummation discussed previously, whose implications seem to have so troubled the author of the *Scriftboc*.

Why the "nights of Tobias" seized the imaginations of the early medieval public may never be fully known.[54] Popular superstition, along with the receptiveness to laws drawn from the Old Testament discussed in Chapter 2, may have led some in Anglo-Saxon England to heed the counsel of the Angel Raphael that continence after the wedding will result in healthy children.[55] That the practice was understood as offering such benefits to married couples is evident from Pseudo-Evaristus, a text known to have shaped the thinking of Hincmar, Archbishop of Rheims (806–82).[56] The reception of the Eucharist at the conclusion of the couple's period of continence – only an implicit feature of the *Penitential*'s Latin sources, and perhaps the invention of its author – was, perhaps, seen as fortifying

[54] It has been observed that abstention at least during the wedding night, and in some cases longer, is a custom known to Indo-European and non-Indo-European cultures alike, typically enacted for the good fortune assumed to accrue to the married couple: see Saintyves, "Les trois nuits de Tobie ou la continence durant la première ou les premières nuits du mariage." It is thus possible, if unlikely, that its appearance among the Anglo-Saxons may be somewhat independent of ecclesiastical influence.

[55] Three nights of abstinence are elsewhere suggested in the Old Testament as a ritual means of obtaining divine favor (Exodus 19:15; 1 Samuel 21:4–5). For a discussion, see Pierre Payer, *Sex and the Penitentials: The Development of a Sexual Code, 550–1150* (Toronto: University of Toronto Press, 1984), 23–6. It is possible that the *Scriftboc*'s addition of a three-day period of abstinence prior to a Quadragesimal fast owes something to the example of the Old Testament.

[56] "et biduo vel triduo orationibus vacent et castitatem custodiant, ut bonae soboles generentur et domino suis in actibus placeant." *Decretales Pseudo-Isidorianae et Capitula Angilramni*, ed. P. Hinschius (Leipzig: Bernhard Tauchnitz, 1863; repr. 1963), 87.

the couple's bodies against the corruption of sin as they proceeded to the potentially soul-destroying business of begetting children.[57]

In the clauses just reviewed, we see some of the ways in which vernacular texts established independent juridical traditions, in this case fashioning treatments of marital sexuality ultimately distinct from those of their supposedly more prestigious Latin sources. Both the *Scriftboc* and the *Penitential* depart from their respective anchor-texts in requiring "the nights of Tobias," by this point a likely element of folk law. Meanwhile, Theodore's own innovations seem to recede. His assignment of Quadragesimal fasting for the newly married couple may not have enjoyed much favor during the period in which the Old English penitentials were composed, for it appears not to resurface in non-Theodorean collections of canons. The clause of the *Penitential* may show its complete rejection by the late Anglo-Saxon period. Indeed, it is just possible that one may see in the *Penitential*'s treatment of the wedding night developments anticipating the elevation of marriage from a necessary evil to a sacrament.[58]

MARITAL SEXUALITY BEYOND THE "NIGHTS OF TOBIAS"

The intricate periods of fasting and abstinence that followed the wedding and would accompany married couples for the rest of their lives afforded a relative handful of opportunities for intimacy. These, as Brundage has demonstrated, were beset by a web of proscriptions, many of which were codified in the penitential canons attributed to Theodore. Of these, the most persistent was the prohibition of intercourse during the three Quadragesimal fasts as well as on Fridays, Sundays, and the three days prior to reception of the Eucharist.[59]

During the few days in which intercourse was permitted, couples found themselves subject to a further layer of prohibitions. All were directed at

[57] On superstitious uses of the Host in this period, see most recently Neil Xavier O'Donoghue, *The Eucharist in Pre-Norman Ireland* (Notre Dame: University of Notre Dame Press, 2011), cap. 3.

[58] It is probably not coincidental that the *Old English Penitential* (cap. 20) forbids marriage more than twice, a prescription very much in contrast to Theodore's and also in opposition to the rule of his immediate source, which had permitted third and fourth marriages while prescribing increasing penances for each.

[59] *PT* II, xii, 1–2. A fine overview of the sexual environment evident in the English penitentials is Anthony Davies, "Sexual Behaviour in Later Anglo-Saxon England," in *This Noble Craft ...: Proceedings of the Tenth Research Symposium of the Dutch and Belgian*

ensuring that the couple took little pleasure in begetting children – ideally, as Gregory the Great had asserted, none at all.[60] Given the requirement, faithfully reproduced by most penitentials, that couples never see one another unclothed, intercourse was not permissible during the day.[61] The couple was also obliged to eschew all positions deemed unorthodox because of their association with prostitutes.[62] Only in their inner lives did laypersons seem to enjoy some measure of liberty in contrast to the regular and secular clergy. To entertain erotic thoughts seems not to have been deemed as grave an offense for laypersons as it was for priests, though the sources' silence on this matter offers no positive evidence; certainly there is evidence (to be explored in Chapter 6) for views peculiar to the Anglo-Saxon clergy concerning the nature and moral status of desire.

Whether these norms would have conflicted or agreed with those obtaining among the earlier Anglo-Saxons is difficult to know. As has been suggested in Chapter 2, the conversion-era English may already have been acquainted with a purity code that rivaled in severity what was urged on them by Gregory the Great through his emissaries. It has been said, though never with reference to the Old English penitentials, that the Anglo-Saxons manifested a reserve about sexuality unusual among their contemporaries.[63] The vernacular penitentials do much to complete this picture, for they occasionally seem to regard even the regulations stipulated in their sources as insufficiently strict. In the Old English penitentials, these statements are corrected in ways that perhaps suggest the existence of another set of norms governing sexual behavior to which the Latin evidence does not attest. This is most visibly the case with the author of the *Canons*, who alters his source material radically, combining provisions from various portions of the *Penitential of Theodore* that leave us with a substantially different set of regulations than those envisioned by his exemplar.

His rewriting of prohibitions on fantasizing perhaps shows the tendency of his thought most plainly. These originally had as their objects

University Teachers of Old and Middle English and Historical Linguistics, ed. Erik Kooper (Amsterdam: Rodopi, 1991), 83–105.

60 Gregory the Great suggests in the *Libellus Responsionum* that husbands who have intercourse solely with the aim of procreation should perhaps be exempted from the rule requiring their absence from Mass. *Bede's Ecclesiastical History of the English People*, ed. and trans. Colgrave and Mynors, 96–9 (I.27).

61 *PT* II, xii, 31.

62 Brundage, "Let Me Count the Ways," 81–93.

63 Hugh Magennis, "'No Sex Please, We're Anglo-Saxons?' Attitudes to Sexuality in Old English Literature," *Leeds Studies in English* n.s. 26 (1995), 1–27.

members of the secular and regular clergy and were meant to preserve the Host from defilement. But in the translator's hands they appear to become incumbent upon the laity as well; certainly the penance indicated is more severe than in Theodore.[64] On other occasions, he supplements his translation of Theodore's penitential with provisions from others that seem to have possessed the necessary severity. The clearest instance of this occurs in the *Canons'* treatment of illicit practices. The language of Theodore's *Penitential* is quite plain (*PT* I, xiv, 21–22):

Si vir cum uxore sua retro nupserit, XL. dies peniteat primo. Si in tergo nupserit, penitere debet quasi ille qui cum animalibus.

"If a man should have intercourse with his wife from behind, let him do penance for forty days for the first offense. If he should have intercourse with her *in tergo,* he should do penance as one who has violated animals."

In the hands of the *Canons*-author, this becomes:[65]

Gif se wer mid his wife hindan hæme, .xl. daga fæste. On oðre stowe hit cwyð þæt he scule hreowsunge don swa se ðe mid nytenum hæmð.

"If a man should have intercourse with his wife from behind, let him fast for forty days. In another place it says that he should repent as one who violates animals."

We have seen that Theodore prohibited irregular positions while likening intercourse *in tergo* to offenses with animals. The *Canons*, however, go a step further. The Old English author's equation of the nonmissionary position with bestiality constitutes one of the rare moments in this text in which we see him acknowledging his use of more than one source. He may have made use of the *Penitential of Egbert*, which says on this question: "Si vir cum muliere sua retro nupserit, peniteat, quomodo cum animalibus, id est, si consuetudine erat, III. annos," "If a man has intercourse with his wife from behind, let him do penance as one who violates animals, that is to say for three years (if the offense was habitual)."[66] As had been the case with the "nights of Tobias," we once again see a compiler perhaps expressing his dissatisfaction with the excessively lenient provisions of the original, this time employing source material from other penitentials that took a harder line toward irregular positions. We also

[64] A 44–5. These clauses refer to the curious offense of self-pollution *per violentiam cogitationis,* "by means of the violence of one's thoughts" (see *PT* I, viii, 7), prescribing a longer penance than had been stipulated in Theodore. But absent Theodore's organization of the canons into explicit categories, it is no longer clear whether the author of the *Canons* means to refer to clerics (as had been the case in Theodore) or laypersons.

[65] A 115–16.

[66] *Egbert* VII.10 (*Bußordnungen,* ed. Wasserschleben, 239).

see, perhaps, the shrewdness of an experienced confessor. The statement immediately following this one in the *Canons* – "Gif he on ðam monðe ær þam beorðre hire mid hæmð, .xl. daga fæste," "If he should have intercourse with her in the month before his child is born, let him fast for 40 days" – appears merely to confuse Theodore's "time of menstruation" (*menstruo tempore*) with the prohibited *tres menses* before and after childbirth.[67] But this rendering may be more than accidental. Given that this canon is preceded by a quite severe condemnation of illicit coital positions, it would seem that the *Canons*-author, like the translator of the *Scriftboc*, here sought to align the clause with more stringent views on ritual purity than were found in his source. If deliberately contrived by the author, this statement might well reflect his awareness of how the physical difficulties of intercourse in the advanced stages of pregnancy threaten to increase the appeal of what was, in his view, among the most heinous of practices. The Old English penitentials say surprisingly little about marital sexuality, but where they do, the translators attempt more or less regularly to exceed their exemplars in severity.

TOLERANCE FOR CONCUBINAGE?

We may conclude this chapter with some remarks on what has seemed to prior commentators the most Germanic of marital irregularities. Though its nature remains a subject of contention, there is general agreement that marriage existed alongside (and perhaps, in some households, coincided with) a more elastic type of union for which the only available term is *concubinage*, doing so in spite of the hostility toward all manifestations of the erotic documented throughout this chapter. Speculations that these arrangements were practiced by elite laypersons in early England and even countenanced by ecclesiastics have a long history.[68] The thesis was adopted without reservations by Felix Liebermann, who held even King Alfred, possessed though he was of a "chaste mind," unable in the Mosaic Prologue of his laws to condemn his contemporaries' practice of using slaves as sexual partners.[69] It is hard to say what underlies this remark

67 A 117. The source is *PT* I, xiv, 23: "Si menstruo tempore coierit cum ea, XL dies iei[u]net," "If he should have intercourse with her during menstruation, let him fast for forty days."

68 Karras ("The Myth of *Friedelehe*," 123) draws attention to Tacitus's observation that the Germans were unique among the barbarian peoples of western Europe in being satisfied with monogamous relationships; the exceptions to this, he observes, occurred only at the top of the social hierarchy. See Tacitus, *Germania*, in *Opera Minora*, eds. M. Winterbottom and R. M. Ogilvie (Oxford: Clarendon, 1975), 46 (c. 18).

69 F. Liebermann, "King Alfred and Mosaic Law," *Transactions of the Jewish Historical Society* 6 (1912), 21–31 at 27–18.

because the evidence in question, as I have shown elsewhere, does little to substantiate it.[70] Liebermann's thinking may well owe something to that of his masters in the field of Germanic legal history, many of whose work suffered from the same fatal indifference to chronology and geography referred to at the outset of this chapter.

A century later, a foundational study of this institution by Margaret Clunies Ross would contend that the *Old English Penitential* also functioned under similar constraints whose descent she traces back to Alfred:[71]

> Clerical marriage was a type of concubinage which the church itself made possible. The equation of mistresses of priests with concubines is clear in Alfred 8–8.3 and in the Northumbrian Priests' Law 35, and this classification, together with the persistent references to concubinage in penitentials throughout the Anglo-Saxon period, suggests that the church had not been altogether successful in persuading the English to give up their concubines. The true state of affairs in England between the ninth and eleventh centuries is probably expressed by the Old English *Penitential of Pseudo-Egbert,* ii, 9, in which concubinage is both acknowledged and partially tolerated.

Clunies Ross here suggests that the Anglo-Saxon church may have been somewhat complicit in the preservation of concubinage among the English, a thesis repeated approvingly in more recent scholarship.[72] Her remarks mostly paraphrase Liebermann's entry on *Konkubinat* in the legal encyclopedia that occupies volume II of his *Gesetze der Angelsachsen.* Whether Liebermann's views merit treatment as conventional wisdom is open to question. The Alfredian clause is merely a denunciation of those who abduct nuns and forcibly marry them: it is an admonition against "marriage by capture" analogous to those occurring elsewhere in Old English legislation, aggravated in this case by the offense against God inherent in the act.[73] No explicit mention is made here of the nun's reduction to a concubine, though her being pointedly denied a widow's

[70] "Slavery, Learning and the Law of Marriage in Alfred's Mosaic Prologue."

[71] Margaret Clunies Ross, "Concubinage in Anglo-Saxon England," *Past and Present* 108 (1985), 3–34 at 23.

[72] See Wyatt, *Slaves and Warriors*, 132, where it is suggested (on the basis of similar evidence, including the *Old English Penitential*) that "despite consistent complaints regarding secular concubinage and other extra-marital relationships, many ecclesiastics appear to have been relatively accepting and even accommodating toward such behaviour."

[73] See Brundage, *Law, Sex, and Christian Society*, 132: "Sexual relations with a nun constituted adultery, presumably on the theory that a consecrated virgin was the bride of Christ; the brunt of punishment for this kind of adultery fell upon the man." Brundage finds this principle attested in Lombard and Bavarian law.

inheritance may perhaps be seen as Alfred's attempt to abrogate an earlier sense that such unions had a kind of legitimacy.[74] As for the chapter of the Northumbrian Priests' law, I see in this only a required excommunication of a priest who marries and then abandons his spouse. The woman in question is not explicitly referred to as his lawful wife, but neither is she called a concubine (*cyfese*).[75]

For its part, the *Old English Penitential* offers in the passage adduced by Clunies Ross an unusually faithful translation of Halitgar. The possibility exists, therefore, that we may attribute to Halitgar whatever tolerance of concubinage seems evident in this clause (though I am not sure that the passage in question shows any willingness to countenance the institution at all).[76] More important, I think, is what happens when Old English penitentials address themselves to this issue in ways that disregard the instruction of their sources. These have to my knowledge not received any attention from specialists interested in the matter of concubinage. The earliest example occurs in the *Scriftboc* (V.6.h.):

Swa hwylc man swa mid his mennen gehæme, fæste án winter; gif heo bearn hæbbe, gefreoge hy and swa þeah fæste an winter.

74 [8] "Gif hwa nunnan of mynstere ut álæde butan kyninges lefnesse oððe biscepes, geselle hundtwelftig scill', healf cyninge, healf biscepe 7 þære cyrican hlaforde, ðe ðone munuc age. [8,1] Gif hio leng libbe ðonne se ðe hie utlædde, nage hio his ierfes owiht," "If anyone takes a nun from a monastery without the king's leave or the bishop's, let him pay 120 shillings, half to the king, [the other] half to the bishop and to the lord of the church where the nun resided. If she should outlive the man who took her out, she is not to have a whit of his inheritance." The text goes on to assert that a child born to the nun is similarly to enjoy none of the inheritance. The argument here seems plainly to be that these kinds of unions are in no way to be reckoned legitimate marriages through which property could descend to widows or heirs. I am unable to see on what basis Clunies Ross suggests that this section of Alfred's code refers to "mistresses of priests." See *Gesetze,* ed. Liebermann, I: 54.

75 [35] "Gif preost cwenan forlæte 7 oðre nime, *anathema sit!*" The text here requires that a priest be degraded and perhaps excommunicated if he leaves his wife for another woman. Concubinage seems not to be even implicitly at issue here. *Gesetze*, ed. Liebermann, I: 382.

76 The clause to which Ross refers (cap. 9 of the *Old English Penitential,* which translates Halitgar IV, 12) requires that those having both a wife and a concubine be denied communion, whereas those who are unmarried but have a concubine (*pro uxore concubinam habet* in Halitgar) should not be denied communion but urged to confine themselves to one partner only, "either the concubine or a wife" (*tantum aut unius mulieris, aut uxoris aut concubine, ut ei placuerit, sit conjunctione contentus*). True concubinage, as understood by historians of Liebermann's generation, would have been polygamous; this provision, however, regards concubinage as an informal monogamous marriage. Given the informality of most marriages well into the late Middle Ages, there seems nothing particularly irregular here. On the informality of marriage even in the later Middle Ages, see

"Any man who has intercourse with his slave should fast for one year; if she should have a child, let him free her and nonetheless fast for one year."

Spindler gives as its source Bede III.15:[77]

Si uxoratus ancillam suam, I et III XLmas postea ac legitimas ferias, tribus mensibus primis et a sua se continens, illa autem, si invita passa est, XL dies, si cum consensu, III XLmas et legitimas ferias. Si genuerit ex ea, dimittat liberam et peniteat ut supra.

"If a married man [violates] his slave, [let him do penance for] one and three Quadragesimas afterwards and for the days of the week that are devoted to fasting, [and] for the first three months of this penance let him abstain from his own wife; as for the slave girl, if she suffered the deed unwillingly, [let her fast] for forty days, and if willingly, [let her fast] for the three Quadragesimas and the usual days of fasting. If he has a child with her, he shall let her go free and do penance as described above."

Pelteret notes that the Old English clause "attempted to protect slave women against sexual abuse by imposing a year's fast on a master who seduced his bondwoman."[78] The context of this clause, and the specific nature of the protection offered, shed further light on the peculiarities of the English version. Bede's penitential had concerned a sexual encounter between a *married* man (*uxoratus*) and his slave. Whether this clause holds fornication with a slave to be a particularly grave offense in itself, or regards the husband's adultery as the principal moral problem, Bede leaves unclear. But adultery is plainly not the concern of the *Scriftboc*'s version. The clause addresses itself to "any man who has intercourse with his slave" and omits the instruction that the penitent abstain from his wife.

Clauses surrounding this one in the *Scriftboc* suggest that it was devised specifically to deal with the unmarried man who seduces his slave. Earlier in this subsection of nine clauses dealing with sexual irregularities, the translator had added to his discussion of married men who sleep with other men's wives a curious seven-year penance for a *hægsteald* ("unmarried") man guilty of the same offense (V.6.c.). This penance is much higher than that prescribed for the married adulterer, straying far

James Brundage, *Medieval Canon Law* (New York: Longman, 1995), 72–3: "Canon law by the late twelfth century deemed that two people were married when they exchanged mutual consent to marry one another ... Alternatively a couple might exchange consent in the future tense, in which case they became husband and wife the next time they had sexual intercourse with each other."

[77] Spindler, *Das altenglische Bussbuch*, 30; for the text, see *Bußordnungen*, ed. Wasserschleben, 222.

[78] Pelteret, *Slavery*, 104.

indeed from the instruction of Bede's penitential that the *vacans* undergo a mere two years' fast. Spindler attributes the discrepancy to the translator's disregard for this source.[79] But the appearance in this section of two clauses altered to deal more severely with the offenses of the unmarried seems unlikely to be coincidental. I would suggest that this passage as well shows the translator's particular concern for the sexual behavior of unmarried men and, in doing so, reveals something of his attitude toward the legal position of female slaves with respect to their masters. For the translator of the *Scriftboc,* fornication with slaves, and not adultery, was the problem.

The *Scriftboc*'s understanding of masters' obligations to their female slaves is not a product of the penitentials attributed to Theodore. Fasts for unmarried men who had intercourse with their slaves are absent from the Theodorean collections.[80] The offense seems to have occasioned some uncertainty for earlier compilers of penitential canons, something that is plainly the case when we turn to the transmission of the penitential of Uinniau. Two versions of this penitential, known under the sigla **V** and **S**, serve as our principal witnesses to the text, and the handling of relations with slaves furnishes one of a few instances in which these texts disagree substantially. While **V**, according to Bieler the older and more authentic of the two, requires of "anyone" (*Si quis* ...) a year-long penance and sale of the slave, **S** carefully qualifies this provision to encompass a much more limited group of persons (*Si quis laicus cum uxore propria* ... , "If any layman with a wife of his own ...").[81] This evidence, along with the omission in Theodore of penances for unmarried men having relations with their slaves, suggests that those who compiled the earlier collections of canons struggled to classify this offense: Should it be remedied as an act of adultery or fornication?

It is revealing, then, that the *Scriftboc,* confronted with a clause that treated relations with slaves as a species of adultery, responded by expanding the scope of its application in order to ensure that even unmarried

[79] Spindler, *Das altenglische Bussbuch*, 29.

[80] The offense is discussed in Theodore's penitential at I, xiv, 12: "Si ancilla eius sit, liberet eam et VI menses ieiunet," "If it is his slave [whom the husband violates], let him free her and fast for six months." As it occurs in a section devoted to the offenses of the married, it seems unlikely that it would have been understood as referring to any other category of persons. Finsterwalder (308) observes that this clause is part of a cluster found in no other Theodorean collection.

[81] *The Irish Penitentials*, ed. Bieler, 88–9; the manuscripts are discussed at 15. V = Vienna, National Library, Lat. 2233 (Theol. Lat. 725), "c. 800"; S = St. Gall, Stiftsbibliothek 150, "saec ix."

masters not use their slaves sexually. Indeed, his treatment of the offense agrees very much with the **V** version of Uinnau's penitential, whose clause on fornication with slaves resurfaces unchanged in a collection to which the translator seems likelier to have had access, the *Excarpsus Cummeani*.[82] The lone exception is its failure to reproduce the requirement in the *Excarpsus* that the slave, once violated, be sold (*venundet eam*). But this is probably a purposeful change, reflecting in all likelihood concerns about the subsequent sale of slaves who have been used sexually that are manifest elsewhere in Old English texts, most explicitly in Wulfstan's *Sermo ad Anglos*.[83] The **S** version of Uinniau perhaps clarifies what is at issue here with its assertion that, once the master has had one or more children with his slave

> ... oportet eum libera fieri ancilla, et si uoluerit uenundari eam, non permittatur ei, sed separentur ab inuicem et peniteat annum integrum cum pane et aqua per mensuram; et non intret amplius ad concubinam suam, sed iungatur propriae uxori.
>
> "he is to set her free, and if he wishes to sell her it shall not be permitted to him, but they shall be separated from each other, and he shall do penance an entire year on an allowance of bread and water; and he shall have no further intercourse with his concubine but be joined to his own wife."[84]

The text seems to indicate that when a master has a child with a slave, her legal position with respect to the master is somehow elevated thereby; it is only now that she is referred to as his *concubina,* and possibly the author of the penitential means for this term to indicate her enjoyment of increased protection from the master and from the church. She is not to be used sexually, but she remains a part of his household, and most importantly, she cannot be sold.[85]

[82] "Si quis intrat ad ancillam suam, venundet eam, et annum I peniteat; si genuerit filium ex ea, liberet eam," "If anyone violates his slave, let him sell her and do penance for one year; if he has a child with her, let him free her" (III.32). This collection is occasionally referred to as "Pseudo-Cummean." *Bußordnungen,* ed. Wasserschleben, 474.

[83] See my "Slavery, Learning and the Law of Marriage" for a full exposition of these. The clearest example of such thinking seems evident in Wulfstan's denunciation of those who purchase women for sexual purposes only to sell them again "for money"; the prelate held this not only to be a grievous act of fornication but an offense against the dignity of the slave's soul, which had been truly "purchased" by Christ: see *The Homilies of Wulfstan,* ed. Bethurum, 270; also Chapter 3, 110.

[84] *Irish Penitentials*, ed. and trans. Bieler, 88–9.

[85] Payer (*Sex and the Penitentials,* 21) reads this clause somewhat differently: "[T]he longer version of the canon dealing with the female slave who begets a child indicates that the slave was actually serving as a concubine." I find it difficult not to see, however, a change in the slave's status occasioned by her bearing her master's children, whatever

This condition is used elsewhere to signify a slave's elevation to something approaching wifely status. In the Breton compilation known as the *Excerpta de Libris Romanorum et Francorum*, for example, female slaves are treated with no particular regard. Once married, however, the text affords them protections analogous to those mentioned in the later version of Uinniau's penitential:[86]

Si quis ancellam suam in matrimonio sibi habere uoluerit et de suis rebus habet potestatem, si noluerit postea habere eam [uoluerit uenundare eam BX], non conceditur; quod si eam uenundare uoluerit, eum uenundari iubemus et ancellam illam in sacerdotis ponimus potestatem.

"If anyone who has power in his own affairs is resolved to have his slave woman in marriage, if he afterwards does not want to have her [should wish to sell her BX], it is not allowed; but if he is resolved to sell her, we command that he shall be sold, and we make that slave woman the ward of a priest."

If this offense is greeted with silence where the unmarried are concerned in Theodore's penitential, it may be because sexual relations between a slave and an unmarried man were understood to result, under some circumstances, in a kind of informal marriage between the two; a logical outcome given Brundage's definition of Germanic marriage as "sexual intercourse accompanied by an intention to live together permanently."[87] As is made clear in the passage from Halitgar referred to earlier, the sole concern of the church throughout most of the earlier Middle Ages was that the man in question limit himself to one sexual partner. In a legal environment in which consummation and marriage were at times difficult to distinguish, we may suppose that intimacies between masters and slaves might have been understood by some clerics to have triggered such conditions, at least for the purposes of pastoral care.[88]

the meaning of the notoriously fraught term *concubina* might be in this instance; at the very least, it is difficult to see why this label should be applied to her after the master is instructed to avoid all contact with her. The usage is perhaps clarified by the clause from Halitgar to be discussed subsequently, which implies the presence of women in a household who exist under the protection of a lord in some servile capacity but are not to be used sexually by him.

86 *The Irish Penitentials*, ed. and trans. Bieler, 149.

87 Reynolds (*Marriage in the Western Church*, 334) has asserted, perhaps more suggestively, that one finds in the medieval law of marriage "the notion that sexual intercourse *per se* creates some form of permanent union."

88 Underlying the logic of such provisions one may discern a literal application of I Corinthians 6:16: "Do you not know that whoever is united to a prostitute becomes one body with her? For it is said, 'The two shall be one flesh.'" Use of the passage in discussions of fornication is an early medieval commonplace. See *Two Ælfric Texts*, ed. and trans. Mary Clayton (Cambridge: D.S. Brewer, 2013), 84.

We may suspect that the *Scriftboc*'s provision tends toward the understanding of relations between slaves and masters evident in Uinniau and the *Excerpta* given its omission of an allowance very likely present in his source to sell the violated slave. As the *Scriftboc*, for reasons established in Chapter 2, may well have been extant during the reign of Alfred – a supposed period of relative tolerance for concubinage – it seems fair to wonder, particularly given the weakness of Liebermann's arguments to this effect, whether tolerance of sexual relations with slaves, where this did not raise them to the condition of (quasi-)wives, should be imputed to his era at all.[89] The *Scriftboc*'s treatment of this offense reflects prohibitions on the sale of slaves that have entered into permanent unions of any kind.[90] Such norms, as I suggest, are most apparent in the long hostility of the Western Church toward separating married slaves by sale, and underlie the corrective addition (sometimes regarded as a mistranslation) made by the *Scriftboc* to a clause that takes up this matter. Whereas his source had allowed that a married slave, once manumitted, might seek another spouse (*libero licet ingenuo conjungere*), the Old English makes the remarkable assertion that "heora swa hwæðer swa freoh byð mot þam ðeowan freols gewinnan," "whichever one of them is free may obtain freedom for the slave."[91] Echoed here may be a principle articulated in Latin canons to which the translator may have had access: "[I]n venditione vel emptione videtur observari debere, ut, quando quis maritum emerit, emat pariter et conjugem, nisi forte alterius ancilla fuerit," "In the sale or purchase [of slaves] it certainly seems that care must be taken, so that when someone purchases a husband, he should purchase together with him his wife, unless by chance she were another's slave."[92]

As our last item of evidence concerning the toleration of informal unions or concubinage in Anglo-Saxon England, we may turn to a passage of the *Old English Penitential*, which translates Halitgar IV.17 (itself canon 27 of the Council of Chalcedon):[93]

89 Use of *mennen* makes composition in the Alfredian period rather than tenth-century revival of prose writing only more likely; see Chapter 2, 76. Pope Leo I, in a letter excerpted in later canon collections, had required that unions with slaves result in their manumission in order to continue legitimately: for a discussion see Reynolds, *Marriage in the Western Church*, 162–5.

90 See "The Old English Penitentials and the Law of Slavery," 113–17. Cap. A 110 of the *Canons of Theodore* probably reveals little, as it faithfully translates the requirement of *PT* I, xiv, 11 that a married man who fornicates with his slave manumit her and fast for six months.

91 The source is *PT* I, xiii, 4; for the Old English, see Spindler, *Das altenglische Bussbuch*, 181 (xiii.16.b).

92 Regino of Prüm, *De synodalibus causis*, ed. Wasserschleben, 262.

93 *Bussbücher*, ed. Schmitz, I: 725.

De his qui rapiunt puellam. Eos qui rapiunt mulieres sub nomine simul habitandi cooperantes aut cohibentes raptoribus decrevit sancta Synodus, ut si quidem clerici sunt, decidant gradu proprio; si vero laici, anathematizentur.

"Of those who seize girls. Those who capture women for the purpose of having them in their households immediately, whether [the women in question] have been taken by force or have conspired with their captors, the holy synod has decreed that if they are clerics they are to be degraded; and if they are laymen, let them be excommunicated."

The *Old English Penitential* gives the following version:[94]

Be þam men þe þæne wifman fram his hlaforde aspanð þe his wicnere bið, for unrihtum hæmede. – Gif hwa mid his lotwrencum oðres manes folgere fram him apæce for hæmedðinge, 7 hire unwilles wið hi hæme: gif h(e) bið gehadod man, þolige his hades; gif he beo læwede, beo heo amansumod.

"Concerning those men who separate from her lord a woman who is his steward, for the purpose of an unlawful union. If anyone deceitfully seduces another man's attendant for sexual purposes, and has intercourse with her [or 'marries' her] against her will: if he is a man in orders, let him lose his office; if he is a layman, let him be excommunicated."

Though this clause does not surface in any discussion of early English slavery of which I am aware, it may refer to female members of the servile class, for *wicnere* translates *servus* in the Old English Genesis, while *folgere* can have the meaning "landless (and therefore dependent) churl."[95] Raith seems to have considered the women referred to in it as servile, seeing in this clause an occasion to remind readers of the conflict between the traditional Germanic law of the household and practices envisaged by the Church: "The situation was somewhat different in this respect regarding one's own female slave, as here there obtained for the lord a certain right of disposal; moreover, canon law for the most part favored manumission for the slave."[96] Raith suggests here that there were few obstacles to slaves belonging sexually to their masters until the intervention of the church, and hints that this clause may have countenanced seduction of the bondwoman by her master, though not by others.

A different principle may be at work in this clause. The chapter immediately preceding this one in the *Old English Penitential* had laid

94 *Die altenglische Version*, 23 (cap. 14).

95 *The Old English Heptateuch*, ed. Marsden, 50–1. Charles McLean Andrews saw the condition of the *folgere* as little better than that of a slave "de jure," a possibility that leaves persons of this class essentially servile. The uncertainty of the term, however, permits little beyond speculation. See *The Old English Manor: A Study in English Economic History* (Baltimore: Johns Hopkins University Press, 1892), 177.

96 *Altenglische Version*, 23 (ch. 14).

down that anyone who by force (*neadinga*) places a *wif* or a *mæden* in *unriht-hæmede*, "an unlawful union," is to be excommunicated (the source had given *uiduarum uel uirginum*). The subsequent clause had gone on to *puellae* – presumably expanding the ambit of protection from *raptus* to young women or children. Rather than repeat the prohibition, the author of the *Old English Penitential* seems to have adapted this portion of Halitgar to argue that *raptus* of a slave was equal in its seriousness to *raptus* of a free-born woman. His doing so is consistent with the tendency of all of the Old English penitentials to urge that the same sexual and marital norms be incumbent on slave and free, even if doing so meant rewriting substantially the stipulations of sources. I find it hard to see any concessions to concubinage here. Having previously said that unions arranged forcibly are illegitimate when involving the free, the translator does the same for slave women, widening the scope of their ecclesiastical protections and possibly conferring on them a status that seems to have been the privilege of the free (perhaps in a manner not unlike the passage from the late version of Uinniau's penitential referred to earlier).[97] The chapter considered in the preceding text confirms the interest of Anglo-Saxon translators in protecting consent in marriage and shows that this rule was understood to apply even to slaves. It is difficult to see how open engagement in concubinage would have been countenanced by the church (as Clunies Ross and Liebermann imply) given the tendency of vernacular canon law to regard norms of sexual conduct as incumbent on slave and free alike. All of the clauses discussed in this section confer protections on slaves from sexual exploitation that are not present in their sources, and they likely show the Anglo-Saxon church to have been peculiarly concerned with the possibilities for sexual immorality opened up by the uncertain legal status of slaves.[98]

[97] The laws of Æthelberht (caps. 10–12) impose fines on those who sleep with servile women of the king's household, but the description given here of the rather prosaic duties of one of the slaves (grinding corn) suggests that these did not include making themselves sexually available to him – nor would such an arrangement likely have been countenanced by Æthelberht's Frankish Christian wife! Oliver (*Beginnings of English Law*, 89) suggests that these slaves were valued "because they had responsibilities in the area of food and drink, which would require slaves not only with certain skills but also with a high degree of trustworthiness, since poison would constantly have been feared as a method of assassination." The translator of the *Old English Penitential* may have had some analogous arrangement in mind as he rewrote this portion of Halitgar's collection.

[98] Such concerns are perhaps evident also in cap. III.6 of the *Old English Penitential* (*Die altenglische Version*, ed. Raith, 39). See the discussion in Chapter 6, 193.

CONCLUSIONS

The work undertaken in this chapter offers some support to earlier descriptions of "Germanic marriage" by Brundage and Reynolds. But the Old English penitentials are not wholly in keeping with what these and other historians would have us expect of Germanic law. Their rather severe handling of matters of sexual purity agrees with much of what has been said over the past few decades regarding the peculiarities of Anglo-Saxon sexuality, usually with reference to verse and hagiography. Aiming to surpass their sources in rigor, the authors of the Old English penitentials brought to these texts their own uncompromising horror of defilement. Yet they can also be seen pursuing different ends, in some instances exceeding their sources' concern for the elevation of consensual marriage and expanding the range of persons (the unmarried, slave women) to be understood as explicitly subject to sexual norms urged by the Church.

The origins of such attitudes are difficult to trace. In their views of marital sexuality we may see some residue of the Levitical purity code arguably taught by British monastic missionaries to which Gregory the Great and subsequently the penitential of Theodore seem to react.[99] It is perhaps due to such habits of mind that the Old English penitentials regularly deliver more rigorous judgments on matters of marital sexuality than are found in their sources. Their inclusion of the "nights of Tobias" agrees with such aims and may also furnish another example of how secular law was shaped in this period by that of the Old Testament. All of the Old English canons described in this chapter attest to the relative independence of Anglo-Saxon clergy when it came to defining the boundaries of the acceptable in the lives of married laypersons.

99 On this, see especially Chapter 6.

5

Caring for the Body

Law, Penitentials, and English "Sick-Maintenance"

While the school of legal-historical scholarship established by Jakob Grimm and Heinrich Brunner has received much criticism over the last few decades, somewhat less attention has been paid to the effects of its parent discipline, comparative Indo-European philology, on our sense of how disputes were resolved before the Conquest.[1] Scholarship in this vein regards practices attested within multiple members of the same language family in much the same way as the cognate words for "father" and "heart" shared by Latin, Sanskrit, and Greek, both types of evidence allowing in theory for the reconstruction of usages obtaining millennia before the birth of Christ.[2] This chapter is concerned with one such practice, the reconstruction of which by Indo-Europeanists constitutes one of the few instances in which members of this field engaged directly with Anglo-Saxon evidence, and whose most familiar attestation is in a text far removed from early medieval Europe:[3]

When individuals quarrel and one strikes the other with a stone or fist so that the injured party, though not dead, is confined to bed, but recovers and walks around

[1] The transition from eighteenth-century historiographers' and lawyers' use of Anglo-Saxon materials as evidence for England's constitutional history to the comparative approach of the early nineteenth century is narrated in Wormald, *Making,* 4–14. For an overview of the Göttingen school of legal history in which the methods of comparative philology were first wedded to historiography, see Daniela Fruscione, "Liebermann's Intellectual Milieu," in Jurasinski, Oliver, and Rabin, eds., *English Law before Magna Carta,* 15–26. The foundation of nineteenth-century historical jurisprudence in Indo-Europeanist studies such as those of Sir Henry Maine is asserted in Lawrence Krader, "Introduction," *Anthropology and Early Law,* ed. Krader (New York: Basic Books, 1966), 7.

[2] On the history of the comparative method, see Oswald Szemerényi, *Einführung in die vergleichende Sprachwissenschaft* (Darmstadt: Wissenschaftliche Buchgesellschaft, 1980), 1–10.

[3] *The New Oxford Annotated Bible,* 3rd ed., ed. Michael D. Coogan (Oxford: Oxford University Press, 2001).

outside with the help of a staff, then the assailant shall be free of liability, except to pay for the loss of time, and to arrange for full recovery.

That it has become customary to refer to Exodus 21:18–19 as an instance of "sick-maintenance" shows how decisively our understanding of this institution has been shaped by studies less interested in the biblical ordinance than its supposed analogues within various Indo-European traditions.[4] The term *sick-maintenance* is a close translation of the Irish *folog n-othrusa,* "maintenance of sickness," and although it postdates the events of Exodus by millennia, Irish tradition has long been held to retain a more archaic form of the institution than is found even in the laws of Moses. According to D. A. Binchy, whose article of 1934 remains the authoritative discussion of the subject, "the Old Irish law preserves for us … the relics of a more primitive system [than is found in Exodus]. In the earliest texts we find that the injurer, instead of paying the 'leech-fee', must undertake the duty of nursing his victim back to health and providing him with medical attendance."[5] That the requirement in Old Irish law of personal care of the victim rather than payment, and of a man to work in the victim's stead, may be the survival of an older tradition concerning "sick-maintenance" is suggested by an ordinance composed in Hittite (1500 BCE):[6]

If anyone injures a (free) person and temporarily incapacitates him, he shall provide medical care for him. In his place he shall provide a person to work on his estate until he recovers. When he recovers (his assailant) shall pay him 6 shekels of silver and shall pay the physician's fee as well.

Similar provisions in sources as far-flung as the code of Manu led Calvert Watkins in 1976 to label sick-maintenance "an inherited feature of Indo-European customary law."[7] Though this conclusion has since found wide acceptance, the views of Binchy and Watkins are not always repeated without reservations in present-day scholarship.[8] In the absence

4 E.g., Doris Edel refers to "the institution of sick-maintenance, which is also found in the early Germanic laws and in the Old Testament (Exod. 21: 18–19), albeit in modernized form." "The Status and Development of the Vernacular in Early Medieval Ireland," in *The Dawn of the Written Vernacular in Western Europe*, eds. Michèle Goyens and Werner Verbeke (Leuven: Leuven University Press, 2003), 351–78 at 355n17.

5 See D. A. Binchy, "Sick-Maintenance in Irish Law," *Ériu* 12 (1934), 78–134 at 78.

6 *The Laws of the Hittites: A Critical Edition*, ed. and trans. Harry Angier Hoffner Jr. (Leiden, The Netherlands: Brill, 1997), 23.

7 Calvert Watkins, "Sick-Maintenance in Indo-European," *Ériu* 27 (1976), 21–5.

8 See Stefan Zimmer, "Glimpses of Indo-European Law," in *The Law's Beginnings*, ed. Ferdinand Joseph Maria Feldbrugge (Leiden, The Netherlands: Brill, 2003), 115–36 at

of a genuinely cognate term to describe the institution in the various Indo-European witnesses, one recent commentator has noted the "rather weak linguistic basis for the reconstruction of a Proto-Indo-European rule of sick-maintenance."[9]

No less troublesome, I would argue, is the assumption of both scholars that traces of Indo-European sick-maintenance are evident in Anglo-Saxon materials.[10] The written output of Anglo-Saxon England, which neither Binchy nor Watkins considered in much detail, does not in fact offer much support for this conclusion. Of the four attestations of sick-maintenance within the corpus of Old English prose, three occur in texts relying in some fashion on the language of Exodus 21:18–19. Of these, two are translations of the biblical text, the earliest occurring in the Mosaic Prologue to the laws of King Alfred and the second in the much later "Old English Heptateuch." Each translates the Vulgate version of Exodus rather differently, though only the first of these may offer any insights regarding contemporaneous practices because the second is a straightforward translation:[11]

ALFRED: Gif hwa slea hys ðone nehstan mid stane oððe mid fyste, 7 he þeah utgongan mæge bi stæfe, begite him læce 7 wyrce his weorc þa hwile þe he self ne mæge.

"If someone should strike his neighbor with a stone or with a fist, and the latter may nonetheless walk about with a staff, let [the attacker] obtain a physician for him and perform his work while he is unable."

OLD ENGLISH HEPTATEUCH: Gif men cidað and hira oðer hys nextan mid stane wyrpð oþþe mid fyste slicþ, and he dead ne bið ac lið on bedde seoc, gif he arist and ut gæþ mid his stafe, he bið unscildig þe hine sloh; gylde swa þeah his weorc and þæt hine man hæle.

"If men quarrel, and one of them throws a stone at the other or beats him with his fist, and he is not dead but lies sick in his bed; if he rises and goes out with his

127–8, and *Encyclopedia of Indo-European Culture*, eds. J. P. Mallory and D. Q. Adams (Chicago: Fitzroy Dearborn, 1997), s.v. "medicine."

9 Zimmer, "Glimpses of Indo-European Law," 128. See also the word of caution in Ferdinand Joseph Maria Feldbrugge, *Law in Medieval Russia* (Leiden, The Netherlands: Brill, 2009), 9.

10 Binchy, "Sick-Maintenance," 78n3; Watkins, "Sick-Maintenance," 23.

11 Liebermann, *Gesetze*, I: 32 (Einleitung, cap. 16); the version given here is Liebermann's transcription of MS E, the "Parker Manuscript" (Cambridge, Corpus Christi College MS 173); *The Old English Heptateuch*, ed. Marsden, 117. The Vulgate version is as follows: "Si rixati fuerint viri et percusserit alter proximum suum lapide vel pugno et ille mortuus non fuerit sed iacuerit in lectulo: si surrexerit et ambulaverit foris super baculum suum innocens erit qui percusserit ita tamen ut operas eius et inpensas in medicos restituat."

staff, he who injured him is without blame; let him pay nonetheless for his work and so that he may be healed."

Another Old English treatment of sick-maintenance is found in the *Scriftboc*. Of all the apparent attestations in Anglo-Saxon sources, it is by far the most detailed, and the strangest:[12]

Swa hwylc man se ðe in gecynde oðerne gedo wánhalne oððe hine womwlite on gewyrce, forgylde him þone womwlite, and his weorc wyrce oð þæt seo wund hal sy, and þæt læcefeoh ðam læce gylde, and fæste twa ǽfestena oððe þreo; gyf he nyte hu he hit gylde, fæste XII monað.

"Whoever renders a man injured in his genitals or inflicts *womwlite* upon him, let him compensate his victim for the *womwlite*, and let him perform his victim's work until the wound has healed, and let him make payment to the physician, and let him fast for two or three of the ordained fasting periods; if he does not know how he might make compensation for the injury, let him fast for twelve months."

Though the *Scriftboc* also relies in some measure on Exodus, in this case the biblical provisions have been filtered through another layer of influences. This portion of the *Scriftboc* recasts one of the many virtually identical clauses circulating in Latin penitentials that adapted the language of Exodus 21:18–19 to the realities of postconversion Europe. Some, but not all of the *Scriftboc*'s peculiarities are traceable to this tradition, as will be shown later.[13]

All the evidence that remains for the existence of sick-maintenance in pre-Conquest England is limited to single words occurring in two texts at opposite ends of the Old English period. The first surfaces in the seventh-century laws of King Æthelberht, and the second in the Old French *Leis Willelme* – a text composed perhaps a century after the death of William the Conqueror that in the opinion of most modern commentators contains few authentic descriptions of earlier English law.[14] While

[12] Spindler, *Das altenglische Bussbuch*, 186 (cap. XIX.20.d). The text appears also in Thorpe, *Ancient Laws and Institutes*, at 148–9 (cap. 22).

[13] The most recent discussion of this clause may be found in Lisi Oliver, "Sick-Maintenance in Anglo-Saxon Law," *Journal of English and Germanic Philology* 107 (2008), 303–26 at 326: "The extant Germanic clauses lack the third requirement of Hittite and Old Irish sick-maintenance clauses that the perpetrator either provide a man to work in the wounded man's stead or compensate the work.... The one Old English instance that we seem to have, from the *Confessional of Egbert*, turns out to have been borrowed from the Irish penitential tradition, which itself had been influenced by Irish secular law."

[14] On the date of the *Leis Willelme* and the various theories concerning its composition, see Jakob Wüest, *Die Leis Willelme: Untersuchungen zum ältesten Gesetzbuch in*

the occurrence of the word *cearwund* in Æthelberht's code may offer some indication that sick-maintenance was an element of English law, there is at best a trace of the institution in this compound; one perhaps unrecognized by those who devised the ordinance in which it occurs, as this clause imposes on the assailant no obligation beyond payment of 30 shillings to a man so wounded.[15] In spite of its lateness, the *Leis Willelme* is the only English source referred to in the studies of Binchy and Watkins, both of whom mention its use of the term *læcefeoh* (if only in the garbled form *lecheof*) and nothing else.[16] The relevance of this text to the history of sick-maintenance has been called into question by Lisi Oliver. For Binchy, the *conditio sine qua non* of sick-maintenance legislation in Ireland and throughout the Indo-European world was the presence of an incapacitating injury: "[I]t is obvious that before any question of increased liability for the defendant can arise, the condition of his victim must be sufficiently serious to demand medical attention and nursing over a period of time."[17] Yet as Oliver notes, the injuries referred to in the *Leis Willelme* must have been of little lasting significance. Her conclusion is borne out by the brief text given its requirement that the plaintiff swear he is not exaggerating the seriousness of his wounds, a condition

französischer Sprache (Bern: Francke Verlag, 1969), where the text is dated no earlier than the middle of the twelfth century given its use of learned texts of Roman law (74); also Ralph V. Turner, "Roman Law in England before the Time of Bracton," *Journal of British Studies* 15 (1975), 1–25; repr. in idem, *Judges, Administrators, and the Common Law in Angevin England* (Rio Grande: Hambledon, 1994), 45–70 at 49–50.

[15] Oliver discusses at length this *hapax legomenon* attested at cap. 63 of the laws of Æthelberht and argues from the suggestions of earlier scholars that the compound must mean "wound causing a person to be bedridden" (308), which suggests (given the apparently cognate Old Norse term *kör* "sickbed") awareness in seventh-century Kent of "an inherited regulation of sick-maintenance" (311).

[16] See Watkins, "Sick-Maintenance," 23: "[W]e must recognize the primitive institution of sick-maintenance as a feature of Indo-European customary law, remarkably preserved intact in Irish and Hittite, and in other cognate Indo-European legal systems commuted, with Binchy, to the later 'leech-fee' alone (OEng. *læce-feoh,* Skt. *samutthāna-vyayam* Manu 8.287)." Watkins does not mention the source of the Old English compound, which occurs in legislation, as Binchy (78) notes, only in the likely irrelevant *Leis Willelme.*

[17] Binchy, "Sick-Maintenance," 91–2. A convalescence in excess of nine days qualified a victim for sick-maintenance in Irish law, which shows just how severe injuries of this sort needed to be: see Fergus Kelly, *A Guide to Irish Law* (Dublin: Institute for Advanced Studies, 1988; repr. 1991), 130. That the *Leis Willelme* have little in common with Irish law is also evident in the latter's requirement that a victim's entitlement to sick-maintenance be first determined upon a physician's examination, a feature of early Gaelic law discussed in Robin Chapman Stacy, *Dark Speech: The Performance of Law in Early Ireland* (Philadelphia: University of Pennsylvania Press, 2007), 34.

presupposing a victim who was not, as in Exodus, hovering between life and death:[18]

[10] Si hom feit plaie en auter e il deive faire les amendes, primierement lui rende sien lecheof. [10a] Et li plaez jurra sur seinz, que pur meins nel pot feire ne pur haur si cher nel fist.

If a man injures another and is obliged to make amends, first let him render [to the victim] the leech-fee. And the injured party must swear on the holy relics, that it could not be done for less nor has he made [the amount] so expensive because of hatred.

Ultimately, there is no way out of the difficulty that what little survives of sick-maintenance in Anglo-Saxon England seems the product of influences external to the British Isles. Even if *cearwund* and *lecheof* suggest some faint awareness of sick-maintenance in Anglo-Saxon law, the possibility that such a practice arrived through Exodus cannot be disproved and indeed seems strong given the influence of the biblical text upon early ecclesiastical law.[19] Divergences from biblical norms in Anglo-Saxon texts only make the Indo-European descent of whatever practices obtained less likely. The application of the "leech-fee" to injuries much less significant than those requiring sick-maintenance in Irish law leaves English "sick-maintenance," if it merits the name at all, far removed from the provisions either of Mosaic or Irish law.

Such a conclusion is surely disappointing should our aim be to find in English law traces of Indo-European antiquity. If, however, we accept the limitation that sick-maintenance as it existed in England was thoroughly contaminated by ecclesiastical canons originating in the laws of Moses, the Old English evidence may still have much to offer the historian of pre-Conquest law. The independence of Anglo-Saxon thought concerning sick-maintenance is evident in the fact that no two Old English discussions of this institution agree entirely as to its form even though each translates a text, whether Exodus 21:18–19 or the penitential clauses derived from it,

[18] *Gesetze*, ed. Liebermann, I: 498–501. The translation given here owes something to that of Robertson, *Laws*, 259. For analysis of the passage, see Oliver, "Sick-Maintenance," 315n40: "[A]lthough the term *lecheof* echoes (probably unrelatedly) Egbert's ruling on sick-maintenance, this stipulation from the *Leis Willelme* would seem to apply to all injuries inflicted by another, whether debilitating to the point of incapacitation or not. The clause that follows even implies that at least in some instances the damage might even have been healed so quickly that the perpetrator could not himself bear witness to the cure."

[19] The earliest references to sick-maintenance extant in ecclesiastical law occur in the penitential of Cummean, a likely source of the *Scriftboc*'s provision that will be discussed in more detail in the following pages. Though the Cummean to whom this penitential was attributed by tradition has been lost to history, it may be assumed that this text antedates considerably the cycle of Theodorean penitentials given the latter's partial reliance upon

whose authority should have made divergent translations unlikely. If those who translated these passages were indeed recording distinctly English views in their departures from source material, the evidence afforded by the *Scriftboc* – evidence that has so far received the least attention in studies devoted to the history of sick-maintenance – would seem to be the most revealing. That its translator renders independently even norms of ecclesiastical law that were likely seen as binding upon his contemporaries suggests that its clause on sick-maintenance may well record something of the customs of his time. The result is a clause showing how biblical, ecclesiastical, and secular norms combined to establish an institution unique to pre-Conquest England that has yet to be acknowledged as such. That the description of sick-maintenance in the *Scriftboc* shows some agreement with the other Old English texts discussed previously makes the existence of an independent English variant of sick-maintenance quite likely.

EXODUS AND THE LATIN PENITENTIALS ON SICK-MAINTENANCE

Making sense of what the *Scriftboc* and other Old English texts have to say about sick-maintenance requires that we consider again the biblical clause that served as the template for all later ecclesiastical legislation. All treatments of sick-maintenance in the Latin pentientials derive in some manner from the Vulgate version of Exodus 21:18–19, of which the Douay version gives the following translation:

> If men quarrel, and the one strike his neighbor with a stone or with his fist, and he die not, but keepeth his bed; if he rise again, and walk abroad upon his staff, he that struck him shall be quit (*innocens erit qui percusserit*), yet so that he make restitution for his work (*restituat … operas eius*), and for his expenses upon the physicians (*inpensas in medicos*).

Dependence on this ordinance is particularly close in the penitential of Cummean, whose clause on sick-maintenance likely served as a basis for what occurs in the *Scriftboc*. I give the text as edited by Ludwig Bieler in 1975 as well as his translation:[20]

> Qui per rixam ictu debilem uel deformem hominem reddit, inpensa in medicos curat et maculae pretium et opus eius donec sanetur restituat et dimidium anni peniteat. Si uero non habeat unde restituat haec,.i. annum peniteat.

Cummean for some of its provisions. On the debt of Theodore's penitential to Cummean, see Flechner, "The Making of the Canons of Theodore," 129–30.

[20] *Irish Penitentials*, ed. Bieler, 120–1.

"He who by a blow in a quarrel renders a man incapacitated or maimed shall meet [the injured man's] medical expenses and shall make good the damages for the deformity and shall do his work [better: 'compensate him for his work'] until he is healed and do penance for half a year. If he has not the wherewithal to make restitution for these things, he shall do penance for one year."

Bieler's translation shows some of the hazards of conflating the Latin tradition of penitentials – a body of texts perhaps relying less on Irish ideas than has often been assumed – with the Irish tradition in which he was a formidable expert. Before moving to the problems posed by Bieler's rendering, we should note the overall aims of this clause, which are evident even in this less-than-ideal translation. Some of the changes Exodus has undergone in Cummean's penitential are plainly meant to accommodate the understanding of violence characteristic of Christian teaching in postconversion Europe. In Exodus, the assailant had been considered *innocens* if his assault did not result in the death of his victim. The arrival of Christianity brought with it an understanding that violence of this sort was prompted by desires that were themselves culpable, and thus such a formulation is unacceptable to the author of Cummean's penitential, who adds to the clause, perhaps to ensure that there is no ambiguity, a penance even for those acts of violence from which no injury results: "Qui ictum proximo suo dederit et non nocuit, .i. uel .ii. uel .iii. xlmis in pane et aqua peniteat," "He who gives a blow to his neighbour without doing him harm, shall do penance on bread and water one or two or three quadragesimas."[21] Imposition of a year of penance on an assailant unable to undertake the obligations of "sick-maintenance" similarly targets as of primary importance the spiritual condition that caused the penitent to do harm, while the material condition of his victim retreats into the background as an area of concern.

These additions result in an understanding of sick-maintenance quite different from what may have obtained in ancient Israel, the Hittite empire, or even early Ireland. In the Penitential of Cummean, sick-maintenance restores the penitent to spiritual health by compelling him to help a man he has wronged and thus curing with its opposite the disordered passion that brought about his evil act.[22] Along with the obvious debt to the

[21] *Irish Penitentials*, ed. Bieler, 120–1.

[22] On the association of penitential and medical thought, see John T. McNeill, "Medicine for Sin as Prescribed in the Penitentials," *Church History* 1 (1932), 14–26. Here McNeill considers the belief, characteristic of most penitentials, that sinful passions are to be cured with their opposites. McNeill traces this *topos*, derived ultimately from Greek medical thought, into the writings of Cassian and thence to the Celtic church, where such thinking finds its first expression in the British Isles (16–18).

Vulgate version of Exodus manifest in its use of the verb *restituere* and the phrase *inpensa in medicos*, the presence of such ideas raises doubts about Thomas Oakley's suggestion that sick-maintenance appears in Latin penitentials as a result of influence from Irish secular law.[23] Indeed, Oakley's description of the practice as maintained in the penitentials is unintentionally misleading. While his summary account suggests that "do[ing] the work of the injured" is characteristic of all members of this corpus, in fact this obligation is required of a penitent only in the *Scriftboc,* which Oakley cites (as "Conf. ps. Egb.") alongside the manuals attributed to Bede and Uinniau as if it were a member of the Latin tradition (which Oakley may indeed have taken it to be, as did many of his contemporaries). The penitential of Uinniau, in any case, does not prescribe anything beyond compensation fixed by an arbiter in cases of wounding and is thus irrelevant to the present discussion. It will be seen later that Cummean's understanding of sick-maintenance as a species of penance, so far unremarked in scholarship on these texts, influenced decisively the peculiar treatment of sick-maintenance found in the *Scriftboc.*

Pastoral ends also lead Cummean to broaden the range of injuries to which the remedy of sick-maintenance may be applicable. Now an injury that renders a victim *deformem* ("disfigured") rather than bedridden may entitle him to sick-maintenance. A somewhat different set of motives is suggested by the penitential's reference to the *maculae pretium,* rendered by Bieler somewhat infelicitously as "damages for the deformity." This phrase probably refers to the system of payments assigned in Frankish secular law to various injuries.[24] Adding a requirement to pay the *maculae pretium* may perhaps be considered an improvement upon Exodus rather than an outright departure from it. The injuries for which one might have expected compensation in Frankish laws of this period – severed digits, ears, noses, and the like – might easily have delayed one's

[23] The point that these phrases show indebtedness to Exodus is made in Oliver, "Sick-Maintenance," 319; on supposed Irish influence, see Oakley, "Cooperation," 522 and n. 12.: "Of particular interest are provisions concerning reparations for wounds. Of Irish origin, and subsequently incorporated into penitentials elsewhere, these demanded that he who wounds another must pay for his medical treatment, do the work of the injured until his recovery, and perform penance, as well as pay the regular secular compensation.... The custom is apparently derived from the requirement of 'sick-maintenance' [in Irish secular law]." For the text of Uinniau, see *Irish Penitentials*, ed. Bieler, 76–7 (caps. 8–9).

[24] The penitential of Theodore (*PT* I, iv, 1) similarly makes concessions to secular custom concerning compensation, lessening the penances of those who pay the "pecuniam æstimationis," taken by McNeill and Gamer (*Medieval Handbooks,* 187n53) to refer to

return to labor even if the victim was not bedridden, and so this ordinance may be seen as preserving the logic of Exodus while making its provisions more merciful. Nonetheless, inclusion of the *maculae pretium* is rather different from the changes so far discussed, for here it is secular legal tradition rather than pastoral concern that shapes the raw materials of Exodus into a provision distinct from its source.

The other remedies assigned by this clause are less certain, with most of the difficulties revolving around the meaning of *restituat*. We have seen that the Douay version translates *restituat* in a pecuniary sense – "make restitution" – in spite of the fact that the verb may have the meaning "restore" or "replace." In Cummean, as in the Vulgate, the objects of *restituat* are *inpensa in medicos* and *opus eius*. While *inpensa in medicos* lends itself to a monetary understanding of the obligation implied by this verb, *opus eius* does not do so with equal ease. Bieler's translation gets around this problem by assigning two meanings to the verb ("shall meet [the injured man's] medical expenses … and shall do his work"). The translation offered by McNeill and Gamer does the same, but their version of an identical passage occurring in the penitential ascribed to Bede gives "make compensation for his work while he is recovering," which suggests that their views on how to render this verb may have wavered over time.[25] I see no reason to doubt that the intended meaning of this provision differs at all from Exodus given the language of Cummean cap. 10 ("Si uero non habeat unde restituat …"), a provision suggesting that completing the obligations of sick-maintenance described in the preceding clause involves giving of one's possessions rather than one's time or efforts.

Some of the ambiguity that twentieth-century scholars have perceived in Cummean's ordinance may be owing to their having followed Oakley in assuming this text to rely upon the Irish tradition of sick-maintenance.

"the 'wergeld' or value in law of the slain man"; see also the *Iudicia Theodori* (cap. 88), wherein the treatment of the offender unable to pay is close to that of Cummean's provision on sick-maintenance: "Qui homicidium vel furtum comisserit et non composuit illis quibus nocuit quando confessus fuerit aepiscopo vel presbitero peccata sua debet illis aut propria reddere vel componere. Si vero non habuerit substantiam unde conponere potest vel nescierit quibus nocuit penitentia plus augeatur"; "He who commits murder or theft and fails to make composition with those whom he has injured, when he has confessed his sins to a bishop or a presbyter, ought either to render them his property or to make composition; if indeed he has not the substance with which to make composition or does not know whom he has injured, his penance is to be the more increased." See *Canones Theodori*, ed. Finsterwalder, 246; trans. McNeill and Gamer, *Medieval Handbooks*, 216.

[25] MacNeill and Gamer, *Medieval Handbooks*, 107 (Cummean) and 225 (Bede).

As Binchy has shown, while one was obliged in "the earliest [Irish] texts ... [to] undertake the duty of nursing his victim back to health and providing him with medical attendance," later "the more primitive obligation to provide sick-maintenance was commuted for a fixed payment, thereby approximating to the practice of the other systems." The shift from personal care to payment in Irish law seems to have happened well in advance of the year 700, though it is doubtful that the former practice died out completely.[26] Bieler's translation seems to have in mind the earlier practice, and the same may be the case for McNeill and Gamer. But we may be sure that nothing other than a pecuniary obligation is implied by the penitentials of Cummean or Bede, whose understanding of sick-maintenance seems in any case rooted in the language of Exodus, and which were set to writing after the obligation to provide sick-maintenance in person had been commuted to a payment in Irish law. The situation is perhaps clarified by the language of the *Excarpsus Cummeani* (cap. VI.23), which does not merely reproduce the language of Cummean as had Bede's penitential: "Si laicus per scandalum sanguinem effuderit, reddat illi tantum, quantum nocuit, et si non habeat unde reddat, solvat opera proximi sui, quamdiu ille infirmus est et postea XL dies peniteat in pane et aqua."[27] The verb *solvere* typically refers to payment in normative texts of this period, as in the *Pactus Legis Salicae* and subsequent works of Frankish legislation.[28] I think we may understand the word to have this meaning here as well: if the culprit cannot afford to compensate his victim in accordance with the value assigned the wound in secular law, let him at least pay him for his lost work as long as he is incapacitated, then proceed to forty days' penance on bread and water.[29]

SICK-MAINTENANCE IN THE *SCRIFTBOC*

We may now revisit the portion of the *Scriftboc* referred to at the outset of this chapter. Here the provisions of Exodus acquire still more traces

[26] Oliver, *Beginnings of English Law*, 105; Stacy, *Dark Speech*, 35.

[27] *Bussordnungen*, ed. Wasserschleben, 480.

[28] See, e.g., the *Pactus lex Alamannorum,* wherein this usage is ubiquitous (as in cap. 21, "Si quartus digitus truncatus fuerit, solvat solidos 5"): *Leges Alamannorum,* MGH Leges V.I, ed. Karl Lehmann (Hanover, Hahnsche Bucchandlung, 1888), 22 and *passim.*

[29] In secular law, offenders unable to compensate their victims might become their slaves, and some temporary period of bondage may be implied by this clause if *solvat* is to be understood as meaning something other than "pay" (which to me seems doubtful). For a discussion of this norm, see Heinrich Brunner, *Deutsche Rechtsgeschichte*, 2 vols. (Leipzig: Duncker & Humblot, 1892), II: 477.

of local custom as they pass from the Latin penitential tradition into the realm of vernacular law. About this clause Spindler had little to say beyond tentative remarks on possible sources; he says nothing about the sweeping changes made by the translator.[30] These deserve extended consideration. We have already seen in the clause on *morð* discussed in Chapter 1 that the translator of the *Scriftboc* was concerned to adapt his materials to the terms and customs of English folk law.[31] The clause on sick-maintenance as well, drawn from the same subsection of this text (*De homicidiis vel livoribus que in homine perfecta sunt*), likely adapts its materials in a purposeful way. However, determining how the *Scriftboc*'s changes assist a priest in the care of souls is not nearly as straightforward a matter as is the case with Cummean.

Before forming some conclusions about the translator's purposes, it will be necessary to describe these changes in some detail. The strangest is the rendering of *debilem ... reddit* as *in gecynde oðerne gedo wánhalne*, a phrase rendered by Thorpe as "alium in genitalibus debilem fecerit."[32] While an injury to the genitals would have prevented work in the short term, the connotations of *in gecynde* suggest that the temporary harm is primarily to the reproductive capacity of the victim.[33] It is rather difficult to know what the author of this canon had in mind, and given ecclesiastics' belief at this time in the sinfulness even of marital sexuality, no churchman holding orthodox views would have regarded the injured party as much harmed by a brief respite from the begetting of children.

The evidence of secular law is not as illuminating as might be hoped. Descriptions of genital wounding in the laws of Æthelberht and Alfred point to injuries that would have been of permanent consequence. The language of Æthelberht's laws offers the faintest suggestion that such wounds met Binchy's criterion for sick-maintenance.[34] But other matters

30 Spindler, *Das altenglische Bussbuch*, 58.

31 See Chapter 1, 44–45.

32 Thorpe, *Ancient Laws and Institutes*, II: 149.

33 See *An Anglo-Saxon Dictionary*, ed. Joseph Bosworth; rev. T. Northcote Toller (Oxford: Clarendon, 1898), s.v. *gecynd.*

34 Wounds to genitals are considered in cap. 64 of Æthelberht's laws, the most severe of which is assigned three wergilds as compensation; to have merely pierced the genitals entails the much less significant payment of six shillings. Alfred's provision (cap. 65) prescribes a substantially lighter penalty than had Æthelberht for the destruction of one's reproductive capacity: eighty shillings is the same amount to be paid for loss of an arm (cap. 66). It is intriguing, but perhaps not ultimately that illuminating in the absence of other evidence, that the clause of Æthelberht's laws in which Oliver detects traces of the Indo-European tradition of sick-maintenance – "Gif man cearwund sie, XXX scill' gebete" – immediately precedes Æthelberht's clause on wounding the *gekyndelice lim.*

were of greater concern. Compensation remedies not the suffering of the victim but the harm done to his kin-group, whose numbers the injury has left him unable to augment: the multiple wergilds thus take the place of persons never born.[35] Some trace of this idea may have attached itself to sick-maintenance within the Irish tradition, for assailants were sometimes required to compensate their bedridden victims for the fact of their being unable to conceive children while incapacitated.[36] These provisions of Irish law, however, do not refer to injury to the genitals; they respond instead to the fact that the victim was expected to recover away from his wife within the culprit's home.[37] At all events, because the *Scriftboc* refers in this instance to a wound whose effects will come to an end (*oð þæt seo wund hal sy*), it seems unlikely that injuries as severe as those described in the laws of Æthelberht or Alfred – injuries that must have involved the permanent destruction or amputation of the generative organ – are what the author has in mind. Perhaps a better question, to be turned to later in this chapter, is why the genitals appear to have been targeted for injury so routinely as to occasion tariffs in royal legislation.

No less puzzling is the transformation of *deformem … fecerit* as *womwlite on gewyrce*. While *macula* may have suggested *wamm*, there is no easy explanation for the translator's substitution of an injury specifically to the face. Like *morð*, *womwlite* is a legal *terminus technicus* of the first order, attested in Frisian as well as English sources and thus likely a shared inheritance of some antiquity.[38] Occurring only in legislation (in the transposed form *wlitewamm*), it designates bruises or other minor wounds to visible parts of the body.[39] That the referent may be something more abstract than bodily injury is implied by the element *wamm/wom*, which may – according to Bosworth and Toller's *Dictionary* – have the meanings "moral stain, impurity, uncleanness, defilement" as well as

[35] As is made explicit in Alfred cap. 65. In any case, the six-shilling fine for piercing the genitals indicates that this wound was – somewhat surprisingly – regarded as rather trivial.

[36] Kelly, *Guide to Early Irish Law*, 131.

[37] Ibid. While the Irish norm, if present, would give an unexpected meaning to the *Scriftboc*'s requirement that the assailant "do the work" of the wounded party, one doubts that such a remedy, if undertaken by his attacker, would have offered much relief to the convalescing victim.

[38] See Horst Haider Munske, *Der germanische Rechtswortschatz im Bereich der Missetaten*, 51, 128–9, 246.

[39] For the English evidence, see Æthelberht caps. 56–60, in Oliver, *Beginnings of English Law*, 72. The discussion of *wamm* here revisits some remarks made in my "Germanism, Slapping, and the Cultural Contexts of Æthelbeorht's Code: A Reconsideration of Chapters 56–58," *Haskins Society Journal* 18 (2006), 51–71.

"blot, disgrace, damage, hurt" when appearing independently. The verb derived from it, *wemman*, refers almost exclusively to the sexual defilement of women, as it does elsewhere in the *Scriftboc*.[40] A curious passage in the Exeter Book poem known as *Maxims I* suggests the association of *wamm*, whatever it may have been, with one's appearance: "word gespringeð, oft hy mon wommum bilihð // hæleð hy hospe mænað, oft hyre hleor abreoþeð" ("Word spreads, often she is encompassed with shameful [accusations], men speak of her insultingly, often her face [complexion?] becomes marred").[41] Some light on this passage, which may show early English thought to depend on notions of causality rather foreign to our own, may be shed by Liebermann's assertion that *wlite* (a noun cognate with Latin *vultus*) might have been understood at this time to designate something more abstract than the face, perhaps having instead the meaning "appearance."[42] Thus the standard gloss of cognate forms of this term in Continental legislation – *deformitas faciei* – should, according to Liebermann, be used with caution when making sense of the English evidence: "*facies* can more broadly be defined as 'outward appearance.'"[43] In the case of the *Scriftboc*, then, we may be dealing, as is the case elsewhere in the Old English corpus, with injuries whose harm resided in the shame endured by those who bore them. However *womwlite* has been realized, it is plain that by the time sick-maintenance arrives in the *Scriftboc* the situation is far removed from that envisaged in either Mosaic or Irish law, where the victim must be gravely injured to qualify for sick-maintenance.

[40] See *Das altenglische Bussbuch*, ed. Spindler, 177 (cap. V.6.a), where according to Spindler *wemman* renders *maculans* in the penitential of Bede: "Læwede man him wife agende gyf he oðres ceorles wif wemme oððe fæmnan, fæste an winter"; also Bosworth and Toller, *Dictionary*, s.v. "wamm."

[41] See *The Exeter Book*, ASPR III, eds. George Philip Krapp and Elliott Van Kirk Dobbie (New York: Columbia University Press, 1936), 159. See also Clare A. Lees and Gillian R. Overing, "The Clerics and the Critics: Misogyny and the Social Symbolic in Anglo-Saxon England," in Thelma S. Fenster and Clare A. Lees, eds., *Gender in Debate from the Early Middle Ages to the Renaissance* (New York: Palgrave, 2002), 19–41 at 22–3.

[42] *Gesetze*, ed. Liebermann, III: 12. An even more abstract definition of *wamm* is suggested by Lees and Overing, who remark that *Maxims I* offers "a tantalizing hint of the rhetorical syncretism of body with moral action in Anglo-Saxon literary culture"; see "The Clerics and the Critics," 23. A shared tradition with Irish thought may be at work here: Lisi Oliver notes that in Old Irish legal prose "the word *enech*, 'face', takes on the legal meaning of honour; 'face-price' is equivalent to 'honour-price.'" See Oliver, *The Body Legal in Barbarian Law*, 102.

[43] *Gesetze*, III: 12; the reference is to *Lex Frisionum*, MGH Fontes Iuris Germanici Antiqui XII, eds. Karl August Eckhardt and Albrecht Eckhardt (Hannover: Hahnsche Buchhandlung, 1982), 84: "(§ 16) Si ex percussione deformitas faciei illata fuerit,

Direct comparison with Cummean's penitential does clarify some of the idiosyncrasies of this portion of the *Scriftboc*. With the use of the term *womwlite,* the *Scriftboc* moves further in the direction intimated by Cummean and its congeners of applying the remedies of biblical sick-maintenance to injuries that do not render victims bedridden or otherwise incapacitated. That the *Scriftboc*'s translator knew what he was doing is suggested by the penance he imposes on the assailant. While in his source the penitent was obliged to undertake a half-year fast (*dimidium anni peniteat*) upon completing the obligations of sick-maintenance, the *Scriftboc* imposes on him the two or three quadragesimal fasts required in Cummean of an assailant whose attack results in no injury at all. Imposition of such a penance suggests that the *wanhalne* done to the victim's genitals is of no more lasting physiological consequence than the *womwlite*, whatever this term means. That both minor injuries to the genitals and *womwlite* are remediable with payments of six shillings in the laws of Æthelberht perhaps narrows down the nature and scope of the injury designated *wanhalne* in this clause of the *Scriftboc.*

No less suggestive of deliberate aims on the part of the *Scriftboc*'s author is the rendering of *opus eius ... restituat.* We have seen that, at the time extant manuscripts of the *Scriftboc* were being prepared, the translator of the Old English Heptateuch regarded this portion of Exodus as a reference to a specifically monetary obligation, as is evident from his rendering: "gylde swa þeah his weorc 7 þæt hine man hæle," "let him pay nonetheless for his work and so that he may be healed." The *Scriftboc* instead obliges the penitent "his weorc wyrc[ean] oð þæt seo wund hal sy," "to do [the victim's] work until the wound is healed" – even though the injury in question is unlikely to have been as incapacitating as those referred to in the biblical source of these provisions on sick-maintenance, as the translator is sure to have understood given his substitution of a penance applied in his source only to attacks resulting in no injuries. This change is of particular interest given its occurrence in the partial translation of Exodus taking up most of the Prologue to Alfred's *domboc*, wherein the attacker faces a similar requirement: "wyrce his weorc þa hwyle he sylf ne mæge," "let him his [the victim's] work while he is unable."[44] In both

quae de XII pedum longitudine possit agnosci, quod *wlitiwam* dicunt, ter IIII solid(is) componat(ur)," "If, because of a beating, a *deformitas faciei* will have been occasioned that can be recognized from a distance of twelve feet – which they call *wlitiwam* – let [the offender] pay thrice four *solidi.*"

[44] Liebermann says little about this aberrant translation in Alfred's *domboc* beyond a description of it in vol. II of his *Gesetze,* s.v. "Arbeit": "Wer jemanden bis zur Arbeitsunfähigkeit

cases, this remedy is not prescribed for a culprit unable to afford compensation, as it arguably was in *Pseudo-Cummean.* I am not sure that this coincidence is best explained by assuming that *restituat* – a term known by the author of the Old English Heptateuch to refer to payment – was misunderstood both by Alfred and by the author of the *Scriftboc.*[45] And while one may speculate that their substitution shows evidence of Irish tradition, such a possibility is complicated by the fact that Irish law, as was mentioned earlier, came to adopt monetary substitutes for personal care of the wounded well in advance of the composition of Alfred's laws. Moreover, Irish law always required that the culprit "provide a substitute to perform the normal work of the victim," as had been the case in Hittite law; he was not obliged to undergo the humiliation of doing the work himself.[46] Thus there is nothing particularly Irish about what Alfred and the *Scriftboc* do with *restituat.*

The other points of similarity between Alfred's Prologue and the *Scriftboc,* none of which has been noted in published scholarship, all seem to derive from the tradition of Latin penitentials rather than Irish secular law. For instance, Alfred has omitted any suggestion that the assailant is *innocens* if he fails to kill his victim, an adaptation made as well by Cummean and related penitentials. That Alfred eliminates such exculpatory language in the immediately following clause as well shows this to be a deliberate change.[47] Though both the *Scriftboc* and the laws of Alfred fail to render *restituat* as "pay, compensate for," insisting instead that the assailant act as a substitute for the victim, this may also show their debt to a tendency of the Latin penitentials, though less directly. We have seen that Cummean's penitential was concerned to establish penalties affecting the soul as much as the purse. By removing money from

verletzt, muss für ihn arbeiten während derselben: aus Exodus AfEl 16 [auch in Bussbüchern, z. B. Merseburg cap. 40]." Liebermann seems mistaken in his assertion that the requirement to perform the work of an injured man is found in Latin penitentials; the one that he mentions (now known conventionally as Merseburg aM) is little different from those so far discussed, requiring of the culprit that he "reddit inpensam in medicum et maculae pretium et opus eius, donec sanetur, restituat et dimidium annum peniteat." See *Paenitentialia minora Franciae et Italiae saeculi VIII–IX,* ed. Kottje et al., 145. I am not sure what Liebermann is referring to in the passage quoted, because there are various Merseburg penitentials, and in none of them does cap. 40 give an ordinance on personal injury.

45 Spindler offers no comment on the changes made by the author of the *Scriftboc* to his source, assuming instead the influence of at least four penitential canons, not one of which comes close to the provisions of the *Scriftboc.*

46 Kelly, *Guide to Irish Law,* 131.

47 For a more detailed discussion of this clause, see my "Violence, Penance and Secular Law in Alfred's Mosaic Prologue."

consideration altogether, the *Scriftboc* and Alfred's laws may have sought to affect the spiritual condition of the penitent more profoundly than was permissible in their sources. That pecuniary remedies advantaged the affluent perhaps led both of these texts to stray from their exemplars in search of more stringent measures.

We are still left, however, with the problem that the injuries referred to in the *Scriftboc* and perhaps in Alfred as well are not necessarily incapacitating, and thus would not have obliged the assailant to perform sick-maintenance in any of the legal environments in which this tradition is attested. Given its appearance in the *Leis Willelme*, this tendency to assign the payment of medical expenses even in cases of milder injuries may be seen as characteristic of sick-maintenance as observed in English law. Unlike the *Leis Willelme*, however, both Alfred's Prologue and the *Scriftboc* insist on a remedy that was probably more demeaning for the assailant than those imposed in other legal traditions even for injuries of greater severity. That the likeliest textual influences on Alfred and the *Scriftboc* had transformed sick-maintenance into a device serving the inner needs of the penitent more than the physical needs of the victim perhaps suggests an explanation.

The recommendations of Alfred and the *Scriftboc* may best be understood in light of the attitudes that surrounded acts of violence in Anglo-Saxon England and the wider Germanic world. According to Carol Clover, whose description of the Norse world may have some bearing on Anglo-Saxon conditions, beatings were under ordinary circumstances reserved for slaves, women, and children: persons who were in a sense feminized by their regularly acting as the objects rather than originators of violence.[48] Even in cases of graver and more lasting wounds, shame seems to have outweighed the suffering and hardship of living with an enfeebled body as a motive for the pursuit of compensation. This is most strikingly the case in cap. 77 of Alfred's laws, wherein one who endures paralysis as a result of an injury is described as *gescynded*, which Oliver has correctly rendered as "shamed" (over Attenborough's "wounded").[49] In such an environment, it is hardly surprising that a class of injuries arose whose sole purpose was to inflict humiliation (often without appreciable bodily injury at all), as is the case with penalties for forcibly tonsuring a man or cutting off his beard "on bismor."[50] Anglo-Saxon law furnishes no

[48] Carol Clover, "Regardless of Sex: Men, Women and Power in Early Northern Europe," *Speculum* 68 (1993), 363–87.

[49] Oliver, "Sick-Maintenance in Anglo-Saxon Law," 325.

[50] See Alfred cap. 35.3–5. Such motives may accompany the act even in the present: see "Hair-Cutting Attacks Stir Fear among Ohio Amish," *New York Times*, October 17,

parallel to a form of abuse familiar from accounts of saga-age Iceland – the lopping off of a rival's buttocks, usually in the heat of battle – but similar acts of ritual humiliation attested in Alfred's laws suggest that both England and Scandinavia shared an understanding of injury as a way of diminishing, in a demonstrative and perhaps ritual fashion, the social status of rivals as well as inflicting pain and fear upon them.[51] As is suggested alike by the forcible shaving of beards in England and by the prohibited insults of the Norwegian "Gulaþing" law, one of which was to liken a man to a mare (*ef hann iamnar honum við meri*), these symbolic injuries had everything to do with stripping victims of the privileges afforded to able-bodied men.[52] Though they are not typically described as having this function, the forcible feminization of victims may reach its apogee within the Germanic world in the wounds to the genitals that surface in the laws of Æthelberht and Alfred; such, at any rate, would seem to be implied by the usage of *macht* to designate the genitals in Old Frisian ordinances concerned with wounding.[53] Such assaults, of which the forcible shaving of beards was probably a lesser variant, make good on the threats hinted at in the prohibited forms of defamation.[54]

Given the associations of the term elsewhere in Old English prose, some similar assault on the social standing of the victim is probably implied by the *Scriftboc*'s reference to *womwlite*. Because the goal of these injuries was to humiliate the victim, the equally humiliating remedy arrived at by Alfred and the *Scriftboc* may perhaps be understood as the

2011. Members of the sect interviewed for this article noted the shame suffered by those whose beards were forcibly shaved.

51 Hrólf's attack on King Aðils of Sweden, which culminates in his slicing off the latter's buttocks, has for some time been regarded as an instance of "symbolic sexual domination of one man by another": see Carl Phelpstead, "The Sexual Ideology of *Hrólfs saga kraka*," *Scandinavian Studies* 75 (2003), 1–24 at 11–12; the foundational study of Norse attitudes toward sexual violence is Kari Ellen Gade, "Homosexuality and Rape of Males in Old Norse Law and Literature," *Scandinavian Studies* 55 (1986), 124–41. Of course, one need not invoke notions of homoeroticism to see just how humiliating such a wound might be.

52 *Norges gamle love indtil 1387*, 5 vols., eds. R. Keyser, P. A. Munch, G. Storm, and E. Herzberg (Christiania: Grøndahl, 1846–95), I: 70 (cap. 196). See also discussion in Clover, "Regardless of Sex," 373–4.

53 "Hversar en man vndad werth ynna sina machte, thet hi nawt tia ne muge, niogen merc to bote for tha niogen bern, ther hi tia machte," "If a man should be wounded in genitals [lit. 'in his power'], so that he may procreate not at all, [the assailant shall pay] nine marks as a remedy for the nine children whom he might have conceived." *Das Emsiger Recht*, Altfriesische Rechtsquellen 3, ed. Wybren Jan Buma and Wilhelm Ebel (Göttingen: Vandenhoeck & Ruprecht, 1967), 187 (cap. 200).

54 The point made here is anticipated somewhat by remarks in Mary Richards, "The Body as Text in Early Anglo-Saxon Law," in *Naked before God: Uncovering the*

sort of "cure" one might expect an experienced confessor to arrive at, forcing upon the attacker the shame of acting for a time as his victim's laborer and thus occupying the same category as the women, children, and slaves of his victim's household.[55] Such a provision is rather different from the *othrus* of early Irish law, in which the offender was obliged to furnish his victim with "[a] substitute sent to his home to do his work" and to host his victim in his own home.[56]

Some sense of why this would be the preferred remedy is afforded by the *Leges Henrici Primi*. Its author imagines pre-Conquest law imposing punishments on both "qui verberat et qui verberatur, ut nec malefaciens inpunitate superbiat nec contumeliatus fedis emendationibus insolescat" ("he who beats and he who is beaten, so that the malefactor will not be made proud in his impunity nor he who is shamed become accustomed to the disgraceful receipt of compensation").[57] While he may have gotten wrong some of the particulars of Anglo-Saxon legislation, the author of the *Leges* knew the centrality of shame to the understanding of violence that prevailed in early England.[58] He was also familiar with the corpus of Latin and Old English penitentials. His perception of assault as an instance of socially destructive *superbia*, if shared by late Anglo-Saxon clerics, may explain why biblical "sick-maintenance" came to be attached in both secular and ecclesiastical law to injuries that are not incapacitating and, in the case of *womwlite*, physiologically trivial. In an environment in which to be injured at all was so humiliating that even a paralytic was regarded as "shamed" by his condition, the physiological severity of an injury could not alone determine the remedy prescribed.[59] We should therefore not be surprised that the *Scriftboc* would complete the tendency of its source to assign "sick-maintenance" for injuries less grave than those in Exodus, here apparently going so far as to apply it to wounds whose "severity" was tied to their capacity to inflict embarrassment.

Body in Anglo-Saxon England, eds. Benjamin C. Withers and Jonathan Wilcox (Morgantown: West Virginia University Press, 2003), 87–115 at 105, where she suggests that wounds to the genitals described in Æthelberht's laws received generous compensation due to "the factors of shame and embarrassment such a wound might involve."

55 An exegetical tradition of this period held the nonresistance to evil required of followers of Christ to exercise a curative function upon the violent: see Abels, "What Has Weland to Do with Christ?," 573–4.

56 Stacy, *Dark Speech*, 35.

57 *Leges Henrici Primi*, ed. and trans. Downer, 260–1 (cap. 84.1).

58 Hyams observes in pre-Conquest law what he calls "proto-trespass," the ability of an aggrieved person to petition the king or a lord for "compensation not just for the injury … but for his shame and loss of honor too." See Hyams, *Rancor and Reconciliation*, 147.

59 For a discussion of this principle, see Oliver, *Beginnings of English Law*, 100.

ENGLISH SICK-MAINTENANCE?

The foregoing has shown that the physician's fee in the *Scriftboc* was very likely superfluous, a meaningless appendage left over from the origins of this clause in Latin penitentials and, ultimately, the laws of Exodus. If the translator of the *Scriftboc* was willing to alter so many other aspects of his anchor text, we may ask why he did not change this one as well. The *Leis Willelme*, which impose, as in the *Scriftboc*, the *læcefeoh* on an offender whose attack has not left his victim bedridden, suggest that this penalty survives in the *Scriftboc* not because of the influence of its source but because payment was expected in secular law for relatively minor injuries. The *Leis Willelme* follows this clause with one showing a clear understanding of the ideology of violence peculiar to pre-Conquest texts:[60]

De sa[r]bote, ceo est de la dulur:–Si la plaie lui vient el vis en descuvert, al pouz tuteveies VIII den., u en la teste u en auter liu, u ele seit cuverte, al puoz tuteveies IIII den.

"With regard to *sarbot,* that is [compensation] for a wound:–If he is wounded on the face, on a part which is visible, for every inch 8 pence shall be paid in every case; if on the head or any other place where it is hidden, for every inch 4 pence shall be paid in every case."

That Old English *sar* and Old French *dulur* refer here to emotional as much as physical suffering is evident from the provision that follows, which describes the manner in which compensation is to be paid: "Puis a l'acordement si lui metera avant honurs … ," "Then at their reconciliation the attacker shall, in the first place, show honour to the wounded man …." The legal environment described in this text, one that made wounds remunerable in accordance with their visibility and that required of the attacker above all that he humble himself before his victim, differs little from that of the *Scriftboc.*

Though they are less-than-ideal witnesses, both the *Scriftboc* and the *Leis Willelme* seem to offer, along with the Alfredian passage discussed earlier, some sense of the form assumed by sick-maintenance in pre-Conquest English law. In all three of these texts, sick-maintenance is applicable to injuries that are not incapacitating and even trivial, and all three require of the culprit that he undertake a more humiliating remedy than mere payment, perhaps because acceptance of compensation was

[60] For Liebermann, the source of this ordinance was "probably Anglo-Saxon" ("wohl Angelsächsisch"); see *Gesetze,* ed. Liebermann, I: 500–1 (cap. 10, 1); trans. Robertson, *Laws*, 259.

held to be a sign of cowardice and thus offered to the assailant a chance to exult once more over his victim's inability to retaliate.[61] To describe the *Scriftboc* as engaging here in the sort of "cooperation" of penance and secular law Oakley perceived in some penitentials of this period would not adequately characterize the complex interactions between written and customary usages manifest in all of these provisions. Rather, the *Scriftboc* has appropriated secular norms only to reframe them so that they furnish priests with a remedy for violence suited to its associations in the Anglo-Saxon world. That the other witnesses to the tradition of early English sick-maintenance, both of which belong ostensibly to the tradition of "secular" ordinances, seem to agree with the penitentials' manner of dealing with wounds in their concern to affect the spiritual condition of the culprit suggests that ecclesiastical laws could do more than merely support laws promulgated by the secular "state."[62] In this instance, the author of the *Scriftboc* combined the precepts of pastoral care with secular law in much the same manner as Alfred in his Prologue.[63]

[61] Contempt for the acceptance of compensation is ubiquitous in much saga literature. See, e.g., *Austfirðinga sögur,* Íslenzk fornrit 11, ed. Jón Jóhanneson (Reykjavík: Hið íslenzka fornritafélag, 1950), 17: "Þorsteinn hvíti kvazk eigi vilja bera Þorgil, son sinn, í sjóði" ("Þorsteinn the White said that he would not bear Þorgil, his son, in (his) purse").

[62] Hyams has considered skeptically claims for "the sharp division of royal government (that is, 'the state') and society," suggesting instead that "assertive royal aspirations [were] compelled to co-exist with something much less than an actual monopoly on the means of violence." Hyams's study does not touch on penitentials or on Oakley's thesis. See Hyams, *Rancor and Reconciliation*, 73.

[63] In the chart that follows, an attempt has been made to represent visually, as a help to the reader, the ways in which textual and cultural influences have been argued (by myself and others) to act upon the texts considered in this chapter.

Appendix

Lines of Influence in the Formation of Old English "Sick-Maintenance"

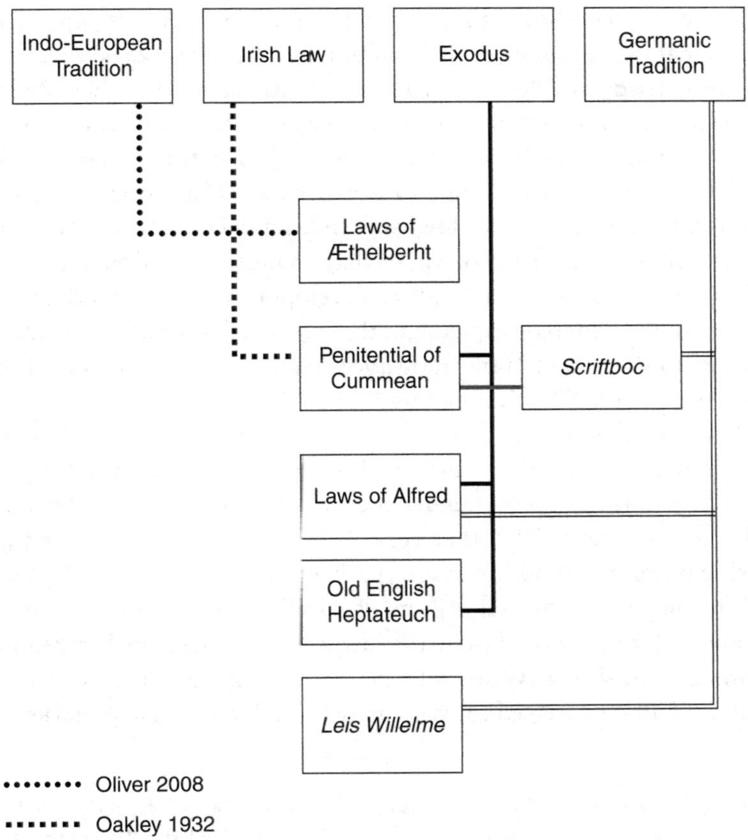

6

Caring for the Mind

Pollution and Mental Liability

This volume has shown that the Old English penitentials offered judgments that varied significantly from those of their sources on several matters of consequence for early medieval Christians. That their divergent translations share certain tendencies suggests that these texts appeared not in a series of haphazard responses to the needs of priests unable to read Latin, but rather as part of a conscious effort to craft a pastoral literature suitable to early English conditions. Underlying the work of the translators was a set of views that changed over time but retained some core features throughout its development. This is, perhaps, most evident in their shared suspicion of the "rights" that Frankish penitentials granted to slaves and in the allowances made for dissolving marriages in cases of physiological dysfunction.[1]

This final chapter will take up a question more elusive than those so far considered: whether the Old English penitentials reveal anything about the role that the mind was understood to play in rendering a person culpable for an offense. That they very likely do, as will be shown in the following pages, has implications for how we view Anglo-Saxon law, whose indifference to the mental aspects of liability has long been assumed. It will be well to consider briefly the history of this doctrine before moving to more critical observations. In the domain of legal-historical scholarship, we find it expressed for what may be the first time in remarks by the

[1] The term *rights* must be used with caution when referring to the early Middle Ages but is not wholly out of place: see Janet L. Nelson, "England and the Continent in the Ninth Century: III, Rights and Rituals," *Transactions of the Royal Historical Society* 14 (2004), 1–24.

great nineteenth-century historian Heinrich Brunner. At the beginning of its development, Brunner argued, English law must have been "closed to the existence of criminal intent" and thus unable to distinguish between accidents and deliberate harm in reckoning liability.[2] That some later legislation indicates otherwise suggested to Brunner that such injunctions for leniency were merely symptoms of the mollifying influence of the Church, indicating nothing about the authentic spirit of Germanic law. For Brunner, the presence in Alfred's laws of punishments even for unintended wrongs showed the force of the primitive tradition.[3] These and other remarks induced Frederick Pollock to conclude that the relationship between motivation and liability for wrongs must have been beyond the grasp of most Anglo-Saxons.[4] Not until well into the twelfth century, Pollock argued, would notions of mental culpability enter English law, leaving much that survives of pre-Conquest legislation, at least in this respect, the product of an essentially barbarian outlook.

Though the notion that the Anglo-Saxons wrote their laws without any sense of the mental aspects of guilt would see frequent repetition by the late nineteenth century, opinion surrounding it was never wholly uniform. Oliver Wendell Holmes rejected some of the assumptions on which this thesis relied, while Percy Winfield's dissent, authored some decades later, proposed that the legislative evidence adduced by Brunner and others did not support their claims.[5] Such remarks seem to have been

[2] "Über absichtslose Missethat im altdeutschen Strafrechte," *Forschungen zur Geschichte des deutschen und franzoesischen Rechtes* (Stuttgart: J. G. Cotta, 1894 [originally published in *Sitzungsberichte der Berliner Akademie* [1890], 817–42]), 487–523 at 488.

[3] The backgrounds of Brunner's views and their implications for the reception of Alfred's laws are considered in my "Noxal Surrender, the *Deodand*, and the Laws of King Alfred," *Studies in Philology* 111 (2014), 195–224. This article considers the provision in Alfred's laws (cap. 13) concerning the disposal of a tree that falls on and kills a woodcutter. Alfred's requirement that the tree be given to the decedent's kin within thirty days or appropriated by the owner of the forest is routinely (and, as I show, rather impossibly) characterized in scholarly literature as an instance of "noxal surrender" analogous to the abandonments of offending slaves and animals in Roman law. That the Anglo-Saxons supposedly treated even inanimate objects similarly has been viewed as a disclosure of their essential primitivism.

[4] "[I]n the case of harm ensuing even by pure accident from a distinct voluntary act, we find that the actor, however innocent his intention, is liable, and that the question of negligence is not considered at all." Pollock and Maitland, *The History of English Law*, I: 54.

[5] "It has been thought that an inquiry into the internal condition of the defendant, his culpability or innocence, implies a refinement of juridical conception equally foreign to Rome before the Lex Aquilia, and to England when trespass took shape. I do not know any very satisfactory evidence that a man was generally held liable either in Rome or in England for the accidental consequences even of his own act." See Oliver Wendell Holmes, *The Common Law* (Cambridge, MA: Harvard University Press, 1881; rev. ed.

met with virtual silence in the years since. While the criminologist Nigel Walker would trace the principle of leniency for insane offenders back to later Anglo-Saxon law in an influential volume (to be discussed in more detail shortly), Walker did not go on to dispute claims by Pollock, Brunner, and others that in earlier Anglo-Saxon England penalties were assessed without regard for the mental states in which offenses were committed.[6] It is unfortunate that an opportunity to challenge these long-held views was missed in what is otherwise a pathbreaking argument.

Commentators even of the present era have sounded a bit more like Brunner than Holmes or Winfield when addressing matters of legal subjectivity. An insightful essay by Richard Abels, noting that a code authorized by Æthelred in 1008 punishes those who abandon their lords in warfare "without reference to the motivation of the deserter," suggests as an explanation that "[t]his disinterest in motivation may reflect an aspect of Anglo-Saxon culture profoundly alien to our own: its lack of a fully developed sense of interiority."[7] Abels goes on to qualify this claim by asserting that some greater awareness of "spiritual interiority" may well be evident in the writings of "late Anglo-Saxon ecclesiastical writers" such as Wulfstan.[8] No such cautions, however, are evident in one often-referenced article on *Beowulf*, which asserts that both the "secular and ecclesiastical law[s]" of Anglo-Saxon England "treat the deed of homicide itself as crime or sin, regardless of the intent or motive. Old English penitentials, for example, distinguish accidental from intentional homicide but nevertheless treat both as punishable offenses."[9] In support of this statement the author quotes only a Latin penitential attributed to

Mark DeWolfe Howe, 1963), 7; Percy Winfield, "The Myth of Absolute Liability," *Law Quarterly Review* 42 (1926), 37–51.

[6] Nigel Walker, *Crime and Insanity in England,* Vol. I: *The Historical Perspective* (Edinburgh: University of Edinburgh Press, 1968), 15–18; also Walker, "The Insanity Defense before 1800," *Annals of the American Academy of Political and Social Science* 477 (1985), 15–30.

[7] Richard Abels, "'Cowardice' and Duty in Anglo-Saxon England," *Journal of Military History* 4 (2006), 29–49 at 46.

[8] Ibid., 46n59. One notable argument for a more developed interiority in this period is Allen J. Frantzen, "Spirituality and Devotion in the Anglo-Saxon Penitentials," *Essays in Medieval Studies* 22 (2006), 117–128 at 121. Here Frantzen regards the tendency of scholars to exclude Anglo-Saxon materials from histories of mysticism or spirituality as symptomatic of "an association of early medieval piety with external discipline and outward conformity, as opposed to piety of the later period with its nuanced regulation of the inner life." Such an outlook has yielded conventional descriptions of penitentials as "crude and mechanical, concerned only with the external or physical side of forgiveness and confession" (121).

[9] Linda Georgianna, "King Hrethel's Sorrow and the Limits of Heroic Action in *Beowulf*," *Speculum* 62 (1987), 829–50 at 837.

Bede. We have seen, of course, that Latin and Old English penitentials were not always of one mind. Nor did penitential canons of this era prescribe "punishments" in all instances. They offered means of soothing wounded consciences and, it was hoped, of reconciling souls to God, more often than not describing their work in medical rather than legal terms.[10] Given these circumstances, we can see why pastoral remedies were requisite even for accidental slayings. That a death was unintended made it no less a source of pain, even of guilt, for everyone involved.[11]

For its part, secular law shows evidence of serious if fitful engagement with matters of intent that is not often recognized. We have already seen that Alfred renders faithfully in his Mosaic Prologue the distinction made in Exodus 24:12–14 between deliberate and unintended homicides while adapting it to the norms of his own day. I have argued that other sections of his *domboc* suggest further attempts to encourage recognition of legal rituals (in this case, the abandonment of one's weapons and entry into the authority or *mund* of one's antagonist) that made manifest the contrition of an offender. If most royal legislation fails to explore at much length the question of intent as a condition of guilt, this is probably owing to its prevailing form in the earlier period, in which kings sought mainly to fix compensations and other remedies for various injuries in the manner of earlier Frankish codes. Questions of intentionality were left to be explored in pastoral literature. Only during the career of Wulfstan, as the West Saxon dynasty found itself beset as never before by threats from abroad, would concern with the spiritual condition of wrongdoers play a more explicit role in the provisions of royal law, with legislation acquiring at this time a distinctly homiletic tone. That such rhetorical purposes underlay Wulfstan's legislative prose requires a more careful attention to context than is sometimes apparent in present-day commentary; clauses examined in isolation from others are prone to disguise Wulfstan's likely aims.

At first, Wulfstan's remarks on intentionality would seem encouraging to those sharing Brunner's view, because the prelate's assertion that unintended wrongs merit leniency implies that his is not the prevailing opinion:[12]

7 gif hit geweorþeð, þæt man unwilles oþþe ungewealdes ænig þing misdeð, na bið þæt na gelic þam þe willes 7 gewealdes sylfwilles misdeð; 7 eac se þe

[10] See, e.g., McNeill, "Medicine for Sin."

[11] The clauses considered at the outset of Chapter 1 in particular seem to have no clear purpose beyond offering couples the means to cope through penance for a misfortune to which their own behavior may or may not have contributed.

[12] *Laws*, ed. and trans. Robertson, 106–7 (VI Æthelred cap. 52); *Gesetze*, ed. Liebermann, I: 258.

nydwyrhta bið þæs þe he misdeð, se bið gebeorhges 7 þy beteran domes symle wyrðe, þe he nydwyrhta wæs þæs þe he worhte.

"And if it happens that a man commits a misdeed, involuntarily or unintentionally, the case is different from that of one who offends of his own freewill, voluntarily and intentionally; and likewise he who is an involuntary agent in his misdeeds should always be entitled to clemency and to better terms, owing to the fact that he acted as an involuntary agent."

It is tempting to see this clause as some attempt to replace traditional with ecclesiastical norms that in the process discloses the real state of things. Doing so would be easier were it found in a straightforward work of secular legislation. But the "code" in which it occurs, VI Æthelred, is concerned primarily with matters of ecclesiastical government and penance. It begins with an injunction "þæt we ealle fram synnum georne gecyrran, þæs þe we don magan, 7 ure misdæda andettan georne 7 geornlice betan," "that we all eagerly turn from the sins that we may do, and eagerly confess our offenses and fervently do penance."[13] One of its few apparent statements on secular law – the somewhat mealymouthed condemnation of those who sell slaves abroad – is, as was shown in Chapter 3, restating a stock concern of penitentials. The same is true of the requirement that punishments be adjusted to fit the conditions of wrongdoers that precedes the provision on intentionality. Both this passage and the one quoted previously are found in the *Handbook for the Use of a Confessor* and were very likely drawn from it.[14] Once viewed in its proper setting, as a statement in a late and fairly condensed member of the tradition of Old English penitentials, its role in Æthelred's laws becomes more apparent. The clause furnishes a summary of the circumstances held in penitentials to make wrongdoing at least partially excusable to aid the work of both confessors and secular judges. That this was the intent is established by the terms used. Compounds in Old English legislation of which *nyd* is the first element designate cases of external compulsion, as in *nydhemede* ("rape") and *nidgild* ("tribute"). In the *Old English Penitential*, a man who *neadunga man ofslyhð* ("slays a man unwillingly") is assigned the same penance as one who accidentally suffocates his child in his sleep, and the editor of the penitential plausibly assumes that this provision refers to one who kills in self-defense or in battle at the urging of his lord.[15] That the interest of VI Æthelred is limited to those who kill or injure accidentally, under orders, or otherwise unwillingly makes sense

[13] *Gesetze*, ed. Liebermann, I: 246.
[14] See Fowler, ed., "Handbook," 19–20; see also Wormald, *Making*, 353.
[15] See *Die altenglische Version*, ed. Raith, 15.

given that these are the forms of unintentional wrongs with which penitentials routinely concern themselves.[16] As for the crucial term *gewealdes* ("deliberately"), it seems significant that use of this term is frequent in homilies and penitentials but quite restricted in Old English legislation. Of its handful of occurrences in this corpus, roughly half are found in the laws of Alfred, whose debt to clerical learning has been shown in Chapter 2; the others are in the text just quoted and a verbatim repetition of it in the "secular" laws of Cnut (cap. 68.2), along with a couple of other unenlightening instances.[17]

Putting the Wulfstanian clause in context leads us to an arresting conclusion: the one case in which royal legislation addresses explicitly matters of motivation is indebted almost entirely to penitentials. Does its derivation from the *Handbook* mean that secular law at this time lacked the tools for dealing with intentionality? To say so, I would argue, assumes a division between secular and ecclesiastical law inappropriate to a period in which bishops bore almost sole responsibility for drafting legislation. While throughout this study I have pointed out reasons to doubt that the role of the church was merely supportive where royal legislation was concerned, there is no question of its cooperation with royal authority. Thus it may be better to say that, in this case, we see how the Old English penitentials furnished royal legislation with developed instruments for talking about matters of intent. It stands to reason, therefore, that the provisions of penitentials will bring us closer than those of legislation to an understanding of how those responsible for the production of normative texts – bishops and the kings they counseled – understood the mental role in culpability.

The usefulness of the Old English penitentials for such investigation has received thus far only limited recognition. The studies by Nigel Walker mentioned earlier, though their focus is unfortunately limited to the early

[16] The provisions of the penitential attributed to Bede are typical: "[IV.4] Qui per iram et rixam subitam [occiderit], IIII annos. [IV.5] Qui casu, I annum. [IV.6] Qui in bello publico, XL dies. [IV.7] Qui jubente domino suo servus, dies XL. [IV.8] Qui liber jubente majore suo, I annum et per duos alios annos XLmas et legitimas ferias," "He who [kills] because of sudden anger and a quarrel, four years. He who [kills] accidentally, one years. He who [kills] in public combat, forty days. He who [kills] at the urging of his master, forty days. He who [kills] at the command of his superior, one year and, for two subsequent years, [fasting during] the quadragesimas and appointed days." See *Bußordnungen*, ed. Wasserschleben, 225.

[17] See *The Dictionary of Old English* [Web Corpus], ed. Antonette diPaolo Healey et al. (Toronto: Dictionary of Old English Project, University of Toronto, 2011), s.v. "gewealdes."

history of the insanity defense, are alone among works of legal-historical scholarship in considering the implications of penitential canons for the standard view that a *mens rea* became the criterion for liability only during the High Middle Ages.[18] Walker's evidence for the leniency of Anglo-Saxon law toward insane (and thus unwilling) offenders came primarily from two sources: the ordinance penned by Wulfstan for Æthelred discussed previously, and a clause from the *Old English Canons of Theodore*. The first of these – essentially the only developed statement in royal legislation on the subjective nature of guilt – establishes clearly enough that questions of motivation might determine the severity of punishments in late Anglo-Saxon ecclesiastical and secular law. For reasons I have touched upon elsewhere, we may doubt whether this clause was intended to deal specifically with the wrongs of the insane.[19] Somewhat less apparent is what is meant by the provisions of the *Old English Canons of Theodore* adduced by Walker.[20] I have argued that they show more consonance with earlier legislative judgments *against* leniency for the insane, but it must be conceded that the available evidence is rather ambivalent. At all events, the views that I think underlie these clauses are not necessarily peculiar to the Anglo-Saxon clergy given how often one encountered elsewhere at this time the notion that insanity was a form of demonic possession and thus the outcome of sinful habits.[21]

[18] See, e.g., Francis Bowes Sayre, "Mens Rea," *Harvard Law Review* 45 (1932), 974–1026 at 981: "[U]p to the twelfth century the conception of *mens rea* in anything like its modern sense was nonexistent."

[19] See my "Madness and Responsibility in Anglo-Saxon England," 100. Put briefly, *gewealdes* is typically used to refer to accidents within this corpus rather than some broader category of unintended offenses that might encompass the acts of the insane.

[20] The texts in question are of very great complexity and uncertain significance: readers may wish to examine this essay, and the notes of the Old English *Canons of Theodore*, for a full explanation.

[21] One possibly representative example is a canon of the Council of Worms (868): "Si quis insaniens aliquem occiderit, si ad sanam mentem pervenerit, levior ei pœnitentia imponenda est, quam ei, qui sana mente tale quid commiserit. Cui quamvis pœnitentia sit imponenda, quia ipsa infirmitas causa peccati, licet fortassis occulta, contigisse creditur, tantum tamen levior, quam ei qui sanus aliquem occiderit, quantum inter insanum & sanum, irrationabile & rationabile, constat esse discriminis," "If someone slays someone while insane, should [the slayer] be restored to sanity, the penance to be applied is to be lighter than that of one who did such a thing with a healthy mind. To him [i.e., the insane person] a penance is, however, to be applied, because this infirmity is believed to have come about through sin, even if it is hidden; however [the penance] should be lighter than that applied to the sane person, because there should be a distinction between the sane and the insane, the rational and the irrational." *Sacrorum Conciliorum Nova et Amplissima Collectio,* ed. J. D. Mansi (Florence, 1759–98; repr. Graz: Akademische Druck- u. Verlagsanstalt, 1960), 15: 874 (cap. 28).

The remaining portions of this study will consider other evidence that potentially reveals much about what Anglo-Saxon churchmen made of the mental role in guilt. As we will see, both Latin and Old English penitential canons in this period were very much interested in having judgments reflect the circumstances that prompted sinful acts. Underlying the differences between Old English and Latin treatments of such questions are distinct views about the role of the will in engendering the spiritual pollutions understood to lie at the root of all sinful actions. Though the Old English texts to be considered show, as in previous chapters, some consistent tendencies, it will be evident that they defy the categories made use of in prior scholarship, being neither indifferent toward inward motivation nor at ease in negotiating the subtler models of intentionality found in some Latin penitentials and pastoral writings. Considered together, they may suggest the habits of mind that Anglo-Saxon clergy brought to bear on questions of intent.

TRANSLATING THE LIBELLUS RESPONSIONUM

That some in the Anglo-Saxon church had their own ways of thinking about the mental aspects of guilt is perhaps nowhere as evident as in their responses to one of the most refined treatises on moral reasoning to have emerged in the early Middle Ages – the collection of recommendations made by Pope Gregory the Great to Augustine during the latter's efforts to establish an episcopal see at Canterbury and reintroduce the ruling elites of Kent to the tenets of the faith. This text, known as the *Libellus Responsionum*, is likely to have circulated independently before becoming appended to Bede's *Historia Ecclesiastica*, where it is reproduced in full.[22] In it we learn of the multitude of problems faced by Augustine and his cohort. Not the least of these was the question of whether a priest should be permitted to celebrate Mass after having been polluted in his sleep, or whether anyone should be able to receive the Host under such circumstances. It seems plain that Gregory's response, and Anglo-Saxon attempts to make sense of it, should reveal much about the implicit

[22] *Bede's Ecclesiastical History*, eds. and trans. Colgrave and Mynors, 78–103. On the transmission of the *Libellus* see Paul Meyvaert, "Bede's Text of the *Libellus Responsionum* of Gregory the Great to Augustine of Canterbury," in *England before the Conquest: Studies in Primary Sources Presented to Dorothy Whitelock*, eds. Peter Clemoes and Kathleen Hughes (Cambridge: Cambridge University Press, 1971), 15–34. I take no position here on whether Gregory authored the *Libellus* and use his name as one is bound to use Alfred's when discussing texts attributed to the king that probably result from composite authorship.

understanding of guilt and the mind likely to have obtained among literate persons in early England.

It will be necessary to review Gregory's reflections at some length before considering what the *Old English Penitential* has done with them. Gregory's answer to Augustine's query about priests administering the Sacrament after having been polluted develops a subtle argument about the origins of sin. Before delivering any judgment, Gregory asserts the necessity of carefully distinguishing the routes by which the dream entered the sleeper's mind (*ualde necessaria discretio, quæ subtiliter pensare debeat, ex qua re accedat menti dormientis*).[23] Gregory goes on to identify three agents that conspire with the wiles of the tempter to bring about such dreams: "gluttony" (*crapula*), "natural superfluity or weakness" (*naturæ superfluitate uel infirmitate*), or waking thought (*cogitatione*). Each clearly involves different degrees of consent by the priest or lay communicant and thus engenders a distinct penitential obligation. A dream arising from "natural superfluity or weakness" is "not to be feared in the least" (*omnimodo non est timenda*). It is without consequence, "for though it is a matter of regret that the mind unwittingly suffered it, it did not bring it about" (*quia hanc animus nesciens pertulisse magis dolendum est quam fecisse*). In cases of gluttony, however, "the mind contracts some guilt [thereby]" (*habet exinde aliquem reatum*). But even in this instance the guilt is so slight that the priest or layman should not be barred from participation in the Sacrament (*non ... ad prohibitionem percipiendi sancti mysterii uel missarum solemnia celebrandi*).[24]

The situation is rather different for one whose dream proceeds "ex turpi cogitatione uigilantis," "evil thoughts while awake," for in this instance we are told:

> patet animo reatus suus; uidet enim a qua radice inquinatio illa processerit, quia quod cogitauit sciens, hoc pertulit nesciens.
>
> "The guilt is clear to the mind; for he sees from what root this defilement sprang because what he thought of wittingly, he experienced unwittingly."[25]

The discourse concludes with a remarkable narrative of how sin is born in the mind. According to Gregory, sin begins with a "suggestion" instigated by the devil or an evil spirit that engenders "delight" in the flesh but does not become fully culpable until the mind gives its "consent" to

[23] *Bede's Ecclesiastical History*, ed. and trans. Colgrave and Mynors, 98–9.
[24] Ibid., 98–9.
[25] Ibid., 100–1.

the act proposed.[26] Thus it is possible for sin to "be brought to completion" (*perfici*) before any act takes place, and even in the absence of an act, because consent alone constitutes the completion of sin and engenders the concomitant obligation of penance.[27] Gregory concludes the discourse with no explicit answer to the questions Augustine had posed, and his mode of response seems to suggest that a solution will perhaps be knowable only to the dreamer, a feature of the text reflective of its pastoral rather than juridical purposes.[28]

However unwieldy as tools of pastoral care, Gregory's responses to Augustine suffice to refute the view sometimes encountered in commentary that "in the penitentials far more attention was concentrated on sinful actions than thoughts."[29] The portion of the *Libellus Responsionum* considering nocturnal pollutions was widely adopted by the authors of Latin penitentials, appearing in various Frankish collections including that prepared by Halitgar of Cambrai, which would serve as the principal source of the *Old English Penitential*. Differences between Halitgar's version and that appearing in Bede's *Historia* are insubstantial.[30] But the rendering of this text in the *Old English Penitential* is, in keeping with the practice of the translator elsewhere, quite independent. The most recent, and perhaps sole, discussion of this text asserts that the *Penitential*'s version

[26] Ibid.

[27] Ibid. Gregory's observations perhaps refine those made in Jerome, *Commentariorum in Matheum, Libri IV*, ed. D. Hurst and M. Adriaen (Turnhout, Belgium: Brepols, 1969), 30–1 (I.5.28). Here Jerome distinguishes between *propassio,* the effect of an external stimulus – in the case of Matthew 5:28, the beauty of a woman – upon the soul, and *passio,* the sin accomplished by consent of the will: "Ergo *qui uiderit mulierem* et anima eius fuerit titillata, hic propassione percussus est; si uero consenserit ... de propassione transiuit ad passionem et huic non uoluntas peccandi deest, sed occasio," "Thus *he who sees a woman* and finds his soul thereby tickled is struck by *propassio;* if, however, he consents [to fornication], he has moved from *propassio* to *passio* and in this instance only the occasion for sin is absent, not the desire."

[28] Remarks by Helmholz on this portion of the *Libellus* should be borne in mind: "In this part of the correspondence, Gregory's responses sometimes seem more theological than legal. A judge in a public court cannot readily draw a distinction between sins according to whether the sinner takes 'delight' in the wrongful acts or regards them with shame, as Gregory suggests should be done." See Helmholz, *The Oxford History of the Laws of England, Vol. 1*, 11. Of course, such distinctions might very well be entertained during a confessional encounter, and it is possible that this text assumes the importance of confession to the oversight of clergy.

[29] John F. Benton, "Consciousness of Self and Perceptions of Individuality," in *Renaissance and Renewal in the Twelfth Century*, eds. Robert L. Benson and Giles Constable, with Carol D. Lanham (Cambridge, MA: Harvard University Press, 1982; repr. 1991), 263–98 at 272.

[30] Because the form of the text used by the translator cannot be known with certainty, and because his narrative frame (see following text) shows his interest in the relationship of

differs from the *Libellus* principally in its "introduc[ing] the notion of an external cause, the devil, who apparently creates the dream experience which in turn causes the physical pollution."[31] Evidence for an even more sweeping reconsideration of its source is abundant. It is, perhaps, significant that the *Penitential* begins by replacing the Latin rubric in Halitgar – *De pollutionibus, interrogatio Augustini, et responsum Gregorii* – with a narrative frame that emphasizes the relevance of these questions specifically to the formation of the church in England.[32] That the order of causes is rearranged to reflect a descent from the least to the most serious instance, with *crapula* moved to second from first place, perhaps also suggests the purposes of the translator.[33] The rearrangement may have been meant as an aid to memory and points to the more practical aims at which the *Penitential*'s version seems directed. Unlike Gregory's text, the *Penitential* does not invite bemusement with questions of ethical speculation. Rather, Gregory's heavily qualified responses are forced into the Procrustean bed of legislative and penitential "if-then" clauses. These are poor vessels for the fine distinctions that Gregory sought to make. The result is a text perhaps intended to provide what Gregory's original response to Augustine lacked: a clear set of protocols for dealing with varieties of pollution that might threaten the sacrifice of the Mass and thus the spiritual welfare of the entire community of Christians.

this text to the early ecclesiastical history of England, quotations are from Bede's version, which may well have had some effect upon the translator's thinking. In any case, neither volume of Schmitz's edition gives the full text of Halitgar's version of this chapter (V.xvii); for this see *Patrologia Latina*, ed. Migne, CV: 689–91.

[31] Malcolm Godden, "Were It Not That I Have Bad Dreams: Gregory and the Anglo-Saxons on Dreaming," in *Rome and the North: The Early Reception of Gregory the Great in Germanic Europe*, Mediaevalia Groningana n.s. 4, eds. Rolf H. Bremmer, Kees Dekker, and David F. Johnson (Leuven: Peeters, 2001), 93–113 at 107.

[32] "Sona swa sanctus Augustinus on engla þeode fulluht gebroht hæfde 7 godes þeowas gehwær gesett 7 geendebyrd hæfde, þa sende he ærendgewrit to Rome to sancte Gregorie þe þa wæs papa 7 bæd hine, þæt he him sende on gewrite, hu him to donne wære ymbe þa nihtlican besmitenesse þe foroft mannum on slæpe gelimpð: hwæðer he þæs on morgen to husle moste gan oððe husel halgian gif he mæssepreost wære," "As soon as Saint Augustine had brought baptism to the English people and established and arranged everywhere God's servants, he then sent a letter to Rome, to Saint Gregory, who then was pope, and bade him send in writing what was to be done concerning the nocturnal pollution that quite often happens to men in their sleep: whether he might go to receive the Host in the morning or consecrate the Host if he should be a mass-priest." *Die altenglische Version,* ed. Raith, 43. The *Penitential* implies that Augustine addressed Gregory for guidance on this problem alone.

[33] "of þreom þingum heo cymð þam slæpendan on mode: hwilon for þære gecyndelican untrumnesse <7 tydernesse>, hwilon for oferflownesse ætes 7 drinces, hwilon eac þæt se man geþencð 7 smeað on dæg idele þing 7 unalyfedlice: þonne þæt he on dæg geþencð waciende,

Impatience with the *Libellus* is particularly evident in the translator's changes to the taxonomy of causes. Gregory had said that pollution resulting from the weakness of the flesh was "not to be feared in the least." Yet the *Penitential* holds it to be an occasion for contrite prayer:

Þonne gif hwa besmiten beo on swefne for þære flæsclican tydernesse, nah he þæs geweald: þingie him georne wið god 7 him forgifenesse bidde.

"Thus if someone is polluted in his sleep because of the weakness of the flesh, he had no control over it: let him eagerly beseech God and ask His forgiveness."

In attributing culpability to this wholly involuntary case of pollution, the *Penitential* is outside the mainstream even of much earlier medieval thought.[34] Yet we may be sure that this rendering is deliberate, for the *Penitential* maintains this approach in dealing with Gregory's judgment on pollution proceeding from gluttony. Gregory had allowed for the possibility that there are some whose minds even under these circumstances may not have been defiled by wicked imaginings (*turpibus imaginationibus non foedetur*).[35] No such qualifications are entertained by the author of the *Penitential*, who holds simply that "gif hit gelimpð for oferflownesse (me)tes oððe drinces, he bið gyltig," "if it [the dream] occurs because of an excess of food or drink, he [the dreamer] is guilty."[36] Though Gregory had recommended no penitential remedy in this case, the Old English exhorts the dreamer "him georne mid his sealmsange 7 mid ælmessan forgifenesse bidde," "eagerly by means of alms and the recitation of psalms [to] ask forgiveness for himself."[37] No less remarkable is the *Penitential*'s recasting of the third cause of polluting dreams:[38]

Gif hit þonne on þa þriddan wisan gelimpð, þæt se man on dæg geseo oððe geþence oððe smeage ymbe unalyfede þing 7 idele lufe þærto nimð 7 lustbærnesse 7 þonne

þæt him becymð on niht slæpende," "Of three things it [the dream] comes to the sleeper in his mind: sometimes because of the infirmity and weakness of our [human] nature, sometimes because of an excess of food and drink, sometimes also because the man thinks and considers during the day an idle and impermissible thing: thus that which he thinks about during the day happens to him during the night while sleeping." *Die altenglische Version*, ed. Raith, 43. I can find this rearrangement of causes in no Latin text of this portion of the *Libellus*.

34 Pierre Payer, *Sex and the New Medieval Literature of Confession*, 76. According to Payer, in the penitential handbooks of the twelfth and thirteenth centuries, most of which make use of older materials, "a distinction was made between involuntary sexual stirrings and feelings on the one hand, and deliberately chosen sexual behaviour on the other. The former were the unfortunate result of original sin, beyond our moral responsibility (but not our control)."

35 *Bede's Ecclesiastical History*, ed. and trans. Colgrave and Mynors, 100.

36 *Die altenglische Version*, ed. Raith, 44.

37 Ibid. The singing of penitential psalms as a remedy for unwilling self-pollution is advised in the penitential of Cummean (cap. II.15): see *The Irish Penitentials*, ed. and trans. Bieler, 115.

38 *Die altenglische Version*, ed. Raith, 44.

þurh þæt 7 þurh deofles hiwunga besmiten bið on slæpe, nis þam alyfed husl to nimanne þæs morgenes þe him on niht swa gelimpð; ac he ah þearfe þæt hit andette 7 bete swa him his scrift tæce.

"If, then, it should happen in the third way, that a man should see during the day or think or consider some improper thing and feel for it some idle desire and delight, and then through that and through the devil's trickery he should be polluted in his sleep, he is not allowed to receive the sacrament in the morning who undergoes such a thing at night: it is needful that he confess it and make amends as his confessor instructs him."

The Old English is more ambiguous about the direct cause of the pollution than the Latin. It is both "through that" – looking at or thinking about an impermissible (*unalyfede*) thing and delighting in it – and through the Devil's trickery that the sleeper is defiled (*besmiten*) in his sleep.[39] The sequence of events in Gregory leading to the realization of sin – a thought prompted by the devil, delight in the thought, and then, crucially, the consent of the will to that delight – is collapsed simply into the act of looking or thinking with delight, a formulation omitting the crucial role Gregory assigns to the yielding of the will to an evil impulse that completed the formation of sin. The thought and the Devil conspire to pollute the dreamer in the absence of his consent, leaving no place for the dreamer's own volition in the reckoning of culpability.[40]

That these divergent renderings of the *Libellus* reflect the aims of the translator seems certain given his subsequent rendering of a clause of Pseudo-Cummean dealing with nocturnal pollutions. Here the source's emphasis on consent (*Qui in somnis voluntate pollutus est …*) is again omitted.[41] It is possible that such changes show the translator following

39 Later confessional manuals require confessors "not to look at the faces of female penitents"; Payer notes that "In early works the rationale for the caution against looking is not entirely clear," speculating that "it was equally intended to spare them from the lecherous predations of some confessors, and to protect the confessor from sexual temptation." A range of views seems to have surfaced on this question, however, with some sources even urging confessors to inspect women's faces while they gave confession as a means of gauging "sincerity." See Payer, *Sex and the New Medieval Literature of Confession*, 54–5. Among the pre-Conquest English, this prohibition seems to have acquired an intensity unknown in later periods, as will be discussed in greater detail subsequently.

40 In its emphasis on the role of pleasure rather than consent in bringing about inward defilement, the *Penitential* perhaps agrees with the thinking of Ælfric as described in Robert K. Upchurch, "Catechitic Homiletics: Ælfric's Preaching and Teaching during Lent," in Hugh Magennis and Mary Swan, eds., *A Companion to Ælfric*, Brill's Companions to the Christian Tradition II (Leiden, The Netherlands: Brill, 2009), 217–46 at 231.

41 In the *Penitential* this becomes "Se godes ðeow þe on slæpe besmiten bið …," "The servant of God who is defiled in sleep …": see *Bussbücher*, ed. Schmitz, I: 620 (II.19); *Die altenglische Version*, ed. Raith, 65 (IV.53).

to the letter Gregory's assertion elsewhere in the *Libellus* that pollutions do not in all instances depend upon consent as they issue from the depravity of the will.[42] But this theological statement surely was not meant to determine the administration of penance. In the *Libellus,* dreams arising from weakness inherent to the flesh are held harmless, and no remedy of any sort is prescribed.

A seeming indifference to the role of consent is not isolated to the *Penitential.* We find traces of it in *Scriftboc* and even in the tradition of Frankish penitentials. All of this suggests that more is at work in the *Penitential*'s treatment of the *Libellus* than inattention to the subtleties of its argument. We may consider, for example, the following clause from the penitential of Cummean concerning the hazards of dealing with women:[43]

Qui per turpiloquium uel aspectu coinquinatus est, non tamen uoluit fornicari corporaliter, .xx. uel .xl. diebus iuxta qualitatem peccantis peniteat; si autem inpugnatione cogitationis uiolenter coinquinatus est, .vii. diebus peniteat.

"He who is polluted by an evil word or glance, yet did not wish to commit bodily fornication, shall do penance for twenty or forty days according to the nature of his sin. But if he is polluted by the violent assault of a thought he shall do penance for seven days."

It is noteworthy that, in this canon, pollution is perceived as arriving in the absence of consent, its single cause being looking at or speaking inappropriately with women; it is even seen as something by which one may be overcome violently (*uiolenter*), presumably without the promptings of external stimuli. The version of this clause in the *Scriftboc* goes in a rather different direction:[44]

Sacerd se ðe ðurh unsyfre spræce oððe þurh gesyhðe oððe sceawunge wifes hine besmiteð and nele gefyrenian, fæste XX daga. Se ðe mid his willan byð besmiten swyðlice, fæste he C daga.

42 "Menstrua enim consuetudo mulieribus non aliqua culpa est, uidelicet quae naturaliter accedit; sed tamen quod natura ipsa ita uitiata est, ut etiam sine uoluntatis studio uideatur esse polluta, ex culpa uenit uitium, in quo se ipsa, qualis per iudicium facta sit, humana natura cognoscat, et homo, qui culpam sponte perpetrauit, reatum culpae portet inuitus," "A woman's periods are not sinful, because they happen naturally. But nevertheless, because our nature is itself so depraved that it appears to be polluted even without the consent of the will, the depravity arises from sin, and human nature itself recognizes its depravity to be a judgement upon it; so man kind having wilfully committed sin must bear the guilt of sin though unwillingly." *Bede's Ecclesiastical History,* ed. and trans. Colgrave and Mynors, 92–3.

43 The passage is also discussed in Chapter 1, though briefly. See *The Irish Penitentials,* ed. and trans. Bieler, 114–15 (cap. II.12–13); slightly different versions of these clauses appear in the "Excarpsus Cummeani," in *Bussordnungen,* ed. Wasserschleben, 469 (cap. II.9).

44 *Das altenglische Bussbuch*, ed. Spindler, 178 (cap. VII.8.a).

"A priest who through filthy conversation or through looking or gazing at women is polluted and did not wish to do wrong, let him fast for twenty days. He who with his consent is greatly polluted, let him fast for 100 days."

The Old English version of Cummean's first clause elaborates upon the sight of women as an avenue for thoughts of fornication. Whereas the Latin presumably refers to gazing lustfully at women (and flirtation), in the Old English it is the mere sight (*gesyhð*) of them – in addition to the more sustained and deliberate ogling suggested by use of the term *sceawung* – that exposes the priest to the risks of unbidden pollution. Indeed, the expansion of *aspectu* into these two types of looking is perhaps meant to disambiguate the Latin by stating the equal dangers of both, lest a cleric suppose one less hazardous than the other. In his version of the second clause, the translator's rendering of Cummean's *uiolenter* as *swiðlice* ("greatly") effectively establishes two types of pollution not explicitly present in his source: one to which the will does not consent that is brought on by looking at women, and a second pollution, more dire because consensual.[45] Cummean had instead contrasted pollutions for which the penitent bore some responsibility (because of his gazing at, or speaking inappropriately with, women under his care) with those arriving at the instigation of the devil and involving the overpowering of the will, here assigned the same penance as pollution *per cogitationem* in the Theodorean canons.[46] The thinking of the Old English translator is revealed in his establishing a new category, "involuntary pollutions arriving from interactions with women," not present in his source.

In the *Scriftboc* and *Penitential* we perhaps see some of the consequences of straying from Gregory's recommendations. Locating culpability on the amorphous ground of "looking with pleasure" (or, in the *Scriftboc*, "looking") rather than consent makes avoiding defilement rather more difficult. The appearance of this tendency in two Old English penitentials appearing at different phases in the development of the genre leads one to suspect that both reflect a shared sensibility drawn irresistibly to such conclusions.

CONSENT AND DEFILEMENT

The texts to be considered subsequently show the further struggles of Anglo-Saxon prose writers with the role of consent. Their difficulties are

[45] Both Thorpe (*Ancient Laws and Institutes,* 347) and Frantzen (in his online edition) translate *swiðlice* as "greatly" (*admodum* in Thorpe) in spite of Cummean's *uiolenter,* a meaning that is conceivable but unlikely for the Old English adverb.

[46] See *PT* I, viii, 3.

unlikely to issue from the fundamental "primitivism" of their outlook. We have seen that early medieval Christendom knew a variety of attitudes concerning the volitional basis of spiritual defilement, with some sources seeming to regard pollution as an inward and intellectual problem and others viewing it as a matter of invasive external influences.[47] The latter seem to have been held capable of afflicting the soul with or without the consent of the penitent. Even Gregory may have come to the more refined view expounded in the *Libellus* rather late; earlier on, his thinking was perhaps not far from that of his Anglo-Saxon translator.[48] The elite clergy of Anglo-Saxon England inherited both views and never consciously sought to reconcile them. If they were disposed to favor nonconsensual models of pollution in some normative texts, the preference likely issued primarily from the inherent appeal of all notions of culpability that demand less of the intellect, and only secondarily from habits of mind native to the Anglo-Saxons, traces of which, as will be shown later in this chapter, are evident in idioms representing mental activity as the effect of external spiritual influences.

Before moving beyond the evidence considered in the preceding section, we should pause to consider some potential counterarguments to conclusions so far ventured. Ostensibly, the *Penitential*'s language seems supportive of those scholars who would continue to hold, as did Brunner and others in the nineteenth century, that developed notions of mental responsibility were foreign to the juridical thought of the Anglo-Saxons. And the *Penitential*'s odd remark in the passage earlier referred to that, though the dreamer did not have "control" (*geweald*) over what happened to him, he must nonetheless beg God's forgiveness, indeed bears an adventitious resemblance to that employed by the twelfth-century *Leges Henrici Primi* as its author breaks into Anglo-Saxon in order to stress the commitment of the English to strict liability: *qui brecht ungewealdes, betan gewealdes*.[49] Within the corpus of Old English penitentials, such views of liability are perhaps manifest in

[47] We may recall that the rules for canons drawn up by Chrodegang of Metz had urged clerics to avoid wedding celebrations, where "unseemly sights and words" might "pollute" their eyes and ears with "contagion": see Chapter 4, n. 36. Some of the tendencies described in this chapter are very likely owing to Carolingian influence.

[48] Paul Meyvaert found evidence that Gregory's thinking as evident in the *Libellus* reflects a shift from an earlier phase in which he was inclined to view the devil, and not the mind or spirit, as bearing responsibility for consent. See Meyvaert, "Uncovering a Lost Work of Gregory the Great: Fragments of the Early Commentary on Job," *Traditio* 50 (1995), 55–74 at 59–60.

[49] "Legis enim est: qui inscienter peccat, scienter emendet, et qui brecht un[g]ewealdes, betan gewealdes," "For it is a rule of law that a person who unwittingly commits a

a provision of the *Canons of Theodore* concerned with rebaptism, a dire offense indeed if undertaken deliberately. The *Penitential of Theodore* had prescribed the harshest remedies only against those whose second baptism had not been an accident.[50] Indeed, the text is in several instances at pains to point out the harmlessness of acts performed without the consent of the will, perhaps because many among the recently converted had imbibed what little they knew of Christian doctrine largely from missionaries whose emphasis on the purity regulations of the Old Testament was more pronounced than their contemporaries across the Channel.[51] As is the case in its treatment of menstruating women who wish to receive the Eucharist, the *Canons* show no patience with the principle so carefully established by its anchor text. Perhaps suspecting that the Theodorean clause furnishes penitents with an unnecessary loophole in prescribing the harshest punishments only for those who deliberately undergo rebaptism, his ordinance imposes lifelong penances even on those who have done so out of ignorance – the very group for whom Theodore had suggested clemency.[52]

The gravity of rebaptism as a threat to orthodoxy doubtless made it a prime candidate for severe measures; Theodore's penitential offers elsewhere no shortage of clauses establishing remedies in proportion to the vaguest motions of desire, and these are, for the most part, faithfully

wrong shall wittingly make amends; he who 'brecht ungewealdes betan gewealdes.'" *Leges Henrici Primi,* ed. and trans. Downer, 282–3 (cap. 90.11a). This quotation, long favored by proponents of Brunner's theory of "strict liability," is somewhat misused. The clause that precedes it urges mercy for unintended offences, and the Old English proverb in any case seems to distantly echo Gregory's "et homo, qui culpam sponte perpetrauit, reatum culpae portet inuitus" (see n. 41), where it is held that human judgment, being defiled by its own sinful nature and by the disobedience of Adam, is not to enjoy before God the privilege of deciding for which offenses it should hold itself in need of expiation.

50 *PT* I, x, 1–2: "Qui bis ignorantes baptizati sunt non indigent pro eo penitere nisi quod secundum canones non possunt ordinari nisi magna aliqua necessitas cogat. Qui autem non ignari iterum baptizati sunt quasi iterum Christum crucifixerint peniteant VII annos IV feria et VI feria; et in tribus XLmis si pro vitio aliquo fuerit; si autem pro munditia licitum putaverint III annos sic peniteant," "Those who have been baptized twice without knowing it need not do penance for this, although according to the canons they may not be ordained unless some great necessity requires it. However, those who are knowingly baptized again, as if they once more crucified Christ: let them do penance for seven years on Wednesdays and Fridays, and during the three *quadragesimae* if [the rebaptism] was for some sin; if, however, they supposed [they would be rebaptized] for purification let them do penance thus for three years."

51 See, e.g., *PT* I, vii, 12, which concerns unintentional ingestion of blood or a polluted substance, held to be without consequence ("nihil est") if done accidentally.

52 "Ða ðe nyton hwæðer hy gefullode beoð, and lætað hi eft fullian – þæt bið swylce hi eft Crist ahon – fæston þonne þa hwile þe hi libbon ælcne frigedæg to anes mæles and þa þreo æfæstenu," "Those who do not know whether they are baptized, and permit themselves to be baptized again – that is as if they again hung Christ – let them fast each

translated in the Old English version.[53] Whatever its similarities to the scant evidence invoked a century ago in favor of the basic primitivism of Anglo-Saxon law on matters of consent, the treatment of the *Libellus* in the *Old English Penitential* seems best explained by analogues that have yet to be mentioned in any commentary. Its logic becomes more apparent when we bear in mind the category of pollutions to which the offense considered in the *Libellus* is likeliest to have belonged in the imagination of the *Penitential*'s author. The nature of this particular sin is perhaps obscured by the idioms with which we describe mental activity today, some of which reflect assumptions about selfhood and subjectivity not shared in the early Middle Ages. We see the challenges these idioms pose when we attempt to render into English clauses of the Latin penitential corpus such as *PT* I, ii, 21, which deals with matters similar to those discussed in the *Libellus* and the portion of the *Scriftboc* mentioned previously. The clause in question, "Qui inludetur fornicaria cogitatione peniteat usque dum cogitatio superetur," is translated by McNeill and Gamer as "He who amuses himself with libidinous imagination shall do penance until the imagination is overcome."[54] The translation is reasonably accurate, but the Latin verb is, of course, in the passive. Who is amusing whom? Use of the passive would seem to indicate that the penitent is not necessarily to be understood as the agent of his own defilement, leaving his situation somewhat like that of the priest in Cummean's penitential who is polluted *inpugnatione cogitationis*, presumably with the help of some evil spirit. As for what is being done to the penitent, we should bear in mind that the verb *inludere* (whose nominal form is *inlusio*, itself the specific concern of the *Libellus*) can also mean "to make game of, speak mockingly of," "to practise upon, fool dupe," and, perhaps most to the point, "to use for sexual pleasure."[55] If the resulting translation, "He who is being molested with thoughts of fornication … ," seems to strain against the grammar and sensibility of speakers of Modern English, it is perhaps because this clause belongs so thoroughly to the mental landscape of the early Middle Ages that its meaning cannot comfortably be transferred into most modern languages.

Friday for the rest of their lives by taking one meal, and also during the three quadragesimal fasts" (*Canons* A 3).

[53] The prime examples of which would be its discussion of autoeroticism, some provisions of which establish the most ineffable distinctions between varieties of sins.

[54] *Medieval Handbooks*, ed. and trans. McNeill and Gamer, 186.

[55] See the *Oxford Latin Dictionary*, ed. P. G. W. Glare (Oxford: Clarendon, 1982), s.v. "inludere." The variety of meanings attached to this word in early medieval treatises on dreaming is noted as well in Godden, "Were It Not That I Have Bad Dreams," 94.

Because he occupied this landscape, the author of the *Canons* was more sensitive to the meaning of Theodore's clause than present-day translators. Here the verb is properly rendered in the passive, but with a change of emphasis: the ambiguous *inludetur*, which seems to reflect either the subjective experience of the penitent or the motive of his demonic tormentor, becomes instead *gebismrad sy*, "should become defiled" or "polluted."[56] In the consequences it imagines for those bemused by erotic thoughts, the rendering in the *Canons* perhaps has some affinities with the *Penitential*. It would seem once again that merely to entertain such thoughts (or be compelled to entertain them by some external agent) left one defiled (the clear implication of Cummean in the clause described previously). As in the *Penitential*, the will plays a role in the birth of sin less significant than that envisaged by Gregory; to be polluted in these vernacular texts is, above all, to be a victim of the Devil's deceptions (*hiwunga*).

The foregoing allows for the possibility that the dreamer referred to in the *Libellus* as well may have been construed by the author of the *Penitential* to be the unwilling party in a kind of demonic attack – a reasonable conclusion given the more pronounced role this text assigns to the Devil (as noted by Godden). Analogies for how to respond to such an event may have been furnished by the more concrete problems posed by human sexual violence, whose victims were sometimes held to incur a penitential obligation of their own even if they bore no responsibility: thus the curious case of the unwillingly violated youth in the penitential of Cummean who must nonetheless perform a week-long fast.[57] (No provision is made for the attacker's penance, though this omission may mean little.) Scholarship has emphasized the exceptionality of this instance, but the clause seems less remarkable when compared with others. A similar provision is to be found in the laws promulgated in the Levant during the early twelfth century concerning male victims of abuse; even these persons are described as having somehow "sinned" unwillingly (*non sponte … peccaverit*).[58] It has already been seen in Chapter 4

[56] See *Canons* cap. A 65: "Se ðe gebysmrad sy fram geligera geþohte, do hreow[e] oð þæt se geþoht sy oferswiðed."

[57] See *The Irish Penitentials*, ed. and trans. Bieler, 128–9 (cap. X.9): "Puer paruulus oppressus a maiore annum aetatis habens decimum, ebdomadam dierum ieiunet; si consentit,. xx. diebus," "A small boy misused by an older one, if he is ten years of age, shall fast for a week; if he consents, for twenty days." The clause is discussed in Allen Frantzen, "Where the Boys Are: Children and Sex in the Anglo-Saxon Penitentials," in *Becoming Male in the Middle Ages*, eds. Jeffrey Jerome Cohen and Bonnie Wheeler (New York: Garland, 1997), 43–66 at 55.

[58] The laws are edited in Benjamin Z. Kedar, "On the Origins of the Earliest Laws of Frankish Jerusalem: The Canons of the Council of Nablus, 1120," *Speculum* 74

that a raped slave was to do penance in spite of her having refused the advances of her master. All of these ordinances perhaps owe something to attitudes underlying Augustine's contention in *De civitate dei* that even those who were unwillingly violated might have experienced some trace of fleshly pleasure and thus have been polluted even as their mind and spirit withheld consent.[59] In the case considered in the *Penitential*'s version of the *Libellus*, the pollution in question might be frivolous if the dreamer were not a priest and thus responsible for the consecration of the Host. Knowing whether he was polluted appears to have seemed to the translator more crucial than knowing how he found himself in this condition. This indifference to whether pollutions were consensual or not may well reflect a notion of pollution as a "contagion," and penance as the means of its containment, that Firey has identified as one of the legacies of Carolingian penitential thought.[60]

Conformity to such views of pollution seems likely even for the *Penitential*'s treatment of the third instance, in which contamination results indirectly from having earlier looked with delight on an attractive body. Once again, consent largely disappears from consideration. Sin becomes instead a matter of thinking about, or even "looking at" – the *Penitential*'s own curious addition – an *unalyfed* thing. That such a category would exist is in itself a significant departure from Gregorian thought given resistance in his *Libellus* to the notion of women as inherent sources of pollution. Indeed, no inherently polluting things exist for Gregory in the external world, whose thinking on this matter relies principally on passages of scripture such as Matthew 15:11: "Nothing outside a man can make him 'unclean' by going into him. Rather, it is what comes out of a man that makes him 'unclean.'"[61] For Gregory, pollution resides so much in the mind that, should a couple unite solely for the purpose of having

(1999), 310–35 at 335 (cap. 9): "Si infans aut quilibet provectus ab aliquo sodomita vi co<m>maculatus fuerit et inde clamorem fecerit, sodomita flammis tradatur. Qui vero non sponte peccaverit, secundum ecclesi<astic>am sentenciam peniteat et legalitatem non ammittat." Kedar paraphrases this clause as follows: "A child or someone older who makes a legal complaint upon having been a victim of an act of sodomy should do penance and should not lose his legal standing" (314).

59 *De civitate Dei contra paganos*, ed. J. E. C. Welldon (London: MacMillan, 1924), I:16. The passage is searchingly considered in Amy Greenstadt, '"Rapt from Himself': Rape and the Poetics of Corporeality in Sidney's Old Arcadia," in *Representing Rape in Medieval and Early Modern Literature*, eds. Elizabeth Robertson and Christine M. Rose (New York: Palgrave, 2001), 311–45 at 317.

60 Firey, *A Contrite Heart*, 94.

61 Gregory adduces this passage (along with Matthew 15:19: "Out of the heart proceed evil thoughts") in support of his contention that purity is a matter wholly of the mind: *Bede's Ecclesiastical History*, ed. and trans. Colgrave and Mynors, 94–5.

children and take no fleshly pleasure in the act, it is possible for neither to suffer any pollution.[62] It could be argued that the *Penitential* agrees with Gregory given its qualification that one must look at a body with delight before the seed of later disturbances in one's sleep is fully established. But even this formulation disregards the primacy of the will's consent (rather than mere delight) as the ultimate agent of guilt. In any case, there can be no doubt that the text implicitly leaves us with a category of "impermissible sights and thoughts" not unlike what is found in the aforementioned clause of the *Scriftboc*, something that does not fit within the schema for which Gregory argues and that makes defilement of the sort that would profane the sacrifice extraordinarily difficult for priests to avoid. With the crucial element of consent more or less disregarded in the vernacular sources considered here, means of distinguishing culpable thoughts from those vaguely entertained would have been unavailable for those who took the instructions of the *Penitential* seriously.

That Gregory should consider the distinction at such length may indicate that he was arguing against those who harbored notions of pollution less dependant upon the role of the mind, some of whom, as Meens has suggested, may have preceded Augustine to Canterbury and introduced the English to their more rigid views.[63] Suspicion of women and the dangers they posed to consecrated spaces, as was suggested in Chapter 2, is manifest elsewhere in the corpus of Old English penitentials, particularly in the *Canons;* here women who are in the later stages of pregnancy are to avoid attending Mass in spite of Theodore's admonitions to the contrary. The *Penitential*'s adaptation should perhaps be seen in such a context. While it is possible that the notion of "impermissible sights" is mentioned casually and is therefore insignificant, its occurring amid an overhaul of Gregory's teachings suggests its role in codifying this new set of norms may have been far from trivial.[64] Evidence within and outside of the *Penitential*, to be considered in the following pages, shows this to be the case.

THE DANGERS OF LOOKING

The force of the norm described in prior sections is evident in the *Penitential*'s treatment of a clause concerned with the hazards posed to

[62] Ibid., 96–7.

[63] See Chapter 2, 80–81, for a full description of Meens's views.

[64] The *Penitential*'s handling of such spiritual dangers differs from the analogous treatments of the later Middle Ages. While these urged watchfulness for "sins that might come through the eyes," always looking requires the accompaniment of desire or enjoyment

priests and other clerics who keep company with women in their household. The source (a provision of the Council of Nicæa) had said the following:[65]

De subintroductis mulieribus. Ex concilio Niceno [cap. III]. Interdicit per omnia magna Synodus non episcopo, non presbytero, non diacano nec alicui omnino qui in clerico est, licere subintroductam mulierem habere nisi forte matrem aut sororem aut amitam vel eas tantum personas que suspiciones effugiunt.

"The great synod forbids entirely to bishops, priests, deacons or any other clerics to have a woman with them [in their household], unless perhaps a mother or sister or aunt or other such persons who are outside of suspicion."

The *Penitential*'s version is quite different:[66]

Soðlice eallunga is forboden on haligum bocum ælcon bisceope 7 abbude 7 mæssepreoste, þæt hi nænigne wifmannes neawiste mid him næbb[an]; ge eac swylce ælcon godes þeowe þe on clænnesse gode þeowian scyle is forboden, þæt he naðer na his magan ne oðerne wifman for nanes weorces þingon [inne] mid him næbbe, þy læs he þurh deofles costnunge þæron gesyngie.

Frantzen translates as follows:[67]

"Truly, it is altogether forbidden in holy books to any bishop or abbot or mass-priest, that he have any cohabitation with women. And also all such (contact) is forbidden to the servant of God who is obliged to minister to God in chastity, that he have neither his kinswoman nor other female servants with him for affairs of work, lest through the devil's temptation he sin on that account."

Here the *Penitential* has reversed the meaning of the latter part of the clause. Whereas female members of one's kin were quite sensibly grouped among those women whose presence in the home of a cleric would provoke no suspicions (*suspiciones effugiunt*), the *Penitential* forbids even these women to dwell with such men lest even they provoke the devil's temptation (*deofles costnunge*). This is a remarkably harsh rule, and its logic is, perhaps, disclosed by the differing reactions provoked by the women in the Latin and the Old English. The former text had taken up this matter presumably to keep ecclesiastics above suspicion of fornication within the communities they served; it is concerned with the outward

for the genuine occurrence of sin. See the summary of such discussions in C. M. Woolgar, *The Senses in Late Medieval England* (New Haven, CT: Yale University Press, 2006), 176.

65 For texts of Halitgar V.viii, see *Bussbücher*, ed. Schmitz, I: 731; II: 288–9 (the latter is given here).

66 See *Die altenglische Version*, 39 (cap. III.6).

67 The translation is to be found in Frantzen's online edition of the Old English penitential corpus.

impressions made by the secular clergy.[68] For the latter, the problem has become the demonic forces that are set loose upon the mind of the individual cleric when he finds himself in close company with women of any sort. Indeed, it is noteworthy that the *Penitential* here aligns itself with an earlier reworking of the Nicene canon by Theodulf of Orléans (750–821), who likewise forbade clergy to cohabit even with female members of their immediate family "quia instigante diabolo etiam in illis scelus frequenter perpetratum invenitur aut etiam in pedisequis earum," "because by the instigation of the devil even among them wickedness is found to be performed or also among their attendants."[69] The *wifman* mentioned in the *Penitential* may thus originate in the *pedisequae* referred to by Theodulf, though the Old English seems not to understand the *wifman* as necessarily an attendant of the priest's kinswoman. The assumed consequences are private rather than public, though they are capable, given the priest's unique role in the community, of having very public implications. We should perhaps doubt whether, in the first clause, "cohabitation" adequately captures the sense of *neawiste,* which is typically translated as "proximity" or "presence" in other Old English texts.[70] There may be in this ruling something of the same tendency at work in the *Canons*' denial of communion to recently delivered women in spite of Theodore's disagreement with the practice, and in the curious canon forbidding priests to share water with pregnant women in the Bigotian penitential, another adaptation of Theodorean materials.[71] All of these

[68] On the backgrounds of the Nicene canons, see Henry Chadwick, *The Church in Ancient Society: From Galilee to Gregory the Great* (Oxford: Oxford University Press, 2001), 198–205. Chadwick notes that the original intent of the canon in question was to ensure that clergy "not have women living with them in ascetic cohabitation" (203).

[69] For the text, see *Patrologia Latina*, ed. Migne, CV: col. 209; also Sauer, *Theodulfi Capitula in England*, which gives an Old English version of an earlier Latin canon of Theodulf (318–19, 420). In both the Latin and the Old English versions in Sauer's edition, the concern is explicitly with the female attendants of kin and not the temptations that might be posed by the kinswomen. The *Penitential* thus opts for the more extreme of Theodulf's views – if he does indeed have in mind Theodulf's, for according to Henry Charles Lea, Theodulf's misgivings about the Nicene canon were far from isolated: see Lea, *An Historical Sketch of Sacerdotal Celibacy in the Christian Church* (Philadelphia: J. B. Lippincott, 1867), 109. In any case, the concerns of the *Penitential* may not have been identical to Theodulf's given its eccentric translation of Gregory's discourse on erotic dreams: the danger posed by women of any sort may have been construed by the author of the *Penitential* as primarily spiritual in nature.

[70] Warrant for such a meaning is amply established by *An Anglo-Saxon Dictionary*, ed. Joseph Bosworth, s.v.

[71] *Irish Penitentials*, ed. and trans. Bieler, 216–17: "Penitentia bibentis quod intinxerat glangella in utero habens filium uel cohabitationis cum ea.xl. cum pane et aqua," "The

judgments seek to wall off priests from a world imagined as offering visual or tactile sources of immediate and, in some cases, nonconsensual defilement, the consequence of which is an entire parish denied the spiritual benefits of the Eucharist.[72] The chief conduits of this defilement were women, even, as in the case of the canon discussed previously, if these were members of one's own family.

The tendencies evident in the *Penitential* and other vernacular manuals have affinities with other examples of Anglo-Saxon thought on the nature of spiritual pollution. It is tempting to see in the *Penitential*'s peculiar treatment of this clause some trace of efforts associated with the Benedictine Reform to discipline priests by imposing on them the norms of the cloister. Certainly the double monasteries known to Bede were brought permanently to an end by the late Anglo-Saxon period; in part, no doubt, due to the efforts of reformers, though it should be borne in mind that they were frowned upon in Bede's time as well.[73] Thus we cannot fix a date at which efforts to segregate more thoroughly men and women within the ecclesiastical establishment began. Traces of such thinking are widespread. Corresponding to the *Penitential*'s view that the mere sight of women threatens priests with immediate defilement is the life of St. Euphrosyne. Here, the heroine, posing as a man in order to enter a monastery and avoid marriage, affords by virtue of her beauty alone the passage by which the devil insinuates himself into the thoughts of the monks while all are assembled to sing the Divine Office.[74]

Þa forþam se sylfe smaragdus wæs wlitig on an-syne. swa oft swa ða broðra comon to cyrcan. þonne besende se awyrgeda gast mænig-fealde geþohtas on heora mód. and wurdon þearle gecostnode þurh his fægernesse. and hi þa æt nyxtan ealle wurdon astyrode wið þone abbod forþam swa wlitigne man into heora mystre gelædde. and he þa gecigde smaragdum to him and cwæð. Min bearn þiu ansyn is wlitig. and þissum broþrum cymð micel hryre for heora tydernyssum.

penance of one who drinks what has been contaminated by a pregnant servant woman, or for cohabitation with her, forty days on bread and water." Bieler's suggestion that the canon should be corrected to read "and (or) by him who cohabits with her" seems unnecessary given the prohibition voiced by the Nicene council.

72 The force of such attitudes shows the dominance of views not unlike those attested in some parts of the Eastern Orthodox world in the later Middle Ages; according to Eve Levin, here "[a]ny sort of association between men and women was fraught with danger; the best solution was simply to stay away from each other." See Levin, *Sex and Society in the World of the Orthodox Slavs*, 55.

73 See the discussion in Frantzen, *Before the Closet*, 80.

74 *Ælfric's Lives of Saints*, ed. and trans. Walter W. Skeat, 4 vols., EETS 76, 82, 94, 114 (London: Oxford University Press, 1890–1900; repr. in 2 vols. 1966), II: 344–5.

"Then, because the same Smaragdus was beautiful in countenance, as often as the brothers came to church, the accursed spirit sent manifold thoughts into their minds, and they were exceedingly tempted by his fairness; and at last they were all stirred up against the abbot because he had brought so beautiful a man into their minster; and he thereupon called Smaragdus to him, and said: 'My child, thy countenance is beautiful, and to the brothers cometh great ruin on account of their frailty.' "

This episode has lately become fodder for work in gender studies given the "homosexual subtext" attributed to it by Frantzen.[75] There can be no doubt that such a subtext is present and seems to have amused the text's author, who assiduously uses masculine pronouns once Euphrosyne has assumed her male persona. I cannot quite agree, however, with Frantzen's assertion that the monks' response to Euphrosyne "reveal[s] their susceptibility to same-sex desires," an outcome of the fact that those whose appearance "occup[ies] an undefined middle ground attract men and women alike"; whether the text may be described as a "direct reference to homosexuality in the monastery" seems to me also uncertain.[76] It should be noted that Euphrosyne's beauty, and its sway over the monks, is at issue in her exchange with the abbot. Hugh Magennis points out that one reference to Euphrosyne's attractive face in the Latin original is omitted in the Old English: for English hagiographers in this era, Magennis observes "a tendency to be careful not to make too much of female physical beauty."[77] Medieval texts may be searched nearly in vain for any evidence that male beauty had the same inherent power to pollute that is attributed by some Old English texts to women's good looks. William of Malmesbury did not feel himself to be in danger of disclosing sinful appetites to his readers when he wrote of the young St. Wulfstan of Worcester:[78]

Cumulabat pectoris gratiam spetiositas corporis, quam licet inter uirtutes non numerem, non tamen omnino excludo, quia sicut ars opificis in commodiore materia elucet, ita uirtus in pulchritudine formae splendidus eminet.

[75] See Allen J. Frantzen, "When Women Aren't Enough," *Speculum* 68 (1993), 445–71 at 466; Andrew Scheil, "Somatic Ambiguity and Masculine Desire in the Old English Life of Euphrosyne," *Exemplaria* 11 (1999), 345–61; Jonathan Walker, "The Transtextuality of Transvestite Sainthood; Or, How to Make the Gendered Form Fit the Generic Function," *Exemplara* 15 (2003), 73–110. Scheil in particular (352–3) develops Frantzen's suggestion that the monks' attraction to Euphrosyne/Smaragdus resides in the appeal of the "eunuch body" and dismisses as naïve the possibility that the monks' distress proceeds merely from their sense that she is a woman. Given the evidence discussed here, I doubt that the simplest explanation may be so easily disregarded.

[76] Frantzen, *Before the Closet*, 84–5; "When Women Aren't Enough," 446.

[77] Magennis, '"No Sex Please, We're Anglo-Saxons?' Attitudes to Sexuality in Old English Prose and Poetry," 3–4.

[78] *William of Malmesbury: Saints' Lives,* ed. and trans. M. Winterbottom and R. M. Thomson (Oxford: Clarendon, 2002), 22–3 (cap. 1.3). In an explanatory note, the editors

"The grace of his heart was capped by the beauty of his body; though I do not count that among his virtues, I do not altogether rule it out, for, just as a craftsman's art shines forth in superior material, so virtue stands out more splendidly in a beautiful form."

Certainly no man in texts from this era of which I am aware was ever reproached in the manner reserved by Wulfstan of Worcester for a woman who sought to use a confessional meeting as a pretext for flirtation: "pretentoque fronti crucis signaculo 'Fuge' inquit 'cum eo quo digna es odio, fomes lasciuiae, mortis filia, uas Sathanae,'" "[A]nd crossing himself [he] said, 'Away with you, and take with you the hatred you deserve, you tinder of wantonness, daughter of death and vessel of Satan.'"[79] The sign of the cross was understood at this time (as it is now) to ward off demonic influences, and Wulfstan's language (*uas Sathanae*) implies that the woman is their conduit.[80] Read in light of the texts considered here, the basic conformity of Euphrosyne's Old English *Life* to early medieval ideas about the spiritual dangers of female beauty is plain enough. However convincing Euphrosyne's disguise (and it is quite convincing indeed as it fools even her father), she can never rid herself fully of the power to ensnare male ecclesiastics in polluting thoughts that seems to have been regarded in this period as peculiar to women.

Though attributing the *Penitential*'s revision of the third Nicene canon to the reforming impulse described earlier is outwardly appealing (and not to be dismissed given the text's demonstrably late appearance), assuming such a cause is made difficult by the presence of very similar conceptions in texts likely to have been composed prior to the activities of Æthelwold and Dunstan. The changes made by the translator of the *Scriftboc* to his source have already been mentioned. Perhaps the most

draw on remarks in C. S. Jaeger, *The Envy of Angels: Cathedral Schools and Social Ideals in Medieval Europe, 950–1200* (Philadelphia: University of Pennsylvania Press, 1985), 106–16, where the notion that refinement in outward appearances reveals one's inner virtue is identified as a Ciceronian *topos* revived in the Carolingian era. There is no reason to disagree, but it should be mentioned that Jaeger focuses on behaviors (table manners, dress) that may be acquired through training. Noteworthy as well are Alcuin's effusions to Bishop Arno of Salzburg, written in 790, whose significance has long been a matter of dispute: for an overview, see David Clark, *Between Medieval Men: Male Friendship and Desire in Early Medieval English Literature* (Oxford: Oxford University Press, 2009), 79.

79 *William of Malmesbury: Saints' Lives*, ed. and trans. Winterbottom and Thomson, 32–3 (cap. 1.6).

80 This aspect of the gesture is emphasized in David F. Johnson, "The *Crux Usualis* as Atropaic Weapon in Anglo-Saxon England," in *The Place of the Cross in Anglo-Saxon England*, eds. Catherine E. Karkov, Sarah Larratt Keefer, and Karen Louise Jolly (Woodbridge, UK: Boydell, 2006), 80–95.

dramatic realization of this tendency occurs outside of penitential texts, in Bishop Werferth of Worcester's translation of Gregory's *Dialogi*, which must be dated to the late ninth century. Here again, a different notion of the role of external sights in the creation of sin seems to drive a translator far from his source. The passage in question is the famous episode concerning St. Benedict's temptations upon becoming a hermit. A devil in the form of a blackbird enters his cell and brings about the spiritual consequences of Benedict's having earlier looked at a woman:[81]

Quadam uero die, dum solus esset, temptator adfuit. Nam nigra paruaque auis, quae uulgo merola uocatur, circa eius faciem uolitare coepit, eiusque uultui inportune insistere, ita ut capi manu posset, si hanc uir sanctus tenere uoluisset. Sed signo crucis edito, recessit auis. Tanta autem carnis temptatio, aui eadem recedente, secuta est, quantam uir sanctus numquam fuerat expertus. Quandam namque aliquando feminam uiderat, quam malignus spiritus ante eius mentis oculos reduxit, tantoque igne serui Dei animum in specie illius accendit, ut se in eius pectore amoris flamma uix caperet.

"One day when he was alone, the tempter appeared. A little black bird, commonly called a *merola,* set about fluttering around him, approaching his face in an annoying manner, so close that the holy man could have caught it in his hand if he had wanted to. He made the Sign of the Cross, and the bird went away. But then, when the bird had gone, a carnal temptation came upon him so strongly that this holy man had never before felt anything like it. Some time before this, he had seen a woman that the evil spirit brought before the eyes of his soul. Such a fire was enkindled in the spirit of God's servant at the memory of this beauty that he could no longer contain the flame of love in his heart."

We are never told who the woman was, or whether Benedict had looked at her with desire, but merely that he had once seen her and forgotten her only to be tormented with her image by the devil with temptations so fierce that the hermit was driven to roll naked in a thornbush. A fairly different sequence of events is found in Werferth. After the blackbird leaves and Benedict finds himself overcome with lust,

Þa at nexstan he geseah sum wif, þæt gelædde se awyrgda gæst beforan þæm eagum his modes 7 mid swa mycclum fyre onælde þam Godes þeowan þæt mod in þæs wifes ansyne, þæt he uneaðe hine sylfne geheald in his agenum breoste for ðam lege þæs wifes lufan.[82]

[81] *Grégoire le Grand: Dialogues,* Sources Chrétiennes 260, ed. Adalbert de Vogüe and trans. Paul Antin (Paris: Éditions du Cerf, 1979), 136 (cap. II.1); *The Life of St. Benedict,* ed. Adalbert de Vogüe, trans. Hilary Costello and Eoin de Bhaldraithe (Petersham, MA: St. Bede's Publications, 1993), 21.

[82] *Bischofs Wærferth von Worcester Übersetzung der Dialoge Gregors den Grossen,* Bibliothek der Angelsächsischen Prosa V, ed. Hans Hecht (Leipzig: George H. Wigand, 1900), 100–1.

"Then afterwards he saw a woman that the accursed spirit brought before the eyes of his mind, and [the devil] burned with such fire the mind of the servant of God in the sight of that woman that he uneasily held himself in his own breast because of the fire of lust for the woman."

Instead of being an image from Benedict's memory subsequently invested by the devil with the power to tempt him, here the woman becomes an apparition bearing no relation to anything Benedict might have seen or done. This is pollution (or near-pollution) *inpugnatione cogitationis*, as opposed to the sort Benedict encounters in the source. Gregory's reference to Benedict's earlier having looked at a woman seems if anything a rueful acknowledgment of the ubiquity of temptations to sin, one meant to cast no aspersions on the reputation of Benedict. But any reader who shared views like those evident in the *Penitential* would probably not have been disposed to see the episode in this way. For these audiences, to have directed one's gaze on an *unalyfed* thing or call such a thing to mind is to be already polluted and perhaps culpable for the pollution.[83] That the author of the *Penitential* was willing to make an ancient ordinance concerning female members of a cleric's household uncompromisingly severe shows the force of these precepts.

It seems quite likely that Werferth's revision was conceived of with a similar set of norms in mind. This text eliminates an aspect of the narrative that might have provoked in audiences suspicion of Benedict's own responsibility for his temptation. A similarly protective approach would likewise be assumed by Ælfric in his version of the story, who tells us only that Benedict was afflicted by temptation while relating nothing of its nature.[84] It seems likely that there prevailed among some early English ecclesiastics an understanding of sin somewhat different from that familiar from sources such as the *Book of Cerne*, wherein the speaker beseeches God, "Guard my eyes lest they look upon a woman with lustful desire" (*Custodi oculos meos ne uideant mulierem ad concupiscendam eam per libidinem*).[85] Here desire remains the crucial element in the formation of sin; whereas in the sources just described, merely to look at a woman makes one's eyes the conduits of unbidden

[83] Levin describes various Old Church Slavonic narratives in which to merely suffer the presence of women threatens the souls of devout monks with destruction: see Levin, *Sex and Society in the World of the Orthodox Slavs*, 55.

[84] See *Ælfric's Catholic Homilies*, ed. Godden, 93.

[85] *The Prayer-Book of Aedeluald the Bishop, Commonly Called the Book of Cerne*, ed. Dom. A. B. Kuypers (Cambridge: Cambridge University Press, 1902), 90; trans. Henry Mayr-Harting, *The Coming of Christianity to Anglo-Saxon England* (State College: Pennsylvania State University Press, 1972; repr. 1991), 184.

demonic influences – something that remains the case, as in the story of St. Euphrosyne, even if one doesn't know that one is in fact looking at a woman. The translator of the *Penitential* perhaps states more forthrightly what is implied in most of these texts. Women pose such immense spiritual hazards to priests that their company is to be avoided even when allowances are made in ancient ecclesiastical canons.

LAW AND SUBJECTIVITY

What notions of legal subjectivity are implicitly present in these texts, and what are their implications for how we might understand pre-Conquest notions of the mental role in guilt? Here it is perhaps worth recalling, as was noted earlier in this chapter, that Old English texts in general share peculiar conceptions of the mind and its workings.[86] Their notion of human subjectivity as fundamentally passive with respect to the images cast up by mental activity, but nonetheless implicated morally in their outcomes and thus obliged to control and subdue them, is one of the most prominent themes of Old English heroic verse. Of hagiographic verse in particular it has been said that "a core principle … is the exercise of spiritual and mental fortitude" – a claim that that might as well be applied to thoroughly secular verse texts such as the *Battle of Maldon* given its seeming understanding of warfare as above all a matter of psychological discipline.[87] Given the foregoing discussion, there is reason to think that these tendencies may be identified with conceptions of mental activity evident in nonliterary texts and thus capable of telling us something about how the pre-Conquest English arrived at their own sense of the mental aspects of culpability.

An especially apt example is afforded by the allusions to the troubled reign of Heremod in *Beowulf*. About this mysterious figure with whom the poet compares the eponymous hero, we are told "hine sorh-wylmas lemede to lange," "Sorrow-waves lamed him too long"; the episode concludes with the remark that "hine fyren onwod," "Sin entered him."[88]

[86] Antonina Harbus notes that "In the Anglo-Saxon mind schema, we see a different understanding of the self or centre of agency and its interaction with the mind than those prevalent in western societies today …"; See *The Life of the Mind in Old English Poetry* (Amsterdam: Rodopi, 2002), 58.

[87] Harbus, *The Life of the Mind*, 90. The same study notes that Maldon "situates the heroic essence in the mind rather than the body. The body may perish, Byrhtwold says, but ideally the intention will remain firm" (84).

[88] *Klaeber's Beowulf and the Fight at Finnsburg*, 4th ed., eds. R. D. Fulk, John F. Niles, and Robert E. Bjork (Toronto: University of Toronto Press, 2008), ll. 904–5 and 915.

That Heremod is in a sense a victim of his own thoughts rather than their agent, as is implied by the poet's repeated placement of Heremod in the object position (*hine*), perhaps was an element of the episode's pathos that only an Anglo-Saxon audience could fully understand.[89] Underlying these passages are mechanisms made more explicit in Anglo-Saxon medical recipes, which hold mental disease and affliction to be the products of external influences – demons and elves that torment one without one's consent – rather than an imbalanced humoral system, an "internal" cause of disorder known to the Anglo-Saxons but derived from foreign sources, principally garbled Galenic teachings.[90]

Given such a cultural environment, it seems hardly surprising that the ecclesiastical hierarchy of early England were inclined to adopt and even develop the notion implicit in some Frankish pastoral texts that a condition of the mind might be fully culpable even while affecting the penitent against his or her will. Whereas classical medicine had looked within for the sources of one's mental condition, Anglo-Saxons – and the Germanic-speaking peoples in general – seem to have looked without, with "externality" here constituting not the space outside one's body but the mental territory over which the will had no control. Though this model of subjectivity has its origins in pre-Christian folklore, the foregoing discussion has shown that, while it was readily adapted to Christian teaching concerning demonic agency, it was probably advanced in earlier and later pastoral manuals at the expense of equally important doctrines about the role of consent in determining culpability. The process was no doubt aided by the view that female beauty was seen as acting on the mind in much the same way as the mischief of elves. This is evident in associations that seem to have surrounded the word *ælfscienu*, a term designating women's good looks that probably connoted as well both the Christian notion of "penetrating demons" and the closely allied English folk-belief in "possessing elves."[91]

[89] This is suggested in Harbus, *Life of the Mind*, 169.

[90] *Leechdoms, Wortcunning and Starcraft of Early England*, Rolls Series 35, 3 vols., ed. and trans. Thomas Oswald Cockayne (London: Longman, 1864–6; repr. Holland Press, 1961), II: 137–9; III: 335.

[91] Heather Stuart, "The Meaning of Old English **ælfsciene*," *Parergon* 2 (1972), 22–6 at 24. Stuart argues against the older view that use of the term to describe the beauty of biblical heroines such as Judith was made possible by positive associations of elves surviving from the pagan era. Stuart notes that both elements of the compound "can refer to both diseases of demon possession and divine inspiration" (24), and so the notion of invasion by an external force remains a part of the term's semantic field. More recently, Hugh Magennis has asserted that the term "suggests a sense of the beguiling power of female

Within the corpus of Old English penitentials, the outcome is a collection of ordinances that seem indifferent to the role of the will where matters of pollution are concerned. Their aberrance inheres in their reliance on a peculiar conception of the mind that could not easily absorb the teachings of Gregory but was particularly suitable to assimilating, and altering into a more extreme form, Carolingian notions of pollution as a kind of contagious disease. The resulting form these assume, I would argue, is not some relic of pre-Conversion beliefs. Rather, it shows the odd paths down which some Anglo-Saxon ecclesiastics were driven as they sought to wed Christian precepts concerning pollution to traditional notions of mental functioning that were not compatible with them. To assume that a thought to which one does not consent leaves one "defiled" and obliged to undertake some penitential remedy – the clear assertion of the *Canons* and *Scriftboc*, and the implication of the *Old English Penitential* – is to depart from standard notions of mental culpability fostered by monastic teaching and advanced in patristic writings, in which the absence of volition separated morally indifferent motions of the soul from consensual sins of thought.[92] Linguistic determinism of some sort may not be ruled out as a stimulus to such developments; at the very least, the peculiarities of early English idioms for mental functioning reveal something of the structures of thought that accompanied them.[93] Surely it is not irrelevant to the inquiry undertaken in this chapter that premodern forms of English share with other early

beauty, but without implying culpability on the part of the heroine": see Magennis, '"No Sex Please," 12.

92 Whether the views ascribed here to some Anglo-Saxon pastoral writers should be classified as "archaic" seems in itself questionable, as the notion of sin implicit in (though in no sense derived from) their writings would compete with the more traditional, consent-based models advanced by Augustine and Gregory in the twelfth century. See Simo Knuuttila, "Remarks on Medieval Discussions of Religious Emotions," in *Medieval Philosophy and Modern Times*, ed. Ghita Holmström-Hintikka (Dordrecht, The Netherlands: Kluwer, 2000), 89–100 at 92.

93 Harbus approves the view of psycholinguist Anna Wierzbicka that "language reflects the human interpretation of the world" and that differences between lexicons "suggest different conceptual universes." See Wierzbicka, *Semantics, Culture and Cognition: Universal Human Concepts in Culture-Specific Configurations* (Oxford: Oxford University Press, 1992), 7 and 20; qtd. in Harbus, *Life of the Mind*, 25. Though Harbus notes the disdain of most linguists for the once-popular Sapir-Whorf hypothesis (from which Wierzbicka's view, as expressed here, differs only somewhat), it should be noted that arguments for determinism never fell wholly out of favor in the field of linguistic anthropology: see Znedek Salzmann, *Language, Culture, and Society: An Introduction to Linguistic Anthropology*, 4th ed. (Cambridge, MA: Westview Press, 2007), 52–69, where linguistic determinism is granted some relevance to ethnographic inquiry. R. D. Fulk has asserted that "it seems necessary to concede some degree of relativity to language" while noting

Germanic languages a tendency to make the thinking or dreaming person the grammatical object rather than subject of verbs associated with mental activity.[94] Having embedded themselves in the English language long before conversion, these notions of the mind as the recipient rather than the source of thoughts may well have constituted the lens through which the English would read Gregory's challenging reflections on the nature of moral responsibility for things thought and dreamt.[95] The resulting concatenation of perhaps irreconcilable ideas would generate an understanding of pollution probably unique in western Christendom – one whose presence across a range of vernacular texts permits us to suppose that it played a role in Anglo-Saxon legal thought on the relationship between subjectivity and liability.

that linguistic determinism, rejected by mainstream linguists because of its "possibly racist implications," "remains, in a form even more extreme [than Sapir had originally described it], the fundamental premise of much poststructuralist literary thought." See Fulk, "Afloat in Semantic Space: Old English *sund* and the Nature of Beowulf's Exploit with Breca," *Journal of English and Germanic Philology* 104 (2005), 315–22 at 315.

94 Impersonal constructions were the norm for descriptions of mental activity in Old English, as in "Þam cynge licodon peran," "The king liked pears," with *cyng* in the dative case and *peran* in the nominative; see Olga C. M. Fischer and Frederike C. Van Der Leek, "The Demise of the Old English Impersonal Construction," *Journal of Linguistics* 19 (1983), 337–68. Representative as well is the usage of *The Dream of the Rood* ll. 1–2: "Hwæt! ic swefna cyst / secgan wille, // hwæt me gemætte / to midre nihte," "Now, I wish to tell of the best of dreams: what I dreamed [literally, "what dreamed me"] at midnight": *The Vercelli Book*, ASPR II, ed. George Philip Krapp (New York: Columbia University Press, 1932), 61. Bosworth and Toller note that Icelandic *dreyma,* the synonym of Old English *mætan* that would come to replace it in later forms of English, requires "acc[usative] of dreamer and of dream": see their *Dictionary,* s.v. *mǽtan.*

95 That Anglo-Saxon sermons and verse alike were peculiarly invested in tropes of the body as a fortress against demonic influences (whose ultimate source is undoubtedly Ephesians 6:16) is argued in Dorothy Whitelock, *The Audience of Beowulf* (Oxford: Clarendon, 1951), 8.

Conclusion

Vernacular Penitentials and Secular Lawmaking

This book has argued that the four Old English penitentials should be considered prescriptive writings comparable in significance to royal legislation and other types of vernacular legal prose that emerged during the Anglo-Saxon period. In particular, I have been concerned to offer an alternative to Oakley's view, popularized nearly a century ago, that Latin and Old English penitentials served merely to "reinforce" the decrees of royal legislation. We have seen that the authors of the Old English penitentials did not wait for royal authorization before offering their own judgments on matters typically seen as the province of "secular law," such as the management of laborers on an estate or the contracting of a marriage. If Alfred's laws show greater deference than the laws of any prior English-speaking king to the prerogatives of confessors, this is probably owing to clerics' having already established (in Latin, and perhaps already in Old English) a tradition of written law whose claims to authority were not as uncertain as those of royal legislation. To place remedies for wrongdoing at least partially in the hands of a literate elite is what we might expect of Alfred, the prologue to whose laws is the culmination of earlier efforts by Kentish kings to establish the supremacy of written law over unwritten custom.

I have also sought in this book to remedy the more general neglect of the Old English penitentials within both philological and historical studies. Its roots are complex. Though Oakley's thesis long served as the rationale for ignoring the differences between Latin and Old English penitential canons, the reception of these texts has been little helped by the tendency of their modern editors to regard them merely as translations whose only purpose was to aid clergy unable to read penitential ordinances in Latin. Against this view, the present study has brought forth an abundance of evidence that the Old English penitentials performed work much more significant than this. Their independence from their exemplars in matters of translation, and their occasional devising of what appear to be wholly original canons, suggest that they enjoyed some authority in their own right. Their survival in a relatively large number of manuscripts when compared with other contemporaneous works of Old English prose, and their appropriation by at least one Norman student of Anglo-Saxon secular law, attest both to the seriousness with which these texts were read and to their being recognized as a distinct genre of legal prose.[1]

Though ecclesiastical history has not been its principal focus, the present study has also shown some ways in which the significance of the Old English penitentials to this field remains unappreciated. That translation was not the principal aim of those who composed the Old English penitentials allows for the possibility that these texts might afford a more accurate view of pre-Conquest pastoral care than what is found in their sources. The survival of several vernacular penitential manuals in England, most of which must have appeared while their sources were condemned abroad, in itself witnesses to the independence of the Anglo-Saxon church in some respects. Certainly the contents of the Old English penitentials suggest much that is in keeping with what other texts have conditioned us to expect of the Anglo-Saxon secular clergy. The far-from-scholarly handling of Latin sources in these texts perhaps reflects the limited capabilities of some members of this estate. That what appears to be folk belief so often displaces written norms in these texts may likewise offer evidence of the worldliness of priests often lamented by reforming bishops. Clauses expressing the unspiritual views of ritual purity that had been dismissed by Gregory the Great and Theodore, along with those establishing a place for practices such as the "nights of Tobias" where no such provision was made in the source, should probably be included in this group. Taken together, these clauses show popular religion to have been, at times, a decisive influence on those who prepared these collections.[2] Given the close ties of priests to secular magnates and

[1] Use of Latin and vernacular penitentials by Wulfstan in legislation written for Æthelred and Cnut offers further evidence of the authority likely enjoyed by these texts.

[2] I use the term *popular religion* as understood by Karen Louise Jolly: "religion … defined not by just its elite leaders but by the behaviors and norms of all of its adherents" (*Popular Religion in Late Saxon England*, 12).

to the lay population in general, such departures from learned norms are perhaps to be expected of their handiwork.[3] The shared disdain of these texts for the rights of slaves in particular seems what we would expect of an environment in which some priests lived within the community of the lord's hall.[4]

The implications of these texts for legal and ecclesiastical history are not necessarily matters for separate consideration. As has been shown throughout the present study, both pose problems for views of Anglo-Saxon royal authority articulated by Oakley. In this conclusion I would like to sketch briefly the significance of the Old English penitentials to claims made in scholarship published after Oakley's. Of contemporary discussions of Anglo-Saxon institutions, some of the most influential may be found in the work of Patrick Wormald, whose sudden death in 2004 deprived the field of early English history of one of its greatest minds. Though scholars are indebted to Wormald principally for his attempt to set right our sense of the manuscript transmission of legislative texts, Wormald spent much of his career developing a view of the Anglo-Saxon legal order that he hoped might compete with that of Frederic William Maitland, whose remarks on the subject in his *History of English Law* and other publications became, in default of any alternatives, the authoritative summation of pre-Conquest institutions.

The need for an alternative to Maitland's thesis was indeed great. Though his interest in pre-Conquest English legal history was deep, the more sophisticated materials of the Anglo-Norman and Angevin periods received more of Maitland's attention for most of his career. Perhaps for this reason, Maitland did not look favorably on Anglo-Saxon law during those few occasions in which he offered published judgments on it. As Wormald maintained in one of the last of his posthumous publications to appear in print, Maitland's work on earlier English law, being itself reliant on the work of Liebermann and Brunner, argued for the essential primitivism of Anglo-Saxon governance, holding it to have been little more than "a system of 'wer, bót and wite,' that is, of feud and compensation with only a marginal 'take' for the king ... essentially unchanged

[3] Blair (*The Church in Anglo-Saxon Society*, 491) suggests that over the course of the tenth century priests were increasingly detached from ministers and thus rendered "ignorant, isolated, cut off even from the basic standards of learning and discipline which [they] would formerly have attained in a minster community."

[4] See ibid., 492.

over the four and a half centuries from the code of Æthelberht to the Conquest and beyond."[5] That Anglo-Saxon law was conceived of by its principal expositor as largely impervious to change and without value for students of later periods did little to draw scholars to the study of its principal monuments for most of the twentieth century.

Wormald found various occasions over the course of his career to argue vigorously against Maitland's thesis. In the legislation and other normative texts of the Anglo-Saxon period, Wormald found an aggressive assertion of royal jurisdiction in the form of forfeitures and a coalescence of ecclesiastical and secular law manifest in the imposition of secular penalties for moral offenses (and *vice versa*).[6] Like many of Wormald's claims, it has been widely repeated and in the process suffered some inevitable distortion. Its novelty has probably been overstated in some published scholarship, for Wormald's arguments for a precocious Anglo-Saxon state are not in all respects a departure from tradition.[7] Nor was the primitivism so destructively assumed by Maitland and his contemporaries entirely banished from Wormald's outlook. Instead, it was pushed back into the earlier phases of Anglo-Saxon lawmaking: even Alfred, as described by Wormald, does not appear wholly immune to it.[8] One in a long line of "barbarian legislators," Alfred is not regarded by Wormald as much given to innovation; in preparing the Mosaic preface to his laws, his aim was merely to offer his contemporaries a "mirror in which West Saxons could … glimpse their own customs."[9] The 120 chapters of his *domboc*, however much they reflect grand ambitions, ultimately amount to "legal nonsense."[10] Forces that would shape Anglo-Saxon England into a polity with institutions of central governance much more developed than was assumed in the second half of the nineteenth century, though

[5] Patrick Wormald, "Anglo-Saxon Law and Scots Law," *Scottish Historical Review* 88 (2009), 192–206 at 193. The classic articulation of this argument, made throughout Wormald's later work on Anglo-Saxon legislation, is to be found in his "Giving God and King Their Due: Conflict and Its Regulation in the Early English State," in idem, *Legal Culture in the Early Medieval West*, 333–57.

[6] See ibid., 341.

[7] Arguments along these lines had been earlier made by James Campbell in a series of studies: see, e.g., "Observations on English Government from the Tenth to the Twelfth Century"; also "The Late Anglo-Saxon State: A Maximum View," *Proceedings of the British Academy* 87 (1994), 39–65, reprinted in Campbell, *The Anglo-Saxon State* (London: Hambledon, 2000), 1–30.

[8] On this aspect of Wormald's scholarship, see Jurasinski, "Sanctuary, House-Peace, and the Traditionalism of Alfred's Laws," 131n7.

[9] Wormald, *Making*, 421.

[10] Wormald, "*Lex Scripta*," 11.

nascent during Alfred's reign, would not be fully realized until the archiepiscopate of Wulfstan, a prelate enabled by the crises of Æthelred's reign to bring royal law into fuller conformity with ecclesiastical ideals and, for this reason, classed by Wormald "in the front rank among early medieval state-builders."[11]

That such a role is granted to Wulfstan perhaps further discloses the pressure of older scholarly habits on Wormald's thinking. For Wormald, as for Oakley, it was through the work of bishops and priests that English kings sought to organize the chaos of a social order still based in feuding and other forms of judicial self-help. As John Hudson has recently noted, Wormald "saw English law as very much a product of deliberate agency. The key agents were the kings and their advisors and officials."[12] That law might instead be as much the outcome of the numberless negotiations undertaken by minor figures outside of the court and the cathedral – a fundamental assumption of much legal-historical scholarship whose focus is on later periods – is a prospect rarely, if ever, entertained in Wormald's studies: "Not for Patrick, therefore, the incremental change of law driven by argument and stratagem in and out of court that has a central place in the views of Milsom, and also of Maitland for the thirteenth century onwards."[13] According to Hudson, this aspect of Wormald's argumentation discloses a curious reliance on methods repudiated by legal historians for the past several decades, many of whom have doubted the efficacy of royal initiative in shaping substantive law, contending instead that "practitioners and participants in cases and transactions are the prime agents of legal change."[14] As a historian of kingship and legislation, Hudson concludes, Wormald was unrivaled. But this virtue in some ways proved a defect when Wormald turned his attention to the development of legal institutions, reliant as he often (and quite understandably!) was on the royal legislation whose nature his work did more to clarify than any scholar of the past two centuries.

Hudson's are only the most recent criticisms leveled against Wormald's so-called maximalist view of the Anglo-Saxon state.[15] For present

[11] Patrick Wormald, "Archbishop Wulfstan and the Holiness of Society," in idem, *Legal Culture in the Early Medieval West,* 225–51 at 226.

[12] John Hudson, "The *Making of English Law* and the Varieties of Legal History," in *Early Medieval Studies in Memory of Patrick Wormald*, eds. Baxter et al., 2009, 421–32 at 425.

[13] Ibid., 425.

[14] Ibid.

[15] See Paul Hyams, "Feud and the State in Late Anglo-Saxon England," *Journal of British Studies* 40 (2001), 1–43.

purposes it is significant that in neither Wormald's studies nor in those offering cautious dissent do Latin or Old English penitentials receive much consideration, in spite of their unique capacity to draw our gaze away from the grand schemes of kings and their bishops and toward those less celebrated places in which law was, in the view of most historians, actually being made. Their inclusion, it must be said, suggests further doubts about the role of episcopal agency in shaping both pastoral and legal practice. That the Old English penitentials survive in manuscripts prepared at the peak of reformist activity – a fact indicating to most commentators of the twentieth century that the texts themselves were composed at this time – is remarkable given their often idiosyncratic judgments. This is certainly the conclusion one might draw from the *Handbook*, a text in all likelihood prepared by Wulfstan that does little to correct the eccentricities of its source. It is difficult to see what use reforming bishops such as Wulfstan would have imagined for the Old English penitentials in general, most of which seem in their indifference to their Latin sources and reliance upon popular law to be products of the secular clerical culture so often disparaged by the prelate and like-minded forebears. Yet the late Anglo-Saxon church furnishes no parallel to the situation of ninth-century Francia, wherein Latin penitentials were condemned for their conflicting and peculiar judgments.

Like the Benedictine Reform, the clerical reform of Anglo-Saxon legal institutions over the course of the tenth century is commonly and rightly regarded as an attempt to model English legislation after Carolingian examples.[16] While such claims are beyond dispute in certain respects, the Old English penitentials invite us to consider the realities that may have confronted such efforts. That the remonstrations of Frankish bishops had no discernible effect on English pastoral care, failing to impede the use of these texts even as Wulfstan sought to shape English pastoral norms after the example of Continental practice, perhaps shows some of the obstacles faced by England's clerical elite.[17] The survival of penitentials in England, while seeming at first to show commonality of practice with the Frankish church, in the end merely offers further proof of just how

[16] See Wormald, "Giving God and King Their Due," 337.

[17] Frantzen contends that a divergence in Wulfstan's "Sermo de Cena Domini" from its source (a homily of Abbo of St. Germain) "confirms the newness of the custom [of public penance] in the tenth-century English church"; elsewhere Frantzen suggests that Wulfstan's interest in reviving public penance in England was owing to the "involve[ment]" of the practice in "the exercise of episcopal jurisdiction, a power in which he believed very strongly." See Frantzen, *Literature of Penance*, 141 and 161, respectively.

removed English pastoral practices were from ideas circulating in the wider West European world.[18] Nor are conclusions such as these wholly against the grain of current scholarly opinion. The likely failure of the revival of public penance in Francia to reverberate across the Channel in spite of Wulfstan's best efforts has for some time been understood to show the resistance of English pastoral practice to external influences.[19] Nonetheless, the use of manuals rejected within Frankish dioceses, and their adaptation to English circumstances – something rarely discussed within this context – may give some sense of why these efforts foundered. By the end of the Anglo-Saxon period, private penance had in all likelihood become entrenched as a distinctly English institution. And among the main evidence for its entrenchment is the survival from this period of a vernacular tradition of penitential canons, all members of which seem to have accommodated the sensibilities of English penitents more than the Latin sources of this literature might allow.

The texts considered in the present study thus leave us with the possibility of an Anglo-Saxon church at times so under the sway of popular tradition that both Oakley's and Wormald's notions of its place in the pre-Conquest English legal order must seem overly optimistic. The way in which these texts handle the treatment of slaves and the law of marriage shows little conformity with norms urged by their sources and suggests that elite Anglo-Saxon clergy did not enjoy quite as much authority as some scholars have imagined to reorganize English life in accordance with their own ideals. Provisions such as these perhaps allow us to see what may have provoked William of Malmesbury's condemnation of the late Anglo-Saxon church for its excessive deference to secular custom and to the lusts of a dissipated aristocracy. While Norman arguments for the "decadence" of the Anglo-Saxon church have been viewed with appropriate suspicion by historians, there is no question that the Old English

[18] A similar point was made by Robin Hodgkin, though without reference to the texts considered in the present study: "It was Theodore who had perceived that the Celtic system of private penance was more tolerable for proud barbarians like the Anglo-Saxons than the public penance which had been the practice of the earlier Church." See Hodgkin, *History of the Anglo-Saxons*, 3rd ed., 2 vols. (London: Oxford University Press, 1952), II: 431.

[19] While Bedingfield has sought to challenge this older view, he concedes that Anglo-Saxon pastoral care was "heavily dominated by private penance"; "For the Anglo-Saxons," he observes, "private penance was the paradigm, and ... descriptions of public penance often treat it as something new, an option to be integrated into the private system." See Bedingfield, "Public Penance," 224 and 229. It should be said that even his sense of how public penance functioned within the pre-Conquest English church shows bishops' understanding of it to be significantly removed from what obtained on the Continent.

penitentials confront us with an at times rather depressing picture of clerical weakness in the face of old attitudes, however cruel or otherwise at odds with Christian ideals.[20] To be sure, the degradation of the church in England at this time was overstated by Frank Barlow, who held that "at its worst the ecclesiastical culture of the eleventh century was a swamp formed by brackish trickles from ancient civilizations ... the stagnant end of an old world."[21] But Norman arguments for the degradation of Anglo-Saxon piety at the time of the Battle of Hastings must have been something more than mere "propaganda," however disingenuously such claims may have been deployed as the new regime seized abbeys and razed ancient English churches.

As was shown in Chapter 3, this weakness may be traced up to the heights of the clerical hierarchy. It was argued here that the Old English penitentials offer some indication of why early attempts in official legislation to suppress Sunday markets were ignored. They also offer a rather different view of Wulfstan's attitude toward slavery than has been customary to assume over the past century. Given that these sentiments, which provoke some of the most radical departures of the vernacular penitentials from Frankish examples, appear to have been shared by the most prolific and influential bishop of late Anglo-Saxon England, it seems fair to wonder whether other peculiarities of this corpus might reflect the views of clerics in all ranks of the English church. For those inclined to take seriously the assertions of William of Malmesbury and other Anglo-Norman voices, the Old English penitentials offer plenty of heretofore unrecognized evidence that the pre-Conquest church was largely cut off from norms advocated on the Continent and left occasionally to drift, as far a concessions to popular superstition are concerned, into what may be classified as heterodox beliefs.[22] They also suggest that the efforts of Wulfstan and his predecessors to distance themselves from the secular clergy should perhaps not be taken too seriously. Even the most exalted of the Anglo-Saxon clergy were not above accommodating the whims of secular magnates, though England's clerical estates pursued this

[20] Skepticism about Normans' claims has been voiced most recently, and in considerable depth, in Mary Frances Giandrea, *Episcopal Culture in Late Anglo-Saxon England*, Anglo-Saxon Studies 7 (Woodbridge, UK: Boydell, 2007), cap. 1, where the hazards of uncritical reliance on Anglo-Norman historiography are brilliantly explored. Giandrea is concerned primarily with narrative, homiletic, and liturgical sources.

[21] Frank Barlow, *The English Church*, 288.

[22] "Heterodoxy" is sometimes attributed to the *Blicking* homilies (see Chapter 2, 78–79) and arguably is a feature of a number of works described in Hollis and Wright, *Old English Prose of Secular Learning*, as is discussed at 3 and 11.

end with varying levels of sophistication and from distinct positions of strength or weakness.

In the final analysis, both Oakley and Wormald run into trouble once they assume the Anglo-Saxon church to have made up for deficiencies in early English secular institutions, whether by transforming pastoral care into an apparatus of the state (Oakley) or by acting as some sort of moral counterweight to the worst impulses of England's secular elite (Wormald). It should be said in conclusion that recent studies of aspects of the early English church having nothing to do with penance offer additional reasons why such models should be used with caution. As Alban Gautier has observed, Wormald's career coincided with a wider (and ongoing) revolution concerning our understanding of the Anglo-Saxon church.[23] Scholars are now more willing than was the case decades ago to question the extent to which the arrival of Roman Christianity within the British Isles constituted a "conversion" of those dwelling therein – and to wonder whether those who brought the trappings of Roman ecclesiastical life across the Channel might in time have undergone a conversion of their own to the ways of those they sought to instruct. What once seemed clear importations from Rome in manuscript art and sculpture, for example, now appear in some cases to have been survivals of the cultures that preceded the arrival of missionaries.[24] Martin Carver in particular has argued that the entire structure of monastic life in northern England – including those elements that seem to belong distinctly to the culture borne there by missionary activity – may best be understood as "not based solely on inspiration from the landscape, nor on conservative tradition, but on the intellectual reconciliation of Christian and non-Christian ideas."[25]

Arguments to this effect are not in themselves wholly new. We find them in the mordant speculation of Seebohm's *Tribal Custom in Anglo-Saxon Law* as to why the recently converted peoples of Western Europe were willing to submit to penances imposed by priests of the new faith.[26] The

[23] Alban Gautier, "La chrétienté anglo-saxonne (viie–xie siècle): à propos de quelques publications récentes," *Médiévales* 56 (2009), 151–68.

[24] Alecia Arceo, "Rethinking the Synod of Whitby and Northumbrian Monastic Sites," *Haskins Society Journal* 20 (2009), 19–30.

[25] Martin Carver, "Early Scottish Monasteries and Prehistory: A Preliminary Dialogue," *Scottish Historical Review* 88 (2009), 332–51 at 332.

[26] Frederic Seebohm, *Tribal Custom in Anglo-Saxon Law* (London: Longmans, 1911), 118–20: "The missionary monks or priests, it might almost be said, *naturally* took the place of the Druids in the minds of the people. They had the power to shut out the criminal from the sacrifices of the Christian altar, just as the Druids could from theirs."

wide acceptance of views such as these, once the exclusive possession of the few English nonconformists who concerned themselves with earlier English history, suggests the waning of what Carver calls "conviction politics" as the determinant of scholarly opinion as far as early ecclesiastical history is concerned – or just a different sort of "conviction politics" reflecting the iconoclastic bent of our time.[27]

Though such ideas lend themselves to reckless use, the sense shared by many scholars (and backed by considerable evidence) of the mixed and compromised nature of early medieval Christianity does require us to qualify our implicit understanding of ecclesiastical legislation in this era. The canons considered in the foregoing chapters certainly show no lack of instances of accommodation and perhaps even of syncretism. And Wormald's most penetrating observations on the nature of secular legislation give us some sense of why this should be the case. In the case of feud, an ancient and nearly ineradicable element of Germanic society, English monarchs could hope in their legislation to do little more, according to Wormald, than "write themselves into the process: as self-appointed instruments of revenge for their people's wrongs, they increasingly demanded compensation for themselves, and also resorted to violence of their own."[28] English bishops would in time do much the same, with wergild imposed "for incest or precipitate second marriage."[29] Whatever spiritual experiences individual Christians may or may not have had were beside the point as far as the business of governance was concerned.[30] Kings' and bishops' labors were directed not at eradicating but at "re-orchestrating" the array of customs by which average people had governed themselves for generations, and written legislation was the tool that made this imaginative recasting of the English social panorama possible.

It is hoped that the present study shows some of the hazards of assuming this work to have been undertaken only by kings and their bishops. The Old English penitentials afford important insights into what this sort of negotiation and compromise, much of it rather distasteful to those attached to older models of the (re-)appearance of institutional

Seebohm was, of course, anything but disinterested regarding questions of sacerdotal authority. The claim was cited approvingly in Oakley, *English Penitential Discipline*, 138.

27 Carver, "Early Scottish Monasteries," 334.

28 Wormald, "Giving God and King Their Due," 336.

29 Ibid., 341.

30 And these should not be trivialized; certainly it is hard to find any trace of syncretism in the motives underlying the martyrdom of King Edmund.

Christianity in England, is likely to have looked like. We should not suppose that these texts show priests and bishops imposing alien observances upon a hostile population cowed only by the fear of divine punishment. Rather, the clergy who devised these canons were insinuating themselves into a range of conversations that had long proceeded without them and were not structured to accommodate their ideas. We should not be surprised if their doing so occasionally required concessions on both sides, sometimes leaving clergy enmeshed within structures of thought rather different from those manifest in Latin canons.

In writing themselves into the daily dramas of pre-Conquest English life, Anglo-Saxon clerics and the vernacular penitentials they composed performed much the same work as royal legislation. But because those who wrote the former were in more frequent contact with average people than kings or secular magnates, they did not enjoy the luxury of stating things as they ought to be. The humbler purposes at which the Old English penitentials were directed allow them to shed more light than any other group of texts on the vacillations and omissions of contemporaneous legislation. They show that Anglo-Saxon statecraft was not a pact between kings and bishops to win the obedience of subject populations, but a far subtler process in which various elite groups sought to bring their competing interests into some sort of fragile equilibrium.

Bibliography

PRIMARY SOURCES

Ælfric of Eynsham. *The Homilies of Ælfric*. Ed. and trans. Benjamin Thorpe. London: Ælfric Society, 1844–6.

Ælfric's Colloquy. Ed. G. N. Garmonsway. 2nd ed. London: Methuen, 1947.

Ælfric's Lives of Saints. Ed. and trans. Walter W. Skeat. 4 vols. EETS 76, 82, 94, 114. London: Oxford University Press, 1890–1900; repr. in 2 vols. 1966.

Ælfric's Catholic Homilies. Ed. Malcolm Godden. EETS ss. 5. London: Oxford University Press, 1979.

The Old English Heptateuch and Ælfric's Libellus de Veteri Testamento et Novo, Vol. 1: Introduction and Text. EETS 330. Ed. Richard Marsden. Oxford: Oxford University Press, 2008.

Ancient Laws and Institutes of England. 2 vols. Ed. Benjamin Thorpe. London: Eyre and Spottiswoode, 1840.

Anglo-Saxon Charters. Ed. and trans. Agnes Jane Robertson. Cambridge: Cambridge University Press, 1956.

The Anglo-Saxon Chronicle, Vol. 6: MS D. Ed. G. P. Cubbin. Cambridge: D. S. Brewer, 1996.

Anglo-Saxon Prognostics: An Edition and Translation of Texts from London, British Library, MS Cotton Tiberius A.iii. Ed. and trans. Roy Liuzza. Cambridge: D. S. Brewer, 2010.

Asser's Life of King Alfred. Ed. William Henry Stevenson. Oxford: Oxford University Press, 1959.

Augustine of Hippo. *De civitate Dei contra paganos*. 2 vols. Ed. J. E. C. Welldon. London: MacMillan, 1924.

Austfirðinga sögur. Íslenzk fornrit 11. Ed. Jón Jóhanneson. Reykjavík: Hið íslenzka fornritafélag, 1950.

Bede's Ecclesiastical History of the English People. Ed. Bertram Colgrave and R. A. B. Mynors. Oxford: Clarendon, 1969.

Biblia Sacra iuxta Vulgatam versionem. Ed. R. Gryson and R. Weber. 4th ed. Stuttgart: Deutsche Bibelgesellschaft, 1994.

Blickling Homilies. Ed. and trans. Richard J. Kelly. New York: Continuum, 2003.

Boniface. *Die Briefe des heiligen Bonifatius und Lullus*. MGH Epistolae selectae 1. Ed. Michael Tangl. Berlin: Weidmannsche Verlagsbuchhandlung, 1916.

Bußordnungen der abendländischen Kirche. Ed. F. W. H. Wasserschleben. Halle and der Saale: Graeger, 1851.

Capitularia regum francorum I. MGH Legum Sectio II, Capitularia I. Ed. Alfred Boretius. Hanover: Hahnsche Bucchandlung, 1883.

Catullus. *The Poems of Catullus*. Ed. and trans. Guy Lee. Oxford: Oxford University Press, 1990.

Chaucer, Geoffrey. *The Riverside Chaucer*. 3rd ed. Ed. Larry D. Benson. Boston: Houghton Mifflin, 1987.

The Chrodegang Rules. Ed. and trans. Jerome Bertram. Aldershot, UK: Ashgate, 2005.

Concilia Ævi Karolini. Ed. Albert Werminghoff. MGH Conc. 2.1. Hanover: Hahnsche Buchhandlung, 1906.

Concilia Ævi Karolini. Ed. Albert Werminghoff. MGH Conc. 2.2. Hanover: Hahnsche Bucchandlung, 1908.

Concilia Ævi Merovingici. Ed. F. Maasen. MGH Conc. 1. Hanover: Hahnsche Buchhandlung, 1893.

Concilia Magnae Britaniiae et Hiberniae. Ed. David Wilkins. London: Gosling, Gyles, Woodward, Davis, 1737.

Councils and Ecclesiastical Documents Relating to Great Britain and Ireland. 3 vols. Oxford: Clarendon, 1871; repr. 1964.

The Cult of St. Swithun. Ed. and trans. Michael Lapidge. Oxford: Clarendon, 2003.

Das altenglische Bussbuch. Ed. R. Spindler. Leipzig: Bernhard Tauchnitz, 1934.

Das Emsiger Recht. Altfriesische Rechtsquellen 3. Ed. Wybren Jan Buma and Wilhelm Ebel. Göttingen: Vandenhoeck and Ruprecht, 1967.

Decretales Pseudo-Isidorianae et Capitula Angilramni. Ed. P. Hinschius. Leipzig: Bernhard Tauchnitz, 1863; repr. 1963.

The Dictionary of Old English. Ed. Antonette diPaolo Healey et al. Toronto: Dictionary of Old English Project, University of Toronto/Pontifical Institute of Mediaeval Studies, 2011.

Die altenglische Version des Halitgar'schen Bussbuches. Ed. Josef Raith. Hamburg, 1933; repr. Darmstadt: Wissenschaftliche Buchgesellschaft, 1964.

Die Bussbücher und die Bussdisciplin der Kirche. Ed. H. J. Schmitz. 2 vols. Mainz: Franz Kirchheim Verlag, 1883–98.

Die Canones Theodori Cantuariensis und ihre Überlieferungsformen. Ed. Paul Willem Finsterwalder. Weimar: H. Böhlau, 1929.

Die Gesetze der Angelsachsen. Ed. Felix Liebermann. 3 vols. Halle an der Saale: M. Niemeyer, 1903–16.

Eadmeri historia novorum in Anglia, et opuscula duo, de vita Sancti Anselmi et quibusdam miraculis eius. Ed. Martin Rule. London: Eyre and Spottiswoode, 1884.

English Historical Documents, Vol. 1, c. 500–1042. Ed. and trans. Dorothy Whitelock. London: Eyre and Spottiswoode, 1955.

Excerptiones de Prisciano: The Source for Ælfric's Latin-Old English Grammar. Ed. David W. Porter. Woodbridge: D. S. Brewer, 2002.

The Exeter Book. Anglo-Saxon Poetic Records III. Ed. George Philip Krapp and Elliott Van Kirk Dobbie. New York: Columbia University Press, 1936.

Grágás: Islændernes Lovbog i Fristatens Tid. Ed. Vilhjálmur Finsen. Copenhagen: Det nordiske Literatur-Samfund, 1852.

Gregory the Great. *Grégoire le Grand: Dialogues*. Sources Chrétiennes 260. Ed. Adalbert de Vogüe and trans. Paul Antin. Paris: Éditions du Cerf, 1979.

The Life of St. Benedict. ed. Adalbert de Vogüe, trans. Hilary Costello and Eoin de Bhaldraithe. Petersham, MA: St. Bede's Publications, 1993.

The Harley Latin-Old English Glossary. Ed. Robert T. Oliphant. Paris: Mouton de Gruyter, 1966.

The Holy Bible. Ed. R. Challoner et al. New York: Catholic Book Publishing Company, 1950.

The Irish Penitentials. Ed. and trans. Ludwig Bieler. Dublin: Dublin Institute for Advanced Studies, 1963; repr. 1975.

Jerome. *Commentariorum in Matheum, Libri IV*. Corpus Christianorum, Series Latina, LXXVII. Ed. D. Hurst and M. Adriaen. Turnhout, Belgium: Brepols, 1969.

Justinian's Institutes. Ed. Paul Krueger, trans. Peter Birks and Grant McLeod. Ithaca, NY: Cornell University Press, 1987.

King Alfred's West-Saxon Version of Gregory's Pastoral Care. EETS o.s. nos. 45 and 50. Ed. and trans. Henry Sweet. London: Oxford University Press, 1871.

Klaeber's Beowulf and the Fight at Finnsburg. 4th ed. Ed. R. D. Fulk, John F. Niles, and Robert E. Bjork. Toronto: University of Toronto Press, 2008.

"A Late Old English Handbook for the Use of a Confessor." Ed. R. Fowler. *Anglia* 83 (1965): 1–29.

The Law of Hywel Dda: Law Texts from Medieval Wales. Ed. Dafydd Jenkins. Llandysul, UK: Gomer, 1986.

Laws of the Alamans and Bavarians. Trans. Theodore John Rivers. Philadelphia: University of Pennsylvania Press, 1977.

The Laws of the Earliest English Kings. Ed. and trans. Frederick Levi Attenborough. Cambridge: Cambridge University Press, 1922; repr. 1963.

The Laws of the Hittites: A Critical Edition. Ed. and trans. Harry Angier Hoffner Jr. Leiden, The Netherlands: Brill, 1997.

The Laws of the Kings of England from Edmund to Henry I. Ed. and trans. Agnes Jane Robertson. Cambridge: Cambridge University Press, 1925.

Leechdoms, Wortcunning and Starcraft of Early England. Rolls Series 35. 3 vols. Ed. and trans. Thomas Oswald Cockayne. London: Longman, 1864–6; repr. Holland Press, 1961.

Leges Alamannorum. MGH Leges Sectio I, Tom. 5/1. Ed. Karl Lehmann; rev. ed. Karl August Eckhardt. Hanover: Hahnsche Buchhandlung, 1966.

Leges Baiwariorum. MGH Leges Sectio I, Tom. 5/2. Ed. Ernst von Schwind. Hanover: Hahnsche Buchhandlung, 1926.

Leges Henrici Primi. Ed. L. J. Downer. Oxford: Clarendon, 1972.

Les statuta ecclesiae antiqua. Ed. Charles Munier. Paris: Presses Universitaires de France, 1960.

Lex Frisionum. MGH Fontes Iuris Germanici Antiqui XII. Ed. Karl August Eckhardt and Albrecht Eckhardt. Hannover: Hahnsche Buchhandlung, 1982.

Lex Salica. 100 Titel-Text. Ed. Karl August Eckhardt. Weimar: Böhlau, 1953.

Lex Salica. MGH Leges Sectio I, Tom. 4/2. Ed. Karl August Eckhardt. Hanover: Hahnsche Bucchandlung, 1969.

The Life of St. Chad: An Old English Homily. Ed. R. Vleeskruyer. Amsterdam: North-Holland, 1953.

Medieval Handbooks of Penance. Ed. and trans. John T. McNeill and Helena Margaret Gamer. New York: Octagon, 1938; repr. 1965.

The New Oxford Annotated Bible. 3rd ed. Ed. Michael D. Coogan. Oxford: Oxford University Press, 2001.

Norges gamle love indtil 1387. 5 vols. Ed. R. Keyser, P. A. Munch, G. Storm, and E. Herzberg. Christiania: Grøndahl, 1846–95.

The Old English Canons of Theodore. EETS ss. 25. Ed. R. D. Fulk and Stefan Jurasinski. London: Oxford University Press, 2012.

The Old English Version of the Enlarged Rule of Chrodegang. Ed. Brigitte Langefeld. Frankfurt: Peter Lang, 1985.

Oxford English Dictionary. Ed. James A. H. Murray. Oxford: Clarendon, 1902.

Paenitentialia minora Franciae et Italiae saeculi VIII–IX. Ed. Raymond Kottje, L. Körntgen, and U. Spengler-Reffgen. Turnhout, Belgium: Brepols, 1994.

Paenitentiale Pseudo-Theodori. Ed. Carine Van Rhijn. Turnhout, Belgium: Brepols, 2009.

Patrologia Latina. 217 vols. Ed. J.-P. Migne. Paris: Garnier, 1844–64.

The Prayer-Book of Aedeluald the Bishop, Commonly Called the Book of Cerne. Ed. Dom. A. B. Kuypers. Cambridge: Cambridge University Press, 1902.

Quellen und Forschungen zur Geschichte der teutschen Literatur und Sprache. Ed. F. Mone. Aachen and Leipzig, 1830.

Regino of Prüm. *De synodalibus causis et disciplinis ecclesiasticis*. Ed. F. G. A. Wasserschleben. Leipzig: Engelmann, 1840; repr. 1964.

Sacrorum Conciliorum Nova et Amplissima Collectio. Ed. J. D. Mansi. Florence, 1759–98; repr. Graz: Akademische Druck- u. Verlagsanstalt, 1960.

Shakespeare's Sonnets. Ed. Stephen Booth. New Haven, CT: Yale University Press, 1977.

Tacitus. *Opera Minora*. Ed. M. Winterbottom and R. M. Ogilvie. Oxford: Clarendon, 1975.

Theodori sanctissimi ac doctissimi archiepiscopi cantuarensis poenitentiale. Ed. Jacques Petit. Paris: Lutetiae Parisiorum, 1667.

Two Ælfric Texts. Ed. and trans. Mary Clayton. Cambridge: D. S. Brewer, 2013.

Varro. *On The Latin Language*. 2 vols. Ed. and trans. Roland G. Kent. Cambridge, MA: Harvard University Press, 1938.

Vatnsdœla saga. Íslenzk fornrit 8. Ed. Einar Ólafur Sveinsson. Reykjavík: Íslenzka Fornritafélag, 1939.

The Vercelli Book. Anglo-Saxon Poetic Records II. Ed. George Philip Krapp. New York: Columbia University Press, 1932.

The Vercelli Homilies and Related Texts. EETS o.s. 300. Ed. D. G. Scragg. Oxford: Oxford University Press, 1992.

William of Malmesbury. *Gesta Regum Anglorum*. 2 vols. Ed. and trans. R. A. B. Mynors, R. M. Thomson, and M. Winterbottom. Oxford: Oxford University Press, 1998.

Saints' Lives. Ed. and trans. M. Winterbottom and R. M. Thomson. Oxford: Clarendon, 2002.

Gesta Pontificum Anglorum. Ed. and trans. M. Winterbottom. Oxford: Oxford University Press, 2007.

Wulfstan, Archbishop of York. *The Homilies of Wulfstan*. Ed. Dorothy Bethurum. Oxford: Clarendon, 1957.

Wulfstan's Canons of Edgar. Ed. Roger Fowler. EETS no. 266. London: Oxford University Press, 1972.

SCHOLARLY WORKS

Abels, Richard. "'Cowardice' and Duty in Anglo-Saxon England." *Journal of Military History* 4 (2006): 29–49.

"What Has Weland to Do with Christ? The Franks Casket and the Acculturation of Christianity in Early Anglo-Saxon England." *Speculum* 84 (2009): 549–81.

Adams, Henry, Henry Cabot Lodge, Ernest Young, and J. Laurence Laughlin, eds. *Essays in Anglo-Saxon Law*. Boston: Little, Brown, and Co., 1876.

Alexander, Michael. *A History of Old English Prose*. Peterborough, ON: Broadview, 2002.

Allard, Paul. "Slavery." IV: 36–9. In Herbermann et al., eds.

Andrews, Charles McLean. *The Old English Manor: A Study in English Economic History*. Baltimore: Johns Hopkins University Press, 1892.

Arceo, Alecia. "Rethinking the Synod of Whitby and Northumbrian Monastic Sites." *Haskins Society Journal* 20 (2009): 19–30.

Barlow, Frank. *The English Church, 1000–1066*. London: Longmans, 1963.

Barrow, Julia. "The Clergy in English Dioceses c. 900–c. 1066." 17–26. In Tinti, ed.

Bartlett, Robert. *Trial by Fire and Water*. Oxford: Clarendon, 1986.

Bately, Janet. "Old English Prose before and during the Reign of Alfred." *Anglo-Saxon England* 17 (1988): 93–138.

Baxter, Stephen, Catherine Karkov, Janet L. Nelson, and David Pelteret, eds. *Early Medieval Studies in Memory of Patrick Wormald*. Aldershot, UK: Ashgate, 2009.

Bedingfield, M. Bradford. "Public Penance in Anglo-Saxon England." *Anglo-Saxon England* 31 (2002): 223–55.

Benton, John F. "Consciousness of Self and Perceptions of Individuality." In *Renaissance and Renewal in the Twelfth Century*. Ed. Robert L. Benson and Giles Constable, with Carol D. Lanham. Cambridge, MA: Harvard University Press, 1982; repr. 1991, 263–98.

Bethurum, Dorothy. "Stylistic Features of the Old English Laws." *Modern Language Review* 27 (1932): 263–79.

Binchy, D. A. "Sick-Maintenance in Irish Law." *Ériu* 12 (1934): 78–134.

Blackstone, William. *Commentaries on the Laws of England: A Facsimile of the First Edition of 1765–1769*. 4 vols. Chicago: University of Chicago Press, 1979.

Blair, John. *The Church in Anglo-Saxon Society*. London: Oxford University Press, 2005.

Bosworth, Joseph, ed. *An Anglo-Saxon Dictionary*. Rev. T. Northcote Toller. Oxford: Clarendon, 1898.

Brackmann, Rebecca. *The Elizabethan Invention of Anglo-Saxon England: Laurence Nowell, William Lambarde, and the Study of Old English*. Woodbridge, UK: D. S. Brewer, 2012.

Brasington, Bruce. "Canon Law in the *Leges Henrici Primi*." *Zeitschrift der Savigny-Stiftung für Rechtsgeschichte. Kanonistische Abteilung* 92 (2006): 288–305.

Breen, Q. "The Twelfth-Century Revival of the Roman Law." *Oregon Law Review* 24 (1944–5): 244–87.

Brooks, Nicholas. *The Early History of Canterbury: Christ Church from 597 to 1066*. Leicester, UK: Leicester University Press, 1984.

"The Fonthill Letter, Ealdorman Ordlaf and Anglo-Saxon Law in Practice." 301–18. In Baxter, Karkov, Nelson and Pelteret, eds.

Brundage, James. "Let Me Count the Ways: Canonists and Theologians Contemplate Coital Positions." *Journal of Medieval History* 10 (1984): 81–93.

Law, Sex, and Christian Society in Medieval Europe. Chicago: University of Chicago Press, 1987.

Medieval Canon Law. New York: Longman, 1995.

Brunner, Heinrich. "Über absichtslose Missethat im altdeutschen Strafrechte." *Sitzungsberichte der Berliner Akademie* (1890): 817–42.

Deutsche Rechtsgeschichte. 2 vols. Leipzig: Duncker and Humblot, 1892.

Bullough, Vern L. "On Being a Male in the Middle Ages." In *Medieval Masculinities: Regarding Men in the Middle Ages*. Ed. Clare A. Lees et al. Minneapolis: University of Minnesota Press, 1994, 31–45.

Bury, J. B. *The Invasion of Europe by the Barbarians*. New York: W. W. Norton, 1927; repr. 1967.

Campbell, Alistair. *Old English Grammar*. Oxford: Clarendon, 1959; repr. 1962.

Campbell, Jackson J. "The Dialect Vocabulary of the Old English Bede." *Journal of English and Germanic Philology* 50 (1951): 349–72.

Campbell, James. "Observations on English Government from the Tenth to the Twelfth Century." *Transactions of the Royal Historical Society* 25 (1975): 39–54.

"The Late Anglo-Saxon State: A Maximum View." *Proceedings of the British Academy* 87 (1994): 39–65.

The Anglo-Saxon State. London: Hambledon, 2000.

Carver, Martin. "Early Scottish Monasteries and Prehistory: A Preliminary Dialogue." *Scottish Historical Review* 88 (2009): 332–51.

Catto, Jeremy. "Andrew Horn: Law and History in Fourteenth-Century England." In *The Writing of History in the Middle Ages: Essays Presented to Richard William Southern*. Ed. R. H. C. Davis. Oxford: Clarendon, 1981, 367–91.

Chadwick, Henry. *The Church in Ancient Society: From Galilee to Gregory the Great*. Oxford: Oxford University Press, 2001.

Charles-Edwards, Thomas. "The Penitential of Theodore and the *Iudicia Theodori*." In *Archbishop Theodore: Commemorative Studies on His Life and Influence*. Ed. Michael Lapidge. Cambridge: Cambridge University Press, 1995, 141–74.

Clark, David. *Between Medieval Men: Male Friendship and Desire in Early Medieval English Literature*. Oxford: Oxford University Press, 2009.

Clayton, Mary. "Suicide in the Works of Ælfric." *Review of English Studies* n.s. 60 (2009): 339–70.

Clover, Carol. "Regardless of Sex: Men, Women and Power in Early Northern Europe." *Speculum* 68 (1993): 363–87.

Colman, Rebecca V. "*Hamsocn:* Its Meaning and Significance in Early English Law." *The American Journal of Legal History* 25 (1981): 95–110.

Conti, Aidan. "The Taunton Fragment and the Homiliary of Angers: Context for New Old English." *Review of English Studies* n.s. 60 (2008): 1–33.

Crawford, S. J. "Review of W. J. Sedgefield, *An Anglo-Saxon Verse-Book*." *The Modern Language Review* 19 (1924): 104–8.

Cross, James E., and Alan Brown. "Literary Impetus for Wulfstan's *Sermo Lupi*." *Leeds Studies in English* 20 (1989): 271–91.

Cubitt, Catherine. "Bishops, Priests and Penance in Late Anglo-Saxon England." *Early Medieval Europe* 14 (2006): 41–3.

Damico, Helen, and Alexandra Hennessey Olsen, eds. *New Readings on Women in Old English Literature*. Bloomington: Indiana University Press, 1990.

Davies, Anthony. "Sexual Behaviour in Later Anglo-Saxon England." In *This Noble Craft ... : Proceedings of the Tenth Research Symposium of the Dutch and Belgian University Teachers of Old and Middle English and Historical Linguistics*. Ed. Erik Kooper. Amsterdam: Rodopi, 1991, 83–105.

Day, David. "Hands across the Hall: The Legalities of Beowulf's Fight with Grendel." *Journal of English and Germanic Philology* 98 (1999): 313–24.

Dumville, David. "On the Dating of the Early Breton Lawcodes." *Études Celtiques* 21 (1984): 207–21.

Dyer, Christopher. "Bishop Wulfstan and His Estates." In *Wulfstan and His World*. Ed. Julia S. Barrow and N. P. Brooks. Aldershot, UK: Ashgate, 2005, 137–49.

Earl, James W. "Violence and Non-Violence in Anglo-Saxon England: Ælfric's 'Passion of St. Edmund.'" *Philological Quarterly* 78 (1999): 125–49.

Edel, Doris. "The Status and Development of the Vernacular in Early Medieval Ireland." In *The Dawn of the Written Vernacular in Western Europe*. Ed. Michèle Goyens and Werner Verbeke. Leuven: Leuven University Press, 2003, 351–78.

Feldbrugge, Ferdinand Joseph Maria. *Law in Medieval Russia*. Leiden, The Netherlands: Brill, 2009.

Fell, Christine. *Women in Anglo-Saxon England*. Bloomington: Indiana University Press, 1984.

Firey, Abigail. *A Contrite Heart: Prosecution and Redemption in the Carolingian Empire*. Leiden, The Netherlands: Brill, 2009.

Fischer, Andreas. *Engagement, Wedding and Marriage in Old English*. Heidelberg: Carl Winter, 1986.

Fischer, Olga C. M., and Frederike C. Van Der Leek. "The Demise of the Old English Impersonal Construction." *Journal of Linguistics* 19 (1983): 337–68.

Fitzgerald, William. *Slavery and the Roman Literary Imagination*. Cambridge: Cambridge University Press, 2000.

Flechner, Roy. "The Making of the Canons of Theodore." *Peritia* 17–18 (2003): 121–43.

"An Insular Tradition of Ecclesiastical Law: Fifth to Eighth Century." In *Anglo-Saxon/Irish Relations before the Vikings*. Ed. James Graham-Campbell and Michael Ryan. Oxford: Oxford University Press, 2009, 23–46.

Fleming, Robin. "Henry Adams and the Anglo-Saxons." In *The Preservation and Transmission of Anglo-Saxon Culture*. Ed. Paul Szarmach and Joel T. Rosenthal. Kalamazoo, MI: Medieval Institute, 1997, 13–36.

Fleuriot, Léon. "Un fragment en Latin de très anciennes lois bretonnes armoricanes du VIe siècle." *Annales de Bretagne* 78 (1971): 601–60.

Foot, Sarah. "The Making of *Angelcynn:* English Identity before the Norman Conquest." *Transactions of the Royal Historical Society* 6th ser. 6 (1996): 25–49.

Æthelstan: The First King of England (New Haven, CT: Yale University Press, 2011).

Frank, Roberta. "Marriage in Twelfth- and Thirteenth-Century Iceland." *Viator* 4 (1973): 473–84.

Frantzen, Allen J. *The Literature of Penance in Anglo-Saxon England*. New Brunswick, NJ: Rutgers University Press, 1983a.

"The Tradition of Penitentials in Anglo-Saxon England." *Anglo-Saxon England* 11 (1983b): 23–56.

"When Women Aren't Enough." *Speculum* 68 (1993): 445–71.

"Where the Boys Are: Children and Sex in the Anglo-Saxon Penitentials." In *Becoming Male in the Middle Ages*. Ed. Jeffrey Jerome Cohen and Bonnie Wheeler. New York: Garland, 1997, 43–66.

Before the Closet: Same-Sex Love from "Beowulf" to Angels in America. Chicago: University of Chicago Press, 1998.

"Penitentials." 362. In Lapidge et al., eds.

"Spirituality and Devotion in the Anglo-Saxon Penitentials." *Essays in Medieval Studies* 22 (2006): 117–28.

"Sin and Sense: Editing and Translating Anglo-Saxon Handbooks of Penance." In *Making Sense: Constructing Meaning in Early English*. Ed. Antonette diPaolo Healey and Kevin Kiernan. Toronto: Pontifical Institute of Mediaeval Studies, 2007, 40–71.

Frantzen, Allen J., and Douglas Moffat, eds. *The Work of Work: Servitude, Slavery, and Labor in Medieval England*. Glasgow: Cruithne Press, 1994.

Fruscione, Daniela. "Liebermann's Intellectual Milieu." 15–26. In Jurasinski, Oliver, and Rabin, eds.

Fulk, R. D., and Christopher M. Cain. *A History of Old English Literature*. Oxford: Blackwell, 2003.

"Male Homoeroticism in the Old English *Canons of Theodore*." In *Sex and Sexuality in Anglo-Saxon England: Essays in Memory of Daniel Gillmore*

Calder. Ed. Carol Braun Pasternack and Lisa M. C. Weston. Tempe, AZ: ACMRS, 2004, 1–34.

"Afloat in Semantic Space: Old English *sund* and the Nature of Beowulf's Exploit with Breca." *Journal of English and Germanic Philology* 104 (2005): 315–22.

"Anglian Dialect Features in Old English Anonymous Homiletic Literature: A Survey, with Preliminary Findings." In *Studies in the History of the English Language IV: Empirical and Analytical Advances in the Study of English Language Change*. Topics in English Linguistics 61. Ed. Susan M. Fitzmaurice and Donka Minkova. Berlin: De Gruyter, 2008, 81–100.

"Localizing and Dating Anonymous Prose: The Evidence of Old English Legislation." 59–80. In Jurasinski, Oliver, and Rabin, eds.

Gade, Kari Ellen. "Homosexuality and Rape of Males in Old Norse Law and Literature." *Scandinavian Studies* 55 (1986): 124–41.

Gautier, Alban. "Manger et boire à la mode étrangère: adoption, adaptation et rejet des pratiques festives continentales dans la Grande-Bretagne du VIIe siecle." *Médiévales* 51 (2006): 37–52.

"La chrétienté anglo-saxonne (viie–xie siècle): à propos de quelques publications récentes." *Médiévales* 56 (2009): 151–68.

Georgianna, Linda. "King Hrethel's Sorrow and the Limits of Heroic Action in *Beowulf*." *Speculum* 62 (1987): 829–50.

Giandrea, Mary Frances. *Episcopal Culture in Late Anglo-Saxon England*. Anglo-Saxon Studies 7. Woodbridge, UK: Boydell, 2007.

Girsch, Elizabeth Stevens. "Metaphorical Usage, Sexual Exploitation, and Divergence in the Old English Terminology for Male and Female Slaves." 30–54. In Frantzen and Moffat, eds.

Glancy, Jennifer. *Slavery in Early Christianity*. Oxford: Oxford University Press, 2002.

Glare, P. G. W., ed. *Oxford Latin Dictionary*. Oxford: Clarendon, 1982.

Gneuss, Helmut. *Handlist of Anglo-Saxon Manuscripts*. Tempe, AZ: ACMRS, 2001.

Godden, Malcolm. "Were It Not That I Have Bad Dreams: Gregory and the Anglo-Saxons on Dreaming." In *Rome and the North: The Early Reception of Gregory the Great in Germanic Europe*. Mediaevalia Groningana n.s. 4. Ed. Rolf H. Bremmer, Kees Dekker, and David F. Johnson. Leuven: Peeters, 2001, 93–113.

Grant, Raymond J. S. *The B-Text of the Old English Bede: A Linguistic Commentary*. Amsterdam: Rodopi, 1989.

Greenstadt, Amy. "'Rapt from Himself': Rape and the Poetics of Corporeality in Sidney's Old Arcadia." In *Representing Rape in Medieval and Early Modern Literature*. Ed. Elizabeth Robertson and Christine M. Rose. New York: Palgrave, 2001, 311–45.

Gretsch, Mechthild. "The Taunton Fragment: A New Text from Anglo-Saxon England." *Anglo-Saxon England* 33 (2004): 145–93.

Grimm, Jakob. "Von der Poesie im Recht." *Zeitschrift für geschichtliche Rechtswissenschaft* 2 (1816): 25–99.

Deutsche Rechtsalterthümer. Göttingen: Dieterichsche Buchhandlung, 1828.

Haines, Dorothy. *Sunday Observance and the Sunday Letter in Anglo-Saxon England*. Woodbridge, UK: D. S. Brewer, 2010.

Hall, Jerome. *General Principles of Criminal Law*. Indianapolis: Bobbs Merrill, 1960.
Hamilton, Sarah. *The Practice of Penance, 900–1050*. Woodbridge, UK: Boydell, 2001.
Harbus, Antonina. *The Life of the Mind in Old English Poetry*. Amsterdam: Rodopi, 2002.
Helmholz, R. H. *The Oxford History of the Laws of England, Vol. I: The Canon Law and Ecclesiastical Jurisdiction from 597 to the 1640s*. Oxford: Oxford University Press, 2004.
Herbermann, Charles George et al., eds. *The Catholic Encyclopedia*. 16 vols. New York: Appleton, 1907–12.
Heywood, Samuel. *A Dissertation upon the Distinctions in Society, and Ranks of the People, under the Anglo-Saxon Governments*. London: W. Clarke and Sons, 1818.
Heyworth, Melanie. "The 'Late Old English Handbook for the Use of a Confessor': Authorship and Connections." *Notes and Queries* 54 (2007): 218–22.
Hill, Rosalind. "Marriage in Seventh-Century England." In *Saints, Scholars, and Heroes: Studies in Medieval Culture in Memory of Charles W. Jones*. 2 vols. Ed. Margot H. King and Wesley Stephens. Collegeville, MN: Hill Monastic Manuscript Library, 1979, I: 67–75.
Hoad, T. F. "West Saxon Dialect." 472. In Lapidge et al., eds.
Hodgkin, R. H. *History of the Anglo-Saxons*. 3rd ed. 2 vols. London: Oxford University Press, 1952.
Hoffmann, Hartmut. "Kirche und Sklaverei im frühen Mittelalter." *Deutsches Archiv für Erforschung des Mittelalters* 42 (1986): 1–24.
Hollis, Stephanie, and Michael Wright. *Old English Prose of Secular Learning*. Woodbridge, UK: D. S. Brewer, 1992.
Holmes, Oliver Wendell. *The Common Law*. Cambridge, MA: Harvard University Press, 1881; rev. ed. Mark DeWolfe Howe, ed., 1963.
Hough, Carole. "The Widow's *Mund* in Æthelberht 75 and 76." *Journal of English and Germanic Philology* 98 (1999): 1–16.
"Penitential Literature and Secular Law in Anglo-Saxon England." *Anglo-Saxon Studies in Archaeology and History* 11 (2000): 133–41.
Howe, Nicholas. *Migration and Mythmaking in Anglo-Saxon England*. South Bend, IN: Notre Dame University Press, 2001.
Hudson, John. *The Formation of the English Common Law*. London: Longman, 1996.
"The *Making of English Law* and the Varieties of Legal History." 421–32. In Baxter, Karkov, Nelson, and Pelteret, eds.
The Oxford History of the Laws of England, Vol. II: 871–1216. Oxford: Oxford University Press, 2012.
Huebner, Rudolf. *History of Germanic Private Law*. Trans. Francis S. Philbrick. Boston: Little, Brown and Co., 1968.
Hughes, Diane Owen. "From Brideprice to Dowry in Mediterranean Europe." *Journal of Family History* 3 (1978): 262–96.
Hurt, James. *Ælfric*. Twayne's English Author Series 131. New York: Twayne, 1972.

Hyams, Paul. "The Common Law and the French Connection." *Proceedings of the Battle Conference on Anglo-Norman Studies* 4 (1982): 77–92.

"Feud and the State in Late Anglo-Saxon England." *Journal of British Studies* 40 (2001): 1–43.

Rancor and Reconciliation in Medieval England. Ithaca, NY: Cornell University Press, 2003.

Innes, Matthew. "'Immune from Heresy': Defining the Boundaries of Carolingian Christianity." In *Frankland: The Franks and the World of the Early Middle Ages. Essays in Honour of Dame Jinty Nelson*. Ed. Paul Fouracre and David Ganz. Manchester, UK: University of Manchester Press, 2008, 101–25.

Jaeger, C. S. *The Envy of Angels: Cathedral Schools and Social Ideals in Medieval Europe, 950–1200*. Philadelphia: University of Pennsylvania Press, 1985.

Jastrow, Ignaz. *Zur strafrechtlichen Stellung der Sklaven bei Deutschen und Angelsachsen*. Breslau [Wrocław]: W. Köbner, 1878.

Jayakumar, Shashi. "Reform and Retribution: The 'Anti-Monastic' Reaction in the Reign of Edward the Martyr." 337–52. In Baxter, Karkov, Nelson, and Pelteret, eds.

Johnson, David F. "The *Crux Usualis* as Atropaic Weapon in Anglo-Saxon England." In *The Place of the Cross in Anglo-Saxon England*. Ed. Catherine E. Karkov, Sarah Larratt Keefer. and Karen Louise Jolly. Woodbridge, UK: Boydell, 2006, 80–95.

Jolly, Karen Louise. *Popular Religion in Late Saxon England*. Chapel Hill: University of North Carolina Press, 1996.

Jost, Karl. *Wulfstanstudien*. Schweizer anglistische Arbeiten 23. Bern: A. Francke, 1950.

Jurasinski, Stefan. "Germanism, Slapping, and the Cultural Contexts of Æthelberht's Code: A Reconsideration of Chapters 56–58." *Haskins Society Journal* 18 (2006): 51–71.

"Madness and Responsibility in Anglo-Saxon England." In *Peace and Protection in the Middle Ages*. Ed. David Rollason and Tom Lambert. Toronto: Pontifical Institute of Mediaeval Studies, 2009, 99–120.

"The Old English Penitentials and the Law of Slavery." 97–118. In Jurasinski, Oliver, and Rabin, eds.

"Sanctuary, House-Peace, and the Traditionalism of Alfred's Laws." *The Journal of Legal History* 31 (2010a): 129–47.

"Violence, Penance, and Secular Law in Alfred's Mosaic Prologue." *Haskins Society Journal* 22 (2010b): 25–42.

"Slavery, Learning and the Law of Marriage in Alfred's Mosaic Prologue." *Secular Learning in Anglo-Saxon England*. Ed. László Sándor Chardonnens and Bryan Carella. *Amsterdamer Beiträge zur älteren Germanistik* 69 (2012): 45–64

"Noxal Surrender, the *Deodand*, and the Laws of King Alfred." *Studies in Philology* 111 (2014): 195–224.

Jurasinski, Stefan, Lisi Oliver, and Andrew Rabin, eds. *English Law before Magna Carta: Felix Liebermann and Die Gesetze der Angelsachsen*. Leiden, The Netherlands: Brill, 2010.

Karras, Ruth Mazo. "The History of Marriage and the Myth of *Friedelehe*." *Early Medieval Europe* 14 (2006): 119–51.

Kedar, Benjamin Z. "On the Origins of the Earliest Laws of Frankish Jerusalem: The Canons of the Council of Nablus, 1120." *Speculum* 74 (1999): 310–35.

Kelly, Fergus. *A Guide to Irish Law*. Dublin: Institute for Advanced Studies, 1988; repr. 1991.

Kemble, John Mitchell. *The Saxons in England*. 2 vols. London: Longman, Brown, Green and Longmans, 1849; rev. ed. Walter de Gray Birch, 1876.

Kennedy, A. G. "Cnut's Law Code of 1018." *Anglo-Saxon England* 11 (1983): 57–82.

Ker, N. R. *Catalogue of Manuscripts Containing Anglo-Saxon*. Oxford: Clarendon, 1957.

Keynes, Simon. "An Abbot, an Archbishop, and the Viking Raids of 1006–7 and 1009–12." *Anglo-Saxon England* 36 (2007): 151–220.

Klinck, Anne L. "Anglo-Saxon Women and the Law." *Journal of Medieval History* 8 (1982): 107–21.

Knowles, David. *The Monastic Order in England*. 2nd ed. Cambridge: Cambridge University Press, 1963.

Knuuttila, Simo. "Remarks on Medieval Discussions of Religious Emotions." In *Medieval Philosophy and Modern Times*. Ed. Ghita Holmström-Hintikka. Dordrecht, The Netherlands: Kluwer, 2000, 89–100.

Kottje, Raymund. *Die Bussbücher Halitgars von Cambrai und des Hrabanus Maurus: Ihre Überlieferung und ihre Quellen*. Beiträge zur Geschichte und Quellenkunde des Mittelalters 8. Berlin: De Gruyter, 1980.

Krader, Lawrence. "Introduction." *Anthropology and Early Law*. Ed. Lawrence Krader. New York: Basic Books, 1966.

Lambert, Tom. "The Evolution of Sanctuary in Medieval England." In *Legalism: Anthropology and History*. Ed. Paul Dresch and Hannah Skoda. Oxford: Oxford University Press, 2012, 115–44.

Lapidge, Michael. "The School of Theodore and Hadrian." *Anglo-Saxon England* 15 (1986): 45–72.

"Latin Learning in Ninth-Century England." In *Anglo-Latin Literature, 600–899*. London: Hambledon, 1996, 409–54.

"Æthelwold." 19. In Lapidge et al., eds.

The Anglo-Saxon Library. London: Oxford University Press, 2006.

Lapidge, Michael, et al., eds. *The Blackwell Encyclopaedia of Anglo-Saxon England*. Malden, MA: Blackwell, 1999.

Lass, Roger. *Old English: A Historical Linguistic Companion*. Cambridge: Cambridge University Press, 1994.

Lea, Henry Charles. *An Historical Sketch of Sacerdotal Celibacy in the Christian Church*. Philadelphia: J. B. Lippincott, 1867.

Lees, Clare A. and Gillian R. Overing. "The Clerics and the Critics: Misogyny and the Social Symbolic in Anglo-Saxon England." In Thelma S. Fenster and Clare A. Lees, eds. *Gender in Debate from the Early Middle Ages to the Renaissance*. New York: Palgrave, 2002, 19–41.

Levin, Eve. *Sex and Society in the World of the Orthodox Slavs, 900–1700*. Ithaca, NY: Cornell University Press, 1989.

Lewis, Charlton T., and Charles Short, eds. *A Latin Dictionary*. Oxford: Clarendon, 1879; repr. 1951.

Liebermann, Felix. *Quadripartitus. Ein englisches Rechtsbuch von 1114*. Halle: Max Niemeyer, 1892.

"Zur Herstellung Canones Theodori Cantuarensis." *Zeitschrift der Savigny-Stiftung für Rechtsgeschichte* 43 [Kanonistische Abteilung 12] (1912): 387–409.

Magennis, Hugh. "'No Sex Please, We're Anglo-Saxons?' Attitudes to Sexuality in Old English Literature." *Leeds Studies in English* n.s. 26 (1995): 1–27.

Maine, Henry Sumner. *Ancient Law: Its Connection with the Early History of Society and Its Relation to Modern Ideas*. Boston: Beacon, 1861; repr. 1963.

Maitland, Frederic William. "The Laws of the Anglo-Saxons." *The Quarterly Review* 200 (1904): 139–57.

Mallory, J. P., and D. Q. Adams, eds. *Encyclopedia of Indo-European Culture*. Chicago: Fitzroy Dearborn, 1997.

Marafioti, Nicole. "Punishing Bodies and Saving Souls: Capital and Corporal Punishment in Late Anglo-Saxon England." *Haskins Society Journal* 20 (2008): 39–57.

Mayr-Harting, Henry. *The Coming of Christianity to Anglo-Saxon England*. State College: Pennsylvania State University Press, 1972; repr. 1991.

Mayvaert, Paul. "Bede's Text of the *Libellus Responsionum* of Gregory the Great to Augustine of Canterbury." In *England before the Conquest: Studies in Primary Sources Presented to Dorothy Whitelock*. Ed. Peter Clemoes and Kathleen Hughes. Cambridge: Cambridge University Press, 1971, 15–34.

"Uncovering a Lost Work of Gregory the Great: Fragments of the Early Commentary on Job." *Traditio* 50 (1995): 55–74.

McNeill, John T. "Medicine for Sin as Prescribed in the Penitentials." *Church History* 1 (1932): 14–26.

McReavy, L. L. "The Sunday Repose from Labor." *Ephemerides Theologicae Lovaniensis* 12 (1935): 291–333.

Meaney, Audrey. "Women, Witchcraft and Magic in Anglo-Saxon England." In *Superstition and Popular Medicine in Anglo-Saxon England*. Ed. D. G. Scragg et al. Manchester, UK: Manchester Centre for Anglo-Saxon Studies, 1989, 9–40.

"The *Ides* of the Cotton Gnomic Poem." 158–75. In Damico and Olsen, eds.

"Old English Legal and Penitential Penalties for Heathenism." *Anglo-Saxons: Studies Presented to Cyril Roy Hart*. Ed. Simon Keynes and Alfred P. Smyth. Dublin: Four Courts, 2006, 127–58.

Meens, Rob. "Ritual Purity and the Influence of Gregory the Great in the Early Middle Ages." In *Unity and Diversity in the Church*. Studies in Church History 32. Ed. R. N. Swanson. Cambridge, MA: Blackwell, 1996, 31–43.

"The Frequency and Nature of Early Medieval Penance." In *Handling Sin: Confession in the Middle Ages*. York Studies in Medieval Theology II. Ed. Peter Biller and A. J. Minnis. York: York Medieval Press, 1998, 35–62.

"'A Relic of Superstition': Bodily Impurity and the Church from Gregory the Great to the Twelfth-Century Decretists." In *Purity and Holiness: The*

Heritage of Leviticus. Ed. M. J. H. M. Poorthuis and J. Schwartz. Leiden, The Netherlands: Brill, 2000, 281–93.

"Penitentials and the Practice of Penance in the Tenth and Eleventh Centuries." *Early Medieval Europe* 14 (2006): 7–21.

Menner, Robert J. "The Anglian Vocabulary of the Blickling Homilies." In *Philologica: The Malone Anniversary Studies*. Ed. Thomas Austin Kirby and H. B. Woolf. Baltimore: Johns Hopkins University Press, 1949, 56–64.

Menzer, Melinda J. "The Preface as Admonition: Ælfric's Preface to Genesis." In *The Old English Hexateuch: Aspects and Approaches*. Ed. Rebecca Barnhouse and Benjamin C. Withers. Kalamazoo, MI: Medieval Institute, 2000, 15–40.

Meyer, Herbert. "Friedelehe und Mutterrecht." *Zeitschrift der Savigny-Stiftung für Rechtsgeschichte*. [Kanonistische Abteilung] 47 (1927): 198–286.

Mezger, F. "Did the Institution of Marriage by Purchase Exist in Old Germanic Law?" *Speculum* 18 (1943): 369–71.

Miller, William Ian. "Choosing the Avenger: Some Aspects of the Bloodfeud in Medieval Iceland and England." *Law and History Review* 1 (1983): 159–204.

"Of Outlaws, Christians, Horsemeat, and Writing: Uniform Laws and Saga Iceland." *Michigan Law Review* 89 (1991): 2081–95.

Mitchell, Bruce. "Old English *Man* 'One': Two Notes." In idem, *On Old English*. Oxford: Blackwell, 1988, 264–8.

Morey, Adrian. *Bartholomew of Exeter, Bishop and Canonist*. Cambridge: Cambridge University Press, 1937.

Morrish, Jennifer. "King Alfred's Letter as a Source on Learning in England in the Ninth Century." *Studies in Earlier Old English Prose*. Ed. P. E. Szarmach. Albany: State University of New York Press, 1986, 87–107.

Munske, Horst Haider. *Der germanische Rechtswortschatz im Bereich der Missetaten*. Berlin: De Gruyter, 1973.

Murphy-O'Connor, Jerome. *Paul: A Critical Life*. Oxford: Oxford University Press, 1996.

Murray, Alexander. "Confession before 1215." *Transactions of the Royal Historical Society*, 6th s., 3 (1993): 51–81.

Suicide in the Middle Ages, Vol. 2: The Curse on Self-Murder. Oxford: Oxford University Press, 2000.

Neff, Charlotte. "Scandinavian Elements in the Wantage Code of Æthelred II." *Journal of Legal History* 10 (1989): 285–316.

Nelson, Janet L. "England and the Continent in the Ninth Century: III, Rights and Rituals." *Transactions of the Royal Historical Society* 14 (2004): 1–24.

North, William. "History, Tradition, and Authority in Bede's Interpretation of the Council of Whitby, 664." *Anglo-Saxon* 1 (2007): 1–53.

Oakley, Thomas Pollock. *English Penitential Discipline and Anglo-Saxon Law in Their Joint Influence*. New York: Columbia University Press, 1923.

"The Cooperation of Medieval Penance and Secular Law." *Speculum* 7 (1932): 515–24.

O'Brien, Bruce R. "From *Morðor* to *Murdrum*: The Preconquest Origin and Norman Revival of the Murder Fine." *Speculum* 71 (1996): 321–57.

"The *Instituta Cnuti* and the Translation of English Law." *Anglo-Norman Studies* 25 (2003): 177–97.

Reversing Babel: Translation among the English during an Age of Conquests, c. 800 to c. 1200. Newark: University of Delaware Press, 2011.

O'Brien O'Keeffe, Katherine. "Body and Law in Late Anglo-Saxon England." *Anglo-Saxon England* 27 (1998): 209–32.

O'Donoghue, Neil Xavier. *The Eucharist in Pre-Norman Ireland*. Notre Dame, IN: University of Notre Dame Press, 2011.

Oliver, Lisi. "*Cyninges fedesl:* The King's Feeding in Æthelberht ch. 12." *Anglo-Saxon England* 27 (1998): 31–40.

The Beginnings of English Law. Toronto: University of Toronto Press, 2002.

"Sick-Maintenance in Anglo-Saxon Law." *Journal of English and Germanic Philology* 107 (2008): 303–26.

"Royal and Ecclesiastical Law in Seventh-Century Kent." 97–112. In Baxter, Karkov, Nelson, and Pelteret, eds.

The Body Legal in Barbarian Law. Toronto: University of Toronto Press, 2011.

Oosthuizen, Susan. "The Anglo-Saxon Kingdom of Mercia and the Origins and Distribution of Common Fields." *Agricultural History Review* 55 (2007): 153–80.

Pasternack, Carol Braun. "Negotiating Gender in Anglo-Saxon England." In *Gender and Difference in the Middle Ages*. Medieval Cultures 32. Ed. Sharon Farmer and Carol Braun Pasternack. Minneapolis: University of Minnesota Press, 2003, 107–44.

Payer, Pierre. *Sex and the Penitentials: The Development of a Sexual Code, 550–1150*. Toronto: University of Toronto Press, 1984.

Sex and the New Medieval Literature of Confession, 1150–1300. Toronto: Pontifical Institute of Mediaeval Studies, 2009.

Pelteret, David A. E. "Slave Raiding and Slave Trading in Early England." *Anglo-Saxon England* 9 (1981): 99–114.

"Slavery in Anglo-Saxon England." In *The Anglo-Saxons: Synthesis and Achievement*. Ed. J. Douglas Woods and David Pelteret. Waterloo, ON: Wilfrid Laurier University Press, 1985, 117–33.

Slavery in Early Mediaeval England. Woodbridge, UK: Boydell, 1995.

"The Image of the Slave in Some Anglo-Saxon and Norse Sources." *Slavery and Abolition* 23 (2002): 75–88.

"Should One Include Unnamed Persons in a Prosopographical Study?" In *Prosopography: Approaches and Applications: A Handbook*. Prosopographica et Genealogica 13. Ed. K. S. B. Keats-Rohan. Oxford: Unit for Prosopographical Research, 2007, 183–96.

Phelpstead, Carl. "The Sexual Ideology of *Hrólfs saga kraka*." *Scandinavian Studies* 75 (2003): 1–24.

Plucknett, T. F. T. *A Concise History of the Common Law*. London: Little, Brown and Co., 1929; 5th ed. 1956.

"The Relations between Roman Law and English Common Law down to the Sixteenth Century." *University of Toronto Law Journal* 3 (1939–40): 24–50.

Pollock, Frederick. "The King's Peace." *Law Quarterly Review* 1 (1885): 37–50.

Pollock, Frederick, and Frederic William Maitland. *History of English Law to the Time of Edward I.* 2 vols. 2nd ed. Cambridge: Cambridge University Press, 1899; repr. 1968.

Pons-Sanz, Sara M. *Norse-Derived Vocabulary in Late Old English Texts: Wulfstan's Works, a Case Study*. Amsterdam: John Benjamins/University Press of Southern Denmark, 2007; repr. 2012.

The Lexical Effects of Anglo-Scandinavian Linguistic Contact on Old English. Turnhout, Belgium: Brepols, 2013.

Rabin, Andrew. "The Wolf's Testimony to the English: Law and Witness in the *Sermo Lupi ad Anglos*." *Journal of English and Germanic Philology* 105 (2006): 388–414.

"Old English *forespeca* and the Role of the Advocate in Old English Law." *Mediaeval Studies* 69 (2007): 223–54.

"Female Advocacy and Royal Protection in Tenth Century England: The Legal Career of Queen Ælfthryth." *Speculum* 84 (2009): 261–88.

"Ritual Magic or Legal Performance? Reconsidering an Old English Charm against Theft." 177–98. In Jurasinski, Oliver, and Rabin, eds.

Reynolds, Philip Lyndon. *Marriage in the Western Church*. Leiden, The Netherlands: Brill, 1994; repr. 2001.

"Dotal Charters in the Frankish Tradition." In *To Have and to Hold: Marrying and Its Documentation in Western Christendom, 400–1600*. Ed. Philip Lyndon Reynolds and John Witte Jr. Cambridge: Cambridge University Press, 2007, 114–64.

Richards, Mary P., and B. Jane Stanfield. "Concepts of Anglo-Saxon Women in the Laws." 89–99. In Damico and Olsen, eds.

"The Body as Text in Early Anglo-Saxon Law." In *Naked before God: Uncovering the Body in Anglo-Saxon England*. Ed. Benjamin C. Withers and Jonathan Wilcox. Morgantown: West Virginia University Press, 2003, 87–115.

Richardson, H. G., and G. O. Sayles. *Law and Legislation from Æthelberht to Magna Carta*. Edinburgh: University of Edinburgh Press, 1966.

Roach, Levi. "Penance, Submission and Deditio: Religious Influences on Dispute Settlement in Later Anglo-Saxon England (871–1066)." *Anglo-Saxon England* 41 (2012): 343–71.

"Law Codes and Legal Norms in Later Anglo-Saxon England." *Historical Research* 86 (2013): 465–86.

Robinson, Fred. "Old English." In *Early Germanic Literature and Culture*. Ed. Brian Murdoch and Malcolm Read. Rochester, NY: Camden House, 2004, 205–34.

Rock, P. M. J. "Bigamy (in Canon Law)." II: 561–4. In Herbermann et al., eds.

Ross, Margaret Clunies. "Concubinage in Anglo-Saxon England." *Past and Present* 108 (1985): 3–34.

Rusche, Philip. "St. Augustine's Abbey and the Tradition of Penance in Early Tenth-Century England." *Anglia* 120 (2002): 159–83.

Ryan, Martin J. "Archbishop Ecgberht and His Dialogus." In *Leaders of the Anglo-Saxon Church: From Bede to Stigand*. Ed. Alexander R. Rumble. Woodbridge, UK: Boydell, 2012, 41–60.

Saintyves, P. "Les trois nuits de Tobie ou la continence durant la première ou les premières nuits du mariage." *Revue Anthropologique* 44 (1944): 266–96.

Salzmann, Znedek. *Language, Culture, and Society: An Introduction to Linguistic Anthropology*. 4th ed. Cambridge, MA: Westview Press, 2007.

Samson, Ross. "The End of Early Medieval Slavery." 95–123. In Frantzen and Moffat, eds.

Sauer, Hans. *Theodulfi Capitula in England. Die altenglischen Übersetzungen, zusammen mit dem lateinischen Text*. Münchener Universitätschriften 8 Munich: Wilhelm Fink, 1978.

Sayre, Francis Bowes. "Mens Rea." *Harvard Law Review* 45 (1932): 974–1026.

Scheil, Andrew. "Somatic Ambiguity and Masculine Desire in the Old English Life of Euphrosyne." *Exemplaria* 11 (1999): 345–61.

Schneider, Karl. "Six Old English Runic Inscriptions Reconsidered." In *Nordica et Anglica: Studies in Honor of Stefán Einarsson*. Ed. Allan H. Orrick. The Hague: Mouton, 1968, 37–52.

Schreiber, Carolin. "Dialects in Contact in Ninth-Century England." In *Bookmarks from the Past: Studies in Early English Language and Literature in Honour of Helmut Gneuss*. Ed. Lucia Kornexl and Ursula Lenker. Frankfurt: Peter Lang, 2003, 1–32.

Scragg, Donald. "The Homilies of the Blickling Manuscript." In *Learning and Literature in Anglo-Saxon England*. Ed. Michael Lapidge and Helmut Gneuss. Cambridge: Cambridge University Press, 1985, 299–316.

Seebohm, Frederic. *The Crisis of Emancipation in America*. London: Alfred W. Bennett, 1865.

The English Village Community. London: Longmans, Green and Co., 1876; 2nd ed. 1883.

Tribal Custom in Anglo-Saxon Law. London: Longmans, Green and Co., 1911.

Sharpe, Richard. "The Prefaces of *Quadripartitus*." In *Law and Government in Medieval England and Normandy: Essays in Honour of Sir James Holt*. Ed. George Garnett and John Hudson. Cambridge: Cambridge University Press, 1994, 148–72.

"The Dating of *Quadripartitus* Again." 81–96. In Jurasinski, Oliver, and Rabin, eds.

Sheehan, Michael M. "Choice of Marriage Partner in the Middle Ages: Development and Mode of Application of a Theory of Marriage." In *Marriage, Family, and Law in Medieval Europe: Collected Studies*. Ed. James K. Farge. Toronto: University of Toronto Press, 1996, 87–118.

Simpson, A. W. B. "The Laws of Ethelbert." In *On the Laws and Customs of England: Essays in Honor of Samuel E. Thorne*. Ed. Morris S. Arnold et al. Chapel Hill: University of North Carolina Press, 1981, 3–17.

Sisam, Kenneth. "The Authenticity of Certain Texts in Lambarde's *Archaionomia* 1568." *Modern Language Review* 18 (1923): 98–104; 20 (1925): 253–9. Repr. in idem, *Studies in the History of Old English Literature*. Oxford: Clarendon, 1953, 232–58.

Spiegel, Flora. "The *tabernacula* of Gregory the Great and the Conversion of Anglo-Saxon England." *Anglo-Saxon England* 36 (2007): 1–13.

Staab, Franz. "Bonifatius, die *regula sancti patris Benedicti* und die Gründung des Klosters Fulda." *Archiv für mittelrheinische Kirchengeschichte* 57 (2005): 55–69.

Stacy, Robin Chapman. *Dark Speech: The Performance of Law in Early Ireland.* Philadelphia: University of Pennsylvania Press, 2007.

Stanley, E. G. "Words for the Dictionary of Old English." In *The Dictionary of Old English: Retrospects and Prospects.* Ed. M. J. Toswell and Antonette di Paolo Healey. Kalamazoo, MI: Medieval Institute, 1998, 33–56.

Steenstrup, Johannes C. H. R. *Normannerne.* 4 vols. Copenhagen: Klein, 1876–82.

Stenton, Doris Mary. *The English Woman in History.* London: George Allen, 1957.

Stenton, Frank Merry. *Anglo-Saxon England.* Oxford: Clarendon, 1943; repr. 1962.

Stevens, Wesley. "Easter Controversy." 157. In Lapidge et al., eds.

Stuart, Heather. "The Meaning of Old English **ælfsciene*." *Parergon* 2 (1972): 22–6.

Sweet, Charles. "The History of the Word 'Law' [II]," *Law Magazine and Review*, n.s. 3 (1874): 644–58.

Szemerényi, Oswald. *Einführung in die vergleichende Sprachwissenschaft.* Darmstadt: Wissenschaftliche Buchgesellschaft, 1980.

Thacker, Alan. "Memorializing Gregory the Great: the Origin and Transmission of a Papal Cult in the Seventh and Early Eighth Centuries." *Early Medieval Europe* 7 (1998): 59–84.

Thijs, Christine. "Levels of Learning in Anglo-Saxon Worcester: The Evidence Reassessed." *Leeds Studies in English* 36 (2005): 105–31.

Thomas, Wilhelm. *Der Sonntag im frühen Mittelalter.* Göttingen: Vandenhoeck and Ruprecht, 1929.

Thompson, Nancy M. "Anglo-Saxon Orthodoxy." In *Old English Literature in Its Manuscript Context.* Ed. Joyce Tally Lionarons. Morgantown: West Virginia University Press, 2004, 37–66.

"The Carolingian *de festiuitatibus* and the Blickling book." In *The Old English Homily: Precedent, Practice, and Appropriation.* Studies in the Early Middle Ages 17. Ed. Aaron J. Kleist. Turnhout, Belgium: Brepols, 2007, 97–120.

Thompson, Victoria. "The Pastoral Contract in Late Anglo-Saxon England: Priest and Parishioner in Oxford, Bodleian Library, MS Laud Miscellaneous 482." 106–20. In Tinti, ed.

Thrupp, John. *The Anglo-Saxon Home: A History of the Domestic Institutions and Customs of England, from the Fifth to the Eleventh Century.* London: Longman, Green, Longman and Roberts, 1862.

Tinti, Francesca, ed. *Pastoral Care in Late Anglo-Saxon England.* Rochester, NY: Boydell, 2005.

Toon, Thomas E. "The Social and Political Contexts of Language Change in Anglo-Saxon England." In *English in Its Social Contexts.* Ed. Tim William Machan and Charles T. Scott. Oxford: Oxford University Press, 1992, 28–46.

Townend, Matthew. *Language and History in Viking Age England: Linguistic Relations between Speakers of Old Norse and Old English.* Studies in the Early Middle Ages 6. Turnhout, Belgium: Brepols, 2002.

Treschow, Michael. "The Prologue to Alfred's Law Code: Instruction in the Spirit of Mercy." *Florilegium* 13 (1994): 79–110.

Turner, Ralph V. "Roman Law in England before the Time of Bracton." *Journal of British Studies* 15 (1975): 1–25. Repr. in idem, *Judges, Administrators, and the Common Law in Angevin England*. Rio Grande: Hambledon, 1994, 45–70.

Upchurch, Robert K. "Catechitic Homiletics: Ælfric's Preaching and Teaching during Lent." In *A Companion to Ælfric*. Ed. Hugh Magennis and Mary Swan. Brill's Companions to the Christian Tradition II. Leiden, The Netherlands: Brill, 2009, 217–46.

Vogel, Cyril. *Les "libri paenitentiales,"* Typologie des sources du moyen âge occidental 27. Louvain: Institut d'études médiévales, 1978.

En remission de péchés. Recherches sur les systèmes pénitentiels dans l'Eglise latine. Ed. Alexandre Faivre. Aldershot, UK: Variorum, 1994.

Walker, Jonathan. "The Transtextuality of Transvestite Sainthood; Or, How to Make the Gendered Form Fit the Generic Function." *Exemplara* 15 (2003): 73–110.

Walker, Nigel. *Crime and Insanity in England, Vol. I: The Historical Perspective*. Edinburgh: University of Edinburgh Press, 1968.

"The Insanity Defense before 1800." *Annals of the American Academy of Political and Social Science* 477 (1985): 15–30.

Wallace-Hadrill, J. M. *Early Germanic Kingship in England and on the Continent*. Oxford: Clarendon, 1971.

Watkins, Calvert. "Sick-Maintenance in Indo-European." *Ériu* 27 (1976): 21–5.

Wenisch, Franz. *Spezifisch anglisches Wortgut in den nordhumbrischen Interlinearglossierung des Lukasevangeliums*. Heidelberg: C. Winter, 1979.

Werckmeister, Jean. "The Reception of the Church Fathers in Canon Law." In *The Reception of the Church Fathers in the West, Vol. 1: From the Carolingians to the Maurists*. Ed. Irena Backus. Leiden, The Netherlands: Brill, 1997; repr. 2001, 51–82.

Whitelock, Dorothy. "Archbishop Wulfstan: Homilist and Statesman." *Transactions of the Royal Historical Society* 24 (1942): 24–45.

The Audience of Beowulf. Oxford: Clarendon, 1951.

Wieacker, F. "*Ratio scripta*. Das römische Recht und die abendländische Rechtswissenschaft." In *Vom römischen Recht*. Leipzig: Köhler and Amelang, 1944, 195–284.

Wierzbicka, Anna. *Semantics, Culture and Cognition: Universal Human Concepts in Culture-Specific Configurations*. Oxford: Oxford University Press, 1992.

Wilberforce, Samuel. *History of the Protestant Episcopal Church in America*. New York: Stanford and Swords, 1849.

Winfield, Percy. "The Myth of Absolute Liability." *Law Quarterly Review* 42 (1926): 37–51.

Wittig, Joseph S. "King Alfred's Boethius and Its Latin Sources: A Reconsideration." *Anglo-Saxon England* 11 (1983): 157–98.

Woolgar, C. M. *The Senses in Late Medieval England*. New Haven, CT: Yale University Press, 2006.

Wormald, Patrick. "*Lex Scripta* and *Verbum Regis:* Legislation and Germanic Kingship from Euric to Cnut." In *Early Medieval Kingship*. Ed. P. H. Sawyer and I. N. Wood. Leeds: Leeds University Press, 1977, 105–38. Repr. in Wormald, *Legal Culture in the Early Medieval West: Law as Text, Image and Experience*. London: Hambledon, 1999, 1–43.

"Æthelred the Lawmaker." *Ethelred the Unready: Papers from the Millenary Conference*. BAR British Series 59. Ed. David Hill. Oxford: British Archaeological Reports, 1978, 47–80.

"Charters, Law and the Settlement of Disputes in Anglo-Saxon England." In *The Settlement of Disputes in Early Medieval Europe*. Ed. Wendy Davies and Paul Fouracre. Cambridge: Cambridge University Press, 1986, 149–68. Repr. in idem, *Legal Culture*, 289–311.

"*Inter cetera bona ... genti suae*: Law-making and Peace-Keeping in the Earliest English Kingdoms." *La Giustizia nell'Alto Medioevo*. 2 vols. Spoleto: Centro Italiano di Studi sull'altio Medioevo, 1994, II: 967–93.

"Frederic William Maitland and the Earliest English Law." *Law and History Review* 16 (1998): 1–25.

"Archbishop Wulfstan and the Holiness of Society." In Wormald, *Legal Culture in the Early Medieval West*, 1999, 225–51.

"Giving God and King Their Due: Conflict and Its Regulation in the Early English State." In Wormald, *Legal Culture in the Early Medieval West*, 1999, 333–57.

The Making of English Law: King Alfred to the Twelfth Century. Oxford: Blackwell, 1999.

"Anglo-Saxon Law and Scots Law." *Scottish Historical Review* 88 (2009): 192–206.

Wrenn, C. L. "Review of Robert Spindler, *Das altenglische Bussbuch*." *Review of English Studies* 12 (1936): 244–6.

Wüest, Jakob. *Die Leis Willelme: Untersuchungen zum ältesten Gesetzbuch in französischer Sprache*. Bern: Francke Verlag, 1969.

Wyatt, David. "The Significance of Slavery: Alternative Approaches to Anglo-Saxon Slavery." *Anglo-Norman Studies* 23 (2001): 328–47.

Slaves and Warriors in Medieval Britain and Ireland, 800–1200. The Northern World 45. Leiden, The Netherlands: Brill, 2009.

Zimmer, Stefan. "Glimpses of Indo-European Law." In *The Law's Beginnings*. Ed. Ferdinand Joseph Maria Feldbrugge. Leiden, The Netherlands: Brill, 2003, 115–36.

Index

Printed in the United Kingdom by TJ Clays Ltd.

In *Work Fame* Leanne Hughes brings the same energy, creativity and pragmatism she brings to her hugely engaging workshops. Packed with tips, techniques, insights and relatable stories it is your go-to-guide for getting noticed and promoted for all the right reasons.

Tim Ferguson, CEO, Audience Group

Work Fame isn't about becoming someone you're not. It's about making sure the real you gets seen. Leanne shows you how to build a reputation so authentically yours that it elevates not just your career, but your whole life.

Matthew Stewart, CEO and Founder, The Custodian Way, Physiotherapist and Chiropractor

In this loud and busy world, those who intentionally build their brands and reputations are the ones who are rewarded. This book will show you how and do it in a fun and entertaining way. I will be recommending it to everyone I know who wants to be successful.

Andy Storch, author of *Own Your Career Own Your Life* and *Own Your Brand, Own Your Career*

In a busy workplace, great work can still go unnoticed. In *Work Fame,* Leanne Hughes shares a practical guide to building a reputation that reflects your strengths — without uncomfortable self-promotion — so you're recognised for the right things and open to new opportunities.

Kathryn Wilson, Managing Director, Aurion

The book challenges the belief that good work will automatically get recognised and provides a simple framework for making your contribution, relationships and ideas more visible. If you've ever wondered why people with similar or even less capability seem to get more opportunities, this book will help explain why and, more importantly, what to do about it.

Petra Zink, Leadership Advisor, Speaker and Author of *The ROI of Trust: How Trust, Decisions, and Influence Actually Work in the AI Age*